Strategic Information Technology Governance and Organizational Politics in Modern Business

Tiko Iyamu
Cape Peninsula University of Technology, South Africa

A volume in the Advances in Human Resources Management and Organizational Development (AHRMOD) Book Series

Managing Director:	Lindsay Johnston
Managing Editor:	Austin DeMarco
Director of Intellectual Property & Contracts:	Jan Travers
Acquisitions Editor:	Kayla Wolfe
Production Editor:	Christina Henning
Cover Design:	Jason Mull

Published in the United States of America by
Business Science Reference (an imprint of IGI Global)
701 E. Chocolate Avenue
Hershey PA, USA 17033
Tel: 717-533-8845
Fax: 717-533-8661
E-mail: cust@igi-global.com
Web site: http://www.igi-global.com

Copyright © 2015 by IGI Global. All rights reserved. No part of this publication may be reproduced, stored or distributed in any form or by any means, electronic or mechanical, including photocopying, without written permission from the publisher. Product or company names used in this set are for identification purposes only. Inclusion of the names of the products or companies does not indicate a claim of ownership by IGI Global of the trademark or registered trademark.

Library of Congress Cataloging-in-Publication Data

Strategic information technology governance and organizational politics in modern business / Tiko Iyamu, editor.
   pages cm
 Includes bibliographical references and index.
 Summary: "This book gives voice to fresh perspectives on the development, implementation, and practice of information systems and technology in organizations, offering a more in-depth understanding of the influence of socio-technical factors on ICT operations"-- Provided by publisher.
  ISBN 978-1-4666-8524-6 (hardcover : alk. paper) -- ISBN 978-1-4666-8525-3 (ebook) 1. Information technology--Management. 2. Knowledge management. 3. Strategic planning. I. Iyamu, Tiko, editor.

  HD30.2.S78788 2015
  658.4'038--dc23

2015010266

This book is published in the IGI Global book series Advances in Human Resources Management and Organizational Development (AHRMOD) (ISSN: 2327-3372; eISSN: 2327-3380)

British Cataloguing in Publication Data
A Cataloguing in Publication record for this book is available from the British Library.

All work contributed to this book is new, previously-unpublished material. The views expressed in this book are those of the authors, but not necessarily of the publisher.

For electronic access to this publication, please contact: eresources@igi-global.com.

Advances in Human Resources Management and Organizational Development (AHRMOD) Book Series

Patricia Ordóñez de Pablos
Universidad de Oviedo, Spain

ISSN: 2327-3372
EISSN: 2327-3380

Mission

A solid foundation is essential to the development and success of any organization and can be accomplished through the effective and careful management of an organization's human capital. Research in human resources management and organizational development is necessary in providing business leaders with the tools and methodologies which will assist in the development and maintenance of their organizational structure.

The **Advances in Human Resources Management and Organizational Development (AHRMOD) Book Series** aims to publish the latest research on all aspects of human resources as well as the latest methodologies, tools, and theories regarding organizational development and sustainability. The **AHRMOD Book Series** intends to provide business professionals, managers, researchers, and students with the necessary resources to effectively develop and implement organizational strategies.

Coverage

- Employee Relations
- Job Enrichment
- Executive Education
- Organizational development
- Talent Identification and Management
- Collaborative Method
- Performance Improvement
- Personnel Retention
- Human Resources Development
- Recruitment Process

IGI Global is currently accepting manuscripts for publication within this series. To submit a proposal for a volume in this series, please contact our Acquisition Editors at Acquisitions@igi-global.com or visit: http://www.igi-global.com/publish/.

The Advances in Human Resources Management and Organizational Development (AHRMOD) Book Series (ISSN 2327-3372) is published by IGI Global, 701 E. Chocolate Avenue, Hershey, PA 17033-1240, USA, www.igi-global.com. This series is composed of titles available for purchase individually; each title is edited to be contextually exclusive from any other title within the series. For pricing and ordering information please visit http://www.igi-global.com/book-series/advances-human-resources-management-organizational/73670. Postmaster: Send all address changes to above address. Copyright © 2015 IGI Global. All rights, including translation in other languages reserved by the publisher. No part of this series may be reproduced or used in any form or by any means – graphics, electronic, or mechanical, including photocopying, recording, taping, or information and retrieval systems – without written permission from the publisher, except for non commercial, educational use, including classroom teaching purposes. The views expressed in this series are those of the authors, but not necessarily of IGI Global.

Titles in this Series

For a list of additional titles in this series, please visit: www.igi-global.com

Handbook of Research on Internationalization of Entrepreneurial Innovation in the Global Economy
Luisa Cagica Carvalho (Universidade Aberta, Portugal & CEFAGE, Universidade de Évora, Portugal)
Business Science Reference • copyright 2015 • 547pp • H/C (ISBN: 9781466682160) • US $335.00 (our price)

Cases on Human Performance Improvement Technologies
Jill E. Stefaniak (Old Dominion University, USA)
Business Science Reference • copyright 2015 • 409pp • H/C (ISBN: 9781466683303) • US $205.00 (our price)

Cases on Sustainable Human Resources Management in the Middle East and Asia
Stephanie Jones (Maastricht School of Management, The Netherlands) and Sheena Graham (Graham Reid Associates, Hong Kong)
Business Science Reference • copyright 2015 • 374pp • H/C (ISBN: 9781466681675) • US $195.00 (our price)

Business Ethics and Diversity in the Modern Workplace
Philippe W. Zgheib (Lebanese American University, Lebanon)
Business Science Reference • copyright 2015 • 326pp • H/C (ISBN: 9781466672543) • US $235.00 (our price)

Impact of Diversity on Organization and Career Development
Claretha Hughes (University of Arkansas, USA)
Business Science Reference • copyright 2015 • 342pp • H/C (ISBN: 9781466673243) • US $215.00 (our price)

Organizational Innovation and IT Governance in Emerging Economies
Jingyuan Zhao (University of Toronto, Canada) Patricia Ordóñez de Pablos (Universidad de Oviedo, Spain) and Robert D. Tennyson (University of Minnesota, USA)
Business Science Reference • copyright 2015 • 304pp • H/C (ISBN: 9781466673328) • US $205.00 (our price)

Utilizing Evidence-Based Lessons Learned for Enhanced Organizational Innovation and Change
Susan McIntyre (Defence Research and Development, Canada) Kimiz Dalkir (McGill University, Canada) Perry Paul (Lessons Learned Consultant, Canadian Armed Forces (Retired), Canada) and Irene C. Kitimbo (McGill University, Canada)
Business Science Reference • copyright 2015 • 323pp • H/C (ISBN: 9781466664531) • US $195.00 (our price)

Approaches to Managing Organizational Diversity and Innovation
Nancy D. Erbe (California State University, USA)
Business Science Reference • copyright 2014 • 387pp • H/C (ISBN: 9781466660069) • US $205.00 (our price)

www.igi-global.com

701 E. Chocolate Ave., Hershey, PA 17033
Order online at www.igi-global.com or call 717-533-8845 x100
To place a standing order for titles released in this series, contact: cust@igi-global.com
Mon-Fri 8:00 am - 5:00 pm (est) or fax 24 hours a day 717-533-8661

Editorial Advisory Board

Thomas Schmidt, *Flensburg University of Applied Sciences, Germany*
Arthur Tatnall, *Victoria University, Australia*
Sharol Mkhomazi, *Tshwane University of Technology, South Africa*
Olayele Adelakun, *DePaul University, USA*
OS Akinsola, *Namibia University of Science and Technology, Namibia*
Nestori Syynimaa, *University of Reading, UK*
Alta van der Merwe, *University of Pretoria, South Africa*
Elayne Coakes, *University of Westminster, UK*

Table of Contents

Preface xiv

Chapter 1
Towards A Contingency Model for Assessing Strategic Information Systems Planning Success in
Medium Enterprises 1
    Ray M Kekwaletswe, University of the Witwatersrand, South Africa

Chapter 2
The Interplay between Human and Structure in IT Strategy 31
    Tiko Iyamu, Cape Peninsula University of Technology, South Africa

Chapter 3
Politicking the Information Technology Strategy in Organisations 51
    Tiko Iyamu, Cape Peninsula University of Technology, South Africa

Chapter 4
Knowledge Requirements for Information Systems Outsourcing 79
    Hanlie Smuts, University of South Africa, South Africa
    Alta van der Merwe, University of Pretoria, South Africa
    Marianne Loock, University of South Africa, South Africa
    Paula Kotzé, CSIR Meraka Institute and Nelson Mandela Metropolitan University, South
        Africa

Chapter 5
Captive Offshore IT Outsourcing: Best Practices from a Case Study 106
    Olayele Adelakun, DePaul University, USA

Chapter 6
The Role of Reference, Imminent and Current Models in Enterprise Conceptual Modelling: A
Case Study of a Namibian Freight Forwarder 121
    Thomas Schmidt, Flensburg University of Applied Sciences, Germany
    Stephan Hofmann, Flensburg University of Applied Sciences, Germany

Chapter 7
Critical Analysis of the Roles of Actors in the Deployment of Software 135
    Tefo Sekgweleo, Tshwane University of Technology, Pretoria, South Africa

Chapter 8
Assessing the Influence of Actors on e-Government Policies: Evidences from Chile and Costa
Rica Experiences 153
    Roberto Cortés-Morales, Costa Rica Institute of Technology, Costa Rica

Chapter 9
Enterprise Architecture for Business Objectives: Understanding the Influencing Factors 171
    Leshoto Mphahlele, Tshwane University of Technology, Pretoria, South Africa
    Tiko Iyamu, Cape Peninsula University of Technology, South Africa

Chapter 10
IT Governance Practices of SMEs in South Africa and the Factors Influencing Their
Effectiveness 188
    Charles Boamah-Abu, University of Cape Town, South Africa
    Mike Tyobe, University of Cape Town, South Africa

Chapter 11
The Interplay of Agents in Improvising Telecommunication Infrastructures' Services to Rural
Community of South Africa 208
    Sharol Mkhomazi, Tshwane University of Technology, South Africa

Chapter 12
Engineering the Services of the Library through Mobile Technology 226
    Eunice Mtshali, Tshwane University of Technology, South Africa

Chapter 13
E-Competences for Organisational Sustainability Information Systems 242
    Zoran Mitrovic, Mitrovic Development and Research Institute, South Africa

Chapter 14
Information Systems Innovations Using Competitive Intelligence 260
    Phathutshedzo Nemutanzhela, Tshwane University of Technology, South Africa

Chapter 15
Competitive Intelligence for Business Enhancement: Deployment Framework 280
    Relebohile Moloi, Johannesburg, South Africa

Compilation of References 293

About the Contributors 319

Index 324

Detailed Table of Contents

Preface xiv

Chapter 1
Towards A Contingency Model for Assessing Strategic Information Systems Planning Success in
Medium Enterprises 1
    Ray M Kekwaletswe, University of the Witwatersrand, South Africa

Strategic planning of information systems is vital in the business environment and this is still an open issue in the management information systems research. Through planning, organisations develop effective long-term use of information systems and subsequently ensuring the support of organisational objectives. This chapter develops a contingency model for measuring the success of strategic information systems planning in the context of medium enterprises. The contingency theory, as an analytical lens, advocates that organisational success can be achieved by matching organisational characteristics to the contextual factors. Drawing from this notion, this chapter postulates that the strategic information systems planning process, as a phase, may lead to successful planning. This relationship is moderated by contingency variables characterised by the presence of environmental uncertainty, organisational structure, government and policies, business strategy orientation and information systems maturity. This chapter studies the moderating role of contingency variables and identifies the influential factors and their effect.

Chapter 2
The Interplay between Human and Structure in IT Strategy 31
    Tiko Iyamu, Cape Peninsula University of Technology, South Africa

Information Technology (IT) has significant impact on organisation's success or failure. However, IT does not operate in a vacuum. It is influenced by non-technical factors, such as of human actions and structure, which are inseparable. Hence the relationship between the factors is critical as revealed in this chapter. Structuration was applied as a lens to examine the types of structures that existed during the development and implementation of IT strategy, and the structures that emerged as a result of human action in the organisation used as the case. The chapter presents that both human actions and structures depends on each other on all processes and activities that are involved in the development and implementation of the IT strategy. Drawing from the findings, the chapter develops a model to illustrate how cultural, policy and personal issues enable at the same time constrain activities in the development and implementation of IT strategy.

Chapter 3
Politicking the Information Technology Strategy in Organisations 51
> *Tiko Iyamu, Cape Peninsula University of Technology, South Africa*

Through IT strategy, many organisations intend to set out key directions and objectives for the use and management of information, communication and technologies. It would therefore seem that IT strategy, for the foreseeable future will remain a key aspect of development within organisations. As a result, there has been more focus on how IT strategy is articulated and formulated. What is missing is that there has been less attention on the implementation of the strategy. Also, in most organisations, technical issues are minor compared to the relationship issues. There are many factors which influence the implementation of the IT strategy. These influencing factors which include organisational politics, determine the success or failure of the IT strategy. This paper focuses on how organisational politics as examined by two underpinning theories, Structuration Theory and Actor-Network Theory, impact the implementation of IT strategy.

Chapter 4
Knowledge Requirements for Information Systems Outsourcing 79
> *Hanlie Smuts, University of South Africa, South Africa*
> *Alta van der Merwe, University of Pretoria, South Africa*
> *Marianne Loock, University of South Africa, South Africa*
> *Paula Kotzé, CSIR Meraka Institute and Nelson Mandela Metropolitan University, South Africa*

Information systems (IS) outsourcing is a complex, multi-layered and a multifaceted concept. An organisation may gain access to knowledge it does not own in-house or be able to obtain it at a lower price by entering into an outsourcing relationship. At the same time, the organisation may risk losing key skills and capabilities unless the outsourcing arrangement is managed strategically and knowledge transferred properly. Knowledge management is valuable in preventing a loss of knowledge when an organisation outsources its information system activities. This chapter analyses and describes the knowledge requirements relevant in an IS outsourcing arrangement.

Chapter 5
Captive Offshore IT Outsourcing: Best Practices from a Case Study 106
> *Olayele Adelakun, DePaul University, USA*

A captive offshore center is a separate business arm of the parent company, wholly owned, to provide IT solutions to its parent company. Some of the reasons for setting up a captive offshore center in the literature include controlling cost and gaining access to low-cost skilled professional but in the case of a Chicago based Company (sears Holdings) it was considered a strategic. One hiding agenda was to lunch a new line of business offering to its US base customers from a low cost location. This chapter reveals how a Sears Holdings lunched a successful captive offshore IT center and why they received outsourcing best practices award from the industry. In achieving the goal of the chapter, interview data was collected from the management team in Chicago and the head of the offshore operation. We compare our result to previous research on offshore best practices and we find many correlations.

Chapter 6
The Role of Reference, Imminent and Current Models in Enterprise Conceptual Modelling: A Case Study of a Namibian Freight Forwarder... 121
    Thomas Schmidt, Flensburg University of Applied Sciences, Germany
    Stephan Hofmann, Flensburg University of Applied Sciences, Germany

Enterprise Resource Planning (ERP) systems constitute a prerequisite for successfully managing business in many industries, including the logistics industry. Since today's standard ERP systems determine a company's business down to the smallest detail, effectively aligning a company's strategy and business processes with software-given processes is imperative for maintaining a competitive advantage. This calls for defining an Enterprise Conceptual Model based on a sound derivation of imminent processes, either directed towards current, reference or ideal processes. The case study exemplifies that an Enterprise Conceptual Model has actually helped to translate strategic goals and operational needs into business processes and, thereby, align imminent and software-given processes. The application of current, reference and ideal process models for definition imminent processes is shown. Insight is drawn from a one-case case study of a medium-sized Namibian freight forwarder and logistics service provider.

Chapter 7
Critical Analysis of the Roles of Actors in the Deployment of Software 135
    Tefo Sekgweleo, Tshwane University of Technology, Pretoria, South Africa

Many organizations resort to software deployment with the intention to simplify their daily activities, and for competitive advantage. The deployment consists of two main phases, development and implementation. Unfortunately, software doesn't always fulfil the organization's intentions. This is attributed to numerous factors, some of complex nature, which happen among humans, non-humans, and between humans and non-humans actors during development and implementation of software. Case study research was conducted to understand the roles of actors, and how their actions and interactions impact the development and implementation of software in the organization. Actor Network Theory (ANT) was employed in the analysis of the data. The theory focused on activities including the negotiation among actors which happened within heterogeneous network.

Chapter 8
Assessing the Influence of Actors on e-Government Policies: Evidences from Chile and Costa Rica Experiences.. 153
    Roberto Cortés-Morales, Costa Rica Institute of Technology, Costa Rica

E-government development, assumed as a public policy problem, has to consider political issues, where actors play a key role for success or failure on such policies. Several political theories admit the importance of actors in their approaches. Although there are efforts to formalize them, the model presented in this chapter looks to integrate a variety of proposals in the context of public policies. The application of the model to e-government cases on Chile and Costa Rica has shown that the characteristics of the process executed in a timeline (with their successes and failures) can be explained from actors' perspective. Issues like promoting new laws, the coordination of multiple agencies or the priority for projects on political context have to be solved with specific actors using their power resources. The explanations found could be considered for characterize future developments on e-government taking on account how critical is the actors' intervention.

Chapter 9
Enterprise Architecture for Business Objectives: Understanding the Influencing Factors 171
Leshoto Mphahlele, Tshwane University of Technology, Pretoria, South Africa
Tiko Iyamu, Cape Peninsula University of Technology, South Africa

The demand for better services by customers and citizens keeps increasing at a rapid rate, enabling organizations the leverage towards competitive advantage. The enterprise architecture (EA) has merged as a possible solution for addressing organizational challenges, as well as for competitiveness and sustainability. The EA deployment involves agents, which are both human and non-human. The agents, based on their interest, influences and determines how the EA is deployed. During the deployment of EA, agents transform themselves in accordance to their interest at the time and space, making the process challenging in achieving the organisational needs. As examined and presented by this chapter, understanding of agents' interests is significant if the challenges that they pose are to be managed for successful deployment of EA. The chapter presents the impact of agents on the deployment of EA in organizations, through the lens of structuration theory.

Chapter 10
IT Governance Practices of SMEs in South Africa and the Factors Influencing Their Effectiveness 188
Charles Boamah-Abu, University of Cape Town, South Africa
Mike Tyobe, University of Cape Town, South Africa

The higher failure rate in SMEs is attributable factors including poor leadership, management and governance. Although IT adoption is prevalent in SMEs, not much is known about its governance. This research investigated IT governance practices in 67 SMEs in selected industries and provinces in South Africa. The findings revealed both sound and poor practices. SMEs with centralised IT departments had better practices, e. g., IT strategic investments; closer interactions among IT and business managers; and training of employees. The other SMEs managed IT opportunities poorly, e. g., irrationally IT investment decision-making; poorly defined IT roles and responsibilities; and noncompliance with IT legislations. It was also found that firm size, industry type and location influenced IT governance practices. Larger SMEs had more effective practices and there were differences in IT resource management among provinces. However, age of a firm and years of IT usage did not have much influence.

Chapter 11
The Interplay of Agents in Improvising Telecommunication Infrastructures' Services to Rural Community of South Africa 208
Sharol Mkhomazi, Tshwane University of Technology, South Africa

The deployment of telecommunication infrastructures is a challenge in many parts of South Africa particularly in the rural areas. The challenge has impact of communities' members as they do not have network coverage for Internet in some areas. The challenge gets worse with individual telecommunication service provider. Hence there is technological proposal for sharing of infrastructure by the service providers. However, the sharing of infrastructure is not as easy as notion by many individuals and groups institutions included. The article presents findings from a study on how a South African telecommunication network service provider could deploy shared infrastructures in the country's rural communities. The sharing of infrastructure is described by the structure and actions of agents within the infrastructure sharing process. Structuration theory was employed as a lens in the data analysis. The key findings include insufficient distribution of infrastructure, ownership responsibility, competitiveness, infrastructure deployment cost, and signification of regulation.

Chapter 12
Engineering the Services of the Library through Mobile Technology 226
   Eunice Mtshali, Tshwane University of Technology, South Africa

Many universities are struggling to response the needs of its users. This is attributed to the rapid change in technological innovations. The growing interest on mobile technology in organisations is at a fast pace, particularly in institutions of higher learning. Mobile technology could be used in academic libraries to provide a better service to their clients or improve the service that they currently provide. Case study research was conducted at Capital University to understand the factors that could influence and impact the adoption of mobile technology in academic library services.

Chapter 13
E-Competences for Organisational Sustainability Information Systems 242
   Zoran Mitrovic, Mitrovic Development and Research Institute, South Africa

The present patterns of economic development are deemed to be 'unsustainable'. It is believed that the concept of sustainability, assisted by the use of information and communication technologies (ICT) through organisational sustainability information systems (OSIS), is a 'cure' for current extraordinary environmental changes. However, the effective use of these systems requires an ICT competent (e-competent) workforce. E-competences, a combination of ICT-related knowledge, skills and attitudes are discussed in a number of studies but the European e-Competence Framework 3.0 is the only known framework that includes a single sustainability related e-competence. This study, however, reveals that, although the E-eCF3.0 sustainability e-competence is relevant, it is not sufficient for the effective use of OSIS as it transpired that the users should also possess other e-competences if these systems are to be exploited effectively.

Chapter 14
Information Systems Innovations Using Competitive Intelligence 260
   Phathutshedzo Nemutanzhela, Tshwane University of Technology, South Africa

The chapter outlines Information System's (IS) innovations using Competitive Intelligence (CI). The theoretical foundation supporting this chapter was reviewed and Information System framework was implemented. Recommendations as to how the framework for Information Systems innovation was implemented have been addressed in this chapter. Knowledge is used as a focal factor for competitive advantage, through effective and efficient performances by employees in many organisations. As a result, knowledgeable employees are expected to share their knowledge with others to increase innovation within the organisation. Unfortunately, this is not always the case. Generally, employees behave differently within an organisation. The main challenge is that no organisation has total control of its employees' behaviour and actions. The behaviour and action has an impact on how Information Systems are deployed for innovation, in creating competitive advantage. As a result, many systems have been deployed by different organisations in attempt to address this challenge for the interest.

Chapter 15
Competitive Intelligence for Business Enhancement: Deployment Framework 280
  Relebohile Moloi, Johannesburg, South Africa

Many organisations employ Competitive Intelligence (CI) to enable and support their goals and objectives, periodically. The CI is deployed by many organisations mainly to collect and analyse relevant data for decision making and competitive advantage. CI products are deployed in various ways in different contexts. CI products differ in many ways such as in terms of compatibility and the functionalities that they offer. The functions of a CI product are considered to be of significant to the organisation that deploys it. Otherwise, it would be short of enabling and supporting its objectives. The compatibility is critical mainly because each environment is unique. Many organisations have acquired CI products which they could not use because of compatibility challenges they encountered during implementation. This is one of the reasons why the criteria for selection and deployment of CI products are very important in many organisations as explored and presented in this chapter.

Compilation of References 293

About the Contributors 319

Index 324

Preface

In the last two decades, much work has been done on organisational politics, as well as on strategic information technology (IT), often separately articulated and presented. Thus, what has been missing is the interaction between strategic IT and organisational politics, making many of the major IT challenges in organisations to remain unresolved. Some of the IT challenges include how networks of both human and non-human actors are formed; how the actors' interacts; structural diverse; and manifestation of environmental factors in the development, implementation, management and use of information systems and technologies in the organisations. It is in this area this book focuses upon, for the benefit of both the academic and corporate domains.

The book presents its contribution from three perspectives, theory, methodology and practice for the benefits of academics and practitioners in both business and IT fields. This was done within context and relevance, to understand how Strategic Information Technology Governance and the associated Organizational Politics could be employed to enable, support and manage modern businesses.

The theoretical contribution comes from both basic and applied research, as presented in this book. The studies explored and examined the ontological and philosophical assumptions to develop models, to improve effectiveness and efficiency of business through IT, while keeping eye on the "necessary evil" called organisational politics. The book reveals that in practice activities in the business world are influenced by conscious and unconsciousness actions of actors, to control and manage processes, using different tools such information technology. These were shown through various frameworks in the book. Methodologically, the studies demonstrate empricalism from theoretical and practical perspectives, showing how the researches were underpinned. Theoretically, organisational transformation through IT was underpinned to understand that the joint effect of the actions of individuals' interacting within institutional structures is fundamental to the business achievements. That both human interaction and institutional structures enable and at the same time constrain the daily actions and thought processes of people, but do not wholly determine the results, which manifest business outcome.

ORGANIZATION OF THE BOOK

The first chapter, "Towards a Contingency Model for assessing Strategic Information Systems Planning success in Medium Enterprises", presents a model which can be used in the development of effective long-term use of information systems, including measuring the success of strategic information systems planning in the context of medium enterprises. The model was guided by contingency theory, as an analytical lens.

Preface

Chapter 2 focuses on the interaction between human and nonhuman agents in the development and implementation of information technology strategy. Thus, how the activities of the agents enable and constrain IT strategy in organisations were examined, from both technical and nontechnical perspectives.

In Chapter 3, two sociotechnical theories, Structuration Theory and Actor-Network Theory were complementarily applied as lenses, to examine and understand the impact of organisational politics on the development and implementation of information technology strategy. One of the largest financial institutions in Africa was used as the case study, to investigate how organisational politics determine the success or failure of the IT strategy. The chapter presents that relative instability of the actor-networks, implementation of the IT strategy can be expected to become increasingly difficult, and that human action produces and reproduces structures which defines IT strategy over time and space.

Chapter 4 covers information systems outsourcing from multi-layered and multifaceted perspectives. The study explores strategic management of information systems outsourcing of resources, such as knowledge, on one hand. On another hand, the impact of retention was examined. The chapter presents knowledge requirements in an IS outsourcing arrangement based on a case study which was conducted in a telecommunication company in South Africa.

Chapter 5 examines how a captive offshore center becomes a separate business arm of the parent company, which is wholly owned, to provide IT solutions to its parent company. A Some Chicago based Company (sears Holdings), which considered the approach to be a strategic move, was used as the case in the study. The chapter presents how a Sears Holdings lunched a successful captive offshore IT center and why they received outsourcing best practices award from the industry. The result was evaluated against previous research on offshore best practices and many correlations were found.

Chapter 6 presents the value of reference process models versus current process models. The empirical data was gathered from an Enterprise Conceptual Model of a medium-sized Namibian Freight Forwarder. The case study exemplifies that an Enterprise Conceptual Model has actually helped to translate strategic goals and operational needs into business processes and at the same time helped to ensure that imminent processes fit to the software-given processes.

Chapter 7 examines why organizations continue to invest in technology, and place less emphasis on non-technical factors in the development and implementation of software. In the study, the lens of ANT, moments of translation was systematically employed in the data analysis to unveil the criticality of the interactions among actors. The study revealed how network of people were consciously and unconsciously formed heterogeneously. This will assist manager to trace activities in order to avoid pitfall, and increase competitiveness.

Chapter 8 covers, from Costa Rica perspective, the roles of actors in E-government development. The study introduces a model which guides the development of E-government project. The success or failure of the E-government development was evaluated based on political issues, which were carried out by the actors.

Chapter 9 focuses on the role of EA in organisations, with specific concetration on monitoring and management of business processes, information flow, technology selection and deployment. In the chapter, a detailed discussion is provided on how the Business and IT units' alignment and organisational structure often have an impact on the deployment of the EA. A framewok which could be used to address factors influncing EA deployment in the organisations.

Chapter 10 contributes to the much work that has been done on IT governance practices in small medium enterprise (SME) over the years, through findings from a study that was conducted in South Africa. Based on the empirical evidence from three regions of the country, a conceptual model was developed, as presented in this chapter. The model can be used to evaluate the operational and strategic value of IT to SMEs.

Chapter 11 empirically unveils the criticality and signification of telecommunication infrastructures sharing in rural areas of South African communities. The chapter highlights that the processes and influencing factors of shared telecommunication infrastructures involve socio-technical factors and the interplay between human action and social systems.

Chapter 12 covers the adoption of mobile technology for teaching and learning in academic institution. It presents a framework which highlights the factors which can guide the adoption of the mobile technology for efficiency and effectiveness purposes. In the chapter, it well emphasised that without the appropriate infrastructure facilities, equipment and staff expertise it will be impossible to adopt mobile technology in academic libraries.

Chapter 13 introduces three dimensions to E-competences for Organisational Sustainability Information Systems. They includes obtaining an initial understanding regarding the sufficiency of the sustainability e-competences (*Sustainability Development*), which is proposed by the European e-Competence Framework 2.0, for addressing sustainability issues in an organisation; identifies the possible need for other e-competences for addressing sustainability issues in an organisation; and provides a theoretical basis for further development and implementation of NeSPA 2013.

In chapter 14, the authors applied diffusion of innovation to examine how competitive Intelligence and Information Systems seem to have a common focus, to meeting the needs of the users in an organisation. It is highlighted that information systems in many ways enables the gathering of information that later becomes competitive intelligence within the environment. Also, competitive intelligence facilitates the creation of information system innovations in the way it is used during the process of improving products and services.

Chapter 15 examines how socio-technical factors manifest themselves, which impacts and sometimes derails the selection and deployment of competitive intelligence products in the organisation. It presents the factors which are critical but are never understood, or are often taken for granted during the selection and deployment of CI products by some of the stakeholders, but are of great importance.

This book will benefit both academic and industry practitioners. The book will be most useful as a learning curve for managers and other IT specialists in the organisations, in terms of understanding why things happen in the way that they do, consciously or unconsciously in the development, implementation, management of information systems and technologies for organisational objectives. Thus, they are able to have deeper understanding and grip of the IT factors that influences their business processes and activities, from both operational and strategic perspectives. Similarly, the academic will benefits from the book, particular from case study perspective. The book can be used to develop and enhance IT related courses curriculum and content, as academics continue to respond to business needs.

Preface

In summary, this book presents the criticality and significance of strategic information technology governance and organizational politics in modern businesses. Thus, the book reveals how information technology is strategically used to govern processes and activities in organisations. In addition, the book contributes to the field of information technology, primarily in the analytical manner it focuses on the factors which manifests themselves into organisational politics, and how the factors are representatively applied in their various contexts of significance. The above points has major impacts on modern businesses, from the perspectives of strategic information technology and governance in organisations.

Chapter 1
Towards A Contingency Model for Assessing Strategic Information Systems Planning Success in Medium Enterprises

Ray M Kekwaletswe
University of the Witwatersrand, South Africa

ABSTRACT

Strategic planning of information systems is vital in the business environment and this is still an open issue in the management information systems research. Through planning, organisations develop effective long-term use of information systems and subsequently ensuring the support of organisational objectives. This chapter develops a contingency model for measuring the success of strategic information systems planning in the context of medium enterprises. The contingency theory, as an analytical lens, advocates that organisational success can be achieved by matching organisational characteristics to the contextual factors. Drawing from this notion, this chapter postulates that the strategic information systems planning process, as a phase, may lead to successful planning. This relationship is moderated by contingency variables characterised by the presence of environmental uncertainty, organisational structure, government and policies, business strategy orientation and information systems maturity. This chapter studies the moderating role of contingency variables and identifies the influential factors and their effect.

1. INTRODUCTION

Information systems use in medium enterprises tends to primarily be for administrative and operational tasks. The most frequent applications in medium enterprises are transactional in nature. Beckinsale, Ram and Theodorakopoulos (2011) have recently stated that the failure to plan the introduction and exploitation of information systems and technologies in medium enterprises is due to the top management limitations. These include management having insufficient time to spend on future business developments and

DOI: 10.4018/978-1-4666-8524-6.ch001

management teams having little experience, expertise or interest in exploiting technology. The age and experience of the owner is often the most influential factor in relation to decisions on IS-based success.

Prior information systems researchers have stated that strategic information systems planning in medium enterprises becomes more critical as technology becomes more central to the medium enterprises' products and processes, and planning needs to be integrated with business strategy. The main problem associated with the lack of strategic information systems use in medium enterprises relates to the relatively poor fit between the offering of information systems and the business need (Levy & Powell, 2005). The increasing demands of the marketplace make it very essential for enterprises to make successful strategic information systems planning (SISP) based on an alignment between information system strategies and the business strategic plan of the organisation. However, the existing literature provides little evidence of information systems (IS) development within medium enterprises. Foong (1999) stated that the introduction of IS into enterprises, like the early introduction into large firms, has tended to be fragmented and based around operational support and transaction processing. Typically, the interest and the enthusiasm of owners tend to drive IS adoption (Premkumar & Roberts, 1999). Not surprisingly, adoption is often not planned strategically. For example, manufacturing businesses invest in systems in order to improve production processing without integrating the order processing system or developing stock control systems (Levy & Powell, 1998).

According to Levy and Powell (2000) high environmental uncertainty is also likely to drive enterprises to change business processes. This chapter argues that paying more attention to SISP may, therefore, increase survival rates of enterprises - supporting the contention that SISP is vital for gaining and maintaining competitive advantage (Agarwal, 1998) – accordingly reducing the environmental uncertainty that challenges managers.

The purpose of this chapter is to develop and validate a contingency model for assessing strategic information systems planning success in the context of a developing country medium enterprise. Strategic Information Systems Planning (SISP) is considered as the first stage in the process of information systems implementation. Strategic Information Systems Planning (SISP) has been defined in several ways. Mohdzain and Ward (2007) perceived Strategic Information Systems Planning (SISP) as activities directed towards recognising organisational opportunities for using information technology, determining the resource requirements to exploit these opportunities, and developing strategies and action plans for realising these opportunities and meeting the resource needs. Teubner (2007), considered Strategic Information Systems Planning (SISP) as an exercise or ongoing activity that enables an organisation to develop priorities for information system (IS) development.

In the context of this chapter, Strategic Information Systems Planning (SISP) is described as a medium or long-term managerial process which identifies an organisation's priorities for developing information systems and information technology, in order to align information systems strategy with business strategy so as to gain competitive advantage (Bechor *et al.*, 2010; Mohdzain and Ward; Teubner, 2007; Zijad, 2007; Newkirk & Lederer, 2006). Many studies (e.g., Hovelja, Rozanec and Rupnik, 2010; Mohdzain & Ward, 2007; Palanisamy, 2005) have been conducted on the topic of success of information systems implementation but there is no consensus about what the appropriate method should be for examining the success of Strategic Information Systems Planning (SISP).

It is inferred, from literature, that the success of Strategic Information Systems Planning (SISP) is difficult to measure and cannot be limited to simple financial aspects such as return on investment

(Segars & Grover, 2005). Strategic Information Systems Planning success (SISPS) has been described in term of the extent to which organisation objectives were achieved (Newkirk & Lederer, 2007). The success of Strategic Information Systems Planning (SISP) in organisation is closely related to the existing link between Strategic Information Systems Planning (SISP) and corporate strategic planning process (Segars & Grover, 2005).

This chapter proceeds as follows: firstly, the theoretical perspectives are presented with the research variables; secondly, the study hypotheses are presented; this is followed by the research methodology discussion; the data analysis is presented; this is followed by a discussion on study findings; a contingency model is then developed; and lastly, implication for practice and research is given.

2. THEORETICAL PERSPECTIVE AND RESEARCH VARIABLES

2.1. Theoretical Perspectives

A strategic information systems planning (SISP) may be broadly considered to be a competitive weapon to cope with uncertain environments (Choe, 2003). It has been argued that organisations can deal with environmental uncertainty by increasing their information processing capability and by creating inter-organizational links between SISP and business strategic planning. SISP is used to obtain competitive advantages over competitors and to prevent competitors from gaining an advantage. Past research suggests the environmental uncertainty often encourages organisations to utilise SISP in order to survive (Grover & Lederer, 1999; Teo & King, 1996; Sabherwal & King, 1992; Reich & Benbasat, 2000).

The present study included one independent variable: Strategic Information Systems Planning Process (SISPP) with five phases namely: strategic awareness, situation analysis, strategy conception, strategy formulation and strategy implementation. One dependent variable was Strategic Information Systems Planning Success (SISPS). The SISPS contain four dimensions, namely: alignment, analysis, cooperation and improvement in capabilities. One moderate variable: environmental uncertainty with three sub-constructs, which are environmental dynamism, environmental heterogeneity and environmental hostility. This chapter puts forward a framework as shown in figure 1 which explores the relationship between SISPP and SISPS under environmental uncertainty.

Figure 1 is a framework exploring the relationship between SISPP and SISPS under environmental uncertainty. The next section discusses the contingency research variables as significant factors affecting management information systems and strategic information systems planning success (Bakar, Suhaimi & Huissain, 2009). A contextual factor is a variable that describes one of the possible ways contexts affect organisations' project performance. The earlier research categorises contextual factors in organisation's internal contexts and factors in the organisations' external context that could be considered for each organisation (Wang, 2006). Literature review provides a wide range of contextual factors that represent attributes of the organisation and its environment. From that investigation, the contextual factors have been characterised by the presence of turbulent environment, environment uncertainty (dynamism, heterogeneity and hostility) in the organisation external aspect and by the existence of organisational structure, IS function structure, orientation of business strategy, IS maturity, IT importance, size, formalisation, centralisation, future role of IS and so on, in the organisation internal aspect (Bechor et al., 2010; Cohen, 2008; Warr, 2005).

Figure 1. Relationship between variables

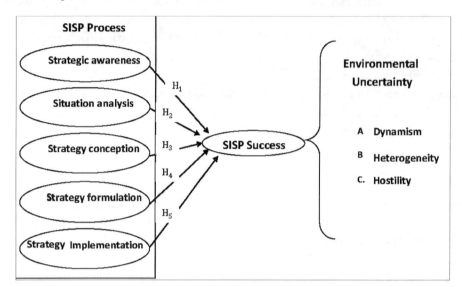

2.2. Research Variables

2.3. Strategic Information Systems Planning Process (SISPP)

SISP can be defined as the process of determining an organisation's portfolio of computer-based applications that will help it achieve its business objectives (Reich & Benbasat, 2000). SISP is a rational process, intended to recommend new information systems linked to an overall corporate strategy, and the SISP helps an organisation to achieve its goal of improved competitiveness, operations and resource management (Mentzas, 1997).

2.4. The Mentzas Model

The Mentzas (1997) model of SISPP describes three process elements, in order to increase detail namely: phases, stages and modules. The phases of SISP are generic strategy formulation steps that can be applied to any corporate strategy development process. Each phase is divided into stages. Stages are considered to be semi-autonomous components of work, which can be planned relatively independently. A stage is defined in terms of the resulting behaviour and appearance of its end-product, and the information structures that underlie it. Stages are further divided into modules. Modules can either be units of work (i.e. activities) or collections of activities.

The observation of the extent to which an organisation carries out each phase and task may be used to assess the state of the SISPP. Therefore, in this chapter, phases and tasks are considered as the basis for assessing the degree of use of the SISPP (following Newkirk & Lederer, 2006; Newkirk, 2001). Table 1 shows the phases and tasks of the SISPP.

Table 1 shows the varied phases and the stages of the strategic information systems planning process. The next section discusses the success dimensions and items.

Table 1. SISPP phases and stages

Phases	Stages
Strategic Awareness	Identification of strategic goals
	Identification of business and IT systems
	Definition of planning process objectives
Situation analysis	Analysis of business systems
	Analysis of organisational systems
	Analysis of IT systems
	Analysis of external business environment Analysis of external IT environment
Strategy conception	Scanning of the future
	Identification of alternative scenarios
	Scenario elaboration
Strategy formulation	Formulation of business architecture
	Formulation of IT architecture
	Formulation of organisational solutions
	Synthesis and prioritisation
Strategy implementation planning	Definition of action plan elements
	Elaboration of action plan
	Evaluation plan
	Definition of follow-up and control procedures

2.4.1. Strategic Information Systems Planning Success (SISPS)

SISPS can be understood in terms of the extent to which the organisation objectives were achieved (Raghunathan & Raghunathan, 1994; Kunnathur and Shi, 2001). Earl (1993) found that SISP embodied three equally important elements for assessing success. These elements were: method, process and implementation. Thus, he used a construct that consisted of all three elements of SISP, which he called "the SISP approach".

Segars and Grover (1998) argue that the benefits of SISP cannot be reduced to such simple financial measures as return on investment, payback or internal rate of return. In this context, they built an instrument and empirically verified a second-order model based on these two perspectives for SISP success. In their instrument, there are four dimensions, namely: alignment, analysis, cooperation and improvement in capabilities. They rigorously tested the model through confirmatory factor analysis in the United States setting. Their test confirmed that planning success is multidimensional (King, 1988) and can be well represented as a second-order factor (SISP success, SISP). Their study has thus provided a theoretical and operational definition for many aspects of SISP success. These four dimensions have been used as basis for the assessment of SISPS in the present study. The dimensions and their items are shown in Table 2.

The understanding of the dimensions and items for the strategic information systems planning process and success informs the conceptual model, figure 2, for assessing process and success.

Figure 2 gives the conceptual model for the SISP process and the SISP success. The following section looks at the contingency variables.

Table 2. SISPS dimensions and items

Dimensions	Items
Alignment	Understanding the strategic priorities of top management Aligning IS strategies with the strategic plan of the organisation Adapting the goals/objectives of IS to the changing goals/objectives of the organisation Maintaining a mutual understanding with top management on the role of IS in supporting strategy Identifying IT-related opportunities to support the strategic direction of the firm Educating top management on the importance of IT Adapting technology to strategic change Assessing the strategic importance of emerging technologies
Analysis	Understanding the information needs of organisational subunits Identifying opportunities for internal improvement of business processes through IT Improved understanding of how the organisation actually operates Development of a "blueprint" which structures organisational processes Monitoring of internal business needs and the capability of IS to meet those needs Maintaining an understanding of changing organisational processes and procedures Generating new ideas to reengineer business processes through IT Understanding the dispersion of data, applications and other technologies throughout the firm
Cooperation	Avoiding the overlapping development of major systems Achieving a general level of agreement regarding the risks/tradeoffs among system projects Establishing a uniform basis for prioritising projects Maintaining open lines of communication with other departments Coordinating the development efforts of various organisational subunits Identifying and resolving potential sources of resistance to IS plans Developing clear guidelines of managerial responsibility for plan implementation
Capabilities	Ability to identify key problem areas Ability to identify new business opportunities Ability to align IS strategy with organisational strategy Ability to anticipate surprises and crises Ability to understand the business and its information needs Flexibility to adapt to unanticipated changes Ability to gain cooperation among user groups for IS plans

Figure 2. Conceptual model for assessing SISP process and SISP success

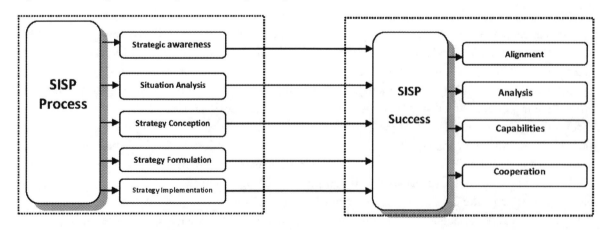

2.3 Contingency Variables

Prescriptive studies have used contingency variables to explore the practices associated with strategic SISP. Wang and Tai (2003) integrated three domains to investigate the effects of contingency variables and planning system dimensions on the effectiveness of IS planning form a contingency perspective. Their model was supported by the empirical data, shown the importance of many contingency factors and planning system dimensions to attaining greater effectiveness of IS planning.

Study conducted by Law and Ngai (2007) proposed that the success of IT projects was affected by contingency factors: management support and the rank of the IS leaders. In many circumstances, the top management team must mediate between technology and business requirements and resolve the conflict of interest among a large number of stakeholders. The seniority of the IS executive can have an effect on the success of IT and business process initiatives. The CIO, as an influential member of the senior management team, must solicit support from the user community and other managers. The direct reporting relationship of the IS executive to the CEO as opposed to other senior leaders moderated the effects of IT investment on the organisation's success (Gefen & Ragowsky, 2005).

Contingency variables are significant variables affecting Management Information Systems and Strategic Information Systems Planning success (Bakar, Suhaimi & Huissain, 2009). A Contingency variable is a variable that describes one of the possible ways contexts affect organisations' project performance (Lee & Pai, 2003). The earlier research categorises contingency variables in two streams of research. First, there is research regarding information systems planning. Second, there is research regarding the strategic use of information resources. Both streams were relevant to this study. Contingency variables examined in previous research are noted in Table 3.

Table 3. Contingency variables used in most management of information systems research

Organisational Characteristics	Industry type Size (Employees, Revenues, Assets) Corporate strategy Corporate structure Corporate culture Attitudes toward change Geographic proximity Information intensity of products or services information intensity of the value chain IS management expertise Is end-user expertise Strategic grid position Strategic role for IT
IS Function	Size (Employees, Budget) Structure Business knowledge of IS managers Locus of control for systems decisions Alignment of the IS plan User satisfaction Implementation history
IT Investment	Investment in technology Strategic grid position Age of systems Connectivity of systems
External Environment	Dynamism Heterogeneity hostility

Following on the contingency variables used in previous studies, Table 3, this chapter examines environmental uncertainty, organisational structure, government and policies, business strategy orientation and information systems maturity as the five contingency variables.

2.3.1 Environment Uncertainty

Every organisation exists in an environment, and the environmental influence on an organisation's performance is critical. There are several environments that may impact on an organisation. Perceptions of, and responses to, environmental problems are evolving rapidly at all levels and can be grouped into categories including social, regulatory, technological, political, economic and industry. Influences of each can negatively affect an organisation, resulting in poor performance or ultimate failure (Kendra, 2004). Researchers (e.g., Cohen, 2008) contend that it is under conditions of environmental uncertainty that strategic planning could come to the fore. Supported by the information uncertainty perspective, they argue that environmental uncertainty increases the need for information gathering and therefore SISP. SISP can be used to reduce uncertainty, and is increasingly recognised as a necessity for organisations to survive and be able to tackle uncertainty quickly and robustly in order to sustain and enhance business competitiveness (Brown, 2008). Chi *et al.* (2005) have described environmental uncertainty as physical and social influences outside the boundaries of the firm that must be taken into consideration in managerial decision-making. Furthermore, uncertainty consists of three components: Lack of clarity; Long time span of definitive feedback; and General uncertainty of causal relationships.

In previous researches, environmental uncertainty has been characterised and studied in terms of three constructs: dynamism, heterogeneity and hostility. These constructs were extensively assessed and validated (Musangu & Kekwaletswe, 2011; Brown, 2008; Newkirk & Lederer, 2007; Newkirk & Lederer, 2006a). Information systems (IS) researchers have used them in their studies of contextual factors that facilitate strategic information systems (SIS) applications, as well as the integration of information systems (IS) and business planning. These three constructs represent the external environment, which includes relevant physical and social factors beyond the borders of the organisation.

2.3.2 Environmental Dynamism

The first construct is termed environmental dynamism by some authors and instability by others. It has been found to impact negatively on comprehensiveness in SISP. It is characterised by the rate of change and innovation in the industry, as well as the unpredictability of the actions of competitors and customers (Newkirk & Lederer, 2006a). Greater dynamism requires higher levels of cooperation and coordination between business and IS (Brown, 2008; Grover & Segars, 2005).

Dynamism has been defined by Brown (2008) as the rate and unpredictability of environmental change, and is especially challenging for managers. Researchers have measured it in terms of the rate of product/service obsolescence, the rate of product/service technology changes, unpredictability of competitors' moves, and unpredictability of product/service demand changes. Dynamic environments increase the firm's need for information resources which can facilitate inter-organisational linkage by improving information processing capabilities such as the building of a knowledge base, the seeking out of new business opportunities, and the development and management of competitive initiatives (Grover & Segars, 2005).

2.3.3. Environmental Heterogeneity

The second construct is termed environmental heterogeneity by some authors and complexity by others. It has been defined as the complexity and diversity of external factors (Newkirk & Lederer, 2006a). Heterogeneity was considered to be a measure of the amount of diversity in a firm's products and markets. It affects the importance of information systems because it creates the need for more extensive analysis or management. Diversity leads to complexity of organisational structures which complicates the administrative task, creating the need for liaison devices such as steering committees (Grover & Segars, 2005).

Newkirk and Lederer (2006b) have showed that environmental heterogeneity has a positive impact on comprehensiveness in SISP. In highly diverse heterogeneous environments, information must be gathered from a wide variety of sources, and various alternative scenarios need to be evaluated. Thus, there is greater comprehensiveness of SISP. Environmental heterogeneity leads also to a more political, rather than rational process in SISP. This again can be explained by the wider variety of diverse and competing interests in heterogeneous environments, which gives rise to political machinations in organisational tasks such as SISP (Brown, 2008).

2.3.4 Environmental Hostility

The last construct is termed environmental hostility by some authors and munificence by others. Environmental hostility has been defined as the availability of resources that permit organisational growth and stability. Hostility involves both the availability of resources and the degree of competition in the external environment (Newkirk & Lederer; 2006a). Environmental hostility indicates the intensity of competition and the exposure of major products or services to economic downturns. Hostile environments are characterised by a scarcity of labour and material resources, making it advantageous for firms to create information partnerships with suppliers (Brown, 2008).

2.4. Organisational Structure

The organisation of work and the arrangements of organisational activities are known to be affected by the implementation of a technological system. Applegate quoted by Pulkkinen (2008) outlined four areas with interrelations between them contributing to information management infrastructure: technical systems, management systems, organisational structure and people. Today, the question is no more of replacing manual systems with computerised ones, but of managing a portfolio of technologies and applications, aligning it to the business strategies and goals, and evaluating alternatives solutions accordingly. However, the challenges of organisational change remain. Sharing information is one of the most crucial factors in change management.

Organisational structure is a fundamental factor influencing SISP effectiveness and strategic information systems applications (Wang & Tai, 2003). Organisational structure refers to the framework typically hierarchical within which an organisation arranges its lines of authority and communications, and allocates rights and duties. Organisational structure determines the manner and extent to which roles, power and responsibilities are delegated, controlled and coordinated, and how information flows between levels of management. A structure depends entirely on the organisation's objectives and the strategy chosen to achieve them (Morton & Hu, 2008; Lee & Pai, 2003).

According to Donaldson (2001) organisational structure is more complicated than distinguishing between centralised and decentralised operations or decisions-making. Other commonly cited structural dimensions include specialisation, standardisation, formalisation, hierarchical levels and span of control. Taking into account of the number of proposed structural dimensions and the variety of their definitions, identifying a definitive set of organisational dimensions is difficult without specific context and objectives (Morton & Hu, 2008).

Previous researchers have developed some dimensions in the structural contingency theory literature and they have considered those dimensions as appropriate starting points. Within the structural contingency literature, the main organisational contingencies are specialisation, formalisation, structural differentiation and decentralisation (Donaldson, 2001). Mintzburg quoted by Morton and Hu (2008) conducted a synthesis of research on organisation design from which he developed five structural configurations that can be treated as a typology of ideal or pure organisational types. These five basic configurations provide a useful framework of organisational structures. The ideal types and their pertinent characteristics are presented in Table 4.

Table 4. Ideal types of organisational structures

Simple Form	Small, simple Low formalisation Highly centralisation Unsophisticated technical systems
Machine Bureaucracy	Perform routine operating tasks Highly formalised Relatively centralised decision-making Automated and integrated technology Highly differentiated structure Standardised work processes used for coordination Operate in stable environments Regulating, non-automated technical system
Professional Bureaucracy	Decentralised decision-making Standardisation of skills used for coordination Highly skilled workers who value autonomy Non-regulating, non-sophisticated technical systems
Divisionalized Form Adhocracy	Centralised headquarters Semi-autonomous, loosely joined divisions Little interdependence or close coordination among divisions Main goals of headquarters is to coordinate goals of divisions with that of its own without sacrificing autonomy Standardised outputs of divisions used for coordination Divisions are generally machine bureaucracies Technical system separated into segment, one for each division Operates as a cohesive group working together Mutual coordination and cooperation Innovative Workers are trained experts from different specialities Ad hoc project teams Low formalisation Decentralised decision-making Operate in dynamic environment Sophisticated and often automated technical system (in the administrative adhocracy)

(Source: Mintzberg quoted by Morton and Hu, 2008)

As stated previously, organisational structure construct has been characterised on a variety of dimensions and using a variety of types. However, two dimensions of organisation structure: formalisation and centralisation have received more theoretical and managerial attention than other characterisations and appear to have the greatest implications for the design of strategic planning systems ((Warr, 2005; Wang & Tai, 2003).

2.5 Government and Policies

Government, political system, regulations and national laws are factors which impact business manager to achieve competitive advantage in the business environment. Political activity interferes with the process of planning organisation business strategy. Planners will design only plans that are politically feasible, and thereby group with some people against others (Mintzberg quoted by Pita, 2007). Most of the time, important strategic change in market is initiated by political activity and that political interference on strategic planning can have negative influence.

Achieving business performance is affected by several political barriers such as: foreign trade policy, tariffs and protection policies, price regulations, investment incentives, trade practice and research and development grants (Pita, 2007). It is the government responsibility to design the appropriate resource management policy instruments that steer the desired economic outcome towards a goal such as sustainable development. Lewis and Harvey (2001) suggested three categories of policy instruments that are available to government to do this namely: full cost pricing, polluter pays principle and command and control.

2.6 Business Strategy Orientation

Competition in medium enterprises sectors has increased considerably because constant adaptation in a turbulent environment requires a continuous flow of new offers (Stevens & Dimitriadis, 2005). Strategy is bound to directly influence an organisation's degree of new offer activity. The task of strategic planning is to assure a stream of new ideas that will allow the organisation to continue to adapt to its uncertain outside world (Frambach *et al.* 2003). Business strategy reflects the actions and choices which firms take to understand and adapt to their environments and to position themselves in markets to achieve high levels of performance (Porter and Kramer, 2006).

Business strategy can be examined using different typologies for the corporate-level strategy and the business-level strategy (Dong *et al.*, 2008). The Miles and Snow's typology of prospectors, defenders and analysers was used to assess business strategy orientation. A prospector has been described as an organisation with an aggressive competitive strategy that attempts to pioneer in the product/market development. Dong *et al.* (2008) have defined defender as an organization with a conservative competitive strategy and engages in little or no new product development. An analyser has been considered as an intermediate type, is an organisation with a moderate competitive strategy that makes fewer and slower product/ market changes than a prospector and less stable than a defender.

The Miles and Snow typology as quoted by Dong *et al.* (2008) combines elements of both corporate and business level strategies. In addition, it is parsimonious but appears to account for significant variations across organisations.

2.7 Information Systems Maturity

Information Technology generally refers to the assistance provided by information systems department to customers and users for IS products and services. These activities include advising and guidance, training, and help-desks for troubleshooting, or resolving user problems (Lertwongsatien, 2000). Information systems maturity is defined as the extent to which the information systems support functions are adequately fine-tuned and planed for supporting user's demands. Information technology support maturity reflects the evolution stages of information systems activities in providing information technology support for customers and users. A higher level of information systems maturity would have evolved from data processing orientation into the strategic IS orientation (maturity) (Cerpa & Verner, 1998). Previous researchers have identified five key indicators of information systems maturity as: formalisation, priority criteria, staffing, performance standard control, and use of technology for customer support.

3. HYPOTHESES

Research Hypotheses

Hypotheses are formulated statements about the relationship between variables or factors. A hypothesis is a refined guess based on assumptions that can be verified or falsified (Sage, 2006). Hypotheses are proven or not proven and repeated results may lead to the development of theory. Relative to determine model fit in structural equation modelling. According to Schumacker and Lomax (2004) hypothesis testing involves confirming that a theoretical specified model fits sample variance-covariance data, testing structural coefficients for significance. Sections 3.1 to 3.5 outline the hypotheses formulated from the proposed contingency framework.

3.1 Strategic Awareness, SISP Effectiveness, and the Moderating Role of Contingency Variables

Managing organisation to achieve competitive advantage require knowledge which often is lacking in adopting organisations. Strategic awareness can help organisation managers to gain appropriate knowledge about competitors, resources, customers, and regulators. Prior researchers have found out that when top managers' knowledge about business environment and IT is high, the planning process will be successful (Newkirk & Lederer, 2006). We therefore hypothesise:

H1. *SISP process in the strategic awareness phase can lead to the SISP success.*

Contingency variables are challenging managers' knowledge about planning and decisions making process and some researchers have suggested that contextual factors can impede managers' to gain appropriate knowledge and achieve organisation performance. We, therefore, further hypothesise:

H2. *The relationship between SISP process in the strategic awareness phase and the SISP success will be moderated by the contingency variables.*

3.2. Situation Analysis, SISP Effectiveness, and the Moderating Role of Contingency Variables

The examination of current business systems, current external environment and IT/IS environment, and extracting information of the present organisation in terms of its requirements will be expected to contribute to the organisation performance. Due to the organisation complexity, a better understanding of business, organisation and information systems, would produce better knowledge about the organisation's requirements and contribute to the SISP success. We formulate the following hypothesis:

H3. *SISP process in the situation analysis phase can lead to the SISP success.*

The basic relationship between situation analysis and SISP effectiveness can be influenced by external and internal factors. Hence:

H4. *The relationship between SISP process in the situation analysis phase and SISP success will be moderated by the contingency variables.*

3.3. Strategy Conception, SISP Effectiveness, and the Moderating Role of Contingency Variables

Strategy conception, with identification and evaluation of opportunities, would provide more realistic alternatives. Identification of information technology objectives would allow the organisation to align future information technology and business objectives. Better alternatives and choices would help the plan produce better results. We formulate the following hypothesis:

H5. *SISP process in the strategy conception phase can lead to the SISP success.*

Contingency variables are influencing the process of identifying IT objectives and misalign information technology and business objectives. Hence:

H6. *The relationship between SISP process in the strategy conception phase and SISP success will be moderated by the contingency variables.*

3.4. Strategy Formulation, SISP Effectiveness, and the Moderating Role of Contingency Variables

Strategy formulation with a careful identification of new business processes, new information technology architectures, and setting priorities for new projects would make it more likely to meet planning objectives. Higher prioritisation level would result in greater chance of attaining SISP success. We formulate the following hypothesis:

H7. *SISP process in the strategy formulation phase can lead to the SISP success.*

The presence of environmental uncertainty, organisation structure, government and policies, business strategy orientation, and IS maturity can influence the basic relationship between strategy formulation and the effectiveness of SISP. Hence:

H8. *The relationship between SISP process in the strategy formulation phase and SISP success will be moderated by the contingency variables.*

3.5. Strategy Implementation, SISP Effectiveness, and the Moderating Role of Contingency Variables

Strategy implementation, with more attention to change management and a better action plan, would be likely to result in good implementation. Better follow-up and control would result in more of the plan being implemented and thus better delivery of planning objectives. We formulate the following hypothesis:

H9. *SISP process in the strategy implementation phase can lead to the SISP success.*

Contextual factors can impact the basic relationship between strategy implementation and SISP effectiveness. Hence:

H10. *The relationship between SISP process in the strategy implementation phase and SISP success will be moderated by the contingency variables.*

The preceding section gave the ten hypotheses driving the study, the next section discusses the research design and the methodology followed in studying the contingencies for assessing strategic information systems planning success.

4. RESEARCH METHODS

This section outlines the research design and methods followed for studying contingencies for assessing the strategic information systems planning.

4.1. Sampling Frame and Procedure

Informed by Newkirk and Lederer (2006), Segars and Grover (1999) as well as Lederer and Sethi (1996), a non-scientific method of sampling was employed for the study. The sampling was framed using the 2010 edition of *"Who Owns Whom in South Africa"*, published by McGregor. This directory contains the names, titles, addresses of top computer executives in South Africa. The entities within the directory include small enterprises, micro enterprises, medium enterprises, large firms, educational institutions, hospitals and governmental agencies.

In developing a desirable sub frame,

1. All large firms, hospitals, educational institutions and governmental agencies were eliminated from consideration.

Table 5. Summary of responses to mail survey questionnaire

Total Number of Questionnaire mailed out	1500
Total Number of Questionnaire Returned	336
Total Number of Returns Useful for Analysis	319
Total Number of Returns Unsuitable for Analysis	17
Gross Response Rate	22.4%
Usable Response Rate	21.2%

2. The job titles of key informants remaining in the frame were examined as a means of determining the level of planning activity.
3. Medium enterprises with a senior executive carrying the job title of chief information officer, vice president, director of strategic planning, director of MIS or head of IS/IT establish in Gauteng province were retained.

A total of 1500 questionnaires were initially mailed out to sample respondents, the overall response to the mail survey was: 336(319 + 17). Thus, the gross responses rate of the research survey was 22.4% (336/1500), of which, 319 (237 + 82) returns, that is, 21.2% (319/1500) were suitable for analysis. A summary of responses to the mail survey questionnaire is presented in Table 5.

The gross response rate and useable response rate received for the present study is quite high as compared with previous and similar SISP studies. A summary of the response rates in previous studies is presented in Table 6.

On the basis of the response rates in prior studies, presented in table 6 above, the response rate for the present study was deemed satisfactory.

5. DATA ANALYSIS

In order to elucidate and qualify the identified research hypotheses, standard statistical tests were conducted using SPSS version 20 and the proposed contingency framework had been analysed using the Structural Equation Modelling (SEM) supported by Analysis of Moment Structures (AMOS). Descriptive statistics (mean, standard deviation, median) were used to assess the normality of the data in order to conform to the assumptions of other statistical methods used. Missing data was initially coded in keeping with

Table 6. Summary of response rate in previous studies

Researcher	Year	Total Number of Questionnaire Mailed Out	Total Number of Questionnaire Returned	Response Rate
Bechor et al.	2010	2300	206	9%
Mirchandani & Lederer	2008	906	131	17%
Cohen	2008	615	121	19.7%
Newkirk & Lederer	2007	1200	220	18%
Kunnathur & Zhengzhong	2001	608	92	15.13%

the recommendations in the SPSS 20 manual; the SPSS option "exclude cases pairwise" was chosen for the missing value. This gave excellent performance and results in all the statistical analytical techniques used in this study. The following statistical procedures were then applied to the data.

5.1. Descriptive Statistics

Descriptive statistics was applied to the data as a means of checking for errors in data entry, which would be detected as out of data. This technique is also used to test for normality of the data via normal probability plots (Coakes, 2005). Tests for central tendency and variability, being mode, mean, median, standard deviation and variance were also performed. The descriptive statistics also describes the distributions of the respondents in terms of demographic data and constructs such as: industries, education level, information systems experience, employment with current company, scope of SISP, planning horizon, gender, age, strategic awareness, situation analysis, strategy conception, strategy formulation, strategy implementation, SISP success and contingency variables. All those data has been presented in cross-tabulates with frequencies, mean, standard deviation, and so on in chapter seven.

5.2. Constructs Validity

Construct validity is defined as the correspondence between a construct and the operational procedure to measure or manipulate that construct. It asks whether the measures chosen are a true construct describing the event or merely artefacts of the methodology itself (Devellis, 2003). Welman and his colleagues (2005) have described the construct validity of the measuring instrument as the degree to which it measures the intended construct rather than irrelevant construct or measurement errors. Mouton (2001) stated that construct validity can be regarded as a synonym to "best approximation to the truth." The rationale for a research design is to plan and structure a research project in such a way that the eventual validity of the research findings is maximised by minimising, or even eliminating, potential errors. Construct validity answers questions such as "Do measures show stability across methodologies?" and "Are the data a reflection of true scores or artefacts of the kind of instrument chosen?" If constructs are valid, we can expect relatively high correlation between measures of the same construct using different methods and low correlation between measures of constructs that are expected to differ (Lertwongsatien, 2000).

There are three general types of construct validity namely: content validity, convergent validity, and discriminant validity. These validity types are described in the following sections.

5.2.1. Content Validity

Content validity represents the comprehensive and reliable measurement of all the dimensions of a construct by an instrument (Lertwongsatien, 2000). It was claimed that the standard of content validity is based on a representation of set items of instrument and employment of sensible methods of scale in constructs. In the present study sixty-four items representing seven variables were used to measure the moderating role of contingency variables in the basic relationship between planning process and SISP success. All of the measurement items of each construct were adapted from previous studies (Musangu & Kekwaletswe, 2011; Bechor *et al.,* 2010; Newkirk & Lederer, 2006; Warr, 2005; Wang & Tai, 2003; Mirchandani, 2000; Mentzas, 1997). A panel of experts' examination within a pilot test was employed to ensure the suitability of the item. This helped justify the content validity of the construct.

5.2.2. Convergent and Divergent Validity

Convergent validity refers to the extent to which multiple attempts to measure the same concept with different methods are in agreement (Hair *et al.,* 2006). To establish convergent validity, correlations between the latent constructs in factor analyses were checked. In this study, multi-factor analyses, such as Exploratory Factor Analysis (EFA) were employed to test the convergent validity of measurement scales.

Hair *et al.,* (2006) have described discriminant validity as the degree to which a concept differs from other concepts. Discriminant validity is established to measures of constructs that theoretically should not be related to each other. To estimate the extent to which any two measures are related to each other, the correlation coefficient is commonly used to observe intercorrelations among measures. Typically, AVE values should exceed the square of the correlations between each pair of latent constructs (Belkin, 2009).

5.2.3. Exploratory Factor Analysis (EFA)

Exploratory factor analysis is a data reduction technique used to reduce a large number of variables to a smaller set of underlying factors that summarise the essential information contained in the variables (Belkin, 2009). Factor analysis is primarily used to analyse the structure of interrelationships among a large number of variables by defining a set of common underlying dimensions, referred to as factors (Hair *et al.,* 2006). Its purpose is to enable the researcher to arrive at a simple factorial structure that facilitates meaningful interpretation (Thurstone quoted by Belkin, 2009). For testing a theory about a structure of a particular domain, confirmatory factor analysis is appropriate.

EFA was used in the present research. There are several different factor analysis methods such as Principal Component Analysis (PCA), Principal Axis Factoring (PAF) and Alpha Factor Analysis (AFA) being the more commonly used techniques (Coakes, 2005). We used Principal Component Analysis (PCA) because of its common use in information systems research as seen in the information systems literature (Belkin, 2009; Rondeau *et al.,* 2006; Wang & Tai, 2003). Principal Component Analysis (PCA) is appropriate if the objective of the analysis is to predict the minimum number of components needed to account for the maximum portion of the variance represented in the set of variables(Hair *et al.,* 2006).

Exploratory factor analysis enables the identification of new factors (variables or constructs) underlying the linear correlation (Belkin, 2009). The factor loadings are the correlation coefficients between the variables and factors. Analogous to Person's r, the squared factor loading is the percent of variance in that variable explained by the factor.

Eigenvalues, also called characteristics roots for a given factor, measures the variance in all the variables that is accounted for by that factor (Kline, 2005). The ratio of eigenvalues is the ration of exploratory importance of the factors with respect to the variables. If a factor has a low eigenvalue, then it is contributing little to the explanation of the variance in the variables and may be ignored as redundant with more important factors. In keeping with the SPSS methodology recommendation, factors with eigenvalues less than one were considered as redundant and not included in any further analysis (Coakes, 2005).

To ensure the suitability and appropriateness of exploratory facto analysis, there are several assumptions which have to be met (Hair *et al.,* 2006); the data correlation matrix has to be greater than .50 to justify the application of factor analysis; the Bartlett's test of sphericity which provides the statistical probability of significant correlations among variables in the entire correlation matrix and the Kaiser-Meyer-Olkin measure of sample adequacy (MSA) which measures the appropriateness of factor analysis should be significant ($p < .05$). Furthermore, a value greater than 0.6 should be expected for factor analysis. Factor extraction, which refers to determining the smallest number of factors that can be used to best represent the inter-relations among the set of variables should be greater than one and together explain 60% of the total variance to be classified as satisfactory. In this study, PCA was employed to determine the number of factors that should be retained.

5.3. Constructs Reliability

According to Rosnow and Rosenthal (1999), reliability is defined as the consistency or stability, whether the measurement can be repeated and confirmed by further competent measurements. The internal-consistency reliability is the degree of relatedness of the individual items in one factor or scale.

The methods of calculating the internal consistency reliability include the Cronbach Alpha and the K-20 tests. As the K-20 test is used when items are scored dichotomously (0 or 1), and items in the current study ranged from 0 to 10 (no extent to great extent, disagree to agree, entirely unfulfilled to entirely fulfilled and much deterioration to much improvement), the Cronbach Alpha was calculated for this study using the Rasch methods. The Cronbach Alpha has a range of 0 – 1, where 0 is no internal consistency and 1 is the maximum internal consistency (Terre Blanche and Durrheim, 1999). Although it depends on what is being measured, as a rule of thumb, 0. 75 is set as an acceptable level for the Cronbach Alpha. Other researchers suggest that a value greater than 0.7 is regarded as a satisfactory level of internal consistency of measure (Hair *et al*., 2000).

6. FINDINGS AND DISCUSSION

The screening of data provided the following information: (i) Sample size of 319 was adequate to run SEM analysis (ii) The data scale was continuous (iii) There was only .3% of missing value in SISP process construct and this case was excluded for the specific analysis. (iv) There was no outlier and the extreme values were checked with 5% Trimmed Mean. Results have shown very little difference between original means and 5% Trimmed Mean, indicating that the extreme values were not influencing the three distributions. (v) All Skewness values were ranged from -1.00 to .036 which complies with Mertler and Vannatta's (2005) requirement, indicating that Skewness values between -1.00 and 1.00 are compared to a normal distribution. (vi) All Kurtosis values were ranged from -1.00 to 1.08. (x) All tests of normality were not significant due to the large sample size of 319 respondents. (xi) All independent variables were checked for multicolinearity.

Descriptive statistics were used to describe the collected data by investigating the distribution of scores obtained for all variables, to determine whether there is any relationship between the variables scores. The aim was to obtain a picture of the data 189 collected during the research. Descriptive statistics were obtained for the demographic data and for the three study variables, namely: planning process, SISP success and contingency variables. SISP Process construct has been evaluated into five phases, as recommended in by Mentzas (1997), and used in various previous researches. These phases were strategic awareness, situation analysis, strategy conception, strategy formulation and strategy implementation. The study used the phases to represent the different factors of SISP process construct. The results provided in Table 6 reveal that responses for each item took the full range of value from 1 to 10. The mean value for the planning process items ranged from 7.297 to 8.305. The highest rated items were defining change management approach (item A21), evaluating opportunities for improvement (item A15) and identifying opportunities for improvement (item A14). The following items were ranked lowest: Identifying new business processes (A17), planning the IS planning process (A1), and organizing the planning team (A4).

Despite these variations, the values of all the means are generally high; giving an indication that on average CIOs in medium enterprises understand the importance of planning process item characteristics. In Table 7, the lowest ranked items were underlined, whereas the highest items were in bold face. The detailed items measuring SISP Process are shown in Table 7, labelled Descriptive data for SISP Process.

6.1. Descriptive of SISP Success Items

SISP Success construct has been divided into four dimensions namely: alignment, analysis, cooperation and capability. Table 8 provides the SISP Success descriptive results.

The results shown in Table 7 indicate that responses for each item took the full range of value from 1 to 10. The mean value for the SISP Success items range from 7.167 to 7.679, being slightly lower than the means values of SISP Process. The highest rated items were: Maintaining open lines of communication with other departments (B7), coordinating the development efforts of various organizational subunits (B8), and Ability to understand the business and its information needs (B11). Ability to anticipate sur-

Table 7. Descriptive data for SISP Process

Phases	Items	N	Mean	Std	Min	Max
Strategic Awareness						
Planning the IS planning process	A1	319	7.328	1.5286	4.5	14.0
Determining key planning issues	A2	319	7.554	1.1687	5.0	10.0
Defining planning objectives	A3	319	7.633	1.1852	5.0	10.0
Organizing the planning team(s)	A4	319	7.398	1.6032	.5	10.0
Obtaining top management commitment	A5	319	7.724	1.5070	2.0	10.0
Situation Analysis						
Analyzing the current environment	A7	319	7.653	1.1799	5.0	10.0
Defining current business organizational systems	A9	319	7.913	1.2625	3.8	10.0
Strategy Conception						
Identifying major IT objectives	A13	319	7.905	.9669	5.8	10.0
Identifying opportunities for improvement	A14	319	**7.992**	.9945	5.0	10.0
Evaluating opportunities for improvement	A15	319	**8.041**	1.0092	5.0	10.0
Identifying high level IT strategies	A16	319	7.943	1.0751	5.0	10.0
Strategy Formulation						
Identifying new business processes	A17	319	7.297	1.5725	2.0	10.0
Identifying new IT architectures	A18	318	7.546	1.3634	3.0	10.0
Identifying specific new projects	A19	319	7.819	1.3306	2.0	10.0
Identifying priorities for new projects	A20	319	7.727	1.2698	2.0	10.0
Strategy Implementation						
Defining change management approach	A21	319	**8.305**	6.2668	2.0	52.0
Defining action plan	A22	319	7.564	1.4489	2.0	10.0

Table 8. Descriptive data for SISP Success

Dimensions	Items	N	Mean	Std	Min	Max
Alignment						
Adapting the goals/objectives of IS to changing goals/objectives of the organization	B1	319	7.461	1.4216	4.0	9.5
Maintaining a mutual understanding with top management on the role of IS in supporting strategy	B2	319	7.777	1.2752	4.0	10.0
Adapting technology to strategic change	B3	319	7.887	1.4116	2.5	10.0
Analysis						
Development of a "blueprint" which structures organizational process	B4	319	7.286	1.9828	.5	10.0
Maintaining an understanding of changing organizational process and procedures	B5	319	7.171	1.7297	2.0	9.9
Generating new ides to reengineer business processes through IT	B6	319	7.302	1.9032	1.0	9.9
Cooperation						
Maintaining open lines of communication with other Departments	B7	319	**7.679**	1.4412	2.0	9.9
Coordinating the development efforts of various organizational subunits	B8	319	**7.496**	1.5722	1.0	9.9
Identifying and resolving potential sources of resistance to IS Plans	B9	319	7.344	1.7180	2.0	9.9
Capabilities						
Ability to anticipate surprise an crises	B10	319	7.167	1.8058	2.0	9.9
Ability to understand the business and its information Needs	B11	319	**7.403**	1.6118	2.0	9.9
Flexibility to adapt to unanticipated changes	B12	319	7.229	1.6854	2.0	9.5

prises and crises (B10), maintaining an understanding of changing organizational process and procedures (B5) and flexibility to adapt to unanticipated changes (B12) were ranked lowest. All effectiveness items means have been rated above 7.166.

6.2. Descriptive of Contingency Variables Items

Contingency variables describe the external and internal factors which can affect the decision making process of management and impede enterprise to gain competitive advantage in the business environment. In the context of this study, Contingency variables construct were characterized by the presence of five variables namely environmental uncertainty, organizational structure, government and policies, business strategy orientation, and information systems maturity. Table 9 provides descriptive results for the contingency variables.

The Table 9 provides descriptive results for the contingency variables. The results indicate that responses for each item took the full range of value from 1 to 10. The mean value for contingency variables items were ranged from 6.593 to 7.948. The highest rated items were; the responsibility to make the decisions concerning hiring and firing of senior personnel is centralized at the top-most levels of man-

Table 9. Descriptive data for contingency variables

Variables	Item	N	Mean	Std	Min	Max
Environmental Uncertainty						
Products and services in our industry become obsolete very quickly	C1	319	6.990	2.0942	1.0	9.9
The product/services technologies in our industry change very quickly	C2	319	7.387	1.8208	2.0	9.5
We can predict when our products/services demand Changes	C4	319	7.606	1.5080	2.0	10.0
Customer buying habits	C5	319	**7.735**	1.3563	2.0	10.0
Nature of competition	C6	319	7.264	1.8456	1.5	9.9
Organisational Structure						
Whatever situation arises we have procedures to follow in dealing with it	C8	319	7.037	1.8889	1.5	9.9
When rules and procedures exist here, they are usually Written	C9	319	6.839	1.9673	1.2	9.9
The responsibility to make the decisions concerning capital budgeting is centralized at the top-most levels of management	C12	319	**7.635**	1.4472	2.0	9.9
The responsibility to make the decisions concerning new product introductions is centralized at the top- most levels of management	C13	319	7.451	1.5760	2.0	9.9
The responsibility to make the decisions about entry into major new markets is centralized at the top-most levels of management	C14	319	7.476	1.5376	2.0	9.9
The responsibility to make the decisions about pricing of major product lines is centralized at the top-most levels of management	C15	319	7.317	1.5624	2.0	9.9
The responsibility to make the decisions concerning hiring and firing of senior personnel is centralized at the top-most levels of management	C16	319	**7.948**	1.1892	2.0	10.0
Government and Policies						
Ability of the party in power to maintain control of the government	C17	319	7.067	2.0764	1.5	9.9
Monetary policy	C18	319	6.866	2.1405	1.0	9.9
Prices controlled by the government	C19	319	6.593	2.2265	1.5	9.9
Business Strategy Orientation						
Seeking market share position at the expense of cash flow and profitability	C22	319	7.634	1.6908	.5	10.0
Using cost control to monitoring performance	C24	319	7.208	1.9748	.5	10.0
Information systems provide support for decision making	C26	319	7.459	1.5874	2.0	9.9
When making a major decision, we usually try to develop thorough analysis	C27	319	7.4873	1.6483	1.50	9.90
Information Systems Maturity						
We have well defined service quality criteria for all information systems support tasks	C29	319	7.528	1.3358	2.5	9.9
We have established service level agreements with all user groups for information systems support	C30	319	7.441	1.3776	2.5	9.9
We have sophisticated systems to record, track and respond to service requests	C31	319	7.426	1.7995	.2	9.9

Table 10. Summary of new measurement model

Observed Variables	Items
SISP Process	
New Strategic Awareness (NSAW)	A4 + A5 + A18+ A21 + A22
New Situation Analysis (NSAN)	A1 + A2 + A3 + A17
New Strategy Conception (NSCO)	A4 + A13 + A14 + A15 + A16
New Strategy Formulation (NSFO)	A7 + A9
New Strategy Implementation (NSIM)	A19 + A20
SISP PROCESS = SAW + SAN + SCO + SFO + SIM	
SISP Success	
New Alignment (NALIGN)	B2 + B3 + B10 + B11
New Analysis (NANALY)	B5 + B6 + B9 + B12
New Cooperation (NCOOPE)	B1 + B4
New Capabilities (NCAPAB)	B7 + B8
SISP SUCCESS = ALIGN + ANALY + COOPE + CAPAB	
Contingency Variables	
New Environmental Uncertainty (NENV_UNCERT)	C8 + C9 + C18 + C29 + C30
New Organizational Structure (NORGA_STRUCT)	C2 + C6 + C12 + C13 + C14 + C15 + C16
New Government And Policies (NGOV_POL)	C17 + C19 + C22 + C24 + C26
New Business Strategy Orientation (NBUS_STRAT)	C27 + C31
New Information Systems Maturity (NIS_MAT)	C1 + C4 + C5
SISP CONTEXT = ENV_UNCERT + ORGA_STRUCT + GOV_POL + BUS_STRAT + IS_MAT	

agement (C16), Customer buying habits (C5) and The responsibility to make the decisions concerning capital budgeting is centralized at the top-most levels of management (C12). Prices controlled by the government (C19), when rules and procedures exist here, they are usually written (C9), and monetary policy (C18), were ranked lowest. Table 10 summarises the variables and items for the proposed model.

The revised confirmatory model, figure 3, did not fit the data adequately, as reflected in the summary shown in Table 10. The ration of minimum discrepancy to the degree of freedom (*CMIN/DF*) was greater than the acceptable level of 3.5. The goodness-of-fit index (*GFI*), adjusted goodness-of-fit index (*AGFI*), and normed fit index (*NFI*) were all less than the acceptable level of .90. The parsimonious goodness-of-fit index (*PGFI*) was not close 1. However, comparative fit index (*CFI*) and incremental fit index (*IFI*) were both acceptable at .91. The root mean square residual (*RMR*) was also acceptable at .03. The root mean squared error (*RMSEA*) was adequate since it was ranged in the interval between .06 to .08. All the indicator variables loaded highly and significantly onto their respective factors. In addition, all the constructs were positively and significantly correlated with each other.

Figure 3 shows the revised confirmatory model. From ten hypotheses tested, seven were supported and three were not supported. The overall results suggest that the improvement of planning process phases is positively related to the effectiveness of SISP. However, this relationship is moderated by several

Figure 3. Revised confirmatory model

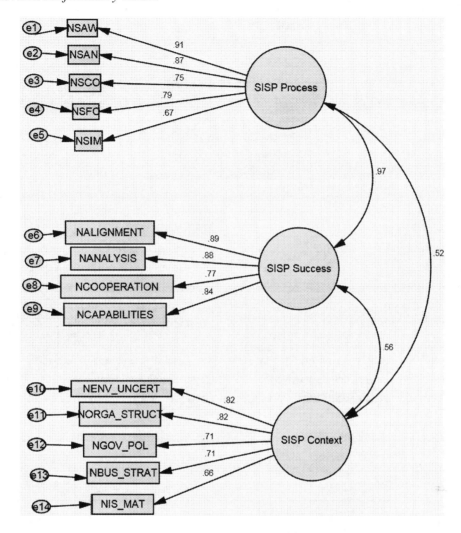

contextual factors demonstrating that the South African medium enterprises sector is not out of environmental uncertainty, organisational structure, government and policies, business strategy orientation and information systems maturity influence. To enable medium enterprises sector to stay and be competitive in the world market, top manager (most of the time medium enterprise owner) and chief information officer (CIO) must work together to (i) identify the internal and external environmental factors which are more influencing their immediate business environment; (ii) develop an explicit business strategy and keep awake that the information systems strategy is aligned with the business strategy, vice versa.

Further, the results and findings of the study have some implications to MIS including SISP researchers. SISP researchers can apply the model for further testing of assessing the effectiveness of SISP under various contextual factors by checking why hypotheses H4, H7 and H8 were not supported in this study and if possible by modifying constructs and variables and proposing new hypotheses between these constructs.

7. TOWARDS A MODEL FOR ASSESSING SISP SUCCESS IN MEDIUM ENTERPRISES

This section gives a contingency model for assessing strategic information systems planning, informed by the empirical evidence and the obtained results. In the basic relationship side the hypothesised H7; *SISP process in the strategy formulation phase can lead to the SISP success* has been excluded from the model; the hypothesised H4 *relationship between SISP process in the situation analysis phase and SISP success will be moderated by the contingency variables* and H8 *relationship between SISP process in the strategy formulation phase and SISP success will be moderated by the contingency variables*, have been excluded as well. The motivation behind the exclusion decision was the no statistical significance of those relationships (H4, H7 and H8). Subsequently, therefore, Figure 4 is characterised as the contingency model for assessing strategic information systems planning success.

The contingency model, Figure 4, may be used to inform further research on the SISP effectiveness and success. In the model, contextual factors may negatively influence the decision making process. Taking into account the importance of information systems investment in medium enterprises and the fact that Strategic Information Systems Planning (SISP) can bring a competitive advantage in the market, the practical contribution of the model is in assisting medium enterprises to understand and identify specific and important contextual factors. The developed contingency model provides clarification to those contingency variables that can significantly impede medium enterprises to gain competitive advantage (Levy & Powell, 2005). It is recommended that chief executive officers (CEOs), chief information officers (CIOs) and others managers may use the model to measure the effectiveness of SISP and improve their decision making process, in order to monitor the impact of internal and external environments.

Figure 4. Contingency model for assessing strategic information systems planning success

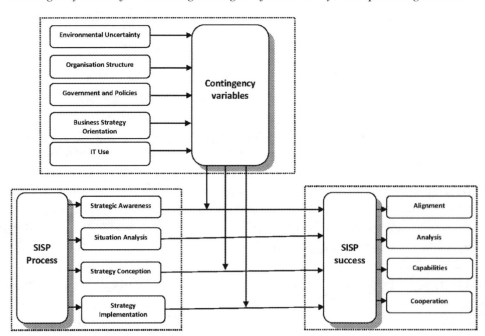

8. CONCLUSION

This chapter was envisaged with the goal of developing and validating a contingency model for assessing strategic information systems planning success in medium enterprises. The objective was to provide a validated contingency model which will help business managers to measure the success of SISP. Contingency theory was adopted as the underpinning theory for the study. Literature review highlighted some significant gaps in the previous strategic information systems planning studies, and these gaps were addressed in the chapter by developing a contingency model for assessing the success of strategic information systems in the medium enterprises. The developed contingency model tested ten hypotheses separated in two groups. The first hypothesis group (H1, H3, H5, H7 and H9) tested the basic relationship between planning process phases and SISP success and the second group (H2, H4, H6, H8 and H10) tested the moderating role of contingency variables in the first hypothesis group.

Three constructs were adopted from previous strategic information systems planning (SISP) literature; namely, organisation management, organisations theories, and business strategy. The three constructs were developed and validated following the Churchill methodology as suggested by Devillis (2003). Exploratory Factor analysis was carried out to the developed constructs. From 66 items developed 15 were dropped and 51 were retained. Structural equation modelling (SEM) with AMOS was used to validate the developed contingency model and test the research hypotheses. Of the ten research hypotheses, seven were supported and three were not supported. The overall results of the study have shown that there is indeed a positive relationship between planning process phases and SISP success. The chapter argued and have shown that this positive relationship is moderated by contingency variables.

REFERENCES

Agarwal, R. (1998). Small firm survival and technological activity. *Small Business Economics*, *11*(3), 215–224. doi:10.1023/A:1007955428797

Bakar, F. A., Suhaimi, M. A., & Huissain, H. (2009). Conceptualisation of strategic information systems planning (SISP) success model in public sector: An absorptive capacity approach. Proceeding of *European and Mediterranean Conference on Information Systems 2009 2009 (EMCIS)*. July 13 – 14, 2009. Izmir.

Basu, V., Hartono, E., Lederer, A. L., & Sethi, V. (2002). The impact of organizational commitment, senior management involvement, and team involvement on strategic information systems planning. *Information & Management*, *39*(6), 513–524. doi:10.1016/S0378-7206(01)00115-X

Bechor, T., Seev, N., Moshe, Z., & Glezer, C. (2010). A contingency model for estimating success of strategic information systems planning. *Information & Management*, *47*(1), 17–29. doi:10.1016/j.im.2009.09.004

Beckinsale, M., Ram, M., & Theodorakopoulos, N. (2011). ICT adoption and ebusiness development: Understanding ICT adoption amongst ethnic businesses. *International Small Business Journal*, *29*(3), 193–219. doi:10.1177/0266242610369745

Belkin, M. (2009). *The assessment of information systems effectiveness in private and hospital pathology* [PhD Thesis]. RMIT University.

Brown, I. (2008). Investigating the impact of external environment on strategic information systems planning: A qualitative inquiry. Proceedings *SAICSIT – ACM Conference*, Wilderness, 8 – 15. doi:10.1145/1456659.1456661

Cerpa, N., & Verner, J. M. (1998). Case Study: The Effect of Is Maturity on Information Systems Strategic Planning. *Information & Technology.*, *34*, 199–208.

Chi, L., Kiku, G. J., Lederer, A. L., Pengtao, L., Newkirk, H. E., & Sethi, V. (2005). Environmental assessment in strategic information systems planning. *International Journal of Information Management*, *25*(3), 253–259. doi:10.1016/j.ijinfomgt.2004.12.004

Choe, J. (2003). The effect of environmental uncertainty and strategic applications of IS on a firm's performance. *Information & Management*, *40*(4), 257–268. doi:10.1016/S0378-7206(02)00008-3

Clark, L. A., & Watson, D. (1995). Constructing validity: Basic issues in objective scale development. *Psychological Assessment*, *7*(3), 309–319. doi:10.1037/1040-3590.7.3.309

Coakes, S. J. (2005). *SPSS: Analysis without anguish: Version 12.0 for Windows*. Australia: John Wiley and Sons.

Cohen, J. (2008). Contextual determinant and performance implications of information systems strategy within South African firms. *Information & Management*, *45*(8), 547–555. doi:10.1016/j.im.2008.09.001

Dekovic, M., Janssens, J. M., & Gerris, J. R. (1991). Factors structure and construct validity of the block child rearing practices report. *Psychological Assessment*, *3*(2), 182–187. doi:10.1037/1040-3590.3.2.182

Devellis, R. F. (2003). *Applied social research methods: scale development theory and applications* (2nd ed.). Thousand Oaks, CA: International Educational Professional Publisher.

Donaldson, L. (2001). *The contingency theory of organisation*. Thousand Oaks, CA: Sage Publications. doi:10.4135/9781452229249

Dong, X., Liu, Q., & Yin, D. (2008). Business performance, business strategy and information systems strategy alignment: An empirical study on Chinese firms. *Tsinghua Science and Technology*, *13*(3), 348–354. doi:10.1016/S1007-0214(08)70056-7

Earl, M. J. (1993). Experiences in Strategic Information Systems Planning. *Management Information Systems Quarterly*, *17*(1), 1–23. doi:10.2307/249507

Foong, S. Y. (1999). Effect of end-user personal and systems attributes on computer-based information system success in Malaysian SMEs. *Journal of Small Business Management*, *37*(3), 81–87.

Frambach, R. T., Prabhu, J., & Verhallen, T. M. M. (2003). The influence of business strategy on new product activity: The role of market orientation. *International Journal of Research in Marketing*, *20*(4), 377–397. doi:10.1016/j.ijresmar.2003.03.003

Gibbs, B. (1994). The effects of environment and technology on managerial role. *Journal of Management*, *20*(3), 581–604. doi:10.1177/014920639402000304

Grover, S. K., & Lederer, A. L. (1999). The influence of environmental uncertainty on the strategic use of information systems. *Information & Management*, *40*–68.

Hair, J., Black, W., Babin, B., Anderson, R. L., & Tatham, R. (2006). *Multivariate data analysis* (6th ed.).

Holvelja, T., Rozanec, A., & Rupnik, R. (2010). Measuring the success of the strategic information systems planning in enterprises in Slovenia. *Management, 15*(2), 25–46.

Kendra, S. A. (2004, May–June). Environmental scanning: Radar for success. *The Information Management Journal, 38* – 45.

Kerlinger, F. N., & Lee, H. B. (2000). *Foundations of behavioural research*. Fort Worth: Harcourt College Publishers.

King, W. R. (1988). How effective is your information systems planning? *Long Range Planning, 21*(5), 103–112. doi:10.1016/0024-6301(88)90111-2

Kunnathur, A. S., & Shi, Z. (2001). An investigation of the strategic information systems planning success in Chinese publicly traded firms. *International Journal of Information Management, 21*(6), 423–439. doi:10.1016/S0268-4012(01)00034-2

Lederer, A. L., & Sethi, V. (1996). Key Prescriptions for Strategic Information Systems Planning. *Journal of Management Information Systems*, 35–62.

Lee, G. G., & Pai, J. C. (2003). Effects of organisational context and inter-group behaviour on the success of strategic information systems planning: An empirical study. *Behaviour & Information Technology, 22*(4), 263–280. doi:10.1080/0144929031000136548

Levy, M. & Powell, P. (1998). SME flexibility and the role of information systems.. *Journal of Small Business Economics, 183* – 196.

Levy, M., & Powell, P. (2000). Information systems strategy for small and medium sized enterprises: An organisational perspective. *The Journal of Strategic Information Systems, 9*(1), 63–84. doi:10.1016/S0963-8687(00)00028-7

Levy, M., & Powell, P. (2005). *Strategy for growth in SMEs*. Oxford: Elsevier Butterworth-Heinemann.

Mentzas, G. (1997). Implementing an IS strategy—a team approach. *Long Range Planning, 10*(1), 84–95. doi:10.1016/S0024-6301(96)00099-4

Mirchandani, D. A. (2000). *Information systems planning autonomy in US-based subsidiaries of competing globally firms* [Phd Thesis]. University of Kentucky.

Mirchandani, D. A., & Lederer, A. L. (2008). The impact of autonomy on information systems planning effectiveness. *International Journal of Management Sciences, 36*, 789–807.

Mohdzain, M. B., & Ward, J. M. (2007). A study of subsidiaries' views of information systems strategic planning in multinational organisations. *The Journal of Strategic Information Systems, 16*(4), 324–352. doi:10.1016/j.jsis.2007.02.003

Morton, N. A., & Hu, Q. (2008). Implications of the fit between organisational structure and ERP: A structural contingency theory perspective. *International Journal of Information Management, 28*(5), 391–402. doi:10.1016/j.ijinfomgt.2008.01.008

Musangu, L. M., & Kekwaletswe, R. M. (2011). Strategic information systems planning and environmental uncertainty: The case of South Africa Small, Micro and Medium Enterprises. In the Proceedings of *IADIS Information Systems Conference*, Avila, Spain 11 – 13 March, 70 – 78.

Newkirk, H. E. (2001). *Environmental uncertainty and strategic information systems planning comprehensiveness.* Thesis, University of Kentucky.

Newkirk, H. E., & Lederer, L. L. (2006). The effectiveness of strategic information systems planning under environmental uncertainty. *Information & Management, 43*(4), 482–501. doi:10.1016/j.im.2005.12.001

Newkirk, H. E., & Lederer, L. L. (2007). The effectiveness of strategic information systems planning for technical resources, personnel resources, and data security in environment of heterogeneity and hostility. *Journal of Computer Information Systems, 47*(3), 34–44.

Palanisamy, R. (2005). Strategic information systems planning model for building flexibility and success. *Industrial Management & Data Systems, 105*(1), 63–81. doi:10.1108/02635570510575199

Pita, Z. (2007). *Strategic information systems planning in Australia: Assessment and Measurement* [PhD Thesis]. RMIT University.

Porter, M. E., & Kramer, M. R. (2006). Strategic and society: The link between competitive advantage and corporate social responsibility. *Harvard Business Review, 1*, 1–14. PMID:17183795

Premkumar, G., & Roberts, M. (1999). Adoption of new information technologies in rural small businesses. *Omega International Journal of Management Sciences, 24*(5), 467–484. doi:10.1016/S0305-0483(98)00071-1

Pulkkinen, M. (2008). *Enterprise architecture as a collaboration tool: Discursive process for enterprise architecture management, planning and development* [PhD Thesis]. University of Jyvaskyla.

Raghunathan, B., & Raghunathan, T. S. (1994). Adaptation of a planning success model to information systems planning. *Information Systems Research, 5*(3), 326–340. doi:10.1287/isre.5.3.326

Reich, B. H., & Benbasat, I. (2000). Factors that influence the social dimension of alignment between business and information technology objectives. *MIS Quartely, 24*(1), 81–111. doi:10.2307/3250980

Rondeau, P. J., Ragu-Nathan, T. S., & Vonderembse, M. A. (2006). How involvement, IS management effectiveness and end-used computing impact IS performance in manufacturing firms. *Information & Management, 43*(1), 93–107. doi:10.1016/j.im.2005.02.001

Rosnow, R. L., & Rosenthal, R. (1999). *Beginning behaviour research: A conceptual primer*. Englewood Cliffs: Prentice Hall.

Sabherwall, R., & King, W. R. (1992). Decision processes for developing strategic applications of information systems: A contingency approach. *Decision Sciences, 23*(4), 917–943. doi:10.1111/j.1540-5915.1992.tb00426.x

Sage, T. A. (2006). *A model of factors affecting business and information technology alignment enabled by enterprise architecture: a structural equation modelling analysis* [PhD Thesis]. Capella University.

Schumacker, R. E., & Lomax, R. G. (2004). *A beginner's guide to structural equation modelling*. Mahwah, NJ: Prentice Hall.

Segars, A.H. & Grover, V. (1998, June). Strategic information system planning success: An investigation of the construct and its measurement. *MIS Quartely*, 139-163.

Segars, A. H., & Grover, V. (1999). Profiles of Strategic information system planning. *Information Systems Research, 10*(3), 199–232. doi:10.1287/isre.10.3.199

Teo, T. S., & King, W. R. (1997). Integration between business planning and information systems planning: An evolutionary-contingency perspective. *Journal of Management Information Systems, 14*(1), 185–214.

Teo, T. S. H., & King, W. R. (1996). Assessing the impact of integrating business planning and IS Planning. *Information & Management, 30*(6), 309–321. doi:10.1016/S0378-7206(96)01076-2

Terre Blanche, M., & Durrheim, K. (1999). *Research in Practice: Applied Methods for the Social Sciences*. Cape Town: UCT Press.

Teubner, R. A. (2007). Strategic information systems planning: A case study from the financial service industry. *The Journal of Strategic Information Systems, 16*(1), 105–125. doi:10.1016/j.jsis.2007.01.002

Wang, E. T. C., & Tai, J. C. F. (2003). Factors affecting information systems planning effectiveness: Organisational contexts and planning systems dimensions. *Information & Management, 40*(4), 287–303. doi:10.1016/S0378-7206(02)00011-3

Warr, A. (2005). A study of the relationships of strategic IS planning approaches, objectives and context with SISP success in UK organizations. Proceedings of *European Conferences on Information Systems*.

KEY TERMS AND DEFINITIONS

Business Strategy: The means by which an organization sets out to achieve its desired goals and objectives.

Contingency Theory: Is a theory that claims that there is no best way to organize an organization, to lead an organization or to make decisions. Instead, the optimal course of action is contingent (dependent) upon the internal and external situation.

Environmental Uncertainty: Situation where the management of a firm has little information about its external environment or the changes in the existing environment.

IS Strategy: Is an organizational perspective on the investment in, deployment, use, and management of information systems.

Medium Enterprise: The definition differs but the general definition of medium-size is any organisation with employee numbers between 50 and 250, annual turnover of between USD10m and 50m, and a balance sheet between USD10m and USD43m in assets. In most countries, Medium enterprises are categorised as part of the SME grouping.

Organisational Structure: Outlines how activities such as task distribution, coordination, control and administration are directed towards the achievement of organizational objectives.

Strategic Information Systems Planning: Is an activity used to identify strategic applications and effective information systems to align an organization's strategy and objectives.

Chapter 2
The Interplay between Human and Structure in IT Strategy

Tiko Iyamu
Cape Peninsula University of Technology, South Africa

ABSTRACT

Information Technology (IT) has significant impact on organisation's success or failure. However, IT does not operate in a vacuum. It is influenced by non-technical factors, such as of human actions and structure, which are inseparable. Hence the relationship between the factors is critical as revealed in this chapter. Structuration was applied as a lens to examine the types of structures that existed during the development and implementation of IT strategy, and the structures that emerged as a result of human action in the organisation used as the case. The chapter presents that both human actions and structures depends on each other on all processes and activities that are involved in the development and implementation of the IT strategy. Drawing from the findings, the chapter develops a model to illustrate how cultural, policy and personal issues enable at the same time constrain activities in the development and implementation of IT strategy.

1. INTRODUCTION

IT strategy is intended to set out key directions and objectives for the use and management of information technologies in the organisation that deploys them. According to Luftman & Kempaiah (2008), technology advances continue to alter and shape the nature of organizations. IT strategy development planning includes the process of introducing the required disciplines, controls and new techniques, establishing good relationships and identifying tasks and responsibilities (Ward & Peppard, 2002). Through human action and within structure, the strategy allow all parts of the organisation to gain a shared understanding of priorities, goals and objectives for both current and future states as defined in the strategy.

IT strategy is developed and implemented for particular purposes by particular users or groups. It is therefore expected that there will be conflicts with the goals of other users and groups, and that such conflicts will be the key to understanding many otherwise unexpected situations. This leads to the importance of non-technical context in the adoption of any technology in an organisation (Weiss & Anderson, 2002).

DOI: 10.4018/978-1-4666-8524-6.ch002

From the development to implementation of IT strategy there exist joint effects of the actions of individuals and groups interacting within institutional structures (Jones & Karsten, 2008). It is therefore not surprising that the interaction between human and structure has a substantial degree of influence on the formulation and implementation of IT strategy. The impact of this influence could be negative or positive depending on how the interplay is exercised in the organisation. This impact forms the focal point of this study.

The interpretations and meanings by individuals and groups of users within an organisation have impact on the technology that they use (Weiss & Anderson, 2002). The stumbling, the compromises, the way non-technical interests get dressed up and disguised in IT strategy require analytical means to understand these issues. To explore this interplay between human and structure, impact of non-technical factors (human and structure) on IT strategy, a theoretical perspective, Structuration Theory (ST) was employed. From the perspective of ST, structures enable and constrain the daily actions and thought processes of people, but do not wholly determine the results. Individual choices are not independent of the structures within which people operate but they can move towards impacting (maintaining, reinforcing, changing or even destroying) the results.

Regardless of the degree to which an employee may commit him or herself to the objectives of the organisation, personal interests are likely to be different from those of the employer, hence the interaction is important. According to Mosindi and Sice (2011), it helps to view organisations as complex social networks of interactions, where amongst employees is considered seriously. Employees seek to satisfy not only the organisational interests, but also their own wants and needs which are driven by self-interest. Mintzberg (2000) points out that people apply strategy in several different ways. Also, it is the management of the powerful resources (technology, capital, people, for example) and the environment they create that allow a difference to be made. According to Iyamu & Adelakun (2008), People's willingness to accept or reject the IT strategy will therefore be highly influential in the outcome of the IT strategy.

Structuration Theory holds that human actions are enabled and constrained by structures, but emphasises that these structures are the result of previous actions (Orlikowski, 1992). According to Jones & Karsten (2008), structures are not implacable or immutable; they are sustained by their ongoing reproduction by social actors, and that it is difficult for humans alone to determine exactly the way in which structures are produced and reproduced.

The research has two key motivations. Firstly, many organisations formulate and develop their business goals, objectives and visions, and then attempt to achieve them based on, amongst other things, the IT strategy. This research, by identifying key components, seeks to contribute to the attainment of the development and implementation of IT strategy. Secondly, while many organisations are developing and implementing their IT strategy, little is known about the extent of the interplay of non-technical (human and structure) and their impacts. The study seeks to make a contribution in this regard. To do this, Structuration Theory was employed to examine the interplay between human and structure during the development and implementation of IT strategy.

The remainder of the paper is structured into six sections. Sections one and two cover the research methodology and approach. It outlined the research approaches and describes the case study strategy. The third and fourth sections present and examine the findings of the case study through Structuration Theory perspectives. Finally, sections five and six discuss the implications of the findings and presents the contributions of the study, respectively.

2. RESEARCH APPROACH

Structuration Theory was applied in the analysis to examine the types of structures that exist during the development and implementation of IT strategy, and the structures that actually emerge as a result of human action in the computing environment of the organisation. The primary aim was understand how the cultural, policy and personal issues enabled and at the same time constrain activities in the computing environment during development and implementation of IT strategy.

The key elements of Structuration Theory are Agency, Structure and Duality of Structure. These elements were used in the analysis. Agency refers to humans' ability to act. According to Giddens (1984), human agency has the 'capacity to make a difference'. Also, the loss of the capacity to make a difference is powerlessness. Hence, agency is intimately connected to power. In this study, the agency was used to identify activities including the roles, responsibilities and procedures in the development and implementation of IT strategy in the computing environment.

Structures are described by Giddens (1984) as rules and resources, instantiated in recurrent social practice. They only have virtual existence, as 'traces in the mind'. Structures both enable and constrain the daily actions and thought processes of people, but do not wholly determine them. Individual choices are not independent of the structures within which they take place but they can move toward maintaining, reinforcing, changing or even destroying them. This was applied to examine the rules and regulation that existed, and the enactment of the structures enabling or constraining in the development and implementation of IT strategy.

The duality of structure was used to understand the contextual dynamics within which organisational dilemmas interplayed; how structures embodied the organisation's norms, which were influenced by actions; whether these actions by agents led to changes in how rules and resources influence interactions and to the reinforcement of the norms upon which these interactions are based, during the development and implementation of IT strategy in the organisation.

For analytical purposes, Giddens distinguishes different structurational dimensions, namely, signification, domination and legitimation. Associated with each structural dimension are mediating components, which are interpretative schemes, facilities, and norms, whereby concepts embedded in the structure are given specificity by social agents through their actions (see Figure 1). These are at the same time, enabled and constrained by the structural properties. The notion of embodied structure was complemented with that of emergent structure, and the notion of user appropriation with that of enactment.

Figure 1. Dimensions of the duality of structure
(Giddens, 1984)

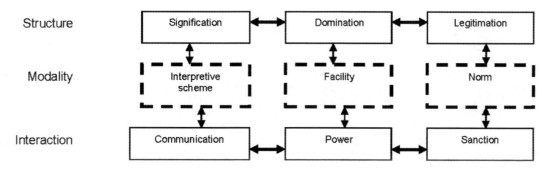

Thus, as human actors communicate, they draw on interpretative schemes to help make sense of interactions. These interactions at the same time produce and reproduce structures of signification. Similarly the facility to allocate resources is enacted in the wielding of power, and produces and reproduces social structures of domination. Finally, moral codes (norms) help determine what can be sanctioned in human interaction, which iteratively produces and reproduces structures of legitimation.

Structuration Theory views groups or organisations as systems with observable patterns of relationships and communicative interaction among people creating structures. Only through the activities of human actors can structure exist (Orlikowski, 1992). Giddens (1984) argues that structure and agency are a duality that cannot be conceived of apart from one another. Through human activities, individuals create both their consciousness and the structural conditions that make their activities possible.

Rose & Hackney (2002) argue that Structuration Theory has a very important role and is very substantial to the development and use of technology in the organisations that deploy it. Orlikowski (2000) extended the structurational perspective on technology to a "practice-oriented understanding of the recursive interaction between people, technologies, and social action".

The dimensions of the duality of structure as shown in Figure 1 was applied in vertical and horizontal basis in the analysis of the case study.

3. RESEARCH METHODOLOGY

The research problem emphasises the complexity of the interplay between IT strategy and non-technical factors in the context of the organisation. The study adopted qualitative case study method. The case study method was chosen because of its advantages in creating novel and profound insights and its focus on examining the rich contextual influences (Yin, 2003). The case study used in the research is an insurance organisation in South Africa. The data collection was from primary and secondary sources, interviews and documentations respectively, within the organisation.

The primary data collection sources were structured and Semi-structured interviews, tape recordings, and documentation. A total of 23 interviews were carried out in the organisation. A set of balanced respondent demographics was formulated and adhered to, as it was a key factor in achieving a true reflection of the situation. The demographics included the different races and genders and the various levels in the IT organisational structure, which included IT Executives, IT Managers, Business Managers, Senior and juniors IT specialists including IT Architects, Project Managers, Programmers and Network Administrators. Others include programmers and analyst, who were in the junior staff category. Table 1

Table 1. Case study demographics

	Case Study Demographics		
	Job Title	White	Non-White
Male	Senior	4	2
	Junior	3	2
Female	Senior	3	2
	Junior	4	3
Total		**14**	**9**

contains a breakdown of interviewees in the case study. The overall number of interviewees was reached when no new information was coming from the participants.

Roode's (1993) description of a process-based research framework for information systems research was used to generate the most appropriate questions for this research. There were three main questions, each with subsidiary questions. The interview questions explored and examined the views of different actors on IT strategy and how they understood it. The study further investigated which factors were involved in the development and implementation of the IT strategy; what influences the initiative of the IT strategy; some of the problems encountered during implementation of the IT strategy and the perceptions employees within the computing environment have of IT strategy.

The secondary sources included documents about organisational structure, Business and IT strategic alignment and IT strategy materials. The materials were used to develop the background information on the human and non-human context of the sites and the organisational hierarchy, which helped to construct the history of the computing environment. This helped to understand the organisational hierarchy as presented in the Agent and Structure subsections of the analysis section.

The research questions deny the separability of the social and the technical elements in a network of actors. The findings constitute a learning curve, and are expected to benefit the computing industry, and through it, contribute to the body of knowledge in this sub-field.

The purpose of the study was to create a better understanding of the impact of structure on IT strategy. This is expected to have implications which include how to leverage the effectiveness and efficiency of both technical (IT strategy) and the non-technical factors interplay with each other.

The study applied Structuration Theory (ST) in the analysis. ST was selected primarily because, it holds: that human actions are enabled and constrained by structures, and emphasises that these structures are the result of previous actions (Orlikowski, 1992). Structure is only manifested in the structural properties of social systems and consists of the rules and resources that human agents use in their everyday interaction. These rules and resources do not exist independently of human action, nor are they material entities. Giddens (1984) describes them as 'traces in the mind' and argues that they exist only through the action of human beings (Jones, 1999). They mediate human action, while at the same time they are reaffirmed through being used by human agents (Orlikowski, 1992).

4. FINDINGS

The findings from the empirical data are presented in this section. There were six factors which impact structures in the development and implementation of IT strategy. These are discussed as follows:

i. Control of Resources

Control of resources was prevalent in the computing environment. This was based on how significant the resources were in the implementation of IT strategy.

The structures within the computing environment determined and defined the tasks allocated to individuals during the implementation of IT strategy in the organisation, and actors enacted these structures in their everyday practice. The IT Director and IT Executive had the mandate to develop and implement IT strategy for the organisation. This mandate allowed them (the IT managers) to make particular operational rules for the various departments, and also gave them autonomous control over resources under their auspices. In some instances, the resources were used according to individual interests. IT managers also used their mandate to determine employees' access to facilities in their interactions with colleagues, with authorities, and with technology during implementation of IT strategy. This meant that the participation of individual employees in the implementation of IT strategy was influenced by factors outside their control. At the same time, employees used their individual knowledge such as technical know-how and information within their reach to gain advantage over others.

Tasks for employees were allocated to the various IT managers, who in turn allocated the tasks with timeframes to their team members. IT managers were granted the authority of control over financial budgets, and the authority to allocate tasks to employees under their control. Coupled with the fact that the prevailing culture in the organisation did not allow for the questioning of any decisions by managers, this meant that managers dominated employees during the implementation of IT strategy. The practices were considered irrational and as such, were not sanctioned by many of the employees, particularly at the lower levels.

The prerogatives of IT managers as mandated by the structures of the organisation meant that they were vulnerable to favouritism and nepotism towards employees. This created conflict of interests.

ii. Human Interference

The organisational hierarchy in the computing environment allowed the management team to coerce employees to adhere to instructions. Thus, older employees had to work with a younger generation of employees, which created tension because of differences in approach and understanding. This "generation gap" co-operation was therefore based on a foundation of unwillingness to work together and led to the younger employees not getting enough information from their older colleagues who were more knowledgeable about the organisation and its needs.

Based on the limited information made available to them, some employees could not easily understand how to carry out their individual tasks during the implementation of the IT strategy. This was a serious problem for some of the employees within this group and it affected the larger computing environment in terms of the processes and activities of the implementation of IT strategy. According to an interviewee, *"In a situation where there is a strategy but you don't understand what the strategy is or the strategy isn't clear or there is conflicting reports about the strategy, you are confused and do not know exactly how to position yourself"*.

There was also a growing concern of ownership and control of the available resources between the older and younger generations. Some of the older generation felt insecure and as a result, acted in their own self-interest in order to achieve and satisfy their own goals and objectives. For example, some of the older employees knew that certain senior managers had more respect for them because of their age, and that whatever they said would be taken more seriously than the words of a younger employee. They exploited this, and were driven by personal interests in their actions.

In the organisation, power was exercised in many ways. For example, there was the exercise of power that came with knowledge. The older employees were more knowledgeable about the organisation as a result of their many years of working in the computing environment of the organisation. Thus, they used their knowledge to maintain job security and to dominate younger employees.

Between the younger and older employees there was also a difference of understanding of what had to be done to implement the IT strategy. Younger employees had limited experience, and were often overruled by older employees on the basis of their pre-understanding of the nature of things that had to be done. This meant that different interest groups were formed which were at a cross purpose in terms of what they thought the task required of them.

This divergence between the formal description and the reality of the workplace, carrying out tasks for the implementation of IT strategy was problematic. Formal procedures, policies, and rules reflected the way the organisation was supposed to function, which was different from how tasks were performed before the younger employees joined the organisation. Coupled with the domination by older employees, this meant that considerable tension existed between the two generations and this played a major role in the legitimacy of events and activities that both parties were involved in during the implementation of the IT strategy.

Certain actions were clear manifestations of non-technical factors. These actions included differences between the employees in the discriminatory use of Afrikaans and domination by a particular age group. As a result, there was sharp division, which led to serious lack of cooperation between the different groups in the computing environment.

iii. Organisational Rules

The prevailing culture within the computing environment meant that the actions and decisions of IT managers could not be questioned by lower level employees. Consequently, some of the IT managers had a nonchalant attitude towards their subordinates. Preferences were accorded to employees as they wished. The IT managers and their preferred employees became dominant.

Language was one of the issues through which the rules of the organisation were constraining. This derailed processes and activities in the implementation of the IT strategy in the organisation. English and Afrikaans were legitimised as official languages for communication in the computing environment, but unfortunately, some employees were not fluent in Afrikaans and found it difficult to understand and interpret documents relating to the IT strategy related documents. It also made it difficult for the English speaking employees to participate in development and implementation of IT strategy meetings where the discussed was in Afrikaans.

Some of the IT Executive team members and the IT managers applied their personal discretion in the way information was shared and how Afrikaans was used as a medium of communication. This obviously affected the actions of some of the employees during the implementation of IT strategy. Some employees felt that they were being dominated and that Afrikaans was used to exclude them from being part of the implementation of the IT strategy. Other employees felt that the IT managers deliberately accorded preferential treatment to certain employees when they used Afrikaans in meetings.

Those who had the advantage of fluency in the language took control and became more popular, and used that as their source of power to dominate others. Thus, Afrikaans was very influential in the implementation of the IT strategy in the organisation. Some of the managers preferred to allocate critical tasks to people they could easily communicate with. Also, in terms of team work, language took preference. Afrikaans speaking employees preferred to work with those who could also communicate in Afrikaans.

The rules of the organisation applied to different processes and activities in the development and implementation stages of IT strategy. For example, not all the employees who were involved in the implementation partook in the development of the IT strategy in the organisation. This, the employees felt, was irrational and as such, they found it difficult to sanction the development and this clearly affected the implementation of IT strategy. IT managers were absolutely unquestioned by lower level employees. This made some of them to apply organisational rules at will.

iv. Cultural Diversities and Conservatism

As evident in the data about the organisation, it is about hundred years old. There is a rich cultural diversity in the computing environment of the organisation, but instead of celebrating their diversity, pervasive elements of conservatism counteracted the advantages that could have been gained from the diversity.

Historically, only Afrikaans speaking people were employed in the organisation. Accordingly, processes and activities were conducted in Afrikaans. As a result, conservative (Afrikaans speaking) employees objected to documents written in English. In the new setting of the computing environment, these employees were found it difficult to adjust and accept the changes that were taking place. Their response to these changes results to lack of co-operation. As such, they were not contributing their knowledge which had been gained from experience. On the other hand, the new intakes into the environment also had difficulty in performing their individual tasks in the new cultural setting. For example, in the past, instructions were given according to seniority of position and those instructions were not queried. The new setting allowed for a process of negotiation. The older employees did not appreciate this. As such, they used the Afrikaans language indiscriminately, including in the meetings. This had an effect on some of the employees. One of whom stated: *"That is a very serious problem; let's take the language issue; you are in a meeting where a lot of people are and you need to contribute and you are sidelined by the language. For example, if you don't speak Afrikaans and the meeting is conducted in Afrikaans".*

The diversity in the computing environment contributed to how tasks for the implementation of IT strategy were allocated in the organisation. This included age generation, cultural differences and the use of spoken and written languages. As a result, getting the employees to be interested in the IT strategy was very difficult, with implementation suffering as a result

There was also a cultural conservatism among the employees in the computing environment. This was particularly prevalent among the older generation of employees. The conservatism, which was about "doing things like we always did", created little or no support for transformation in the organisation. This became a dominant factor because those who indulged in the practices of the old culture were more knowledgeable about the organisation and they were not interested in change. As such, they reluctantly enrolled in the implementation of the IT strategy.

At the time of this study, the new and old cultures had not found accepted point of compromise. The non-acceptance of the new culture created considerable barriers for implementation of the IT strategy in the organisation.

v. Historical Effects

The historical shift in the politics of South Africa forced the organisation to amend some of its traditions. Traditionally, non-white people were not employed in the computing environment of the organisation. In the new dispensation, the organisation embarked on transformation in order to align with the government policy of 'Affirmative Action', and more non-whites were employed in the computing environment. The transition from the old to the new political dispensation has been a challenge and has affected the development and implementation of IT strategy in the organisation with 'new intakes' having to learn about the organisation while at the same time being allocated tasks.

During the study, the organisation was in a process of transformation which had been initiated to balance the number of employees in the computing environment along racial lines. One way in which this transformation process was implemented was through the employment of 'affirmative action' candidates. The Employment Equity Act, Act 55 of 1998, applies to all employers and workers and protects workers and job seekers from unfair discrimination, and also provides a framework for implementing affirmative action. In terms of the Act, employers must make sure that designated groups (black people, women and people with disabilities) have equal opportunities in the workplace. Designated groups must be equally represented in all job categories and levels.

The affirmative action employees felt they were being discriminated against. This led to lack of co-operative actions and manifestations of defensive behaviour by the affirmative action employees. Between them and the rest of the employees, an antagonism developed. The affirmative action candidates claimed that because of the discrimination information about the IT strategy was not appropriately circulated or shared with them. They felt that their white colleagues had more power as a result of the resources within their reach. In response to this domination, the affirmative action candidates acted in their individual interests and half-heartedly supported the implementation of IT strategy in the organisation.

The reluctance to co-operate, or the complete lack of co-operation from both the affirmative action candidates and other employees, including managers, who had jurisdiction over the resources available to them, was used by these same managers as a source of power to exclude unco-operative employees from the implementation of IT strategy. An employee explained as follows: "... my *experience is that senior people have got most of the knowledge and the juniors are not really reaping the benefits and growing; as such, to get the junior programmers and so forth through to the ranks where they can acquire more knowledge is almost impossible"*.

vi. Irregularities Caused by Personal Interests

Through employees' actions IT strategy was annually developed and implemented in the organisation. Unfortunately, employees were influenced by different personal interests, which had detrimental effects, especially for the implementation of IT strategy. IT managers' personal interests manifested themselves through irregularities such as favouritism and nepotism, while the rules of the organisation protected them in the execution of these acts.

Personal values, beliefs and attitudes sanctioned human actions and produced and reproduced structures of legitimation. Naturally, these norms were seldom articulated, but nevertheless were used to sanction human actions that then reproduced the structures of legitimation. Similarly, personal interests mediated early decisions about IT strategy in the organisation that eventually wielded their greatest influence during the implementation stage. The general perception was that managers gain personal benefits, as expressed by an interviewee: *Managers show a lot of excitement on the development and definition of IT strategy because they are inclusive; because they play a role and a part in it and it serve their interest. They will go there with a full understanding of what the strategy is all about.*

In developing and implementing IT strategy in the organisation, the relationships between IT management and employees revolved around rules, regulations and available resources. Between IT managers and employees, IT strategy was interpreted, tasks were negotiated and allocated, and information was shared and communicated. However, this all happened with varying degrees of success.

When it came to mobilisation of employees for the implementation of IT strategy in the organisation, this was sometimes done amongst age groups, with older people considered more senior and afforded preferential treatment. Also, employees rendered more support to colleagues of their own age group causing major problems of imbalance in terms of experience and knowledge about the organisation.

There was no performance contract for employees in the computing environment of the organisation. As a result, employees did not believe that the organisation could fairly judge their performances and qualification for salary increases and promotion. Consequently, employees resorted to manoeuvring because they believed that managers had no objective way of differentiating effective people from those who were less effective, and were in fact practising nepotism and favouritism.

5. ANALYSIS

The findings from the empirical data was analysed using Structuration Theory. The analysis focuses on the actions of the structures, agents that existed within the structures, how the agents acted and were acted upon, (this included employees as well as the rules and regulations,) and resources associated with the development and implementation of IT strategy in the organisation.

5.1. Agency

The agents were intimately connected with rules and resources. The agents involved in the development were different from those who were responsible for the implementation of IT strategy in the computing environment of the organisation. The employees involved in the development and implementation of IT strategy had different backgrounds and skills, including managerial and technical skills. Further, the employees were made up of different races, generations and a range of ages.

The Executive Committee (Exco) of the organisation mandated the IT division through the IT Director to be responsible and accountable in all activities, including IT strategy, in the computing environment of the organisation. The IT Director used the mandate to include the IT Executive in the responsibility of developing and implementing IT strategy in the organisation.

The computing environment of the organisation was hierarchically structured. There were several teams and each member of these teams was responsible for the management of the area(s) allocated to him or her. In the development and implementation of IT strategy, processes and activities were carried out by individuals and teams (units) of employees including the IT managers. Within the hierarchy, roles and responsibilities were respectively accorded and mandated, on the basis of the rules and regulations of the organisation.

The IT Director, IT Executive, IT managers, IT technical staff and the rest of the employees were involved either in the development or implementation of IT strategy in the organisation. However, some employees, such as the IT managers were involved in both the development and implementation of IT strategy.

During implementation of IT strategy, the roles and responsibilities were spread across the teams in the computing environment. The IT Executive team delegated responsibilities and authority to their various managers in the development and implementation of the IT strategy. Authority was wielded primarily by the exploitation of rules and resources in the development, as well as in the implementation of IT strategy in the organisation.

5.2. Structure

There were rules and regulations, which guided the development and implementation of IT strategy in the organisation. Based on these rules, resources and regulations the IT Director was mandated to develop and implement IT strategy through which business processes and activities were enabled and supported.

The resources in the computing environment of the organisation were managed by the IT Director through the rules of the organisation. Management was part of her role and responsibility. In the order of hierarchy, the responsibilities were further delegated to the IT Executive team and other IT managers for the implementation of IT strategy in the organisation.

Members of the IT Executive team had employees that carried out the various task. The IT division was divided into four (systems development, services, facility and architecture) main sections, which were further, divided into teams and units of IT managers and their subordinate employees. Also, within the IT division, there were forums, which were linked to one another, and each of them had responsibilities in the development and implementation of IT strategy.

The employees were allocated to the different units within the computing environment according to their individual skills. Similarly, the financial budget was allocated according to the needs of the units. The IT Director mainly carried out these allocations and management of tasks. The different activities including responsibilities were conducted within rules. The rules were used as benchmarks for the measurement of events in the development and implementation of IT strategy in the organisation.

The various responsibilities, accountabilities and management in the development and implementation of IT strategy originate from the IT Director, based on the rules in the organisation. This spreads across all levels of employees in the computing environment of the organisation. The IT managers including the employees relied on these rules in order to carry out their group and individual responsibilities in the development as well as in the implementation of IT strategy.

The individuals in the computing environment used the resources within their reach to carry out their responsibilities in the development and implementation of IT strategy in the organisation. The rules were as important as the resources as they depended on each other in the development and implementation of IT strategy. As a result of the dependencies, how the rules were interpreted and used by the different employees was critical. This led to the use of the dimensions of the duality of structure in the case study, as follows:

5.3. Dimensions of the Duality of Structure

Structure and human interaction in the computing environment was divided into three dimensions for the primary purpose of analysis. The recursive character of these dimensions is illustrated by the linking modalities.

Also, the structures including interactions that took place in the development were not necessarily the same as during the implementation of IT strategy in the organisation. Thus analysed through the concept of the Duality of Structure are summarised in Tables 2 and 3. The discussion that follows after the tables should be read in conjunction with the tables to get a better understanding and a full appreciation of the duality of structure during IT strategy development and implementation, respectively.

Table 2. IT strategy development

Signification	Domination	Legitimation
As a result of the importance attached to IT strategy in the organisation, development was done by the IT Director and the IT Executive team.	Only the IT Director and IT managers had the mandate to make decisions regarding the development of IT strategy.	Only the IT Director or her delegate was responsible and accountable for the IT strategy.
Interpretive Scheme	**Facility**	**Norms**
IT strategy sets the direction for the computing environment of the organisation, and it was intended to align with the business strategy to achieve its aims.	The IT Director had the authority to allocate resources in the development of the IT strategy.	The rules and regulations of the organisation were mandatory. It was difficult to change or resist.
Communication	**Power**	**Sanctions**
During development, there was little if any communication between the IT Director and the IT Executive team, who develop the IT strategy, and the rest of the employees.	The IT Director used her mandate to develop the IT strategy together with the IT Executive team.	IT strategy is developed and approved by the IT Director and IT Executive team, and then presented to the rest of the employees at a workshop.

IT Strategy Development

As a result of the importance attached to IT strategy in the organisation, development is done by the IT Director and the IT Executive team. IT strategy sets the direction for the computing environment of the organisation, and it was intended to align with the business strategy in order to achieve its aims. During development, there was little, if any communication between the IT Director and the IT Executive team, who develop the IT strategy, and the rest of the employees.

Only the IT Director and IT managers had the mandate to make decisions regarding the development of IT strategy. The IT Director had the authority to allocate resources to the development of the IT strategy. The IT Director used her mandate to develop the IT strategy together with the IT Executive team.

Table 3. IT strategy implementation

Signification	Domination	Legitimation
Technical aspects received priority due to the technical interests of lower levels of decision makers, not because they match with a particular aspect of the IT strategy.	Implementation is dictated by knowledge about the organisation and technical skills.	IT strategy implementation is carried out by employees at lower levels who have not been involved in the development of the strategy.
Interpretive Scheme	**Facility**	**Norms**
Employees relied on technical abilities and understanding when interpreting their implementation tasks. Language affected the way things were understood.	IT managers can coerce employee to implement IT strategy by making aspects thereof an individual's only task.	Implementation of IT strategy was done through teams and individual allocation of tasks, which is enforced through performance appraisal methods.
Communication	**Power**	**Sanctions**
During implementation, communication in the computing environment was one-way, which was from the IT Director and the IT Executive team to the rest of the employees.	Employees including IT managers protect individual interests. The managers used the authority bestowed on them and employees used their technical ability to protect their individual interests.	Employees accepted their individual tasks to implement IT strategy without full understanding of the strategy. Issues of mistrust permeated the ranks of employees, severely hampering implementation.

IT Strategy Implementation

Technical aspects received priority due to the technical interests of lower levels of decision makers, not because they matched with a particular aspect of the IT strategy. Many of the employees relied on technical abilities and understanding when interpreting the tasks allocated to them for implementation. Language affected the way things were understood. During implementation, communication in the computing environment was one-way, which was from the IT Director and the IT Executive team to the rest of the employees.

Implementation was dictated by knowledge about the organisation and technical skills. IT managers could coerce an employee to implement IT strategy by making aspects thereof an individual's only task. Employees including IT managers protected individual interests. On one hand, the managers used the authority bestowed on them. On another hand, employees used their technical ability to protect their individual interests.

IT strategy implementation was carried out mostly by employees at lower levels who had not been involved in the development of the strategy. Implementation of IT strategy was done through allocation of tasks to teams and individual, which was enforced through performance appraisal methods. Employees accepted their individual tasks without full understanding of the strategy. Issues of mistrust permeated the ranks of employees, severely hampered implementation.

Duality of Structure: Signification and Communication

The Executive Committee (Exco), which was the highest decision making body of the organisation, assigns responsibility for the development and implementation of IT strategy to the IT Director and IT Executive. The relevance of IT strategy to the organisation required it to have a wide range of input and audience within the computing environment of the organisation. The IT Executive ensured that this input was managed.

The approval of the IT strategy by the Exco permitted the IT Director and IT Executive team to communicate the initiatives which included the objectives and development to the next level of management (the IT managers). Subsequently, the various IT managers did the same by providing the necessary information to the rest of the employees.

The development of IT strategy was divided into different components. Members of the IT Executive team were responsible and accountable for these components. Some of the components included business applications, hardware and network aspects. The main purpose for dividing IT strategy into components was to assign roles and responsibilities as guided by the rules of the organisation. Another reason was the availability of resources for the different IT Executive team members.

Employees within the computing environment of the organisation were made aware of the developed IT strategy. Different media such as the company intranet and team meetings were used as communication platforms. According to some of the employees, the most popular and value-adding communication platform was the departmental workshop.

Some of the employees were not satisfied with the level of awareness that was created by the IT Executive team. These employees thought (perspective) that the IT Executives could do more to create awareness about IT strategy in the organisation. However, on the other hand, some employees felt that there was enough access to information on IT strategy in the organisation.

The main aim for creating the awareness was for the employees to understand the importance of IT strategy in the organisation so that they could contribute to its implementation in their various ways. Some employees were also concerned about the flow of information. Those who were concerned said that they would prefer a two-way information flow between the junior and senior employees in the computing environment. Most of the junior employees interviewed emphasised that such flow of information could enhance their understanding of IT strategy in the organisation.

Some of the senior managers acknowledge that there was a problem with communication in the computing environment. This was attributed by some, to the dominant language used in the organisation. In addition to these oral communication problems, there was also a problem of understanding some of the documentation relating to IT strategy. This was also attributed to language. Some of the Afrikaans speaking employees found it difficult to read and understand documents that were written in English, and *vice versa*. According to one of the managers, *"One of the problems in my opinion was that it's an Afrikaans company and our strategy was written in English. When I go to speak to my manager to explain or help explain the document, my manager is not able to explain it to me in my own language; he's explaining it to me in his second language, which creates problems"*.

Duality of Structure: Legitimation and Sanction

The IT Director was responsible and accountable for IT strategy in the organisation. As such, she ensured that IT strategy was accepted in the organisation, starting with the Executive Committee (Exco). The IT Director presented IT strategy to Exco for approval.

Upon approval, the IT Executive team then tried to get the buy-in of the IT managers reporting directly to them, and encouraged the various IT managers to get the buy-in of their employees. Even though incentives were offered, some employees were reluctant and others, for various reasons, did not accept the IT strategy. For example, some employees felt that the information shared or communicated to them was either not complete or was incorrect; as a result, they did not trust the IT Executive team. During the interviews, an employee explained as follows: *"Because, you have a vote of no confidence in your IT management then whatever strategy they put forward you immediately have a vote of no confidence in that strategy because you believe the IT managers are not capable of developing an IT strategy."*

There was obviously a strained relationship between the IT Executive team and the rest of the employees, and both parties realised that. Even though the rules of the organisation mandated the IT Executive to allocate tasks, it became difficult to do so as the employees were either unwilling or reluctant to accept their individual tasks.

The strained relationship between the IT Executive team and the rest of the employees led to lack of trust and confidence. This affected the capacity and capability to share information, as well as to carry out task in the development and implementation of IT strategy. As one of the employees said, *"At the end of the day, IT Executive or EXCO can decide on a strategy but if what the people are doing everyday does not support the strategy then it will never be implemented; it will only be words on paper for the rest of our lives; we must align what we do with strategy; and the people must believe that the strategy is the right direction to move and they must know their impact on the strategy"*.

Many of the employees who did not sanction the IT strategy alleged that they could not read or understand the document as it was written in the language they were not fluent in.

Duality of Structure: Domination and Power

The authority to develop and implement IT strategy in the organisation was mandated from the Exco to the IT Director and the IT Executive team. To communicate the developed IT strategy, IT Executive organised a workshop. Attendance at the workshop was a success as almost every employee in the computing environment attended. All IT managers, as instructed by the IT Director, applied the performance appraisal approach. This enabled the IT managers to use their authority to coerce employees to implement the IT strategy by allocation of tasks and resources.

Some employees who had been in the organisation for a long time were more knowledgeable and had more information about the organisation and its businesses and activities than some of their colleagues, particularly those with less number of years of service in the organisation. Their stocks of knowledge created a feeling of superiority toward their colleagues during the implementation of IT strategy in the organisation. The majority of the employees felt that the rules of the organisation gave them little or no room to negotiate their differences.

Understanding of the developed IT strategy was critical for successful implementation. There were concerns that if information was not properly shared or communicated in terms of a two-way flow, IT strategy may not be well understood, leading to incorrect implementation acts. Some of the employees pointed out that incorrect implementation could hamper the business processes and activities that IT strategy was supposed to enable and support. According to one of the employees, *"From my personal experiences because your role is sometimes so small in the company, your power is minimal, you don't really have much say in things like that so you have to follow your leader; even if you don't see it as the correct way, you can't really do anything, you can't impact it to a point of change because higher up that's the way it works and that's the way it's going to continue to work"*.

The implementation of IT strategy in the organisation first of all required the acceptance of the developed IT strategy by employees. The level of acceptance formed the basis for the actions of individuals, teams and groups, and, therefore, their participation, which was essential for successful implementation. However, with a low level of acceptance, and issues of mistrust permeated the ranks of employees, implementation was bound to be severely hampered. The IT Executive therefore used its authority to enforce acceptance. Using the performance appraisal approach, IT managers, as instructed by the IT Director, allocated tasks and resources to employees involved in the implementation of the IT strategy. Employees accepted instructions or commands with little or no negotiation. It was clear, however, that employees at the lower levels in general did not have a good understanding of the IT strategy they were supposed to be implementing.

Using the Duality of Structure from ST, we were able to analyse the recursive relationship between structure and human actions during the development and implementation of IT strategy. This forms the remainder part of the analysis as presented from the next paragraph.

During development of the IT strategy, the IT Director and her IT Executive Team were in full control, as mandated by the organisation. Communication was restricted to intra group communication, which excluded the rest of the employees. These communicative actions reproduced the structures of signification that says that development of the IT strategy would be undertaken by the IT Director and her Team. Using the power bestowed on her by the organisation, the IT Director took responsibility for the development of the IT strategy with her team. These actions produced and reproduced the structures of domination which put all decisions regarding the development of the IT strategy in the hands of the IT Director and her Team. Finally, when the Team approved the developed strategy, it was presented to the rest of the employees at a workshop as an accomplished fact, reproducing the structure of legitimation which recognises the IT Director as being solely responsible and accountable for the IT strategy.

During implementation of the developed IT strategy, employees were mobilised by their managers to undertake the implementation of aspects of the IT strategy by allocating these as tasks to them. Communication was one-way, from the managers to the employees, and issues of language often affect the way things were understood by employees. These communicative actions reproduced structures of significance, which were that employees saw things through technical lenses, regardless of their actual match with the developed IT strategy. Employees used their technical abilities to protect their own interests, and managers their authority to safeguard their positions. These actions reproduced the structures of domination, based on technical skills and knowledge of the organisation, respectively. Finally, employees accepted their tasks, mainly because their performances will be appraised, and continued with their work without full understanding of the developed IT strategy. Their work was affected by issues of mistrust towards their managers who often provided, in their opinion, incomplete or incorrect information about the developed IT strategy. This reproduced the structure of legitimation that employees at lower levels, who have not been involved in the development of the strategy, but were involved in the implementation.

6. IMPACT OF NON-TECHNICAL FACTORS ON IT STRATEGY

The organisation had defined processes and procedures in place to develop and subsequently implement IT strategy. The actions of the IT Director, IT Managers and employees, who acted within these procedures, were influenced and affected by non-technical factors. This sometimes derailed certain procedures, or erected barriers to the effective and efficient execution of procedures. There were many divides observed between the employees of the organisation, caused by a great diversity within the workforce. While it was possible to capitalise on diversity and exploit this to the benefit of the organisation, this was unfortunately not the case. Rather, the diversity was used in many subtle and not-so-subtle ways to undermine procedures and co-operative works.

The diversity also transformed itself into manifold divides. A divided workforce could spend a lot of energy on attempts to cross the divides and ensure some form of co-operation between the different factions. If it does not do so, the separate factions could potentially work in isolation without or with a modicum of co-operation. Either way, such a state of affairs cannot be conducive to the development of IT strategy which by its very nature requires the co-operative efforts of many groups of different expertise and skills.

One can point to a generation divide, a racial divide, and a language divide within the organisation's computing environment. Language, however, was perhaps the single most important factor that caused division. As mentioned before, historically, only Afrikaans speaking people were employed in the organisation, but to accommodate new appointments in terms of the organisation's compliance with the stipulations of the Employment Equity Act, both Afrikaans and English were accepted as official languages of communication. In reality, this policy was to accommodate the previous generation of Afrikaans speaking employees. The consequences of the policy were many. Employees who were not fluent in Afrikaans found it difficult to understand and interpret IT strategy related documents. It was difficult for them to participate in meetings where the development and implementation of IT strategy were discussed in Afrikaans. They were seen to be un-cooperative, and were excluded as managers preferred to allocate critical tasks to people they could easily communicate with. The implementation of the organisation's affirmative action policy brought in many new employees, who invariably were not Afrikaans speaking. This aggravated the situation, and the older generation of Afrikaans speaking employees (including some managers) turned more and more inwards towards their own people.

IT managers had autonomous control over resources under their auspices. This rendered them vulnerable to favouritism and nepotism and created conflicts of interest. Some of the IT managers practised favouritism as they wished, and some, as observed above, preferred to allocate critical tasks to people they could easily communicate with. In the absence of performance contracts, some employees acted in ways to ingratiate themselves with their managers, who they believed practised nepotism and favouritism.

The changes in the computing environment – brought about to a large extent by the implementation of the affirmative action policy – caused feelings of insecurity in some employees from the older generation. They exploited their greater knowledge of the organisation and the computing environment to achieve personal objectives, to maintain job security and to dominate younger employees. Such practices were not restricted to individuals. Various groups, divided along language, race or age lines, all pursued their group interests first and not that of the organisation and the implementation of the IT strategy.

Employees at the lower levels, who mainly came from non-white (coloured, Indian and black) origins, and who were appointed in terms of the organisation's affirmative action policy, formed such a group. They were "forced" into a group by the actions of other employees, who referred to them as affirmative action candidates. While this was considered to be discriminatory, these employees were also considered as not having the same organisational values or ways of operating as their white colleagues. Few tasks or opportunities in the implementation of IT strategy were therefore allocated to them, virtually excluding them from any participation. Quite rightly, the affirmative action employees felt they were being discriminated against. The affirmative action candidates claimed that because of the discrimination, information about IT strategy was not appropriately circulated or shared with them. In response to this domination, the affirmative action candidates acted in their own interest by only half-heartedly supporting the implementation of IT strategy in the organisation.

In presenting human interaction with structure, as analysed and found on the case study, we necessarily have to move to a higher level. Figure 2 shows that the various factors of non-technical factors that influence and impact the development and implementation of IT strategy have been accommodated in three main components, namely, organisational culture issues, internal policies and personal issues. This represents a generalisation of the results of the case study, and puts forward the proposition that these three main components would also accommodate non-technical factors that would be found in other organisations.

The various non-technical factors are, as has been shown, not independent, but deeply inter-dependent. The three main components proposed in Figure 2 are similarly not independent. Certain factors of a personal nature need a particular organisational culture in which to thrive, or would feed on particular internal policies. Similarly, certain internal policies would only be possible within a particular organisational culture. In the case study, the latter was illustrated forcefully: the organisation's policy of acknowledging both Afrikaans and English as official languages had serious consequences – not so much as a result of the policy itself, but as a result of the organisational culture in which this policy was promulgated. The culture in the organisation coped poorly with diversity, and the additional diversity created through the policy transformed into, another divide, linking with existing divides and reinforcing them and itself.

Figure 2. Impact of non-technical factors on IT strategy

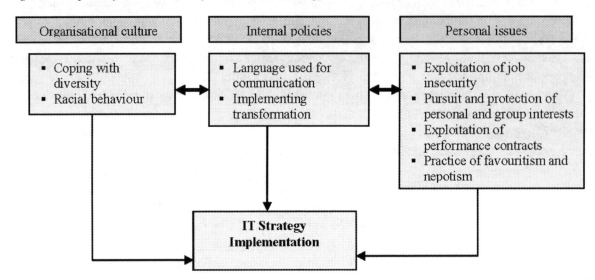

The advantage of a general framework such as shown in Figure 2 is that it enables a greater understanding of how non-technical factors manifest in the implementation of IT strategy. While non-technical factors could never be eradicated, using a framework such as Figure 2 could assist in removing some of the feeding grounds of non-technical factors, or counteracting them with appropriate measures.

7. CONCLUSION

The study investigated the impact of non-technical factors on IT strategy and probed the interaction between these issues in the development and implementation of IT strategy. It vividly exposed the fact that culture, policy and personal issues enable IT strategy as much as it constrains it, whether consciously or unconsciously.

Structuration Theory was identified as suitable theory to underpin the research. As such it provided an ontological and epistemological basis for the research: both an understanding of the essence of what is investigated in the study, and how to obtain knowledge about the phenomena studied. This means that the data collection, subsequent analysis of the data and interpretation of the results of the analysis were guided by Structuration Theory.

Some of the findings, such as cultural diversity, of the study are known facts in many organisations. But it was thought to be known by few. As a result, it was easy to turn a blind eye to the practice. Other matters were considered to be too sensitive to address. The findings of the study will instil confidence in IT managers to boldly confront the signs such as language manipulation.

The empirical findings of this study contribute to the understanding of the impact and influence of people and process both in the development and implementation of IT strategy in organisation. In addition, the study contributes to a better understanding of human implications, the roles of actors, structures and the individuals and groups of individuals involved in the implementation of IT strategy. Also, the study revealed an insight, which professionals including IT managers would not have detected or observed.

REFERENCES

Giddens, A. (1984). *The Constitution of Society: Outline of the Theory of Structuration*. Cambridge, UK: John Polity Press.

Gottschalk, P. (1999). Implementation Predictors of Formal Information Technology Strategy. *Information & Management, 36*(2), 77–91. doi:10.1016/S0378-7206(99)00008-7

Iyamu, T., & Adelakun, O. (2008). The Impact of non-Technical Factors on Information Technology Strategy and E-business, *Proceedings of the 12th Pacific Asia Conference on Information Systems (pp. 1214-1222). China*

Jones, M. (1999). Structuration Theory. In W. L. Currie & R. D. Galliers (Eds.), *Rethinking Management Information Systems* (pp. 103–134). United Kingdom: Oxford University Press.

Jones, M. R., & Karsten, H. (2008). Giddens's Structuration Theory and information systems review. *Management Information Systems Quarterly, 32*(1), 127–157.

Kohli, R., & Grover, V. (2008). Business value of IT: An essay on expanding research directions to keep up with the time. *Journal of the Association for Information Systems, 9*(1), 24–38.

Lederer, L., & Sethi, V. (1988). The implementation of strategic information systems planning methodologies. *Management Information Systems Quarterly, 12*(3), 445–461. doi:10.2307/249212

Luftman, J., & Kempaiah, R. (2008). Key Issues for IT Executives 2007. *MIS Quarterly Executive, 7*(2), 99–112.

Mintzberg, H. (2000). *The rise and fall of strategic planning*. Englewood Cliffs, London: Prentice-Hall.

Mosindi, O., & Sice, P. (2011). An Exploratory Theoretical Framework for Understanding Information Behaviour. *International Journal of Technology and Human Interaction, 7*(2), 1–8. doi:10.4018/jthi.2011040101

Myers, M. D. (1997). Qualitative Research in Information Systems. *Management Information Systems Quarterly, 21*(2), 241–242. doi:10.2307/249422

Orlikowski, W. (1992). The Duality of Technology: Rethinking the Concept of Technology in Organizations. *Organization Science, 3*(3), 398–427. doi:10.1287/orsc.3.3.398

Orlikowski, W. (2000). Using Technology and Constituting Structures: A Practice Lens for Studying Technology in Organizations. *Organization Science, 11*(4), 404–428. doi:10.1287/orsc.11.4.404.14600

Roode, J. D. (1993). Implications for teaching of a process-based research framework for information systems. *Proceedings of the 8th annual conference of the International Academy for Information Management. Orlando, Florida*

Rose, J., & Hackney, R. (2002). Towards a Structurational Theory of Information Systems: a Substantive Case Analysis. Proceeding of the 36th Hawaii International Conference on System Sciences, Track 8, vol. 8, p. 258, USA; Washington. doi:10.1109/HICSS.2003.1174746

Scarbrough, H. (1998). *Linking strategy and IT-based innovation: The importance of the "management of expertise". Information Technology and Organisational Transformation: Innovation for the 21st Century Organisation*. West Sussex, England: John Wiley & Sons Ltd.

Walsham, G., & Waema, T. (1994). Information Systems Strategy and Implementation: A Case Study of a Building Society. *ACM Transactions on Information Systems, 12*(2), 159–173. doi:10.1145/196734.196744

Ward, J., & Peppard, J. (2002). *Strategic Planning for Information Systems* (3rd ed.). West Sussex, England: John Wiley & Sons.

Weiss, J., & Anderson, D. (2002). CIOs and IT Professionals as Change Agents, Risk and Stakeholder Managers: A Field Study, proceedings of the 36th Hawaii International Conference on System Sciences, Track 8, vol. 8, USA; Washington.

Yin, K. (2003). *Case Study Research, Design and Methods* (3rd ed.). Newbury Park, California: Sage Publications.

KEY TERMS AND DEFINITIONS

Development: The process and procedure through which an organization formulate IT Strategy, periodically.

Implementation: This is the operationalization of the formulated items and technology artefacts in an organisation, with a period of time.

IT Strategy: Is an organisation's articulated intent to achieving its goals and objectives at both short and long terms, through information technology.

Non-Technical Factors: These are factors that are not technological, but are related to the deployment and use of technologies. They includes processes, procedures, rules, as well as human.

Organisation: A legal business entity with employees, which have its goals and objectives mandate.

Structuration Theory: Is a theory that focuses on human and technical factors as agents, and defines structure as rules and resources. The theory postulates that factors enables and constrain activities in the production and reproduction of events.

Structure: The rules and resources that are involved in the development and implementation of IT Strategy.

Chapter 3
Politicking the Information Technology Strategy in Organisations

Tiko Iyamu
Cape Peninsula University of Technology, South Africa

ABSTRACT

Through IT strategy, many organisations intend to set out key directions and objectives for the use and management of information, communication and technologies. It would therefore seem that IT strategy, for the foreseeable future will remain a key aspect of development within organisations. As a result, there has been more focus on how IT strategy is articulated and formulated. What is missing is that there has been less attention on the implementation of the strategy. Also, in most organisations, technical issues are minor compared to the relationship issues. There are many factors which influence the implementation of the IT strategy. These influencing factors which include organisational politics, determine the success or failure of the IT strategy. This paper focuses on how organisational politics as examined by two underpinning theories, Structuration Theory and Actor-Network Theory, impact the implementation of IT strategy.

1. INTRODUCTION

IT strategy is a term that refers to a complex mixture of thoughts, ideas, insights, experiences, goals, expertise, memories, perceptions, and expectations that provide general guidance for specific actions in pursuit of particular ends within the computing environment (Ward & Peppard, 2002). IT organisations have many and diverse stakeholders and this makes politics inevitable. IT strategy helps to set direction (Straub & Wetherbe, 1989), comprehension and focus on the future in the wake of change in the organisation that it supports. Walsham & Waema (1994) argue that IT needs strategy to achieve its aims and objectives. No doubt, "IT Strategy" is a significant factor in driving towards a specific direction. What is even more important is the outcome of the IT strategy. The question is, what influences or causes the IT strategy outcome (implementation)? Orlikowski (1993) argued that organisational politics has

DOI: 10.4018/978-1-4666-8524-6.ch003

an important influence on the degree to which IT, through its strategy, can be used. It is argued that the danger of politics is that it can be carried to extremes, and can then seriously harm the effectiveness of an organisation (Armstrong, 1994). In a study by Robbins et al. (2001), many employees and employers confirmed the recognition of legitimate and illegitimate politics in the organisations.

The way in which the IT strategy is developed and implemented have a significant impact on its success, and can have a direct impact on the organisational culture. According to Gottschalk (1999), implementation is key to the success or failure of IT strategy. Those who develop the IT strategy will probably be different people from those who carry out the implementation. If the IT strategy is understood or interpreted differently, the implementation is likely to encounter problems (Walsham & Waema, 1994). Implementing IT strategy depends on key people within the organisation (Daniels, 1994). In essence, unless all major stakeholders are involved, successful implementation is unlikely. However, analysing the peoples' perspectives opens the door for political intent within the organisation. Where there are different people and technologies, there are conflicts and difficulties (Orlikowski & Gash, 1994). It is inevitable that people are influenced and driven by different forces, such as 'politics', in the organisations. Orlikowski (1993) argued that organisational politics has an important influence on the degree to which IT, through its strategy, can be used. Where people are involved, politics exists. Scarborough (1998) argues that IT strategy needs other elements with a strong influence such as politics to achieve the set goals and objectives.

It is a serious oversight to pretend that politics does not exist. Since the beginning of time, politics has been a part of every human equation (Butcher & Clarke, 1999). Politics is the means; power is the end. Organisations are the most fertile breeding ground for politics. This is due to the fact that the actors seek different personal interests such as success, professional growth and financial security (Kling & Iacono, 1984). According to Hanbury (2001), "If a project is not facing a lot of organisational politics, it is a sure sign that it is not doing anything significant". The study explored the impact of organisational politics on the implementation of IT strategy.

Regardless of the degree to which an employee may commit him or herself to the objectives of the organisation, personal interests are likely to be different from those of the employer. Employees seek to satisfy not only the organisational interests, but also their own wants and needs which are driven by self-interest. According to Morgan (1986), "organisational politics arise when people think differently and want to act differently."

It has been demonstrated, analytically as well as empirically, that technical issues get caught up in a host of organisational issues such as politics. Orlikowski & Barley (2001) state "... to include insight from institutional theory, IT researchers might develop a more structural and systematic understanding for how technologies are embedded in complex interdependent social, economic and political networks, and consequently how they are shaped by such broader institutional influences".

Organisational politics involves those activities undertaken within organisations to acquire, develop, and use power and other resources to obtain one's preferred outcomes in a situation in which there is uncertainty, lack of clarity or a lack of consensus about choices. Organisational structure is a key component of organisational politics, and power is the focal point of organisational structure. According to Holbeche (2004), politics is a fact and part of life in organisations.

Much work has been done on organisational politics, such as Markus (1983), Pfeffer (1992), Hardy (1994), Butcher & Clarke (1999), Mintzberg (2000) and Lewis (2002) and on IT strategy, such as Ciborra (1996), Lederer & Sethi (1988), Boar (1998), Lederer & Gardiner (1992), Gottschalk (1999), Wolff & Sydor (1999) and Mack (2002). These works are often separately articulated. What is missing is the interaction between IT strategy and organisational politics. It is in this area that further research is vital to both the academic and corporate domains.

Of the numerous, including the above mentioned works, there is no clear definite definition of IT strategy, and most literature and discussion have focussed on Strategic Information Systems Planning (SISP) (Orlikowski & Robey, 1991). The research therefore defines IT strategy as follows: *"IT strategy is the technical design which serves as the road map over a period of time for the implementation of information technology and information systems by people using a formal process."* The research adopts this definition to examine the development and implementation of IT strategy for the following reasons:

1. It recognises that IT strategy can neither be formulated nor implemented in isolation from IS.
2. It recognises the inseparable relationship between the social construction of the IT environment and technology.
3. It acknowledges the role of human involvement (Rosser, Kirwin & Mack, 2002).

The primary aim of this study was to understand how organisational politics impact IT strategy. The study was shaped by three key issues, how IT strategy is implemented, which includes the people and structures; the influencing factors, such as organisational politics, in the implementation of IT strategy; and the impact of these influencing factors on the implementation of IT strategy in the organisation. The research question: "What influence, impact does organisational politics have on IT strategy in the organisation that deploys it"?

2. RESEARCH APPROACH

The study adopted a qualitative, case study involving a financial institution in South Africa. The selection of the organisation for the case study was based on the following factors: the first is that the organisation have a wide range of cultural diversity within its information technology (IT) environment; secondly, the organisation provide a very good representation of the particular financial sector in it operate; thirdly, the selection of the organisation for the research was a matter of accessibility. Many organisations were approached, but research access was not easy to obtain. In particular, the nature of this study did not help matters either, as it has to do with organisational politics, which is considered a sensitive issue in many organisations.

The study has three lines of investigation: it applied an interpretive perspective to investigate the relationship between technical and non-technical factors in the implementation of IT strategy; it investigates the organisational politics within the computing environment in the implementation of IT strategy. This area of investigation was more carefully phrased because of the sensitive nature of the subject (politics); and it focused on the impact of organisational politics on IT strategy.

Primary data was collected through semi-structured interviews with employees of the organisation. The questions for the collection of data were grouped into three categories. Roode's (1993) description of a process-based research framework for information systems research was used to generate the most appropriate questions.

A total of 31 interviewees were carried out in the organisation. As shown in Table 1, a set of balanced respondent demographics was formulated and adhered to, as it was a key factor in achieving a true reflection of the situations. The demographics included different races and genders and various levels

Table 1. Case study demographics

	Job Title	White	Non-White
Male	Senior	6	2
	Junior	4	4
Female	Senior	5	3
	Junior	4	3
Total		19	12

in the IT organisational structure, in the number associated to them, they included senior employees: IT Executives, IT Managers, Business Managers, IT Architects and Project Managers; and junior employees: Programmers, Business Analysts, Analyst Programmers and Network Administrators. Table 1 contains a breakdown of interviewees in the case study.

The first group of questions focused on interviewees' understanding of IT strategy as understood by the respondents: the purpose was to measure the meaning and definition of IT strategy. The second group of questions followed an inductive logic with the objective of allowing any relevant information on the topic of how IT strategy is implemented within the organisation to surface. The last group of questions aimed to explore in more depth the nature of influence of actors within the implementation of IT strategy. An interview guide was used to avoid losing focus, and to ensure that all relevant questions were asked. Questions were both closed and open-ended. Indeed, while some questions required a brief and precise answer, it was also desirable to let information emerge. Respondents were thus given the opportunity to express their thoughts on the topic of interest as freely as possible.

The interpretive approach was selected for this study. The approach proved useful to the study in the following ways: to observe, capture and explain participants' behaviour, which cannot be easily identified with other research approaches; it allowed for an in-depth analysis of the case studies to be presented, a factor necessary due to the nature of the topic; to study individuals in their natural setting, which involves physical interaction and gathering of material and to emphasise the researcher's role as an *active learner* who can tell the story from the participants' view rather than as an 'expert' who passes judgment on participants. According to Klein & Myers (1999), information systems researchers should explore 'how' and 'which' principles may apply in any particular or different situation.

The case study approach was applied. It enables in-depth exploration of complex subject such as "IT strategy and Organisational politics". Yin (1994) defines a case study as an empirical inquiry that investigates a contemporary phenomenon within its real-life context, especially when the boundaries between phenomenon and context are not clearly defined. Structured and semi-structured interviews, tape recordings, and documentation were used for the research data collection. A set of balanced respondent demographics was formulated and adhered to, as it was a key factor in achieving a true reflection of the situations. The demographics included the different races and genders and the various levels in the IT organisational hierarchy.

Figure 1. Duality of Structure
(Giddens, 1984)

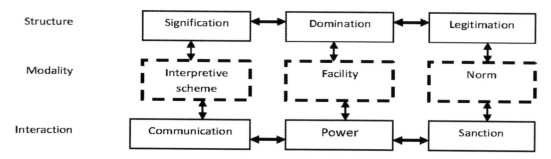

3. METHODOLOGY

The research employed two theories, Structuration Theory (ST) (Callon and Law, 1989) and Actor–Network Theory (ANT) (Giddens, 1984) for the analysis and interpretation of the case study at two different levels: through the 'duality of structure' concept of ST, and the concept of 'translation' of ANT. The aim was not to compare and contrast the two theories, but to use them in a complementary fashion. Their importance and usefulness to the research are highlighted below.

Giddens' (1984) *'dimensions of the duality of structure'*, Figure 1 *was* applied in the analysis. The action and interaction of actors and the interplay between agency and structure were established and recognised in the different situations in terms of time and place. Giddens (1984) described what is involved in exploring and exposing the duality of structure that may exist based upon an analysis of the situated actions of a designated group of actors. This analysis, concentrating on the emergent regularities of the situation, is an interpretative scheme and dealt with how the understanding of agents was exhibited.

No organisation has the total power to determine what the choice(s) of an actor will be in a particular circumstance. Giddens (1984) advocates an action and structure duality; the actor by virtue of interaction with the organisation being both constrained by and, in a sense, creating the structure(s) of the organisation. This results from modalities that link particular types of interaction with particular structural elements Giddens (1984). The three key types of modality are *interpretative schemes, facilities* and *norms*. This is diagrammatically shown in Figure 1.

The second analysis, using ANT, focused on the relationships between institutional properties, human agents and technology, and highlights the different interests such as politics and power in the computing environment of the organisations. Interactions between actors are the primary building blocks of actor-networks and their many manifestations are called 'translations' (Callon 1986; Latour 1987; Latour 1997). Bowker & Star (1996) suggest that treating classifications and standards with ANT allows political and ethical issues to be addressed, in part by making infrastructure non-transparent. From the perspective of ANT, the study used the moments of translation as shown in Figure 2 for the second analysis.

Figure 2. Moments of Translation
(Callon, 1986)

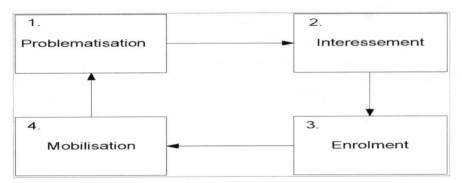

1. **Problematisation:** This is an act of indispensability, which brings about a compulsory situation, which Callon (1986) refers to as Obligatory Passage Point (OPP), a situation that has to occur in order for all the actors to satisfy the interests that have been attributed to them by the focal actor.
2. **Interessement:** Allies are locked into place, set of actions by which an entity attempts to impose and stabilise the identity of other actors in the same network for the cause of problematisation.
3. **Enrolment:** Defines and coordinates the roles. It involves the consolidation of the alliances through bargaining and mutual concessions. As defined by the focal actor, the solution is accepted as a new concept through the process of negotiation. A new network of interests is created or generated. Actors accept the roles defined for them when enrolling in the network (Callon, 1986).
4. **The Mobilisation:** The stage where actors become delegates or spokespersons for the focal actor. The new network starts to operate in a target oriented approach to implement the solution proposed. According to Callon (1986), through mobilisation of allies, actors become legitimate spokespersons of the groups they claim to represent. This leads to strengthening and stabilisation of the network.

The different theoretical concepts of ST and ANT emphasise different social contexts and facilitate different types of explanations. A limitation of ST is that it is a theory of social organisation that explains change in a social system over time (Jones, 1999). As a result of this limitation, ST does not allow for the examination of relationships between people and technology, and, for example, how power and values are embedded in the use of technology. Monteiro and Hanseth (1996) argued that ST simply does not provide a fine grained analysis of the interaction between individuals and technology. An interrogation of the relationship between individuals and technology, which ST lacks, was complemented by ANT. ANT is concerned with the interactions between technology and individuals (Law, 1992), and contains a wealth of concepts for understanding the relationship between technology and individuals. The combination and complementary use of both theories allowed for a more complete analysis of the study.

4. DATA ANALYSIS

Using ST and ANT from the perspectives of duality of structure and moments of translation, respectively, findings from the case study are presented as follows:

Analysis through Structuration Theory

The computing environment was structured as a hierarchical system, within which activities took place and were managed by individuals and groups (units) of employees. Responsibilities were accorded on the basis of the organisation's rules and regulations. Within IT department, there were rules, regulations, processes and procedures, which were enforced through organisational structures. The IT executive committee formulates these policies, which were binding and all employees including the managers were expected to adhere to them.

Agents

Agents were intimately connected with rules and available resources. Within these rules, the available resources were applied. In the computing environment, the employees involved in the development of the IT strategy included the CIO, IT managers and IT Architects. The employees that were involved or responsible for the development of the IT strategy were not necessarily the ones who were involved in the implementation of the IT strategy in the organisation. The implementers of the IT strategy included employees such as IT managers, IT Architects, IT Technical staff and users (employees).

The CIO of the organisation has mandate to decide on any unclear instances in the development and implementation of the IT strategy. The CIO delegates responsibilities for the various components of the IT strategy to the IT managers who report directly to him. The responsibilities include exploitation of resources and execution of policies.

These agents do not act in a vacuum but within a structure (rules and resources). Structure and agency, according to Giddens (1984), are a duality that cannot be conceived of apart from one another.

Structure

The word 'structure' must not be confused with its obvious connotation of organisational hierarchy in the English language. Structure in Structuration Theory are rules and resources, instantiated in recurrent social practice (Giddens, 1984).

In conjunction with available resources, the organisation has rules and regulations within which IT strategy was developed as well as implemented. The development or review of IT strategy was done bi-annually - at the end of alternate calendar years IT strategy was developed or reviewed against the organisational requirements for the following year. To achieve this objective, time frames were set and information required by individuals was provided. At the end of each calendar year, the CIO and some of the IT managers (his direct reporting line) meet, usually for two days. Heads of business units are invited.

The office of the CIO was responsible for the development as well as the implementation of the IT strategy in the organisation. The CIO identifies and invites relevant actors, and initiates the creation of the IT strategy. The resources for achieving the development and implementation of the IT strategy in the organisation include technical and non-technical factors, such as technology and people, respectively. The organisation has rules and regulations through which the development and implementation including resources were managed. There was a period of consultation with IT managers, but the decision was essentially a top-down one, taken on the basis that the organisation must have an IT strategy to support and enable the organisational processes and activities.

The CIO, in accordance with the organisation's mandate to him, defines the rules within which the IT strategy was developed and allocates tasks to the different IT managers. The management practices of the development of the IT strategy were recognised by the IT managers, and there were effective practices for making changes to the IT strategy.

The CIO's approval of the developed IT strategy leads to its implementation. There was a gap between those who develop and those who implement IT strategy in the organisation, because many of those implementing IT strategy were not involved in the development. Also, the computing environment does not have complete and necessary structures for implementing the IT strategy. There were no defined rules and processes within which the IT strategy could be implemented. The implementers tend to work around the information that was laboriously provided by individual managers, rather than follow their information needs and requirements. As a result, there were no effective practices.

Relevant technical personnel were available, but some of the units didn't have enough of them. The IT managers were not experienced in managing implementation of IT strategy and lacked awareness of either technical or non-technical possibilities in the implementation of the IT strategy. While development of the IT strategy in the organisation was undertaken by the CIO and his direct reporting line of IT managers, each of the IT managers was allocated part of the IT strategy to be implemented. The CIO instructs the IT managers to enforce performance contracts for the implementation of the IT strategy. Based on the organisation's rules, the CIO was mandated to allocate the available resources for the development and implementation of the IT strategy. On another level, the organisation's rules permits the IT managers to make decisions concerning different resources.

The mutual dependency of agency and structure, and their link via modalities within the computing environment of the organisation, are discussed:

Dimensions of the Duality of Structure

For the primary purpose of analysis, social structures and human interactions in the development as well as in the implementation of IT strategy are divided into three dimensions and the recursive character of these dimensions is illustrated by the linking modalities – Structure and Interaction: Signification and Communication; Legitimation and Sanction; and Domination and Power.

Duality of Structure: Signification and Communication

After the development of IT strategy, it was communicated to all employees through their various managers, including the organisation's intranet site, and there was a presentation by the CIO to the wider audience of the computing environment in the organisation. IT strategy was communicated for the sole purpose of implementation. The means through which the implementation was carried out was also presented and communicated to all employees in the computing environment including business managers who receive the services of the IT department.

For awareness and implementation purposes, the managers of the various units within the computing environment presented only that part of the IT strategy that concerns their unit to their employees: The CTO presented the architectural strategy aspect of the IT strategy to the Architects; The IT manager for Application presents the business applications strategy aspect of IT strategy to employees within the application unit.

In implementing IT strategy, each unit was allocated a task and each unit further allocates part of its task to individual employees. Deadlines were set for the individual tasks. During task allocation and deadline fixture, negotiation took place between the managers and the employees involved. The performance contract was signed at consensus by the employee and the manager, listing the various tasks and timeframe within which duties will be carried out and completed. At the point of agreement between both parties, the performance contract was enforced. The implementation of IT strategy in the organisation was critical in order for objectives to be achieved. However, there were problems. Implementing IT strategy was largely dependent on the employees, who have widely differing levels of interest and technical skills. Some were rather interested and happy to carry out (implement) their allocated task. Others didn't see any personal value in it and simply regarded it as an extra burden in their already complicated activities in the computing environment. Deadlines came and went, and many of the tasks were not completed.

IT strategy plays an important role in the organisation by supporting and enabling its business processes and activities. The employees believe that IT strategy was the platform upon which to set goals and use the scarce resources to satisfy the business needs. The general opinion was that IT strategy was very important and thus it must be aligned with the business strategy.

During the development of IT strategy, decisions were reached through the IT Exco meetings and processes. Based on the rules and regulations of the organisation, employees did not necessarily had the right and privilege to contribute to those decisions, and not every employee was allowed to participate in the development of the IT strategy. Collective choice was involved in defining the needs and allocation of resources in the development of IT strategy to meet the business strategy needs. Debate, discussion, pressure and protest were all part of the process of collective action, which determines which needs should be met or at least each need's priority, and the distribution of resources.

The employees were not merely workers of the organisation, but were a part of the organisation, and it was through their input to the implementation of IT strategy that they contributed to the organisation. Some employees were very experienced and others were technically skillful. IT managers and their various subordinates (employees) engage in interactions in terms of the performance contracts to achieve the objectives of the IT strategy. An interviewer explained: "The components of IT Strategy are implemented through the various teams and groups according to performance contract. The IT strategy implementation starts with the IT managers and they bring it down to our level and we discuss who will do what."

The technical component of IT strategy was given more priority than the non-technical factors in the development and implementation. No doubt, the development as well as the implementation of IT strategy has primary technical activities. In the computing environment, non-technical factors were regarded as secondary issues. Ironically, these components make the rules and regulations of development and implementation of IT strategy effective or defective.

Employees felt they were neglected in the development and as such, they lacked the interest to try and gain an understanding of IT strategy. The different levels of interests and understanding made communication difficult. In this situation, achieving the necessary cooperation of the employees was potentially difficult. As a result, the rules, regulations and resources to implement IT strategy were not appropriately adhered to. In addition, some of the employees were of the opinion that there was poor communication in the computing environment and that the poor communication contributes to the different levels of interest:

There is no broad base communication. If we had a communication strategy that reached to everybody the same message across the organisation, I think we would have less of people going against the IT strategy because even if your interest was low as for instance you wouldn't have an excuse because it would have been communicated so that you can understand it, I think that's what it really boils down to.

It became clear from discussions with interviewees that conflict exists between the employees and IT managers across the different 'units' in the computing environment. While the latter can be seen to encapsulate the positive qualities of management and superiority as they strive to provide quality service to the business needs, the former encompasses the more negative aspects.

Duality of Structure: Legitimation and Sanction

IT strategy was important to the organisation. As such, the responsibility and accountability for IT strategy, including the development and implementation, was mandated to the highest authority, which was the office of the CIO in the computing environment. In developing IT strategy in the organisation, the CIO applies the mandate accorded to him by the organisation to ensure that the managers reporting to him abide by the rules and regulations within which IT strategy was developed.

In the development as well as implementation of IT strategy in the organisation, the CIO presents mandatory rules and regulations to which IT managers and the rest of the employees abide. These rules and regulations were seen and accepted as an obligation within which IT strategy was developed and implemented in the organisation. The rules and regulations allowed for how the tasks of developing and implementing of IT strategy were allocated to the employees. The allocated tasks were treated as non-negotiable and built into individual performance contracts of each employee.

Though mandatory rules and regulations exist with respect to the development and the implementation of IT strategy in the computing environment of the organisation, getting buy-in from the employees was still very necessary and vital. The mandatory rules and regulations without buy-in remind the researcher of an adage that says 'you can drag a horse to the river but you cannot force it to drink the water'. As a result of the imposed rules and regulations, some of the employees were proactive participants and others were reluctant or antagonistic in the development as well as in the implementation of IT strategy in the organisation. Some of the employees at the junior level were interested in more active roles in the development of IT strategy. Unfortunately, the rules of the organisation do not allow their participation in the development of IT strategy.

Employees didn't have an option, they had to accept the rules and regulations, as provided by the computing environment, which guide the development and implementation of IT strategy in the organisation. However, some employees felt left out and thought they had ideas that could had contributed, particularly to the development of IT strategy. As a result, there were mixed reactions from the employees. One of the employees expressed the situation as follows:

Some staff support and as such are interested in the IT strategy mainly because it personally benefits them. On the other hand, some people reject the IT strategy in any form due to the fact that it seems to alienate or does not benefit them.

It seems unlikely that there will be improvements in how IT strategy is currently developed and implemented in the organisation. This is because implementation of IT strategy in the organisation was not easy and some of the managers seem unable to identify what and where mistakes and problems are.

The results revealed an imbalance between technology and people, with an overemphasis on technology. However, some employees do understand the problems. This is due to their ultimate involvement in the problems. The employees were aware of the criticality of their roles, particularly in the implementation of IT strategy. They felt that the managers do not realise or are ignorant of the difference that they, the employees, could make to the implementation of IT strategy. According to one of the employees,

The people impact is huge. Only the person involved can control his/her activity in whole. The manager can only control it to a certain extent. If the person applies his/her frustration, the impact is negative. Frustration can be due to lack of incentive and unhappiness.

Duality of Structure: Domination and Power

The organisational rules and regulations bind the computing environment, which was managed by the CIO. The CIO and the IT Exco manage and controlled the broad strategic decision-making of IT strategy. The CIO made the final decision on all matters relating to IT strategy in the organisation.

The IT managers had lesser authority (as compared to the CIO), which they used to respond to conflicting demands of the employees. The CIO has maximum authority to demand from his employees the deliverables for the development and implementation of IT strategy in the organisation.

Within the level of management, the IT managers didn't have equal power to contribute and make decisions in the development and implementation of the IT strategy in the organisation. Some IT managers were directly involved in the development of IT strategy and others were not. IT managers such as the CTO and Risk Manager were specifically mentioned by many of the interviewees. They were seen and regarded as more popular and powerful than others. This was due to the extent of their involvement in IT strategy. There were about thirty IT managers on the same level in the computing environment of the organisation. As a result of unequal power and popularity on the management level within the computing environment of the organisation, IT managers were struggling to attain power, influence and control. This was evident in the interviews:

There are too many 'power' struggles and personal interests within the IT department in the organisation. People are afraid to change. People will sabotage or refuse to contribute to any work because they are not in agreement or it does not favour them. These groups of people are the ones that have been in the organisation for a long period.

Some of the power struggles were manifestation of racial acts. This was experienced at the senior level, as a result of the replacement of a white-male CIO with a black-male CIO. Similarly, the employees share unequal power in the implementation of the IT strategy. Some of the employees were seen and considered to have more privilege than others. This was perceived to relate to technical skill, stocks of knowledge or an established relationship with the IT manager and or other employees concerned in the particular implementation.

The control of activities in IT strategy was evidently unequal in the two fields of development and implementation. The CIO and the senior IT managers were more in control of the development of IT strategy, while implementation issues were often controlled by employees at lower levels. An interviewee opined:

The implementation is more likely to be where the personal side comes in, the building of the kingdoms, the personal gain because that is where the IT strategy is more measurable than the defining or the development of the strategy.

IT strategy was regarded as a critical tool for the enabling and support of the business processes and activities in the organisation. As such, interpretation and sense making of IT strategy in the computing environment were vital. Also very important was how the strategy was communicated to the employees and who were involved in the development and implementation.

The development and implementation of the IT strategy was done through allocation of tasks and all employees in the computing environment were involved, but at different levels. Employees at the senior levels carried out the development and the rest of the employees were largely involved in the implementation of IT strategy. All employees accepted their individual and group tasks as defined by their performance contracts.

The rules and regulations dictated 'power' through the allocation and control of resources during the development and implementation of IT strategy. Another important factor was how employees, including managers, applied resources within their reach and control. Managers dominated according to the resources they had at their disposal.

In this analysis, some of the difficulties of IT strategy were exposed, including the autonomy of the managers and the varying degrees of interests of employees within the units headed by the managers. It is evident that employees (non-managers) are marginalised in the development of IT strategy. It is also evident that rules and regulations were very important factors in the development as well as the implementation of IT strategy in the organisation.

Using the Duality of Structure from ST, we were able to analyse the recursive relationship between structure and human actions in the development and implementation of IT strategy.

During development of the IT strategy, the CIO and his direct line of reporting IT managers were in full control, as mandated by the organisation. Communication was restricted to intra group communication, excluding the rest of the employees. These communicative actions reproduce the structures of signification that says that development of the IT strategy would be undertaken by the CIO and his Team. Using the power bestowed on him by the organisation, the CIO takes responsibility for the development of the IT strategy and assembles an elite group – those IT managers reporting directly to him – to develop the IT strategy. These actions produce and reproduce the structures of domination which put all decisions regarding the development of the IT strategy in the hands of the CIO and his Team. Finally, when the CIO and IT Exco approved the developed strategy, it was filtered through to the rest of the employees as an accomplished fact, reproducing the structure of legitimation which recognises the CIO as being solely responsible and accountable for the IT strategy.

During implementation of the developed IT strategy, employees were mobilised by their managers to undertake the implementation of aspects of the IT strategy by allocating these as tasks to them. Communication was one-way, from employees to the IT managers, and focuses mainly on technical issues. These communicative actions reproduce structures of significance, which were that technical aspects received priority due to the technical interests of employees, regardless of their actual match with the developed IT strategy. Employees and managers use their technical abilities and information to protect their own interests, reproducing the structures of domination, based on technical skills and knowledge of the organisation, respectively. Finally, employees work according to their individual performance contracts without full understanding of the developed IT strategy. Their work was affected by politics of rivalries which create an environment of non-cooperation during implementation. All of this reproduces the structure of legitimation that employees at lower levels, who have not been involved in the development of the strategy, will implement the strategy.

A more detailed analysis is now undertaken through Actor-Network Theory.

Analysis through ANT

This section analyses this case from an ANT perspective by drawing upon the sociology of translation as described in the methodology section. The focus is on how 'the actor-network' grows, changes and possibly stabilises during development and implementation of IT strategy within the computing environment of the organisation.

The main goal and objective of IT strategy is to align it with the business strategy of the organisation. To achieve this, a set of requirements is formulated. The requirements are problematised by the CIO for the employees. IT strategy is developed and implemented as a solution for these requirements. The most important actors involved in the actor-network are first identified. This is followed by the analysis, using the four moments of translation.

The actors in the development and development of IT strategy in the organisation included Business Managers, Chief Information Officer (CIO), Chief Technology Officer (CTO), IT Managers, IT Architects, IT Employees others include Technology (which were selected in the development and implementation of IT strategy), Performance Contract and Skill-set.

ANT Translation: Problematisation

The business managers presented the CIO with the organisation's strategy, with which he must align IT strategy. The CIO introduces the business strategy to his executive (IT Exco) team, which included the CTO and certain IT managers (Risk and Strategic Manager, Application Development Manager and Service Delivery Manager). The IT Exco was requested to develop the IT strategy for the organisation and ensure that it aligns with the business strategy.

For the purpose of development, the IT Exco splits IT strategy into components such as Architecture, Application and Infrastructure. IT strategy components were allocated to the appropriate authority as defined by IT Exco. The heads of the units were responsible and accountable for the various components that were allocated to his or her unit.

All IT-based solutions in the organisation were dictated by the IT strategy of the organisation. All issues and matters relating to the IT strategy were addressed through appropriate channels (units) such as Architecture, Application and Hardware as defined by the IT Exco. The head of each of these units has a mandate to approve/disapprove decisions pertaining to issues relevant to their individual unit. The CIO makes the final decision within the computing environment of the organisation.

Employees were allocated tasks in the development and implementation of the IT strategy in the organisation. For example, all architectural work in the organisation had to go through the Architecture department for approval.

The performance contract was engaged to ensure that each employee performs his/her individual tasks in the development and implementation of the IT strategy. The IT managers manage the performance contract of their individual employees. The CIO manages the performance contract of the IT managers. During this stage, the CIO uses the main goal and objective of IT strategy, namely to align with the business strategy of the organisation, to formulate a set of requirements. These requirements were problematised by the CIO, and under the leadership of the CIO, the development and implementation of IT strategy was presented as a solution to the problematised issue. The processes of development and implementation of the IT strategy were defined as the Obligatory Passage Points (OPP) through the implementation of individual performance contracts in which agreed upon tasks related to the development and implementation of the IT strategy were assigned to all employees.

ANT Translation: Interessement

In the computing environment of the organisation, the IT strategy was currently developed and reviewed annually. Sometimes, the implementation was not completed until the following year. The performance contract, which was instituted by the organisation, was used to carry out tasks in the development and implementation of IT strategy in the computing environment. The outcome of individual performance contracts was used to determined employees' annual salary increases and financial bonuses. As a result, some employees became interested in the development as well as implementation of IT strategy.

With regard to the development and implementation of the IT strategy, employees were required to have a performance contract. To a certain extent, negotiation was allowed but it was highly restricted. This process involves every team, unit and individual including the CIO and the IT managers in the computing environment of the organisation.

The various interests in IT strategy were either individual or team based. Individual interests were mostly based on 'stocks of knowledge', which makes the employee concerned more comfortable in carrying out his/her tasks. The team interest was according to roles, responsibilities and skill-set. In all cases, however, the performance contract and its outcome, with attached possible salary increases and financial bonuses, could be seen as a major driver of the interest of employees.

ANT Translation: Enrolment

The participation of employees in the development and implementation of IT strategy was key in achieving its aims and objectives. The CIO and the IT Exco used the performance contract as a system which enables them to persuade and convince employees at all levels to engage in the development and implementation of IT strategy in the organisation.

Development and implementation of IT strategy in the organisation was done through allocation of tasks to employees and managed by IT managers. The task allocation was done in accordance with individual and teams roles and responsibilities within the computing environment. This was based on performance contracts as outlined by the rules and regulations.

Heads of the different teams in the computing environment report the activities and progress of events of the teams to their immediate managers and the IT Exco. The activities and progress reports include the allocated tasks in the development and implementation of IT strategy. This was done in order to assess elements such as risks and gaps, including participation levels of employees in the development as well as in the implementation of IT strategy in the organisation.

However, some of the employees still did not or only reluctantly participated in the development and the implementation of IT strategy. Some employees attributed reasons for their lack of participation in the development and implementation of IT strategy to a lack of opportunity to participate - often caused by racial prejudices. Other employees, mostly on the senior level admitted that there were factors and circumstances that sometimes prevented individuals from participating in IT strategy in the organisation:

Some people don't like working with other people. My case is an example. Some people do not like working with me. The reasons are partly a power struggle, partly ignorance, personal and staff capabilities.

In addition, some employees at times get mixed messages from different sources in the development and implementation of IT strategy in the organisation. These messages were attributed to personal interests. There were some instances in which decisions were not reached by the parties (stakeholders) involved in the different tasks of development and implementation of IT strategy. In such cases, the action and reaction of the employee or managers responsible became a matter of individual choice. One of the interviewees explained:

Some IT managers will decide that they have their own view of what technology to achieve and they may not map directly to the IT strategy so they will follow their own direction, it's a common process.

The majority of employees at the lower levels did not have a full understanding of how IT strategy was developed, yet they enrolled in the implementation. The high level of enrolment and participation were due to the performance contract, which forced every employee to enrol accordingly and complete the allocated tasks in the development and implementation of the IT strategy. The low level of commitment, however, causes division and the pursuit of individual interests among the employees.

ANT Translation: Mobilisation

The realisation of the annual salary increase, including financial incentives, motivated many employees to be committed to the IT strategy in the organisation. Also, IT managers in the various units were tasked to encourage employees in their various units to be committed to the development and implementation of IT strategy. The tasks were linked to the performance contract. As a result of the potential impact of the performance contract, the IT managers spoke positively on behalf of their superior (CIO) and the computing environment on the need, aims and objectives of IT strategy in the organisation.

Employees in the organisation understood the development and implementation of IT strategy differently. Some of the employees thought it was too complex and therefore will not meet its goals and objectives. Others, who were believed to be more experienced, consider the development and implementation of the IT strategy to be in order and excellent.

Even though understanding was at different levels/stages, employees were encouraged to participate in IT strategy development and implementation. The IT managers performed the allocation task on a one-on-one basis and in the group meetings with their employees. This process gave the IT managers the opportunity to persuade each of the employees twice. This led to increased employee participation in IT strategy. For example, the employees (particularly the technical specialists) who did not understand how decisions about IT strategy were made in the organisation were now knowledgeable about it. Each IT manager represents their unit or group at the management level in the development and implementation of IT strategy.

The rules of the organisation, through the performance contract, enable the IT managers to mobilise employees in the implementation of the IT strategy. Also, some employees were able to mobilise their colleagues based on their stock of knowledge. The mobilisation was, however, more around the attainment of performance contract outcomes than about the IT strategy as such. In other words, the actor-network mobilises around loosely coupled individual and/or group targets more than around the solution proposed during problematisation.

It could also be argued that the solution and the OPP proposed during problematisation had within it the seeds of such a fragmented mobilisation: a holistic IT strategy, properly communicated to all levels, was not put forward as the solution to be attained; rather, with the development of the IT strategy done "behind closed doors", this was poorly communicated to the different levels with the emphasis then shifting to the implementation. More specifically, the processes of implementation (the OPP) became the solution to the problematised issue of supporting the business strategy. This meant, *a priori*, that the focus of individuals and groups would be on their tasks within the relative process (es), without necessarily paying attention to the broader picture (which they did not have) and their role therein. Added to this the performance contract and individually negotiated targets meant even more that individual interests and rivalries between managers and groups led to a fragmented mobilisation of the network. One of the senior employees in the computing environment of the organisation had this to say:

There is politics in the IT environment. It is about ownership of roles and it touches on innocent people. This politics becomes a stumbling block and pushes projects out of deadlines.

From the point of view of the focal actor, the CIO, this was not a problem, as the network would indeed operate relatively stable and in a target oriented manner to implement the solution proposed. This does not mean, however, that a coherent and holistic IT strategy would be the result of the implementation process.

5. FINDINGS

From the above analysis, some findings are extracted. The most critical of these findings are presented below:

i. The Importance of Human Interactions

The human interaction was very important in the implementation of IT strategy in the organisation. Through interactions, understanding was gained, allocated tasks were communicated and information was shared between the actors involved in the implementation of IT strategy. At the same time, poor interaction between the top and lower levels meant that lower ranked employees in general had a poor understanding of the IT strategy, which affected the implementation.

While employees in the computing environment have a common understanding of the aims and objectives of IT strategy, they do not necessarily have the same understanding and interpretation of the IT strategy. In particular, the way in which it was communicated to them affected their interest and fuelled the pursuit and protection of self-interests. Also, the working relationship among the employees, including the management, was influenced by diverse human interests, intentions and actions. A good working communicative relationship among the employees was vital due to the interdependency of individual tasks, activities, responsibilities and accountabilities when implementing the IT strategy.

The computing environment consisted of employees of several races – white, black, coloured and Indian. Even though all processes and activities of the organisation were non-racist, racial domination was prevalent, and it became an influencing factor during implementation of the IT strategy. Racial domination played itself out because the employees who indulged in the acts were able to associate themselves with the dominant actors, heads of autonomous departments. Some employees resorted to racial discrimination to ingratiate themselves with superiors including colleagues of the same racial identity because they lacked confidence and feared competition in their talents and skills. As a result of these actions, employees who did not belong to this racial group could not enrol in some of the activities during the implementation of the IT strategy.

There was a lack of racial integration and trust among the employees. As a result, negative relationships existed among the employees. Some members of the white race at times excluded employees of other races in communicating some of the processes and activities during the implementation of IT strategy. Similarly, some of the people of the black, coloured and Indian races segregated themselves from the white race, which made it difficult for them to be interested in and enrolled in the allocation of tasks.

ii. The Organisational Rules and Hierarchy

The organisational hierarchy was a determining criterion for the allocation of roles and responsibilities. In turn, larger parts of tasks were allocated according to roles and responsibilities of the actors involved in the implementation of IT strategy in the organisation. Employees' actions, which the organisational hierarchy allows for, had an impact on IT strategy. Irrespective of individual interests, all levels of employees acted within the constraints and enabling structure of the rules and resources. Their various actions, required by their individual roles, had an impact on and shaped the implementation of the IT strategy.

The CIO, or his delegates, make(s) the final decision on the use of facilities in the implementation of IT strategy. The availability of these facilities, which are made scarce to some employees, makes the other employees with free access powerful. While the IT strategy is handled by the CIO and certain IT Executives, all employees are involved in the implementation. This is the normal practice and is generally accepted in the computing environment.

The organisation applies the rule of equality, but, they were often modified in accordance with departmental functions. For example, only the Architecture department was allowed to deploy and use any kind of facility such as a technological resource, which was not the case with other departments in the computing environment. This practice was accepted, but perceived as discriminatory by many employees.

There was inequality of power among the departments and employees including the IT Managers, which led to the departments and employees competitiveness. As a result of such acts of rivalry, many employees used resources such as the performance contract to achieve their individual goals. One department head indicated that he preferred other departments to perform poorly so that his department could dominate others and be seen as being more productive and hence be awarded more incentives. In the same vein, more and more managers responded to such ideas, which created a prevalence of competitiveness and rivalry fuelled by the need to gain advantage in the computing environment of the organisation. Employees typically followed the lead of their various managers. When one department introduced a technology based on their interpretation of the IT strategy, other departments exercised their prerogative to either comply with it, or not. Most of the actions of the employees were deliberate, in the full awareness that their actions could lead to either success or failure of the technology in the organisation.

The personal interests of the different departments were therefore dominant and controlled during implementation. This ultimately wielded the greatest influence over the trajectory of initiative and innovation. Departments were not able to accept each other and were not able to see the impact of integration, a collaborative approach and dependencies. As such, each department created a barrier in the implementation of IT strategy in the organisation.

iii. The Effect of Autonomy

The rules of the organisation allowed autonomy in every department in the computing environment. Thus, the various heads of departments were autonomous in their actions during implementation of the IT strategy. As a result of this autonomy, the IT managers were dominant in the allocation, as well as the carrying out of tasks in their various units. Because of the autonomy granted to the IT managers, they sometimes ignored tasks that were not of personal interest or priority to them and relegated or allocated others to their subordinates who sometimes lacked the necessary skills and or experience to carry out the allocated talks.

The rules of the autonomy made the IT managers dominant in their various departments and mandated the CIO to make the final decision in the computing environment of the organisation. The allocation of tasks was done virtually at random. There was no formal method or process of allocating tasks and responsibilities to employees. What was also missing was the process of measurement of progress with the allocated tasks. The individual managers used their power as mandated by the structure in allocating and measuring employees' tasks and performances.

Employees were positioned within structures, but they were not necessarily positioned in equal ways and didn't have equal opportunities. Some employees had greater access to more resources and knowledge or information than others. These individuals drew from different structures or from the same structures in ways which gave them an advantage, not only with respect to their peers, but also with respect to their superiors.

Also, there was a pervasive and accepted rule in the organisation that dictated that subordinates at all times had to obey their managers, which allowed for all IT employees to accept IT strategy without question or objection. This means that a manager at any level is able to prevent aspects of the IT strategy from being implemented and all employees at a lower level will oblige to comply with the decisions made by the manager. Therefore, resistance of any type was limited when it came to complying with dictates of the IT strategy.

The performance contract was measured on a timescale shorter than the period of IT strategy implementation, which was problematic. In the organisation, IT strategy was developed and implemented within a period of between one and three years. Based on the performance contract employees were appraised and incentives were awarded, which included salary increases and financial bonuses. The appraisals were done on a bi-annual basis. This meant that most tasks and assignments were not completed when the appraisal was conducted. As a result, some of the employees indulged in lobbying their colleagues and managers for good ratings.

iv. Exercise of Power

In the computing environment, facilities are processes, procedures and capabilities, and they were vital in the implementation of IT strategy. Based on the rules of the organisation, IT managers had access to these facilities. Also, some employees were more knowledgeable about these facilities than their colleagues. Those who had access to these facilities used it as a source of power and domination. Some facilities were acquired through factors which are a manifestation of organisational politics. During the implementation, power was exercised to protect individual interests, which shaped the outcome of IT strategy in the organisation.

Control over facilities such as financial budgets, the use or availability of employees with specific technical skills and the use of technology, was critical as these were the determining factors for the allocation of responsibilities and accountabilities. These facilities were used as a source of influence through which power of authority was exercised. As a result, lobbying and negotiation for these facilities were paramount.

During implementation, facilities as modalities of power refer to the authority to allocate resources to agents and to dominate the actions of others. This produces and reproduces structures of domination. During implementation, these structures of domination include the domination of some employees by others, the availability and use of resources and the relationships between people and technology. Thus, for example, both IT Managers and employees used their individual authority to protect their individual interests.

v. The Implication of Networks of People

Many social networks of people were identified in the computing environment, formed along various lines such as hierarchy, departmental affiliation, skill-sets and racial groups. Through these networks, employees formed interactive groups through their right of association. These networks of people were difficult to manage and as such contributed more negatively than positively to the implementation of IT strategy. For example, race diversity was misconstrued to be a political racial divide, with actions often interpreted as acts of racism.

The rules of the organisation mediated in the relationships between the employees and how they interacted during IT strategy implementation. The interaction went along these lines of networks and also followed the hierarchical lines in the organisation, making the immediate superior (IT Manager) dominant.

Prior to the research, the CIO (a white male) was replaced by a black male. Many of the white employees feared that they may lose their jobs. Others thought that there would be radical changes causing them to lose control of responsibilities of the facilities used in the implementation of the IT strategy in the organisation. As a result, employees at different levels intensified their actions to protect their individual interests: actions in certain processes and activities were personalised to protect individual employment, responsibilities, accountabilities and control of facilities. Some of the employees chose to provide the CIO and other IT Managers with incorrect information in order to achieve these aims.

vi. Alignment of Different Interests

There were different interests, which were demonstrated during the allocation and execution of tasks in the implementation of IT strategy.

Employees' actions constituted the practice, as an enactment of the structures enabling and constraining the implementation of IT strategy in the organisation. Inevitably, individual employees responded and reacted differently to the practice. For example, because of the autonomy possessed by the IT Managers, to some of them, personal interest superseded the objectives of the organisation. At best, a loose alignment of interests was achieved, held together by a joint adherence to the requirements of individual performance contracts.

The levels of interest of and participation by employees in the implementation of IT strategy were different. Many of the employees had personal interests which conflicted with the interest of the organisation. Others put group interests first. The alignment of interests, given these circumstances, was not very successful. Alignment requires a translation of interests so that individuals and groups would see their own interests in the interests of the organisation.

The performance contract was used coercively to align the various interests during the implementation of IT strategy. However, even though employees were appraised based on their performance contracts, enrolment and mobilisation were low. As a result, many employees only reluctantly accepted their allocated tasks associated with implementation.

vii. Superiority Issues

The superiority exhibited by certain individuals and groups, in the implementation of IT strategy, was a dominating factor as levels of superiority were used to intimidate employees at the lower levels, which daunted their confidence in carrying out their various tasks. This superiority was, unfortunately, often a manifestation of racial behaviour.

The employees were dominated by senior management in their activities (such as allocation of resources, sharing of services and information and use of mandated authority) associated with the implementation of IT strategy. As a result of the domination, some employees could not freely express themselves, which affected their contribution to the implementation of IT strategy.

The superiority issues had an impact on the implementation of IT strategy. Such issues were prevalent among the IT managers. The different personalities of these managers played a role as they ranked themselves. The ensuing rivalries were counterproductive with considerations of expediency often dictating the implementation of the IT strategy.

Employees were dominated by senior management in their activities (through allocation of resources, sharing of services and information and use of mandate authority) associated with the implementation of IT strategy. This had a negative effect on many of the employees, particularly, on those at the lower levels. The superiority issues led to reduced productivity, created a lack of trust, increased internal conflict and led to greater resistance in the implementation of IT strategy in the organisation.

6. INTERPRETATION OF THE FINDINGS

The above seven findings are interpreted and mapped onto four factors, as shown in Figure 3 and Table 2. These factors were manifestations of organisational politics and they were the critical factors which impact the implementation of the IT strategy in the organisation. The factors of organisational politics are Racial behaviour, Exploitation of job insecurity, Exploitation of performance contracts and Pursuit and protection of personal and group interests. The mapping was done to make sense of the interrelationship between the findings and the interpretation (factors of organisational politics).

Figure 3. Mapping of factors of organisational politics

Findings		Factors of organisational politics	
Human interactions	pursuit and protection of self-interests; diverse human interests, intentions and actions; racial domination and racial discrimination; lack of racial integration; negative relationships	Race diversity misconstrued as a political racial divide, with actions often interpreted as acts of racism; racial domination and racial discrimination; lack of racial integration	**Racial behaviour**
Organisational rules and hierarchy	modification of rules for some departments; inequality of power among the departments and employees; acts of rivalry to achieve their individual goals; prevalence of competitiveness and rivalry to gain advantage; facilities used as a source of influence; dominance of personal interests; barriers created by departments	measurement of progress determined by managers; inequality of power among the departments and employees; disinformation	**Exploitation of job insecurity**
Effect of Autonomy	dominant IT managers focus on tasks of personal interest or priority; measurement of progress determined by managers; the dialectic of control; allocated tasks for the implementation of IT strategy bound by performance contracts; performance contract measured on timeframe shorter than the period of IT strategy development and implementation	performance contract used coercively; allocated tasks for the implementation of IT strategy bound by performance contracts; performance contract measured on timeframe shorter than the period of IT strategy development and implementation	**Exploitation of performance contracts**
Exercise of Power	domination of some employees by others; availability and use of resources	personal interests in conflict with the interest of the organisation; group interests put first; counterproductive rivalries; lack of trust, increased internal conflict	**Pursuit and protection of personal and group interests**
Implications of networks of people	social networks contributed more negatively than positively; race diversity misconstrued as a political racial divide, with actions often interpreted as acts of racism; change of CIO initiated actions to protect individual interests; disinformation		
Alignment of Different Interests	personal interests conflicted with the interest of the organisation; group interests put first; alignment of interests not very successful; performance contract used coercively; reluctant acceptance of allocated tasks		
Superiority issues	counterproductive rivalries; expediency dictating implementation of IT strategy; reduced productivity, lack of trust, increased internal conflict		

Table 2. Mapping the findings on factors of organisational politics

Findings	Racial Behaviour	Exploitation of Job Insecurity	Exploitation of Performance Contracts	Pursuit and Protection of Personal and Group Interests
Human interactions	X			X
Organisational rules and hierarchy		X		X
Effect of Autonomy		X	X	X
Exercise of Power		X	X	
Implications of networks of people	X	X		X
Alignment of Different Interests			X	X
Superiority issues	X			X

i. Racial Behaviour

Although the organisation advocated racial integration in the computing environment, racial diversity was misconstrued as a political racial divide, and actions were often interpreted as acts of racism. Some employees resorted to racial discrimination to ingratiate themselves with their superiors. This resulted in negative relationships and a lack of trust among employees in the computing environment. Some whites at times excluded employees of other races in communicating some of the processes and activities in the implementation of IT strategy. Similarly, some blacks, coloureds and Indians segregated themselves from the whites, which made it difficult for them to be part of the allocation of tasks. All of this added up to a divided workforce. This was not conducive to productivity, especially with respect to the implementation of the IT strategy.

ii. Exploitation of Job Insecurity

The absence of any process of measuring progress with tasks allocated to employees meant that individual managers used their power to decide how to measure employees' performances. With appraisals in terms of the individual employee's performance contract also measured on a timescale shorter than the period of IT strategy implementation, employees resorted to seeking the approval of their managers instead of focusing on the task at hand. Power was unequally distributed among the different departments, and this, coupled with an unhealthy competitiveness and rivalries to gain personal advantage meant that employees and managers alike were constantly insecure about what they had to do and about their jobs as such. This situation was not improved by acts of disinformation. Some employees were dominated by others, which meant that those dominated were often deprived of the resources needed to do their job, adding to their insecurity.

iii. Exploitation of Performance Contracts

The performance contract was regarded as a *sine qua non* in the organisation. All employees, including managers, were obliged to conform and sign their contracts. However, employees were not forced to perform the tasks as stated in their individual contracts. This depended on the agenda of individual managers, who might coerce employees to perform tasks aligned with their (the managers') interests. Using their power and authority, and the "threat" of performance appraisal, managers therefore exploited the performance contracts. At the same time, employees did their bit of exploitation as well.

Employees who had more organisational knowledge and information related to the implementation of IT strategy at their disposal, and those highly skilled employees whose expertise were heavily relied upon during implementation, became dominant and they used that as power to dictate activities and processes during implementation, regardless of specific performance contract stipulations.

iv. Pursuit and Protection of Personal and Group Interests

IT managers, especially heads of departments, promoted their individual interests through the facility to allocate and authorize the use of available resources. These actions led to counterproductive rivalries, where personal and group interests, often in conflict with the interests of the organisation, were put first. The driving force behind this pursuit of individual and group interests was often the feeling of superiority of one manager or the particular group over others. This had a negative effect on many of the employees, particularly, on those at the lower levels. It led to reduced productivity, created a lack of trust, increased internal conflict and negatively affected the implementation of IT strategy in the organisation.

7. THE IMPACT OF ORGANISATIONAL POLITICS ON THE IMPLEMENTATION OF IT STRATEGY

The four factors of organisational politics identified are, of course, not independent. In order to discover the relationships between the factors, they were further analysed. From the literature reviewed, the author identified the concepts related to organisational politics: domination, inequality of power, disinformation, coercion, self-interests, rivalries, lack of trust and conflict (Pfeffer, 1992). Table 3 shows the analysis where each factor, regarded as a category, shows the concepts that make up that category.

In terms of the analysis, the relationships as shown in Table 3 hold between the factors of organisational politics. The implementation of IT strategy is the results of peoples' actions, through procedures, processes, activities and use of resources. Even though the CIO, IT Managers and other employees acted

Table 3. Relationships between factors of organisational politics

	Racial Behaviour	Exploitation of Job Insecurity	Exploitation of Performance Contracts	Pursuit and Protection of Personal and Group Interests
Domination	X	X	X	
Inequality of power		X	X	
Disinformation				
Coercion			X	
Self-interests	X		X	X
Rivalries	X	X		X
Lack of trust	X	X		X
Conflict		X		X

within the defined processes and procedures, organisational politics influenced and negatively impacted the implementation of IT strategy in the organisation.

The participation or enrolment of employees in the implementation of IT strategy was marked by different negotiations, but mainly, the performance contract was the basis for all negotiations. And here the rules allowed the IT managers to use their discretion (as they saw fit) in certain scenarios. The performance contract did not permit any employee to avoid participating or enrolling in the implementation of the IT strategy, forcing them to be committed individually and collectively. While this made it easier to involve all employees in the implementation of IT strategy, individual actions resulting from the performance contract did not guarantee a positive outcome. First, employees were not forced to perform the tasks as stated in their individual contracts – this, in many cases, depended on the agenda of individual managers, who might coerce employees to perform tasks aligned with their (the managers') interests. Second, using their power and authority, and the "threat" of performance appraisal, in other words, exploiting the job insecurity of employees, managers exploited the performance contracts, often to achieve their own objectives, which did not necessarily align with that of the organisation in terms of IT strategy implementation. Third, employees did their bit of exploitation as well. Some employees who were privileged shared and communicated information with colleagues of their choice, while the information was supposed to be made available to the entire department. Some highly skilled employees whose expertise was heavily relied upon in the implementation of IT strategy in the organisation, used their power to dictate activities and processes in the implementation of IT strategy, regardless of specific performance contract stipulations. Through their actions they inhibited and dominated other individuals.

Due to the huge dependency on people, technologies and processes in the implementation of IT strategy, relationship was key and fundamental. As the analysis revealed in Table 3, the feeble relationship which was a manifestation of organisational politics was instrumental to the derailment of IT strategy in the organisation.

Some employees, including some IT managers, felt insecure about their jobs or financial aspects related thereto. As a result, their actions were based on furthering their personal interests rather than those of the organisation. For example, some managers felt that they could not report the truth about the activities in and the state of their department, in case it might have an adverse effect on their employment.

Managers exploited performance contracts by using their power to decide how to measure employees' performances. There were stiff and unhealthy competitiveness and rivalries, which led to constant insecurity. This situation was not improved by acts of disinformation or non-information, which, as pointed out above, were often racially motivated. Some employees were dominated by others, excluded and deprived of the resources needed to do their job, adding to their insecurity.

The flow of information during implementation was top-down in approach. The autonomy of managers also allowed them to interpret the implementation tasks differently, depending on the interest of the head concerned. IT managers used the mandates and authority bestowed on them to share the information they received and their interpretation thereof as they pleased and in the process, imposed constraints on the performance of those who were not privileged or favoured by them. Such actions were informed by personal interests, exploited the performance contracts of employees and prevented employees from carrying out tasks that the managers would prefer not to undertake.

IT managers, especially heads of departments, also promoted their individual interests through the facility to allocate and authorize the use of available resources. These actions unavoidably led to counterproductive rivalries, where personal and group interests, often in conflict with the interests of the organisation, were put first. The driving force behind this pursuit of individual and group interests was often the feeling of superiority of one manager or a particular group over others. This had a negative effect on employees and increased the job insecurity of many of the employees, particularly, those at the lower levels in dominated departments or groups.

The organisational politics led to reduced productivity, created a lack of trust, increased internal conflict and negatively affected the implementation of IT strategy in the organisation. These factors of organisational politics as captured and illustrated in Figure 3 and Table 2, derailed processes and activities in the implementation of IT strategy. As a result of the derailment, IT strategy is developed or reviewed each year, making it a cost prohibitive exercise.

8. CONCLUSION

In summary, during implementation of the IT strategy, employees were mobilised by their managers to undertake aspects of the implementation by allocating these as tasks to them. Communication was restricted, and the focus was on technical aspects. These communicative actions reproduce structures of significance, which were that technical aspects receive priority, regardless of their match with particular aspects of the developed IT strategy. Employees use their technical abilities and managers their authority to protect their own interests. These actions produced and reproduced the structures of domination, dictating implementation based on pragmatic considerations. Finally, employees accepted their tasks, coupled as they were to performance related incentives, and continue with their work without full understanding of the implementation. Their work is affected by a variety of issues which created an environment of poor cooperation. All of this reproduces the structure of legitimation during the implementation of IT strategy in the organisation.

Due to the relative instability of the actor-networks, implementation of the IT strategy can be expected to become increasingly difficult in time. As pointed out before, the actions of agents always carry within them the seeds of change, but such change, to improve the alignment and hence the stability of the networks, would also require a change in the processes to create new norms, facilities and interpretive schemes. As mediators of the actions of agents, they could contribute to new structures of legitimation, domination and signification, which in turn could lead to a better translation of interests of the actors in the network. The findings from the analysis represent the current regularity in practice, which is likely to continue unless an effort is made to change it.

Much work has been done on organisational politics, such as Markus (1983), Pfeffer (1992), Hardy (1994), Butcher & Clarke (1999), Mintzberg (2000) and Lewis (2002) and on IT strategy, such as Ciborra (1996), Lederer & Sethi (1988), Boar (1998), Lederer & Gardiner (1992), Gottschalk (1999), Wolff & Sydor (1999) and Mack (2002). These works are often separately articulated. What was missing was the interaction between IT strategy and organisational politics, which this study hugely contributes to the body of knowledge through its empirical findings.

The complementary use of Structuration Theory and Actor-Network Theory as lenses through which the analysis was undertaken, revealed a rich context that otherwise would not have been observed. It enabled the explanation of the interaction between technology, human action and organisational structure, affecting the strategic IT direction of the organisation. This represents a contribution to Information Systems Research methodology. The author believes that this approach (combination of both Structuration Theory and Actor-Network Theory) could, in many cases, be used to conduct more in-depth analyses of the social aspects that so often lead to failures of information system projects.

The other contribution of this study aims to be of significance to decision makers, professionals, including managers and employees of the organisation within the computing environment, and IS researchers. It is expected that the key contribution will arise from the understanding of the fundamental of the impact of organisational politics on IT strategy. Through this, a better understanding of the influences in the deployment of IT strategy will be gained.

REFERENCES

Armstrong, M. (1994). *How to be an even better manager* (4th ed.). London: Kogan Page Ltd.

Boar, H. (1998). Information Technology Strategy as Commitment. RCG Information Technology. Retrieved from http://www.rcgit.com/Default.aspx

Bowker, G., & Star, S. (1996). How things (actor-net) work: Classification, magic and the ubiquity of standards. *Philosophia, 25*(4), 195–220.

Butcher, D., & Clarke, M. (1999). Organizational Politics: The Missing Discipline of Management? Cranfield School of Management, Cranfield, Bedfordshire, UK. Industrial and Commercial Training, 31 (1), 9-12.

Callon, M. (1986). Some elements of the sociology of translation: Domestication of the scallops and the fisherman of St Brieuc Bay. In J. Law (Ed.), *A New Sociology of Knowledge, power, action and belief*. London: Routledge.

Callon, M., & Law, J. (1989). On the Construction of Sociotechnical Networks: Content and Context Revisited. *Knowledge and Society: Studies in the Sociology of Science Past and Present, 8*(1), 57–83.

Ciborra, C. U. (1996). Improvisation and information technology in organizations. *Proceedings of International Conference on Information Systems*. USA; Philadelphia.

Daniels, C. N. (1994). Information Technology: The Management Challenge. London; Addison-Wesley publishing Ltd

Giddens, A. (1984). *The Constitution of Society: Outline of the Theory of Structuration*. Cambridge, UK: John Polity Press.

Gottschalk, P. (1999). Implementation Predictors of Formal Information Technology Strategy. *Information & Management, 36*(2), 77–91. doi:10.1016/S0378-7206(99)00008-7

Hanbury, R. (2001). Strategy Clinic: Keeping politics away from project management. Retrieved from http://www.computerweekly.com/

Hardy, C. (1994). Power and politics in organizations. In C. Hardy (Ed.), *Managing Strategic Action: Mobilizing Change*. London: Sage Publications.

Holbeche, L. (2004). *The power of constructive politics*. Horsham, United Kingdom: Roffey Park Institute Publications.

Jones, M. (1999). Structuration Theory. In W. L. Currie & R. D. Galliers (Eds.), *Rethinking Management Information Systems* (pp. 103–134). United Kingdom: Oxford University Press.

Klein, H., & Myers, M. (1999). A set of principles for conducting and evaluating interpretive field studies in Information Systems. *Management Information Systems Quarterly, 23*(1), 67–93. doi:10.2307/249410

Kling, R., & Iacono, S. (1984). The control of Information Systems Developments After Implementation. *Communications of the ACM, 27*(12), 1218–1226. doi:10.1145/2135.358307

Latour, B. (1987). *Science in Action: How to follow Scientists and Engineers through Society.* Cambridge, Massachusetts: Harward University Press.

Latour, B. (1997). On actor-network theory: A few clarifications. Retrieved from http://www.keele.ac.uk/depts/stt/stt/ant/latour.htm

Law, J. (1992). Notes on the theory of the actor-network: Ordering, strategy, and heterogeneity. *Systems Practice, 5*(4), 379–393. doi:10.1007/BF01059830

Lederer, L., & Gardiner, V. (1992). The Process of Strategic Information Planning. *The Journal of Strategic Information Systems, 1*(2), 76–83. doi:10.1016/0963-8687(92)90004-G

Lederer, L., & Sethi, V. (1988). The implementation of strategic information systems planning methodologies. *Management Information Systems Quarterly, 12*(3), 445–461. doi:10.2307/249212

Lewis, D. (2002). *The place of organizational politics in strategic change.* London: John Wiley & Sons Ltd.

Mack, R. (2002). Creating an Information Technology (IT) Strategy: An Alternative Approach. Gartner, Inc. Retrieved from www.gartner.com

Markus, L. (1983). Power, Politics, and MIS Implementation. *Communications of the ACM, 26*(6), 430–444. doi:10.1145/358141.358148

Mintzberg, H. (2000). *The rise and fall of strategic planning.* Englewood Cliffs, London: Prentice-Hall.

Monteiro, E., & Hanseth, O. (1996). Social Shaping of Information Infrastructure: On Being Specific about the Technology. In W. J. Orlikowski, G. Walsham, M. R. Jones, & J. I. DeGross (Eds.), *Information Technology and Changes in Organizational Work* (pp. 325–343). London: Chapman and Hall.

Morgan, G. (1986). *Images of Organization.* London, Beverly Hills: Sage.

Orlikowski, W. (1993). CASE tools as organisational change: Investigating incremental and radical changes in systems development. *Management Information Systems Quarterly, 17*(3), 1–28. doi:10.2307/249774

Orlikowski, W., & Barley, S. (2001). Technology and institutions: What can research on information technology and research on organizations learn from each other? *Management Information Systems Quarterly, 25*(2), 145–165. doi:10.2307/3250927

Orlikowski, W., & Gash, D. (1994). Technological Frames: Making Sense of Information Technology in Organisations. *ACM Transactions on Information Systems, 12*(2), 174–207. doi:10.1145/196734.196745

Pfeffer, J. (1992). *Managing with power: Politics & influence in organizations.* Boston, USA: Harvard Business School Press.

Robbins, S. P., Odendaal, A., & Roodt, G. (2001). *Organisational Behaviour: Global and Southern African Perspectives* (9th ed.). South Africa: Pearson Education.

Roode, J. D. (1993). Implications for teaching of a process-based research framework for information systems. *Proceedings of the 8th annual conference of the International Academy for Information Management*. Orlando, Florida.

Rosser, B., Kirwin, B., & Mack, R. (2002). Business/IT Strategy Development and Planning, Gartner Inc. Retrieved from http://www.gartner.com/DisplayDocument?doc_cd=112300

Scarbrough, H. (1998). *Linking strategy and IT-based innovation: The importance of the "management of expertise". Information Technology and Organisational Transformation: Innovation for the 21st Century Organisation*. West Sussex, England: John Wiley & Sons Ltd.

Walsham, G., & Waema, T. (1994). Information Systems Strategy and Implementation: A Case Study of a Building Society. *ACM Transactions on Information Systems*, *12*(2), 159–173. doi:10.1145/196734.196744

Ward, J., & Peppard, J. (2002). *Strategic Planning for Information Systems* (3rd ed.). West Sussex, England: John Wiley & Sons.

Wolff, S., & Sydor, K. (1999). Information Systems Strategy Development and Implementation: A Nursing Home Perspective. *Journal of Healthcare Information Management*, *13*(1), 2–12. PMID:17283848

Yin, R. K. (1994). *Case Study Research, Design and Methods* (2nd ed.). Newbury Park, California: Sage Publications.

KEY TERMS AND DEFINITIONS

Actor Network Theory: The theory categorises human and non-human actors, and focuses on how networks of actors are created for various purposes. It claims that both human and non-human actors are equal.

Development: The process and procedure through which an organization formulate IT Strategy, periodically.

Implementation: This is the operationalization of the formulated items and technology artefacts in an organisation, with a period of time.

IT Strategy: Is an organisation's articulated intent to achieving its goals and objectives at both short and long terms, through information technology.

Non-Technical Factors: These are factors that are not technological, but are related to the deployment and use of technologies. They includes processes, procedures, rules, as well as human.

Organisation: A legal business entity with employees, which have its goals and objectives mandate.

Structuration Theory: Is a theory that focuses on human and technical factors as agents, and defines structure as rules and resources. The theory postulates that factors enables and constrain activities in the production and reproduction of events.

Chapter 4
Knowledge Requirements for Information Systems Outsourcing

Hanlie Smuts
University of South Africa, South Africa

Marianne Loock
University of South Africa, South Africa

Alta van der Merwe
University of Pretoria, South Africa

Paula Kotzé
CSIR Meraka Institute and Nelson Mandela Metropolitan University, South Africa

ABSTRACT

Information systems (IS) outsourcing is a complex, multi-layered and a multifaceted concept. An organisation may gain access to knowledge it does not own in-house or be able to obtain it at a lower price by entering into an outsourcing relationship. At the same time, the organisation may risk losing key skills and capabilities unless the outsourcing arrangement is managed strategically and knowledge transferred properly. Knowledge management is valuable in preventing a loss of knowledge when an organisation outsources its information system activities. This chapter analyses and describes the knowledge requirements relevant in an IS outsourcing arrangement.

INTRODUCTION

Outsourcing as a business practice is flourishing in almost every domain and organisations are outsourcing software development, innovation and even functional departments [Hirschheim & Dibbern, 2014; Power, Desouza & Bonifazi, 2006]. In an environment where survival depends on cost-cutting and downsizing, information systems (IS) becomes a probable target for outsourcing as it is difficult to measure direct contribution of the IS function to the organisation as a whole [Benamati & Rajkumar, 2002; Dibbern, Goles, Hirschheim & Jayatilaka, 2004].

Outsourcing is defined as the action of transferring organisational work to an outsource vendor [Power et al., 2006]. The scope of work outsourced and the delivery of the outsource vendor against the scope is

DOI: 10.4018/978-1-4666-8524-6.ch004

managed by an outsourcing arrangement that stipulates the contract conditions, the required service levels and the required deliverable quality of the arrangement [Power, Bonifazi & Desouza, 2004]. A special type of outsourcing is IS outsourcing and Sparrow [2003: 1] defines IS outsourcing as "the practice of handing over planning, management and operation of certain functions to an independent third party, under the terms of a formalised service level agreement". Sparrow [2003] maintains that outsourcing should be seen as a strategic management tool. As such, it should be evaluated in the context of the strategic position of the organisation [Power et al., 2006].

In the context of an IS outsourcing arrangement, the focus of value creation no longer remains internal to the organisation, but occurs within the relationship between the client organisation and the outsource partner. The client organisation has to rely on its outsource partner to share knowledge and continually respond to change [Gottschalk, 2006]. Currie and Pouloudi [2000b] observe that one of the emerging issues for management will be how to identify and evaluate knowledge-based assets in the context of IS outsourcing. A part of this emerging research agenda "is due to the growth in outsourcing and the realisation that many contracts have simply failed to take into consideration important issues of intellectual property protection, core competencies, managerial and technical capabilities and skills, and software development and exploitation" [Currie & Pouloudi, 2000b: 162].

However, the use of IS outsourcing as a strategy presents several knowledge management challenges to IS managers since both knowledge management and IS outsourcing are complex, multi-layered and multifaceted concepts [Currie & Pouloudi, 2000b]. An organisation may gain access to knowledge it does not own in-house, or may be able to obtain it at a lower price, by entering into an outsourcing relationship. At the same time, the organisation may risk losing key skills and capabilities, unless the outsourcing arrangement is managed strategically and knowledge transferred properly [Al-Salti, 2009; Currie & Pouloudi, 2000b; Laplante, Costello, Singh, Bindiganavile & Landon, 2004]. Knowledge management is important in preventing a loss of knowledge when an organisation downsizes or outsource its business activities [Aydin & Bakker, 2008; Christopher & Tanwar, 2012]. Currie et al [2000b] identified that one of the emerging issues for management is how to identify and evaluate knowledge-based assets in the context of IS outsourcing.

Knowledge transfer between the organisation and outsource vendor is required for all the phases prior and during an IS outsource arrangement [Beyah & Gallivan, 2001; Dibbern et al., 2004]. Currie et al [2000b] argue that knowledge transfer in all the IS outsourcing phases provides an opportunity to encourage researchers, and managers, to consider the value of knowledge-based assets, and to evaluate the extent to which knowledge can be acquired or lost through IS outsourcing. Aydin and Bakker [2008] concur that, although the importance of knowledge management in IS outsourcing is highlighted by scholars, little research is being done on how organisations deal with managing knowledge in outsourcing situations [Blumenberg, Wagner & Beimborn, 2009].

The focus of this chapter is to address this gap in research with the objective to investigate how organisations manage knowledge in outsourcing activities, with a specific focus on knowledge requirements. In order to analyse and describe the knowledge requirements relevant in an IS outsourcing arrangement, a research study was conducted in a telecommunication company in South Africa. This chapter reports on the knowledge requirements identified pertinent to IS outsourcing. The *background* section provides context for this chapter, the *IS outsourcing strategy and lifecycle section* provides a knowledge management perspective on IS outsourcing and the *study on knowledge requirements in IS outsourcing section* defines the method followed to conduct the research, as well as the findings of the study. The chapter is concluded with the *future research possibilities* and *conclusion* sections.

BACKGROUND

Organisations are constantly searching for ways to grow and maintain their competitive edge. Today's business activities depend greatly on IS enablement [Ang & Cummings, 1997; Aydin & Bakker, 2008; Goles & Chin, 2005]. This demands that IS maintenance be regarded as a critical process that needs to be performed with the highest possible quality. Achieving the desired IS quality requires both organisation-specific knowledge about internal business operations and explicit technical knowledge. In tis context, IS outsourcing is a complex and potentially daunting task if the organisation is unsure about its implications, its required business performance and its essential IS support and knowledge management [Aydin & Bakker, 2008].

IS outsourcing is not a recent management trend and has been present in its different forms from the early 1960's [Akomode, Lees & Irgens, 1998; Aydin & Bakker, 2008; Claver, Gonzales, Gasco & Llopis, 2002]. By IS outsourcing, organisations give way to greater dependence on external service providers. The scope of IS outsourcing varies from data centres to application development, user and desktop support, operations and architecture [Ang & Cummings, 1997; Lacity & Willcocks, 2009; Lam & Chua, 2009]. However, irrespective of the scope of IS outsourcing, roles, responsibilities, governance, organisational relations and the kinds of knowledge required, outsourcing problems have organisation specific characteristics and vary considerably from one organisation to the next [Goles & Chin, 2005; Hirschheim & Dibbern, 2014].

There are many IS outsourcing models and many ways to employ them strategically as a management tool [Fink & Shoeib, 2003]. In the process of choosing an outsourcing model or combination of models, an organisation should consider future strategies, plans and budgets for IS as well as internal skills and capabilities [Cullen & Willcocks, 2003; Zelt, Wulf, Uebernickel & Brenner, 2013]. According to Sood [2005], the choice of outsourcing model can permanently change the way in which the organisation works. There are four main types of sourcing models that are used, namely, (1) onsite model, (2) offsite model, (3) offshore model and (4) hybrid model [Sood, 2005]. Using an *onsite model*, the outsourcing vendor places skilled individuals at the client organisation's location, constantly interacting with the client organisation's teams. In this scenario, the organisation's IS professionals are accountable for the day-to-day management of the outsource vendor, as well as providing logistical support such as offices, computers, software licences and phones [Sparrow, 2003]. With the *offsite model*, the outsource vendor has an office in close vicinity (e.g. same city) to the client organisation's headquarters [Power et al., 2006]. In this instance, the outsource vendor bears the cost of facilities and administration, although some of it may be included in the outsourcing fees [Sood, 2005]. When using the *offshore model*, the entire arrangement is accomplished in a different country that provides a more cost-effective location, with skills and communication infrastructure being readily available at low cost [Cha, Pingry & Thatcher, 2008; Ranganathan & Balaji, 2007]. With the *hybrid model*, the outsource vendor uses a variant of the onsite and the offsite models to enable most of the work to be done offshore [Aalders, 2001]. Several variations of these models have also been deployed in the past based on the nature of the outsourcing requirement and the outsourcing arrangement [Aalders, 2001; Carmel & Tjia, 2005]. Examples include the *near-shore* model that is similar to the offshore model, except that work is moved outside the country to neighbouring locations. The only advantage over the offshore model is that the travel time is just a couple of hours [Power et al., 2006].

IS outsourcing undertakes to leverage the outsource vendor's management practices and skills and the economies of scale arising from using a specialist IS outsource vendor [Aalders, 2001; Drucker, 2010].

However, research has shown that consequential knowledge management and value creation have been disappointing [Cullen & Willcocks, 2003; Drucker, 2010]. Client organisations report their frustration with cost–service debates and significant loss of control over their IS fate, including their knowledge base. Outsource vendors, on the other hand, find it difficult to deliver on promises of innovation and value added, hampered by their lack of knowledge about the client's long-term business strategy [Lacity & Willcocks, 2009]. In this context, Sparrow [2003] noted that the topic of IS outsourcing generates heated deliberation among IS professionals with arguments against and in favour of IS outsourcing. Some IS professionals perceive it as an enlightened approach to the management of routine IS services and a mature development of partnerships with suppliers [Sparrow, 2003]. Adversaries argue that outsourcing involves major risks with loss of control, loss of qualified IS resources, loss of flexibility and loss of competitive advantage in information management [Rao, Nam & Chaudhury, 1996]. Others see it as symptomatic of an organisation that has failed to grasp the strategic importance of IS and a lack of investment in the development of their IS staff, especially where the outsourcing arrangement transfer staff from the organisation to the service provider [Sparrow, 2003].

Knowledge is a crucial factor for IS outsourcing decisions, since organisations acquire external knowledge through this process and share organisational knowledge with the outsource vendor [Beyah & Gallivan, 2001; Dibbern et al., 2004]. The importance of knowledge transfer in an IS outsourcing arrangement becomes observable when the outsourcing lifecycle is examined. Knowledge transfer is vital during the period prior to the outsourcing, when vendors are selected and contracts are drafted, during the implementation phase, when services are transferred to the vendor, and throughout the contract management and maintenance period, where existing practices are optimised and new practices created [Beyah & Gallivan, 2001; Vural, 2010].

However, the outsourcing of IS responsibilities to a vendor can negatively influence the downstream outcomes of IS projects by modifying whether and how retained organisation employees learn and preserve important explicit and tacit knowledge [Sparrow, 2003]. A lack of or insufficient learning by these employees may lead to the deterioration of internal knowledge assets and a loss of organisational memory. Furthermore, it may be difficult to restore a specific organisational competence, which was previously outsourced, when the organisation limits or ceases investing in its own competencies due to the outsourcing arrangement [Beyah & Gallivan, 2001]. The fact that an organisation relies on an outsource vendor does not mean that they should ignore the importance of an ongoing knowledge management programme specifically related to knowledge transfer [Beyah & Gallivan, 2001]. The potential loss of business achievements necessitates continual assessment of the impact of IS outsourcing decisions on the protection and enhancement of an organisation's knowledge base [Aalders, 2001; Beyah & Gallivan, 2001].

Knowledge management constructs are helpful in understanding IS outsourcing performance and provides a sound basis for examining and mitigating some of the risks related to outsourcing [Beyah & Gallivan, 2001; Dibbern et al., 2004]. However, according to Srinivas [1999], organisations lack the means to assign value to the knowledge that is transferred to the outsource vendor, the knowledge received from the outsource vendor, and the new knowledge created or exploited through the outsourcing arrangement. The lack of focus on what happens to knowledge when an organisation outsources is a serious gap in practice, and one that deserves thorough study and analysis [Kess, Torkko & Phusavat, 2007; Lacity & Willcocks, 2009].

Knowledge Requirements for Information Systems Outsourcing

Figure 1. Business, IS, and outsourcing strategy
[Gartner, 2007]

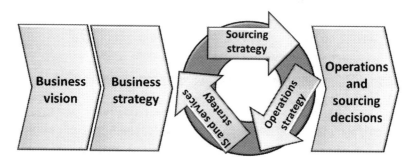

In order to understand the knowledge requirements when an organisation outsources IS, knowledge management concepts can be applied to IS outsourcing phases. In the next sections, *IS outsourcing strategy and lifecycle* are described, as well as *knowledge and processes for organisational knowledge-creation*.

IS OUTSOURCING STRATEGY AND LIFECYCLE

The preparation for IS outsourcing in reality starts long before the first contact is concluded with an IS outsource vendor. The period before the actual involvement of the vendor could be the most valuable time of the entire outsourcing arrangement, as preparation is required before embarking on an IS outsourcing venture [Sood, 2005]. IS outsourcing decisions include many issues, such as competitive threats, latest trends and business changes [Goles & Chin, 2005].

A solid sourcing strategy that aligns with the overall business goals will ensure proper consideration of the different IS outsource models in order to achieve the best results [Gartner, 2007]. Figure 1 shows how organisations should evaluate the complex relationships between operating, IS and sourcing decisions in order to determine the best sourcing model as early as possible. An organisation's IS and sourcing strategies must be derived from, and be connected to, the business strategy. The *business strategy* defines a set of objectives associated with a *business vision*, for example, how to get additional market share, better serve and retain clients, obtain competitive advantage and optimise processes. The *operations strategy* defines what the business will do, when the business will do it and how it will measure success. The *IS strategy* examines how the IS services can support the objectives set by the business strategy. The *sourcing strategy* mainly defines who will fulfil parts of certain objectives, through a set of plans and decisions that define and integrate internally and externally provided services, to fulfil the organisation's business and IS strategies [Gartner, 2007].

Once an IS outsourcing strategy has been defined, an IS outsourcing lifecycle guides an organisation in realising the full value that outsourcing can provide [Gartner, 2002a]. The first step in any outsourcing initiative is to identify the strategic intent and key objectives of the IS outsourcing arrangement, as it will determine what will be outsourced, how success or failure will be measured, how it will guide the choice of outsource provider and facilitate the allocation of appropriate management skills and effort [Cullen & Willcocks, 2003; Gellings, 2007]. Several outsourcing lifecycle models exist, consisting of numerous steps. For example:

- Cullen and Willcocks [2003] identified three distinct phases of outsourcing: (1) the architect phase, (2) the engage phase and (3) the govern phase. The first two phases deal specifically with the decision to outsource, the preparation for the outsourcing arrangement and comprises of the activities required to make the arrangement work. The third phase, govern, comprises of the management of the outsource arrangement [Cullen & Willcocks, 2003].
- Sood [2005] describes an outsourcing lifecycle consisting of seven steps, namely, (1) request for proposal and vendor selection, (2) contracts and negotiations, (3) rates for each type of working profile, (4) setup and logistics, (5) programme execution, (6) implementation and testing, and (7) programme completion. The first 3 steps of the lifecycle deal with the process of evaluating and selecting the vendor on the basis of the match between the vendor's proposal and the organisation's requirements and criteria, agreeing a master services agreement governing the overall terms of conditions of the outsourcing arrangement, as well as statements of work for each engagement included in the master agreement. Steps 4 and 5 focuses on the initial planning and logistics to kick-start the outsourcing process and the planning for the involvement of the in-house team, as well as the definition of a transition plan for the transfer of knowledge to the new team. The last two steps refer to execution i.e. the implementation and monitoring of the outsource arrangement and metrics to measure whether the relationship is working well, as this will assist with enforcing the service level agreements (SLAs) and knowledge transfer [Goo, Huang & Hart, 2008]. If reverse knowledge transfer is not required, then the vendor will undertake to sustain and maintain implementation [Sood, 2005].

In the next section, *knowledge management* and *knowledge creation processes* are described towards understanding knowledge requirements in IS outsourcing.

Knowledge and Processes for Organisational Knowledge-Creation

Information becomes internalised knowledge when it is accepted and retained as appropriate representations of the relevant knowledge [Frappaolo & Capshaw, 1999; Godbout, 1999; Lindvall, Rus, Jammalamadaka & Thakker, 2001]. Knowledge comes with insights, framed experiences, intuition, judgement and values, and encompasses the scope of understanding and skills that are mentally created by people [Clarke & Rollo, 2001]. Knowledge can be categorised as either being explicit or tacit. Explicit knowledge can be articulated in the form of text, diagrams or product specifications for example [Clarke & Rollo, 2001; Nickols, 2001]. Nonaka [1991] refers to explicit knowledge as formal and systematic, like a computer program. Tacit knowledge is far less tangible than explicit knowledge and refers to personal and context-specific knowledge, making it difficult to communicate and formalise [Clarke & Rollo, 2001; Nonaka & Takeuchi, 1995]. Tacit knowledge includes cognitive and technical elements, where the technical aspects refer to concrete know-how, crafts and skills. Cognitive elements include mental models such as paradigms, beliefs and viewpoints and are seated in how individuals perceive and define their world [Polanyi, October 1962]. The articulation of tacit mental models is a key factor in creating new knowledge [Nonaka & Takeuchi, 1995].

The interaction between tacit and explicit knowledge occurs at an individual, and not organisational, level [Nonaka & Takeuchi, 1995]. The management of this knowledge is inherently linked to the sharing of knowledge between individuals and to the collaborative processes involved [Edersheim, 2007; Meihami & Meihami, 2013]. Organisational learning results from a process in which individual knowledge

Figure 2. Knowledge spiral
[Nonaka & Takeuchi, 1995]

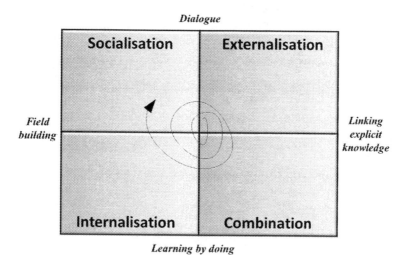

is transferred, enlarged and shared, and is characterised as a spiral of knowledge conversion (Figure 2) from tacit to explicit [Nonaka & Takeuchi, 1995; Nonaka, Toyama & Byosiere, 2001].

The process of knowledge conversion progresses through four different modes as shown in Figure 3: socialisation (tacit to tacit), externalisation (tacit to explicit), combination (explicit to explicit) and internalisation (explicit to tacit) [Nonaka & Takeuchi, 1995].

- *Socialisation* includes shared information and experiences, as well as the sharing of tacit knowledge between people through observation, imitation and practice.

Figure 3. Contents of knowledge created by the four modes
[Nonaka & Takeuchi, 1995]

	Tacit knowledge →	Explicit knowledge
Tacit knowledge ↓	(Socialisation) **Experiential knowledge**	(Externalisation) **Conceptual knowledge**
Explicit knowledge	(Internalisation) **Operational knowledge**	(Combination) **Systemic knowledge**

- *Externalisation* is the process whereby tacit knowledge is articulated as explicit knowledge through collaboration with others by means of conceptualisation and extraction such as converting tacit knowledge into words or numbers. The use of technology to manage and search explicit knowledge bases is well established, and explicit knowledge is shared not only via document management systems, e-mails, in meetings, etc., but also through education, learning and training interventions.
- *Combination* is the enrichment of the collected information by re-configuring it or enhancing it through sorting, adding, combining or categorising it so that it is more usable. In order to act on information, individuals should understand and internalise it.
- *Internalisation* involves the process of creating an organisation's own tacit knowledge. The process is closely related to learning-by-doing, through studying documents or attending training in order to re-experience to some degree what others have previously learned. Individuals are afforded the opportunity to create new knowledge by combining their existing tacit knowledge with knowledge of others [Krogh, Ichijo & Nonaka, 2000; Nonaka & Takeuchi, 1995].

Organisational knowledge creation is a dynamic interaction between tacit and explicit knowledge induced by several triggers as shown in Figure 3 [Nonaka & Takeuchi, 1995].

- Socialisation facilitates the sharing of experiences, technical skill and mental models and usually commences with building a field of interaction. The content of knowledge created through this mode is *experiential knowledge*.
- The outcome of externalisation is *conceptual knowledge* as it is activated through dialogue and collective reflection and facilitates the articulation of tacit mental models.
- By networking newly created and existing knowledge from sections in the organisation, the combination mode is triggered creating *systemic knowledge*.
- Lastly, learning by doing prompts internalisation constructing *operational knowledge*.

In the next section the relationship between IS outsourcing and knowledge management is considered.

A Knowledge Management Perspective on IS Outsourcing

Knowledge transfer has come to the fore in response to the increasing size, complexity and scope of organisations, as well as the increasing capabilities of modern IS to support knowledge-orientated activities [Niederman, 2005]. Knowledge is an important factor for IS outsourcing arrangements, as knowledge flows in both directions between the organisation and the outsource vendor with the aim of increasing the collective knowledge of each other's knowledge domain [Aydin & Bakker, 2008; Blumenberg et al., 2009]. Technology-specific knowledge, such as the IS services provided, flows from the organisation to the outsource supplier, and business-specific knowledge about processes and procedures flows from the supplier to the organisation. The purpose of this knowledge transfer is to increase the knowledge shared by the organisation and the outsource vendor [Bandyopadhyay & Pathak, 2007; Blumenberg et al., 2009]. Knowledge sharing and management in the context of IS outsourcing is not a stand-alone practice; it should be integrated into all aspects of the outsourcing arrangement [Aydin & Bakker, 2008; Balaji & Ahuja, 2005; Blumenberg et al., 2009]. The inseparability of IS from the internal production service in the client organisation implies that, even in situations of total outsourcing, a minimum set of capabilities are retained in-house by the client organisation [Miozza & Grimshaw, 2005].

As the same knowledge is used to solve many different problems, it is recognised that the same IS capability can transform different organisations in different ways. Outsource vendors benefit fully from their knowledge resources as they reuse the same knowledge assets in different contexts for different customers. Similarly, IS functions have to design adequate knowledge transfer strategies to build expertise so that new problems can be solved by reusing the same knowledge. The fact that an organisation relies on an outsource vendor does not mean that it should ignore the importance of an ongoing knowledge management programme specifically related to knowledge transfer [Beyah & Gallivan, 2001]. The importance of a shared knowledge base is highlighted as a basis for performance gains, as it creates sensitivity to the organisational environment of the other party and encompasses goals, constraints, interpretations and behaviour [Cruz, Perez & Cantero, 2009]. Such an environment for knowledge integration is created through a common language and frequent interaction, consequently fostering knowledge transfer and having a positive influence [Beyah & Gallivan, 2001; Blumenberg et al., 2009].

Organisations discover the effective deployment of IS management and derive business value from it through experiential learning and hands-on experience. Often challenges are not appreciated unless they are experienced, as the understanding of the value of an IS innovation tends to materialise in an evolutionary manner. Organisations choosing to outsource may unintentionally fragment this knowledge by missing critical learning opportunities, with a resulting loss of ensuing business gains. This necessitates constant assessment of the impact of IS outsourcing decisions on the protection and enhancement of an organisation's knowledge base [Beyah & Gallivan, 2001]. The delivery of business value is essentially a set of knowledge-based activities in the context of IS, as it involves the integration and harmonisation of knowledge "from many individuals of different disciplines and backgrounds, with varied experiences and expectations, located in different parts of the organisation" [Blumenberg et al., 2009: 344]. The consideration of knowledge-based activities implies and requires a close partnership consisting of both formal processes and informal working relationships between the functional areas in the organisation and IS. These interactions between functional areas in the business and IS are of the utmost importance for cross-functional knowledge transfer, although the impact on IS outsourcing performance has not been researched comprehensively [Blumenberg et al., 2009; Lee, 1996].

STUDY ON KNOWLEDGE REQUIREMENTS IN INFORMATION SYSTEMS OUTSOURCING

In order to understand the cross-functional knowledge transfer between the client organisation and outsource vendor, a research study was conducted with the objective to investigate how organisations manage knowledge in outsourcing activities, with a specific focus on knowledge requirements. The purpose of this research study was to gain an understanding of the knowledge requirements between a client organisation and an outsource vendor as the client organisation already holds knowledge, the outsource vendor brings knowledge and through the process of IS outsourcing, new, joint knowledge is created. In order to define knowledge requirements relevant in an IS outsourcing arrangement, data considering knowledge sources, means of knowledge transfer in an IS outsourcing arrangement and knowledge sharing specific to the IS outsourcing lifecycle, was collected.

The research design, data collection method, respondent profile, respondent feedback and findings are discussed in the following sections.

Research Design

An interpretive case study [Larsen & Myers, 1999; Orlikowski & Baroudi, 1991] was concluded at a large telecommunication organisation within the South African context. The interpretive case study research methodology was chosen, as the study attempted to learn from the current situation in real life [Larsen & Myers, 1999; Olivier, 1997] and the results are expressed using descriptive statements [Olivier, 1997]. Yin [2003] defines five components of research design that are important for case studies namely the questions, the propositions, the unit(s) of analysis, the logic linking the data to the propositions and the criteria for interpreting the findings. The unit of analysis in this single case study is the organisation, with the objective to distil the key knowledge requirements in an IS outsourcing arrangement.

The company where the case study was conducted operates in a competitive telecommunication market in South Africa. Product and services are key differentiators and technology enablement plays a significant and key role within this company. This environment was relevant for data collection as it utilises an outsourced model for IS and applies a multi-sourcing approach for application development projects. A scoping study for the replacement of a legacy retail billing system and the implementation of a customer management system were outsourced to a systems integrator through a procurement process. The scope of work outsourced included business process modelling, high level solution design and architecture, an implementation programme work plan and a data migration strategy. The resource model that the client organisation utilised for this project consisted of a small number of permanent employees with specialist knowledge, outsource vendor resources and independent specialist contractors hired in by the client organisation. A key objective for the outsource vendor was to design a future-proof, integrated and optimised business process set and this requirement emphasised the requirement for knowledge sharing and knowledge flow between all three groups of resources. The target audience for this data collection consisted of permanent employees, contractor and consultant resources, as well as business users and programme sponsors.

IS outsourcing lifecycles were described in the *IS outsourcing and lifecycle section* and the 3-phase lifecycle proposed by Cullen and Willcocks [2003] were utilised to design the questionnaire. The research participant questionnaire consisted of four sections, namely:

1. **Respondent Demographical Information:** General information regarding the research participant e.g. whether from the client or vendor organisation, whether they utilise a knowledge base or not, the source of the knowledge base, e.g. internal, external, the outsourcing model that they operate within.
2. **Knowledge Sources in IS Outsourcing:** This section established what knowledge management systems are referenced, the reasons for using such a knowledge management system and knowledge transfer mechanisms.
3. **Architect, Engage, and Govern Phases of IS Outsourcing Life Cycle:** This section contained three open-ended questions. Firstly, a question relating to the definition of outsourcing key objectives, benefits and the outsourcing business case; secondly, a question referring to the outsourcing model, the outsource arrangement definition and contract negotiation; and thirdly, a question related

Table 1. Identification of research participants

Main Criteria	Sub-Criteria	Rationale
IS outsourcing programme work streams	Business requirements	• Best practice process design knowledge • Business, business process and process modelling knowledge
	Technical requirements	• Solution design concepts and knowledge • Integration of business and technical requirements
	Project management	• Project plan and project artefact management • Deliverable quality assurance
IS outsourcing project commercial management	Business model management	• Business process scenario and process measurement knowledge • Business case for IS outsourcing
	Outsource vendor management	• Outsource vendor management expertise • Contract and payment profile management
Organisational hierarchy	Programme director/owner	End-to-end view of IS outsourcing arrangement, including all components such as business case, commercial management, artefact management and business (organisational) knowledge
	Outsource vendor team members	• Knowledge sharing from outsource vendor to client organisation • Knowledge sharing from client organisation to outsource vendor • Outsource vendor best practice contribution to IS outsourcing arrangement
	Outsourcing project team members	• Knowledge sharing from outsource vendor to client organisation • Knowledge sharing from client organisation to outsource vendor • Business, organisational and business process knowledge

to the monitoring and management of the outsource arrangement, commercial management, the measuring of outsourcing benefits and the termination / exit processes.

4. **General Section:** This section consisted of one open-ended question where the research participants could indicate any further general feedback and comments regarding the knowledge components of the IS outsource arrangement.

The criteria and rationale used to identify the research participants are summarised in Table 1. These criteria informed the typical profile of the research participants. The rationale focused on IS outsourcing project areas where knowledge, knowledge bases and knowledge sharing were the key drivers. In addition, three main selection criteria informed the participant profile:

1. Research participant representation from all IS outsourcing programme work streams, namely business requirements, technical requirements, project management and commercial management
2. Research participants who understand systems with broad business process management knowledge, knowledge and expertise about outsource vendor management and research participants who work in environments where knowledge and knowledge sharing are key priorities
3. Research participants from different levels of the organisational hierarchy in both the client organisation and the outsource vendor organisation, for example programme directors, business analysts, solution architects, and so on, including onsite, near-shore and offshore resources.

This selection ensured that different perspectives on the research questions were obtained in order to contribute to the richness of interview data.

The first column in Table 1 depicts the *main criteria* for research participant selection and it points to the relationship type between the organisation and the research participant. The second column, *sub-criteria*, reflects the specific area of work of the research participant and the last column provides the rationale for including different work areas.

In order to establish the knowledge requirements relevant to an IS outsourcing arrangement, a web link to the questionnaire, together with an explanation of its purpose, was emailed to the identified target audience, which comprised 62 research participants representing multiple roles in the client organisation and the outsource vendor organisation. The survey was completed by 40 respondents, thereby giving a response rate of 65%.

Data Analysis

Quantitative and qualitative feedback was gathered using the questionnaire. Totals of the responses submitted were reported on in the *respondent profile* and *knowledge sources in IS outsourcing sections*, the answers to the open-ended questions were collated, relevant parts of the data were identified and common themes were classified [Flick, 2007]. The process of identifying common themes and classification was concluded through a two-step process. Firstly, descriptive codes were used in order to attributing a theme to a segment of text [Welman, Kruger & Mitchell, 1994]. Secondly, open coding was utilised in order to establish themes from the questionnaire data [Leedy & Ormrod, 2014; Myers & Avison, 2002]. Open coding is a process of reducing data to a small set of themes that describe the phenomenon under examination [Leedy & Ormrod, 2014].

Respondent Profile

The purpose of the first three questions in the questionnaire was to determine the profile of the research participants, that is, their affiliation to the client organisation, the project stream of the outsourcing arrangement to which they were allocated and, lastly, the phase of the outsourcing project they focused on. Of the 40 participants that completed the questionnaire, 22 were permanent employees of the client organisation, 12 were contractors or consultants contracted to the client organisation and seven were employed by the outsource supplier. Business owners and line managers formed part of the permanent employee contingent of the respondents. With respect to the outsourcing arrangement the respondents contributed to, more than one phase could be relevant. Accordingly, ten respondents contributed to the architect phase, 11 to the engage phase and 25 to the govern phase of the IS outsourcing arrangement.

Knowledge Sources in IS Outsourcing

The purpose of the second section of the questionnaire was to establish what knowledge was required for the various phases of the IS outsourcing arrangement, what knowledge bases were utilised and how knowledge was transferred. Accordingly, respondents could select more than one of the options provided.

Table 2 presents the source of the knowledge management systems referenced. Twenty respondents indicated that this was an internal organisational knowledge management system, whilst 16 respondents referenced a knowledge management system external to their organisation (nine utilised web resources and seven the system at the outsource partner). Twenty referred to a subject matter expert within their organisation, and 11 referenced a subject matter expert outside their organisation. Two research par-

Table 2. Knowledge management system source

Knowledge management system internal to your organisation	20
Knowledge management system external to your organisation – web resources	9
Knowledge management system external to your organisation – outsource partner	7
A subject matter expert internal to your organisation	20
A subject matter expert external to your organisation	11
We do not reference a knowledge management system or utilise experts	2

ticipants indicated that they had not referenced a knowledge management system or utilised experts for this IS outsourcing arrangement.

Table 3 presents the knowledge components referenced for IS outsourcing. Best practice operational knowledge (21 respondents) and project documentation (19 respondents) scored the highest in terms of knowledge components referenced. Thirteen respondents referenced a lessons learnt repository, 13 benchmark information, and ten accessed client or outsource vendor intelligence. Only three respondents specified that they utilised a human resource skills database, while five respondents indicated that they had not used a knowledge management system or database for this IS outsourcing arrangement.

The way in which the knowledge required, was transferred, is shown in Table 4. In this instance, the respondents could choose all the relevant options provided. Two respondents indicated that they had all the knowledge required to perform their task on the IS outsourcing arrangement, while 21 indicated that they obtained the knowledge by doing their own research. Direct observation was highlighted by 19 research participants, a documented knowledge repository by 18 and joint execution by 17 research participants. Fifteen indicated that they obtained the required knowledge through learning by doing and by concluding a proof of concept. Nine indicated experimentation and comparison as a means of knowledge transfer, five referred to narration and one respondent indicated imitation as a mechanism for obtaining knowledge.

Architect, Engage, and Govern Phases of IS Outsourcing

The purpose of the third section of the questionnaire was to obtain any additional feedback from research participants on knowledge flows for the architect, engage and govern phases.

Table 3. Knowledge components referenced for IS outsourcing

Best practice operational knowledge base	21
Client / outsource vendor intelligence	10
Human resource skills database	3
Project documentation management	19
Lessons learnt repository	13
Benchmark information	13
We do not use a knowledge management system / base	5

Table 4. Methods of knowledge transfer

Direct observation	19
Narration	5
Imitation	1
Learning by doing	15
Experimentation and comparison	9
Proof of concept	15
Joint execution	17
Documented knowledge repository	18
Lecture	2
My own research	21
I have all the required knowledge	2
We do not transfer knowledge	0

Research participants shared several comments regarding the *architect* phase of the IS outsourcing arrangement. Some of the comments shared include:

Live demonstrations and presentations of the current challenges faced from all parties involved.

A better managed knowledge repository. Knowledge should be more available.

Market the framework used to select the outsourcer. Obtain buy in and adapt the framework where necessary. Define key individuals and work with them in their respective domains

Availability of documented organisation knowledge, crucial business decision making of available options based on an existing business strategy

Knowledge sharing sessions with SME from outsource partner with specific agenda and objectives

Would be ideal to have a centralised repository that contains all the up-to-date business rules, migration plans, etc. that is easy to read and access.

Joint execution, and conducting formal knowledge transfer workshops.

The analysis of comments delivered the following emerging themes for the *architect* phase:

1. **Client Organisation Consideration:** This theme included the client organisation buy-in to the outsource vendor arrangement framework, client organisation to outsource vendor skill gap analysis, a comprehensive outsource business case, detailed planning with appropriate stakeholders and access to a benchmarking repository. Knowledge of the organisational environment and the strategic objectives communicated by top management are key, since decisions on IS outsourcing must be taken in the IS departmental context as well as the organisation as a whole. Knowledge of the vari-

ous cost factors must be considered in terms of development/deployment costs and ongoing costs, with a specific emphasis on licence costs, human resource costs, hardware infrastructure costs, and suchlike for cost analysis purposes. The cost impact of smaller areas of outsourcing rather than 'big bang' outsourcing should be considered. Sensitivity refers to local shareholder and staff expectations and is easier to manage in a start-up organisation as no critical staff volumes are in place. In terms of risk, offshore data is a key concern in terms of regulatory and intellectual property loss.

2. **Client Organisation Preparation to Embrace:** This theme consisted of defining an agile business decision-making process, a detailed understanding of the outsource requirements by the client organisation, client organisation training on joint execution and outsource management, client organisation key resource involvement, as well as the identification of the key resource pool for vendor selection, the client organisation skills database and the outsource skills requirement assessment. Lastly, preparation included the finalisation of the client organisation knowledge repository and organisational documentation.

3. **Client Organisation for Implementing the IS Outsourcing Arrangement:** This theme referred to outsource vendor and outsource model intelligence, as well as a quantified business case with sufficient activity-based costing information, outsource benchmarks and outsource performance measures. It also included an outsource options analysis of which knowledge transfer is a key outsource deliverable.

With regard to the *engage* phase of an IS outsourcing arrangement, research participants shared the following comments:

Transparency of information be it through a shared online portal or other. This must be kept up-to-date at all times, and if any material is hidden, this should be stated clearly (where the gaps are), why, and who has access.

Better, more complete documentation

Culture of knowledge sharing

Defined knowledge transfer channels, which are appropriately transparent, where stakeholders are kept up to date on the processes used and rationale for vendor selection and subsequent contract terms.

Knowledge transfer of key benchmarking that is done i.t.o. best practises specific to industry common repository

Access to a knowledge base of information

Unpacking the key objective of knowledge transfer into measurable services and products to be included in the criteria for vendor selection and contract negotiation.

We have access to a lot of knowledgeable people in the organisation. Internal research should be completed in terms of the expected outcomes and current best practice internationally. This way when selecting vendors etc., the internal resources already know what to expect and aren't so easily mislead

The analysis of the comments provided emerging themes for the *engage* phase in the following areas:

1. **Statement of Work Feedback:** This theme included a clear scope of the client organisation's negotiation position reflected in a comprehensive outsource request for proposal, with the control of knowledge management requirements included in the outsourcing arrangement governance process. Other comments included the formalisation of service level agreements, the definition of detailed and effective measures, as well as the establishment of a formal hand-over plan. Respondents indicated that outsource vendor to client organisation knowledge transfer mechanisms should be formally agreed to and that clear communication of timelines for service delivery by the client organisation is required.
2. **Outsource Vendor Selection:** This theme comments included the establishment of best practice procurement processes for outsource vendor evaluation and selection and the establishment of an expert cross-functional evaluation team and a common understanding of the outsourcing arrangement status between the client organisation and the outsource partner. Research participants highlighted the fact that client organisation knowledge-sharing sessions with outsource vendor customers should be conducted to obtain a view of vendor engagement and delivery.
3. **Outsource Vendor Commercials:** This theme refers to the definition of accurate performance measures and benchmarks for the outsourcing arrangement, the monitoring of benefit realisation within the outsourcing arrangement, and the clear communication of expectations. A dedicated team to manage the outsource vendor, with the support of an external specialist body, should be assembled in order to control the outsourced operational aspects. The monitoring capability and key skills that the client organisation requires to manage an outsource vendor relationship should be embraced or developed where required. In terms of organisational and contract design, knowledge of the supplier and customer organisational structures, knowledge of legislation that may affect the contents of the contract, and robust contracts with exit clauses as well as delivery benefits, are important.
4. **Outsource Vendor Hand-Over:** This theme points to the availability of a client organisation operational knowledge repository, detailed client organisation documentation and the creation of a common knowledge repository shared by the client organisation and the outsource vendor. Respondents maintained that one team consisting of client organisation resources and the outsource vendor should be formed in order to facilitate wider collaboration with detailed documentation and direct access between the outsource vendor and business stakeholders. In addition, there should also be direct access to the business areas affected by the outsourcing arrangement. Formal focus group meetings, knowledge transfer workshops and outsource vendor subject matter expert knowledge sharing sessions should be conducted in order to create a formal training and coaching repository for the IS outsourcing arrangement. Knowledge of the time it takes for resources to be mobilised helps define resource mobilisation realistically. For implementation and transition, knowledge of systems (people, IS systems, processes) and planning as the outsourcing arrangement gains traction, is critical for reducing time to market.

For the govern phase of IS outsourcing, research participants shared the following comments:

Wider collaboration and transparency, with detailed documentation

Shared office space between internal project resources and outsourced project resources, allotted hand over time, joint documentation responsibilities.

Again, transparency of and ease of access to all relevant information; if certain information must be kept to within a restricted set of individuals, this should be clear to all, and why. This mitigates any problems with regard to assumptions and addresses gaps of information and understanding.

Create a team that manages/monitors the outsourcers. They should not have to deal with the day to day running as well as there is not adequate time to do both

Transparency, to appropriate level of management, so that consequences of actions/non-action is known up front.

Determining key knowledge gaps in the organisation and formalising how the knowledge in these areas would be transferred is key.

Better and more complete documentation

Emerging themes based on the analysis of comments for the *govern* phase of IS outsourcing included:

1. **Relationship Management:** This theme pointed to strong relationship management and relationship building between the client organisation and the outsource vendor. Respondents also emphasised transparency at the appropriate management level so that consequences of actions or non-actions are shared.
2. **Deliverable and Commercial Management:** This theme highlighted the understanding of industry norms and trends, an outcome-based analysis of the usability of the end product, a mandated and knowledgeable decision-making body and the management of the scope size of the outsource requirement and the implementation cycles. Outputs are monitored by well-defined and measureable business processes, key performance indicators, service level agreements and requests for key performance indicators sets, as well as by knowledge transfer into measurable services and products. The research participants indicated that a reference model knowledge base and the application of the reference models in a proof of concept should be considered.
3. **Communication and Change Management:** This theme included integration sessions across the outsourcing arrangement work streams, iterative detailed updates to all team members, joint documentation responsibilities and joint execution between outsource vendor and client organisation resources. Respondents indicated that shared office space and a joint team war room facilitate operational integration, expectation-sharing sessions and outsource stage alignment sessions. An inclusive stakeholder plan, including stakeholder feedback, is required for client organisation stakeholder communication and expectation management.
4. **Knowledge Application:** This theme consisted of industry best practice and benchmarking knowledge transfer, access to a lessons-learnt and previous experience knowledge base, as well as an outsource vendor selection framework that is shared with client organisation business stakeholders. Expertise was shared by means of a cross-functional team that defined and drove the process.

5. **Knowledge Sharing:** This theme included access to a client organisation knowledge management repository, a client organisation process documentation knowledge base and a vendor subject knowledge and experience knowledge base. Research participants indicated that key expert knowledge can be formally utilised through consulting and that the outsourcing arrangement should optimise outsource vendor capability and experience.

General Comments

Research participants made several general comments regarding the knowledge management framework for an IS outsourcing arrangement. Respondents maintained that a knowledge management framework should be agreed on early in the outsource process, knowledge transfer buy-in should be obtained from both parties and collaborative tools for knowledge sharing and transfer should be identified. The client organisation should build capability for outsource vendor management, should be trained in joint execution, and the client organisation key man dependencies should be eliminated. A culture of knowledge sharing should be fostered over and above the availability of a client organisation's requirement document repository and secure knowledge repository. The client organisation should use the outsource process to acquire knowledge and, in turn, knowledge transfer should form part of outsourcing arrangement governance.

Research participants also commented on the impact of knowledge transfer on outsourcing models, including onsite, offsite, offshore, near-shore and hybrid on- and offshore.

- Respondents maintained that the *onsite* outsource model is the best approach, as direct engagement can take place. As teams from both the client organisation and the outsource vendor are onsite, it is easier to keep control and ensuring that knowledge transfer objectives are met is more straightforward.
- The *offsite* outsource model requires more discipline to achieve the objectives, but it is often required in order to accommodate skills shortages and complexity. However, when using the offsite model, knowledge sharing may be limited or lacking.
- Research participants indicated that the *offshore* model does not work in the African context, as it has an impact on certain efficiencies such as the increased time required to manage the arrangement. Furthermore, it presents a quality risk, communication is a challenge and there is a lack of knowledge sharing.
- In the use of the *near-shore* model communication presents a challenge and knowledge sharing may not be optimal.
- The *hybrid on- and offshore* model allows a core team to manage offshore when accountability transfers from the onshore team; this frees up the onshore team for other activities and reduces risk. However, communication is vital to ensuring that this model works together with joint execution.

Findings

The way in which knowledge is transferred beyond organisational boundaries in the context of IS outsourcing was highlighted in the outcomes of the study. Patterns of interaction included interactions within the client organisation and within the outsource vendor teams, as well as those between the client organisation and the outsource vendor teams. In order to deliver the business value intended by the IS

Knowledge Requirements for Information Systems Outsourcing

outsourcing arrangement, this team interaction requires both formal and informal processes in order to create shared knowledge from individual team knowledge.

With the aim of reporting the knowledge requirements collected, a framework reflected in Figure 4 was created by using the knowledge spiral for organisational learning shown in Figure 2 combined with the contents of knowledge created as depicted in Figure 3. The framework reflects the four modes of knowledge conversion and the interaction between tacit and explicit knowledge. Furthermore, the content of knowledge created such as experiential knowledge, conceptual knowledge, operational knowledge and systemic knowledge, are expanded by inserting descriptive detail illustrating knowledge conversion between tacit knowledge and explicit knowledge, as well as the contents of knowledge created (adapted from [Nonaka & Takeuchi, 1995]). These knowledge processes are relevant in the knowledge requirements between the client organisation and the outsource vendor [Al-Salti, 2009; Aydin & Bakker, 2008].

Table 5 presents the summary of emerging knowledge requirement themes from the data collected reported by the outsourcing lifecycle steps. For each theme, the content of knowledge created is indicated based on the framework depicted in Figure 4.

Table 5 indicates that the main focus of knowledge content during the *architect*, or initiation phase of an IS outsourcing lifecycle is on articulation of tacit knowledge, creation of a shared vision and translating external knowledge to what it means for the internal process. During the *engagement* phase of the lifecycle, the process of creating explicit knowledge between the client organisation and outsource vendor is reflected, as well as some skills transfer and creation of new tacit knowledge between the two, creating a common understanding between client organisation and outsource partner. In the *govern* phase of the IS outsourcing lifecycle, more emphasis is placed on the enrichment of joint knowledge towards realising the business case benefits of the IS outsource arrangement.

Figure 4. Four modes of knowledge conversion and contents of knowledge created (Adapted from [Nonaka & Takeuchi, 1995])

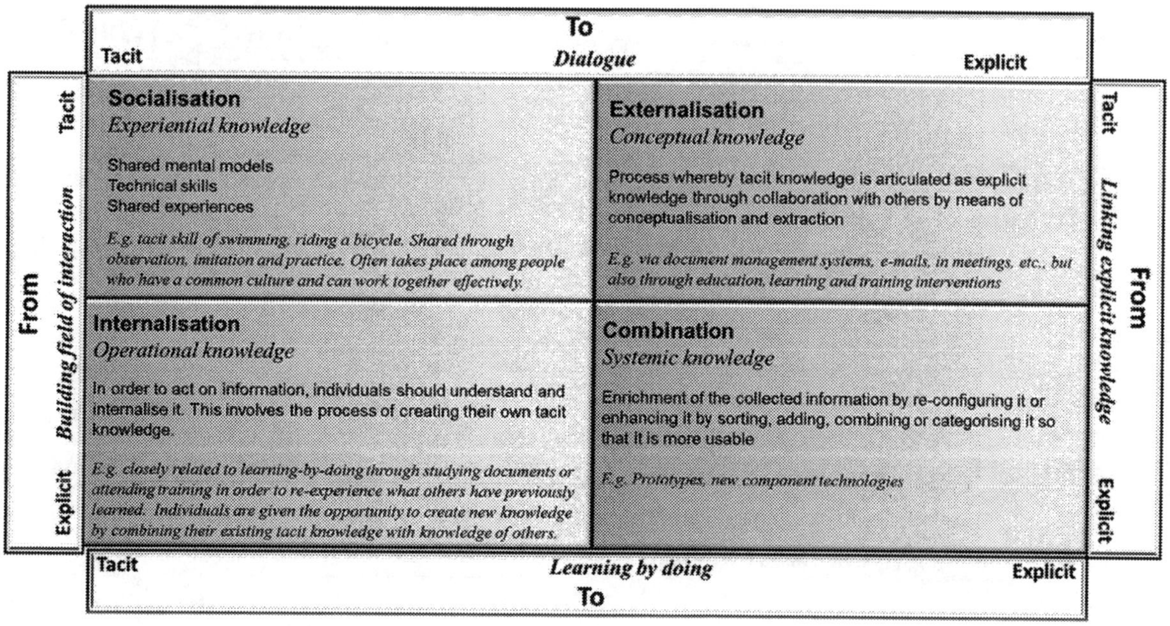

Table 5. Summary of emerging themes for knowledge requirements for IS outsourcing

Lifecycle	Knowledge Requirements for IS Outsourcing	Knowledge Content
Architect Phase	Identification and documentation of client organisation intellectual property	Conceptual
	Market knowledge	Operational
	Knowledge of client organisation environment, strategic objectives as communicated by top management	Experiential
	Knowledge of client organisation structures in order to engage with the correct people Views must be considered in context of the stakeholders' area as well as the organisation as a whole	Conceptual
	Knowledge of the operations in order to derive operational type benefits which can also be lifted up to a strategic level	Operational
	Knowledge sharing session with outsource partner	Operational
	Knowledge of the various cost factors must be considered in terms of development/deployment costs & ongoing costs with a specific emphasis on licence costs, human resource costs, hardware infrastructure costs, etc	Operational
	Understanding of sensitivity around local shareholder and staff expectations	Experiential
	Knowledge of risk related to chosen outsource model e.g. offshore data is a key concern, risk of loss of intellectual property	Experiential
Engage phase	Negotiation knowledge and skills	Conceptual
	Identification and documentation of client organisation intellectual property	Conceptual
	Records management	Conceptual
	Define model for retaining key knowledge and skill in organisation	Conceptual
	Create knowledge repository for organisational key knowledge	Conceptual
	Knowledge of the client organisation is key & ensuring integrity of information is paramount	Conceptual
	Knowledge of SLAs	Operational
	Knowledge of outsourcing processes as inherent knowledge and business relationships take time to develop as does the internal cultural requirements of the organisation	Experiential
	Knowledge of the objectives and mutual benefits of the parties involved	Systemic
	Knowledge of the areas that are core and that need innovation	Operational
	Supplier knowledge & their ability to evolve & offer better services	Systemic
	Knowledge of systems (people, IS systems, processes)	Conceptual
	Planning as gaining traction is critical to reduce time to market	Operational
	Knowledge of the supplier and customer organisational structures	Conceptual
	Knowledge of legislation that may affect the contents of the contract	Operational
	Facilitate wider collaboration by creating one team consisting of client organisation resources and the outsource vendor enabling direct access between the outsource vendor and business stakeholders	Systemic
	Knowledge of the support constructs required from the client organisation perspective	Conceptual
	Knowledge of roughly the time taken for resources to be mobilised helps define this criterion reasonably	Systemic
	Knowledge of the effects that certain actions may have, thereby taking the correct mitigating actions	Operational

continued on following page

Table 5. Continued

Lifecycle	Knowledge Requirements for IS Outsourcing	Knowledge Content
Govern phase	Contract management knowledge and skills	Operational
	Financial and cost management knowledge and skills	Operational
	Knowledge of internal policy and procedures of client organisation	Conceptual
	Learning by doing	Experiential
	Project management knowledge and skills	Operational
	Maintain knowledge repository for organisational key knowledge eg business requirements	Conceptual
	Delivery traceability matrix	Conceptual
	Plan and manage knowledge transfer to operational (support) team	Experiential
	Knowledge of the intricate details held within the contract including products, services, boundaries at which you are allowed to operate	Operational
	Strict contract management (rules of the game), governance re commercials, milestones and performance	Conceptual
	Knowledge of service level agreements	Operational
	Knowledge of escalation paths within the supplier organisation for problem resolution	Conceptual
	Create joint documentation accountability	Systemic
	Conduct formal focus group meetings, knowledge transfer workshops and outsource vendor subject matter expert knowledge sharing sessions in order to create a formal training and coaching repository for the IS outsourcing arrangement	Systemic
	Knowledge of critical metrics in relation to the operational environment to measure performance	Operational
	Knowledge to set clear concise objectives for meetings	Operational

Survey respondents maintained that the knowledge management framework should be agreed on and documented at the start of the outsourcing arrangement. This is a prerequisite, since working on extremely large, complex and transversal projects makes it difficult to outsource the work completely. Accordingly, there is a need for an internal organisational team to be responsible for joint execution, to ensure that the organisation's needs and governance are always considered and that the organisation's risks are mitigated. Templates should be generated for this team and the organisation's core staff should be trained to manage outsourcing arrangements.

Outsource partners usually consider getting the outsourced work done within timelines, irrespective of the damage that may be caused when all requirements are not taken into account. This often leads to rework and incomplete work, which ultimately results in additional costs for the client organisation that erode the savings realised by outsourcing. It also leads to a lack of succession planning within the organisation, as well as a lack of specific skills, which ultimately ends up costing the organisation more.

Participants indicated that one of the biggest challenges was best practice knowledge of the procurement process and the time it takes to conclude outsourcing negotiations and arrangements. A significant challenge was the effort, time and knowledge needed to manage an outsource vendor properly.

FUTURE RESEARCH POSSIBILITIES

The data for this study was collected at a telecommunication organisation in South Africa in order to create the knowledge requirement description. Further research is needed to generalise the knowledge elements contained in it in order to support outsourcing arrangements in general. Another issue accentuated by this research is the applicability of the knowledge requirements for IS outsourcing in industries other than telecommunication and in outsourcing projects other than IS outsourcing.

Client organisation and outsource vendor team members participated in this research and the responses for the two groups varied. The different requirements of such two groups within the IS outsourcing lifecycle and in the context of knowledge sharing, could be researched further.

CONCLUSION

This chapter contributed to the theoretical body of knowledge on IS outsourcing and how organisations deal with managing knowledge in outsourcing situations, by presenting input on knowledge requirements in an IS outsourcing arrangement based on a case study conducted in a telecommunication company in South Africa. The knowledge requirements for all three IS outsourcing lifecycle phases namely the architect phase, the engage phase and the govern phase, were addressed. The knowledge requirements presented can be used as a checklist for an organisation to determine what knowledge is required in the organisation, what knowledge is required by the outsource vendor, and what knowledge should be shared between the two when outsourcing IS or components thereof. By considering and planning for these knowledge requirements, an organisation may mitigate the risk associated with an IS outsource arrangement.

Knowledge requirements are relevant at different levels of abstraction and apply from the IS outsourcing arrangement level right down to the individual phases of IS outsourcing and the operational level in the client organisation. Knowledge required for each of these phases must be considered in order to assist organisations to deal with managing knowledge in IS outsourcing situations.

REFERENCES

Aalders, R. (2001). *The IT outsourcing guide*. West Sussex: John Wiley & Sons Ltd.

Akomode, O. J., Lees, B., & Irgens, C. (1998). Constructing customised models and providing information for IT outsourcing decisions. *Logistics Information Management*, *11*(2), 114–127. doi:10.1108/09576059810209973

Al-Salti, Z. (2009). *Knowledge Transfer and Acquisition in IS Outsourcing: Towards a Conceptual Framework* [Doctoral Symposium PhD]. Brunel University.

Ang, S., & Cummings, L. L. (1997). Strategic Response to Institutional Influences on Information Systems Outsourcing. *Organization Science*, *8*(3), 235–256. doi:10.1287/orsc.8.3.235

Aydin, M. N., & Bakker, M. E. (2008). Analyzing IT maintenance outsourcing decision from a knowledge management perspective. *Information Systems Frontiers*, *10*(3), 293–305. doi:10.1007/s10796-008-9084-5

Balaji, S., & Ahuja, M. K. (2005). Critical team-level success factors of offshore outsourced projects: a knowledge integration perspective. *Proceedings of the 38th Hawaii International Conference on System Sciences*, Hawaii. doi:10.1109/HICSS.2005.178

Bandyopadhyay, S., & Pathak, P. (2007). Knowledge sharing and cooperation in outsourcing projects: A game theory analysis. *Decision Support Systems, 43*(2), 349–358. doi:10.1016/j.dss.2006.10.006

Benamati, J., & Rajkumar, T. M. (2002). A design of an empirical study of the applicability of the Technology Acceptance Model to outsourcing decisions. *Proceedings of the Special Interest Group on Computer Personnel Research*. Kristiansand, Norway. doi:10.1145/512360.512371

Beyah, G., & Gallivan, M. (2001). Knowledge Management as a Framework for Understanding Public Sector Outsourcing. *Proceedings of the 34th International Conference on System Sciences*. Hawaii. doi:10.1109/HICSS.2001.927193

Blumenberg, S., Wagner, H.-T., & Beimborn, D. (2009). Knowledge transfer processes in IT outsourcing relationships and their impact on shared knowledge and outsourcing performance. *International Journal of Information Management, 29*(5), 342–352. doi:10.1016/j.ijinfomgt.2008.11.004

Carmel, E., & Tjia, P. (2005). *Offshoring Information Technology: Sourcing and Outsourcing to a Global Workforce*. New York: Cambridge University Press. doi:10.1017/CBO9780511541193

Cha, H. S., Pingry, D. E., & Thatcher, M. E. (2008). Managing the knowledge supply chain: An organisational learning model of information technology offshore outsourcing. *Management Information Systems Quarterly, 32*(2), 281–306.

Christopher, D., & Tanwar, A. (2012). Knowledge Management in Outsourcing Environment: People Empowering People. *The IUP Journal of Knowledge Management, X*(2), 61–86.

Clarke, T. & Rollo, C. (2001). Corporate initiatives in knowledge management. *Education + Training, 43*(4/5), 206-214.

Claver, E., Gonzales, R., Gasco, J., & Llopis, J. (2002). Information systems outsourcing: Reasons, reservations and success factors. *Logistics Information Management, 15*(4), 294–308. doi:10.1108/09576050210436138

Cruz, N. M., Perez, V. M., & Cantero, C. T. (2009). The influence of employee motivation on knowledge transfer. *Journal of Knowledge Management, 13*(6), 478–490. doi:10.1108/13673270910997132

Cullen, S., & Willcocks, L. (2003). *Intelligent IT outsourcing: eight building blocks to success*. Oxford: Butterworth-Heinemann.

Currie, W., & Pouloudi, A. (2000b). Evaluating the relationship between IT outsourcing and knowledge management. *Journal of Change Management, 1*(2), 149–163. doi:10.1080/714042463

Dibbern, J., Goles, T., Hirschheim, R., & Jayatilaka, B. (2004). Information Systems Outsourcing: A Survey and Analysis of the Literature. *The Data Base for Advances in Information Systems, 35*(4), 6–102. doi:10.1145/1035233.1035236

Drucker, P. F. (2010). *The Drucker lectures: essential lessons on management, society and economy*. McGraw-Hill.

Edersheim, E. H. (2007). *The Definitive Drucker*. New York: McGraw-Hill.

Fink, D., & Shoeib, A. (2003). Action: The most critical phase in outsourcing information technology. *Logistics Information Management, 16*(5), 302–311. doi:10.1108/09576050310499309

Flick, U. (2007). *Designing qualitative research*. Sage Publications Ltd.

Frappaolo, C., & Capshaw, S. (1999). *Knowledge management software: capturing the essence of know-how and innovation*. Information Management Journal.

Gartner. (2007). Best practice process for creating an IT services sourcing strategy. In G00153560 (Ed.), (pp. 1-29): Gartner Inc.

Gellings, C. (2007). Outsourcing Relationships: The Contract as IT Governance Tool. *Proceedings of the 40th Hawaii International Conference on System Sciences*. Hawaii. doi:10.1109/HICSS.2007.421

Godbout, A. J. (1999, January). Filtering Knowledge: Changing Information into Knowledge Assets. *Journal of Systemic Knowledge Management (Journal of Knowledge Management Practice)*.

Goles, T., & Chin, W. W. (2005). Information Systems Outsourcing Relationship Factors: Detailed Conceptualisation and Initial Evidence. *The Data Base for Advances in Information Systems, 36*(4), 47–67. doi:10.1145/1104004.1104009

Goo, J., Huang, D., & Hart, P. (2008). A path to successful IT outsourcing: Interaction between service-level agreements and commitment. *Decision Sciences, 39*(3), 469–506. doi:10.1111/j.1540-5915.2008.00200.x

Gottschalk, P. (2006). Research propositions for knowledge management systems supporting IT outsourcing relationships. *Journal of Computer Information Systems, 46*(3), 110–116.

Hirschheim, R., & Dibbern, J. (2014). *Information Technology Outsourcing: Towards Sustainable Business Value*. Springer-Verlag.

Kess, P., Torkko, M., & Phusavat, K. (2007). *Knowledge transfer for effective outsourcing relationships*. Proceedings of the 29th International Conference on Information Technology Interfaces (ITI). Cavtat, Croatia.

Krogh, G. v., Ichijo, K., & Nonaka, I. (2000). *Enabling Knowledge Creation: How to unlock the mystery of tacit knowledge and release the power of innovation*. New York: Oxford University Press. doi:10.1093/acprof:oso/9780195126167.001.0001

Lacity, M. C., & Willcocks, L. P. (2009). *Information Systems and Outsourcing: Studies in Theory and Practice*. Basingstoke, Hampshire: Palgrave Macmillan.

Lam, W., & Chua, A. (2009). Knowledge outsourcing: An alternative strategy for knowledge management. *Journal of Knowledge Management, 13*(3), 28–43. doi:10.1108/13673270910962851

Laplante, P. A., Costello, T., Singh, P., Bindiganavile, S. & Landon, M. (2004). The Who, What, Why, Where and When of IT Outsourcing. *IT Pro, IEEE, January / February*, 19-23.

Larsen, M. A., & Myers, M. D. (1999). When success turns into failure: A package driven business process re-engineering project in the financial services industry. *The Journal of Strategic Information Systems, 8*(4), 397–417. doi:10.1016/S0963-8687(00)00025-1

Lee, M. K. O. (1996). IT outsourcing contracts: Practical issues for management. *Industrial Management & Data Systems, 96*(1), 15–20. doi:10.1108/02635579610107684

Leedy, P. D., & Ormrod, J. E. (2014). *Practical Research: Planning and Design* (10th ed.). New Jersey: Pearson Education Limited.

Lindvall, M., Rus, I., Jammalamadaka, R., & Thakker, R. (2001). *Software Tools for Knowledge Management: A DACS State-of-the-art report*. Maryland: Fraunhofer Center for Experimental Software Engineering Maryland and The University of Maryland.

Marketplace realities in strategic outsourcing. (2002a). Gartner (pp. 1-22). Gartner Inc.

Meihami, B., & Meihami, H. (2013). Knowledge Management a way to gain a competitive advantage in firms. *International Letters of Social and Humanistic Sciences, 3*, 80–91.

Miozza, M., & Grimshaw, D. (2005). Modularity and innovation in knowledge-intensive business services: IT outsourcing in Germany and the UK. Science Direct, 1419-1439. Retrieved from www.sciencedirect.com

Myers, M. D., & Avison, D. (2002). *Qualitative Research in Information Systems*. London: Sage Publications.

Nickols, F. (2001). The Knowledge in Knowledge Management *Paper commissioned for Knowledge Management Yearbook 2000 - 2001*.

Niederman, F. (2005). International business and MIS approaches to multinational organisational research: The cases of knowledge transfer and IT workforce outsourcing. *Journal of International Management, 11*(2), 187–200. doi:10.1016/j.intman.2005.03.004

Nonaka, I. (1991). The Knowledge Creating Company (Harvard Business Review ed. Vol. Harvard Business Review).

Nonaka, I., & Takeuchi, H. (1995). *The Knowledge Creating Company*. Oxford University Press.

Nonaka, I., Toyama, R., & Byosiere, P. (2001). A Theory of Organisational Knowledge Creation: Understanding the Dynamic Process of Creating Knowledge. In M. Dierkes, A. B. Antal, J. Child, & I. Nonaka (Eds.), *Handbook of Organizational Learning & Knowledge* (pp. 491–517). New York: Oxford University Press.

Olivier, M. S. (1997). Information Technology Research: A practical guide for Computer Science and Informatics (Second Edition 2004 ed.). Van Schaik Publishers.

Orlikowski, W. J., & Baroudi, J. J. (1991). Studying Information Technology in Organisations: Research Approaches and Assumptions. *Information Systems Research, 2*(1), 1–28. doi:10.1287/isre.2.1.1

Polanyi, M. (1962, October). Tacit Knowing: Its Bearing on Some Problems of Philosophy. *Reviews of Modern Physics, 34*(4), 601–606. doi:10.1103/RevModPhys.34.601

Power, M. J., Bonifazi, C., & Desouza, K. C. (2004). The ten outsourcing traps to avoid. *The Journal of Business Strategy, 25*(2), 37–42. doi:10.1108/02756660410525399

Power, M. J., Desouza, K. C., & Bonifazi, C. (2006). *The Outsourcing Handbook: How to Implement a Successful Outsourcing Process*. London: Kogan Page Limited.

Ranganathan, C., & Balaji, S. (2007). Critical Capabilities for Offshore Outsourcing of Information Systems. *MIS Quarterly Executive, 6*(3), 147–164.

Rao, H. R., Nam, K., & Chaudhury, A. (1996). Information Systems Outsourcing. *Communications of the ACM, 39*(7), 27–28. doi:10.1145/233977.233984

Sood, R. (2005). *IT, software and services: outsourcing & offshoring*. Austin, Texas: AiAiYo Books.

Sparrow, E. (2003). *Successful IT outsourcing: from choosing a provider to managing the project*. London: Springer-Verlag. doi:10.1007/978-1-4471-0061-4

Srinivas, H. (1999). Position Paper on Knowledge Asset Management Retrieved September, 2011, from http://www.gdrc.org/kmgmt/km-1.html

Vural, I. (2010). *Success Factors in information Systems Outsourcing*. Saarbrucken, Germany: Lambert Academic Publishing.

Welman, C., Kruger, F., & Mitchell, B. (1994). *Research Methodology* (3rd ed.). Cape Town: Oxford University Press Southern Africa.

Yin, R. K. (2003). Case Study Research: Design and Methods (3rd ed.). Sage Publications Inc.

Zelt, S., Wulf, J., Uebernickel, F., & Brenner, W. (2013). *The Varying Role of IS Capabilities for Different Approaches to Application Services Outsourcing*. Paper presented at the 19th Americas Conference on Information Systems (AMCIS).

KEY TERMS AND DEFINITIONS

Explicit Knowledge: Formal and systematic knowledge that has been codified and articulated in the form of text, diagrams, etc.

Externalisation: The process whereby tacit knowledge is articulated as explicit knowledge through collaboration with others. E.g. education, learning and training interventions.

Implicit Knowledge: Refers to a person's internal state and is knowledge that is deeply embedded in an organisation's operating practices.

Information Systems Lifecycle: The step by step phases and activities an organisation follows when outsourcing its information systems to a 3rd party.

Information Systems Outsource Model: The approach aligned to business objectives an organisation chooses to outsource such as having all the organisation's development, maintenance and operations performed by an outsource vendor, or by simply contracting an external supplier to perform one single task, such as to install a piece of software. E.g. tactical outsourcing, strategic outsourcing, business process outsourcing, etc.

Information Systems Outsourcing: the process in which an organisation delegates a part or all of its information systems to an external service vendor (provider) for the supply of products or services required for effective internal operations in order to achieve its objectives.

Internalisation: The process of combining a person's existing tacit knowledge with knowledge of others.

Knowledge Transfer: The sharing process through which individuals or functional units increase their explicit knowledge.

Knowledge-Based Assets: The collected knowledge within an organisation that the organisation owns or needs to own in order to create value for the organisation.

Tacit Knowledge: A dimension of implicit knowledge and includes relationships, norms, actions, experience and values linked to an individual.

Chapter 5
Captive Offshore IT Outsourcing:
Best Practices from a Case Study

Olayele Adelakun
DePaul University, USA

ABSTRACT

A captive offshore center is a separate business arm of the parent company, wholly owned, to provide IT solutions to its parent company. Some of the reasons for setting up a captive offshore center in the literature include controlling cost and gaining access to low-cost skilled professional but in the case of a Chicago based Company (sears Holdings) it was considered a strategic. One hiding agenda was to lunch a new line of business offering to its US base customers from a low cost location. This chapter reveals how a Sears Holdings lunched a successful captive offshore IT center and why they received outsourcing best practices award from the industry. In achieving the goal of the chapter, interview data was collected from the management team in Chicago and the head of the offshore operation. We compare our result to previous research on offshore best practices and we find many correlations.

INTRODUCTION

A captive center is a wholly owned subsidiary of the parent company in a near-shore or offshore location, with the goal to provide support for to the parent company. Many Fortune 1000 companies in the US and Europe have offshore IT work abroad either to a third party or to their captive offshore center. Companies engage in offshore outsourcing to achieve cost saving and leverage distance talents. Offshore IT centers are setup to support the parent IT operations especially the back office activities. Most offshore centers are located in low cost, high quality, talent rich developing countries like India, Philippines and Brazil. Figure 1 shows some of the countries that US and European companies have established offshore centers. In the recent years there has been an increase in captive offshore centers.

Captive offshore have evolved from the traditional approach of offshoring to a third party. Offshore outsourcing to a third party is used primarily to achieve cost saving while captive outsourcing is used to

DOI: 10.4018/978-1-4666-8524-6.ch005

Figure 1. The 25 most attractive offshore location
Source: At Kearney 2004.

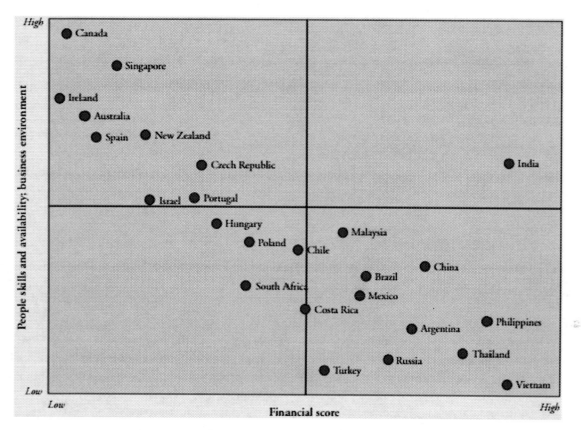

achieve a strategic move in addition to cost saving (Oshri, 2013, Lampel and Bhalla, 2008; and Farrell, 2005 and 2006). Captive offshore outsourcing has been prescribed as a tactical solution for alleviating distance in offshore outsourcing and software development (Carmel and Agarwal 2001).

While captive offshore centers have grown in recent years (Oshri, 2013) it is still a challenging proposition for many companies. Some of the reasons why captive offshore center can be more challenging than offshore to third party include the following (a) hiring employees in a new foreign locations, (b) setting up a physical facility including real estate rental, (c) building IT infrastructure (hardware, software and networks), (e) employee attritions due to lack of local knowledge (f) problems associated with integrating offshore center with the headquarters, and (g) senior executive lack of understanding or support / inadequate involvement (h) inability to obtain/attract additional client outsides the parent company – this is only for companies that setup the captive offshore to generate additional revenue from leveraging its capacity. (Adelakun, 2008, Lacity et al. 2010, Oshri and Uhm (2012).

This research was inspired by the work on offshore outsourcing (Carmel and Agarwal 2002; Rottman, and Lacity 2004; and Oshri 2013). Carmel and Agarwal (2002) looked at how US companies gradually progress through a maturation process to achieve success with their offshore outsourcing. One of the outcomes of the research was the four-stage offshore outsourcing model – offshore bystander, offshore experimenter, proactive cost focus, and proactive strategic focus. Carmel and Agarwal's offshore maturity model was has been used to explain successful relationships between offshore outsourcing client and providers for example Kaiser and Hawk (2004) used it as the bases for successful eight-year relationship between a U.S. financial insurance company and an India based supplier.

Rottman and Lacity (2004) interviewed 27 people in selected large US companies that use India-based vendors for offshore IT outsourcing to identify offshore best practices building on the work of Carmel and Agarwal to develop twenty best practices on how US companies can swiftly move through the various stages of offshore outsourcing maturity model by Carmel and Agarwal (2002).

While several people have studied offshore outsourcing there is not so much studies on captive offshore center development or maturity process (Oshri 2013). While captive offshore centers have some common characteristics with offshore to third party they also have a few unique characteristics. The most important is that they are wholly owned by the parent company. Many of them only provide services to the parent company unlike the traditional offshore to third parties. Captive offshore centers therefore go through a different maturation progress that is different from the maturation process describe by Carmel and Agarwal (2002). Oshri (2013) in his paper at the MISQ executive discuss the three maturity process of captive offshore centers – hybrid, shared or divested.

This research focused on the captive offshore outsourcing centers with the objective to find out the best practices that will enable a captive offshore center to be successful. To do this we study a Chicago based Retail Company that lunched a captive offshore IT center in India. The Chicago based company received international best practices recognition by the International Association of Outsourcing Professional (IAOP) in 2013 because of how they operate and manage their captive offshore center.

To achieve this research goal, interview data were collected from the management team in Chicago and the head of the offshore operation. We compare our data and results to the twenty best practices for offshore outsourcing by Rottman and Lacity (2004). Several of the best practices that applied to offshore outsourcing to third party also applies to captive offshore outsourcing. However, they go through a different maturity model (Carmel and Agarwal 2002; Rottman, and Lacity 2004; and Oshri 2013). The rest of the paper discusses the literature on traditional offshore and captive outsourcing. This is followed by how the research method and the case company analysis.

LITERATURE REVIEW

Questions such as how can organizations swiftly move through the offshore learning curve; how can organizations reduce the risks associated with Outsourcing; how can U.S. organizations work efficiently with foreign partners; what are the tactical approaches to successfully manage offshore outsourcing; and what is the maturation process for offshore outsourcing. These questions have been addressed by several authors (Rottman, and Lacity 2004; Carmel and Agarwal 2001, 2002; Kaiser and Hawk 2004 and Oshri 2013) to name a few. Some of the best practices listed in the literature include creating a central program management office, carefully select a location and hire a legal expert, and picking the appropriate offshore country depending on what is been offshored. Picking a location is not only a factor of cost but also a factor of availability of highly available talents, available infrastructure at reasonable price, government and political stability, business friendly culture and respect of intellectual property (AT Kearney 2004, Adelakun 2008, Joshi and Mudigonda, 2008; Kotlarsky and Oshri, 2008). Figure 1, shows AT Kearney's 25 top offshore locations in 2004. There are very little changes among this site since then.

In general offshore IT outsourcing to third party have significant differences from offshore IT outsourcing to a captive offshore center. First, companies that establish captive offshore centers may have significant higher setup cost than companies that use a third party and therefore not meeting their financial goal in the short run (Apte et al., 2007). Second, captive centers have to quickly figure out how to build local capacity to reduce social-cultural gad and three, they tend to have longer learning curve without strong local connection the quest for high-quality local talent could be an uphill battle. A captive canter is a business unit that is owned and provides services to the parent firm from an offshore location (Oshri, and van Uhm 2012).

Despite the challenges with captive offshore center many Fortune 1000 US companies have setup a captive offshore center with an economic value of over $12.3 billion and employing over 440,000 professionals (Oshri, and van Uhm 2012). Traditional offshore outsourcing and captive outsourcing regardless to their challenges was attractive to US companies because of the opportunity for significant cost saving, high quality talents at relatively low-cost compare to parent company location, availability of decent infrastructure, stable government and political system, respect of law and intellectual property, and other incentives such as tax reduction for a period of time (Jennex and Adelakun 2003; Joshi and Mudigonda, 2008).

The literature on outsourcing has also addressed the what, how, when and where questions. What seems to be missing is a deeper understanding on captive offshore centers and how they evolve with time. Captive offshore have changed from just providing services to parent company to include such as (a) a profit center that not only provide service to the parent company but that also provide similar services to other companies in addition to the parent company; (b) a captive center that is used to service local companies at the host country in particularly multinational companies operating at the host county and that outsource none core activities to local companies; (c) lastly, a captive center that is used to lunch strategic innovative new business offerings (Oshri 2013; Oshri, Kotlarsky and Liew 2008). Figure 2, shows how the captive offshore has evolved over time.

Figure 2. The Evolution of Captive Offshore Center
Source Oshri (2013)

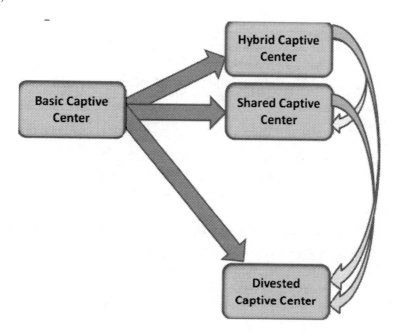

Hybrid captive center is a mix between the traditional outsourcing and captive offshoring. The shared captive center provides services to both parent and external clients. Shared captive center is often used to pursue a growth strategy to a new region or at the parent company's location. Shared captive are often used as profit center. In the divesting captive center, the center is acquired by another firm because buyer believes that the acquired center value will go up especially if they have specialized business knowledge. The buyer could also use the center to explore other lines of business that could be integrated and added to the center capabilities and portfolio of capabilities (Oshri 2013).

RESEARCH METHOD

Empirical data was collected using a semi-structured interview data collection technique from a single case company. The case study was conducted at a Chicago based retail company (Sears Holdings) who has successfully opened a captive offshore IT center in India. Three senior management team members in Chicago were interviewed. The head of the India operation was also interviewed during his visit to Chicago.

The interview data collection technique works well in this case as it allow interviewees to explain the set of activities and best practices but in place to achieve a successful outcome. The case company was considered a best practices by the International Association of Outsourcing Professional (IAOP) of which the author is a member. Therefore, author chooses to study what the Chicago Company did correctly to earn the "Outsourcing Best Practices" award from the industry. The case study is discussed in the next section.

CASE STUDY: SEARS HOLDINGS

Sears Holdings Corporation

Sears Holdings Corporation is a U.S. based company headquartered in the Chicago suburb of Hoffman Estates, IL. With over 2600 retail stores in the U.S. and Canada, Sears is one of the major brands and leading retail stores in the U.S. Sears Holdings brands include Kenmore, Craftsman and DieHard, with a broad apparel offering, including well-known labels such as Lands' End, Jaclyn Smith, Joe Boxer, Sofia by Sofia Vergara, and The Country Living Home Collection. Sears Holdings is also known as a leader in the area of tools, lawn and garden, fitness equipment and automotive repair and maintenance. Sears has been recognized for numerous achievements including 2011 Mobile Retailer of the Year. Sears Holdings Corporation operates through its subsidiaries, including Sears, Roebuck and Co., and Kmart Corporation.

Sears, once a giant and dominant industry leader, has suffered significant business losses in the 1990s. To overcome the financial struggles of the past, Sears has put in place several strategies to move the organization back to a more stable position financially within the retail industry. The retail industry in the U.S. has changed significantly since the mid 2000s. Unfortunately, Sears was not able to change at the rigorous speed of other companies in the industry. This led Sears's executives to turn to the information technology division of Sears Holdings to come up with innovative ways to move Sears to the next level.

Captive Offshore IT Outsourcing

Sears IT Organization (I&TG) and Its Outsourcing Challenge

The Information & Technology (I&TG) group of Sears Holdings Corporation provides software development, support, and maintenance services to Sears' business units. They are the leaders in the technology-based reinvention of Sears. The CIO is responsible and accountable for all IT to Sears's business units either through internal I&TG or to external vendors. Traditionally Sears would collect business requirements from the business units and then plan, design, and deliver the technology solution to the business. Due to cost pressures, Sears outsourced much of the technology design and development to third party technology outsourcing vendors. Sears has hundreds of these third party vendors, some of which are independent contractors. Over time, the independent contractors grew so large to the point that it began to deteriorate in-house technology capabilities and resulted in the loss of intellectual property. In addition to loss of intellectual property, development cost also increased significantly over time because the independent contractors charged a much higher rate than internal resources. Even though Sears is not paying benefits to the contractors it was still not cost efficient over all.

To address this situation in 2010 Sears launched a captive offshore IT center in India called Sears Holdings India (SHI). Sears established SHI as a collaborative partner and focal point for all offshore technology design and development. The launching of SHI is part of the reinvention process at Sears. Using information technology as a driver, SHI has been one of the key elements of the long-term strategy to help Sears regain its top spot by transforming its various businesses. Since its inception, SHI has been delivering high quality software development and support services which bring new innovate ideas to Sears Holdings. This has enabled Sears Holdings to create and launch new business ventures like MetaScale Consulting Services.

The launching of SHI led to additional productivity and value being delivered by the outsourcing vendors as they collaborated and, in some cases, competed with SHI to win contracts. To accelerate SHI's maturity and ability to collaborate and compete with external vendors, Sears embedded best technology and process practices with SHI from inception.

1. Sears Holdings India (SHI)

Strategically located in Pune, India, SHI is a stand-alone subsidiary of Sears Holdings and is headed by a seasoned managing director, Mr. Alok Kumar. Alok works with his Sears US counterpart, Justin Sheppard, to make sure Sears's business is being well handled. Mr. Kumar reports directly to the CIO of Sears Holdings Corporation who is ultimately responsible for all technology initiatives at Sears, including the launching of SHI.

Developing an internal captive IT center in Sears was a challenge for many reasons. First, it is a new and different approach to IT services at Sears. Sears IT managers have been using contractors for many years, and it is a major change in management balance to switch from contractors to offshore IT personnel. This was not only a challenge for management, but also for the IT teams in the US branch. Some employees were hesitant to embrace offshore development because they thought SHI employees were replacing their jobs, but in reality that was not the case. Second, the executive management of Sears Holdings was somewhat unenthusiastic about this change primarily because of the upfront cost of setting up an offshore location. This put a lot of pressure on Justin and Alok, who are responsible for building the offshore location. Luckily, they had the full support of the CIO and the CTO. Third, the executive team at Sears Holdings Corporation demanded to see tangible measurable results in the first year of launching SHI. SHI needed to meet their targeted EBITDA (Earnings before Interest, Taxes, Depreciation and Amortization) every year within the first three years of its launch. To make things more challenging for SHI, the executive team has imposed a travel restriction on Sears Corporation at all levels to reduce cost in 2010 and 2011, the very period SHI was been implemented in India. Fourth, in transitioning to SHI, they also saw some passive aggressive resistance from their former vendors who were trying to keep their business with Sears. Lastly, they have to figure out how to attract top talent in Pune that will stay with them considering the high level of competition and attrition in India.

The management team of SHI understood that they needed to overcome all the above challenges and still meet the target goals set for SHI by the executive team. By the end of 2010 Justin and his team successfully met the EBITDA requirement for that year and thereafter; the numbers of independent IT consultants in Sears were reduced by a significant amount; and the number of services provided by SHI Pune was higher than previously predicted. However they still have to deal with some internal resistance to the change. Below are some of the best practices put in place by Sears I&TG group that helped SHI overcome the mentioned challenges and made them a success and an exemplar company.

Best Practices Put in Place: What Makes It Work

I. Governance Model and Leadership Commitment

From the very beginning the CIO of Sears Corporation was fully behind building Sears Holdings India (SHI). At Sears Corporation's executive level the CIO is held accountable and responsible for the success and failure of SHI. To ensure the success and visibility of SHI's progress at the executive level the following three management and governance structures were put in place: Sears Management Team, SHI Board, and SHI Management Team. These three senior leadership teams at Sears were committed to the success of SHI. They ensured that SHI received the required support and guidance needed to be successful.

Sears Management Team

The Sears Management Team comprised of the General Manager of SHI (Mr. Alok Kumar), the Program Manager of SHI (Mr. Justin Sheppard), and some other key members within the I&TG and Sears business units. This group is responsible for building the SHI from the ground up, operating it, ensuring smooth transitioning of IT services from I&TG to SHI, as well as reporting progress to the SHI Board. The group also needs to ensure that all the resources needed to make SHI a success are acquired both in India and in the US. In addition the group is also responsible for change management within Sears Holdings Corporation, as well as ensuring that personnel in India understands the American business processes and culture and vice-versa.

SHI Board

The SHI Board was comprised of the SHI Managing Director (statutory requirement), Sears Chief Financial Officer (CFO) and Sears Legal counsel; the head of the program office also reports to this group.

Captive Offshore IT Outsourcing

The inclusion of the CFO played a critical role in SHI's success. The CFO ensured that the financial benefits of SHI were achieved and clearly understood by the leadership of Sears Holdings. The CFO became the advocate of SHI in key forums within Sears.

SHI Management Team

The SHI Managing Director heads the SHI management team. He is fully responsible for all local activities and operations in India. One of the responsibilities of this team is to source premium local talent and keep them in SHI. They also have to ensure that the level of attrition is very low. They identify who and how often personnel needs to travel to the US for training and cultural assimilation. The team also assists personnel on the US side to better understand their India counterpart.

II. Metric: Measuring the Right Thing and Measuring It Right

Sears senior leadership has clearly defined objectives and goals for each year from the very beginning. The Sears team, in consultation with SHI, understands these goals and the criteria SHI will be evaluated against. One key measurable goal was the EBITDA for that year. The other four key dimensions against which the SHI performance was measured were: Customer satisfaction, learning & development (Intellectual Property Protection), cost effectiveness (reduction of contractors), and internal business process/quality. The clear objectives and metrics gave clarity to the SHI team on what to focus on and deliver.

The financial objective was relatively easy to measure, however other measurable goals were more challenging. The Sears management team put in additional effort to ensure that each objective was measured and they have data to back it up. For example, they were able to demonstrate how many third party vendors were retired. The number of vendors and contractors that were retired from Sears's long list of vendors were identified, including the date and time they turn in their badge (signifying they were retired). It was important for SHI to ensure customer satisfaction not only for the final customer but also the satisfaction of the internal IT management which was also seen as a customer. Data was collected from business units about their experience with SHI and how satisfied they were. Internally, there were cross functional reviews after every project transition to see how SHI could improve for their next project. SHI from the beginning has embarked on obtaining CMM certification to ensure process quality.

III. Standardization of Processes with Cultural Sensitivity

Under the guidance of the Sears team, SHI internal business processes were implemented with required tailoring for local statutory and cultural requirements: a. HR policies at Sears were extended with India specific modifications b. Policy of the Internet and asset usage was extended without any change to SHI c. Code of Conduct policy was extended with modifications to include India specific changes d. Training and appraisal policies were tailor made for SHI e. Hiring and induction plans were tailor made for SHI. Without these tailored processes it will be very difficult to operate SHI while meeting all the target goals set by the board. Prior to joining Sears, Justin lived in India for two years so he has good understanding of the Indian culture. This made him able to assist US personnel to make the necessary adjustments culturally in order for the program to be successful. For example, communication of achievability in terms of assignments is often a cultural miscommunication between India and US personnel.

IV. PMO (Program Management Office)

The program office is made up of nine personnel, some hired internally as well as some brought in from elsewhere, headed by Justin Sheppard. The primary goal of the PMO is to ensure that SHI was successfully implemented and operational. The program office is also responsible for making sure that SHI gets to the mature stage relatively quickly, while achieving the set goals. In addition they serve as the liaison between Sears US and SHI especially on sensitive political and cultural issues. SHI success was made possible largely due to the honest, open, and transparent communication, facilitated by the PMO, between VPs, directors, and executives. The PMO is also responsible for leading change management initiatives in addition to working with business unit managers and I&TG managers.

V. Internal Change Management

The PMO understands the importance of change management in the successful implementation of the SHI program. Sears management initiated an internal change management process to help employees and stakeholders understand the objectives and guiding principles for the SHI initiative and allay fears of job security and changing roles and responsibilities. Employees were informed that SHI enables Sears to tap into the global talent pool at lower costs, which in turn allows them to serve the Sears business units more effectively. The savings generated would ultimately be invested back in developing new technology platforms and solutions, which would generate new and exciting job opportunities. If the SHI initiative was not successful, Sears would have no option but to depend more and more on 3rd party vendors; a practice everyone knows is more costly. This transparent communication led to enhanced collaboration between Sears US IT group and SHI employees. Teams that excelled in the new collaboration were used as an example for those that struggled with this new way of business. For business units and managers sitting on the fence, the management team brought in the executives on the board to communicate the need for change to them. That helped to move the change process along in the right direction.

VI. Relationship Management (Partnership)

Sears and SHI modeled their relationship as a partnership. Making SHI successful was the responsibility of both Sears and the SHI management teams. They used a "2-in-a-box" peer relationship to keep both sides accountable for each other and allow for maximum communication. The message to the Sears teams was to provide SHI with support and guidance as they would provide any new colleague. At the same time SHI's performance was compared with the performance of 3rd party vendors on cost effectiveness and quality parameters. SHI had to prove its value by competing with external vendors.

VII. Organization and Communication Structure

An important part of Sears's communication model is regular reviews and feedback to both parties. The Sears management team developed a lateral communication structure between the US side and India side. While communication on each side could be vertical, they discourage vertical communications between US side and the India side. This model fosters good relationship and understanding among

Figure 3. Box Communication and Coordination Model

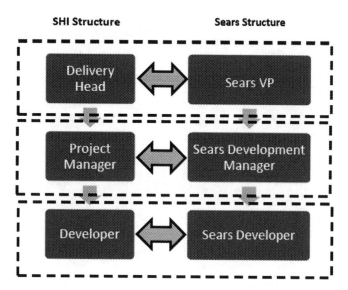

peers. Figure 3 illustrates the organization and communication structure between the two sides. The PMO named this model "2-in-a-Box".

This model contributed significantly to quick success of SHI in reaching an operational maturity level quickly. Despite the travel restrictions, which limit the amount of face-to-face interaction between the India side and the US side, they were able to have relatively reliable communication, including exchange of documents and ideas. Issues that were escalated up to the next management level were also discussed and resolved at that level. Decisions were then passed down and implemented on each side.

VIII. Tools and Method

The Sears team ensured that standard development practices and appropriate tools were inculcated at SHI from its inception. While the work transition to SHI was happening, Sears helped SHI to adopt best development practices – open source adoption, architecture standards, tool standards, knowledge management, scorecards and a continuous improvement philosophy. To train some of the new SHI employees, the shadow and reverse shadow approaches were used. So 3-4 people from India were brought to the U.S or other vendor sites to observe work being done by the position they would be working for at SHI. Then the roles were reversed allowing the vendor to coach the SHI employee. Justin also noted they didn't really have complicated tools for documentation and communication, but they made sure standard communicating and documentation tools were available for virtual global work. A team room for video conferencing was established on both ends allowing for a more personal meeting. It was also vital, especially during the initial stages, to showcase success from SHI. This was achieved through a newsletter approach to let everyone know the accomplishments made by SHI and reassuring trust in SHI. Process standardization was highly emphasized in India. SHI was able to win more contracts over because they demonstrated superior ability to follow standard development processes.

Figure 4. Focus area for successful transition

Skill Level	Team Mix	Development Methodology	Entry/Exit Strategy
• Technology skill • Domain Expertise	• No. of SHI resources • No. of contractor resources • No. of Sears resources • Vendor selection	• Agile	• Onsite/Offsite strategy • Knowledge Transfer

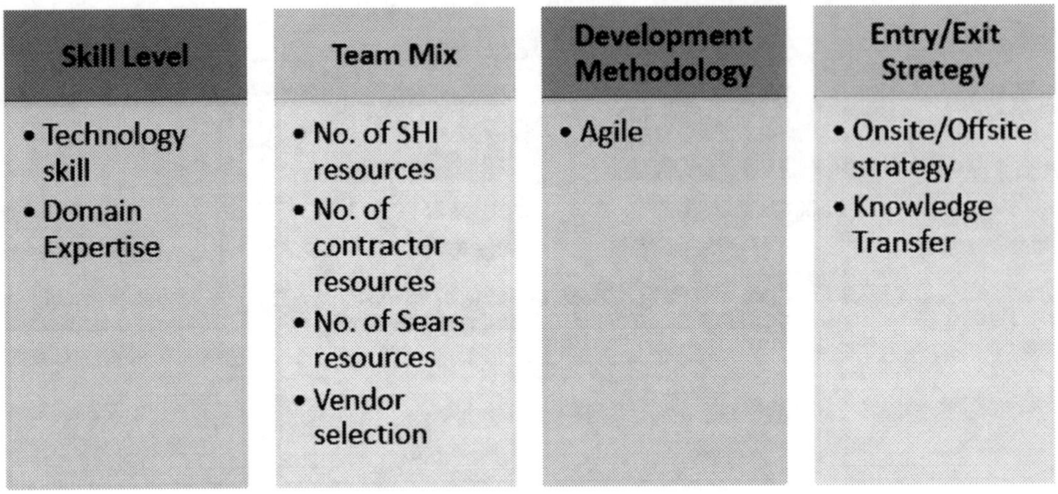

IX. Transition and Operation

The combined team (SHI and Sears) faced a number of challenges with respect to transitioning and operation. One, Sears has no brand recognition in India so hiring quality human resources in time was a key challenge. Two, the executive board demands quick transitioning and operation with results within the first year. Lastly, as the SHI organization grew, managing associate expectations about career progression, compensation and benefits was a key challenge. Below is a brief description of how the combined team (Sears US and India) addressed these challenges.

Transition and Operation Process

The Sears management team identified four major areas for executing successful offshore transitions (Skill level, Team Mix, Development method, and Entry/Exit Strategy). Figure 4, illustrates the four focus areas for successful transition.

The combined Sears and SHI teams collaborated to define and follow the transition process. Before transitioning any program portfolio, analysis was performed. Portfolio Analysis can be defined as the structured process to understand the clients' portfolio of products & solutions and associated complexity. The transition team identified key applications for transitioning and defined order for migrating projects to offshore on the basis of the discussion with the business team. The transition team created exhaustive checklists to support transitions. The applications, which could be easily transitioned, were defined first for quick wins. This helped in building initial confidence and trust between Sears and SHI teams. The detailed & process oriented approach ensured that most transitions were successful.

To address the human resources challenge, the HR team institutionalized key career development processes including a career path framework to provide a choice of career paths to associates. As part of this framework, SHI associates will be assessed across functional and behavioral competencies. The competency measurement is completed by a 3rd party to avoid any internal biases. The results of an employee's assessment will be used to create an individualized career development plan. The Sears and SHI team believe that providing a clear development path to all India employees will build employee loyalty, trust, and productivity. In addition, the combined team paid serious attention to cultural issues. For example, employee family members were regularly involved in SHI social events a practice the US side is yet to fully grab.

Lesson Learned

Overall, Sears Holdings management was satisfied with the outcome of Sears Holdings India (SHI). Here are some of the major results of implementing SHI. One, SHI has met the their financial objectives, which generated multi-million dollar annual cost savings. What is more impressive is that break-even on SHI investment occurred in the first year of its operations.

Two, Sears Holdings business units successfully transitioned development and support of many of their current systems to SHI. Sears is able to send software development and maintenance work to SHI at rates which are substantially less than 3rd party outsourcing rates.

Finally, Sears Holdings now has a better global presence. The knowledge of developing a global presence is something that Sears is planning to leverage internally and externally. For instance, Sears Holdings and SHI are collaborating on a new technology services company, called MetaScale LLC, that will provide planning and operational execution services to companies that seek to launch their own captive center operations.

However, this success also comes with some key lessons. One, travel restrictions early in the program slowed the overall teams' speed and collaboration. Even with the rise of many virtual collaboration tools, relationships are best developed, at least initially, with in-person face-to-face interaction. The travel challenge added another level of difficulty to the program, a situation that could be avoided. Two, place experienced people in key positions. Justin's prior experiences living in India helped Sears Holdings avert many of the cultural challenges that could have derailed the program. Three, employ a local general manager instead of an expatriate in the foreign division. While expatriates have been successful in the past, it is obvious in this case that having an experienced local general manager helps to overcome many of the local operational issues at Sears Holdings India. Lastly, an open, honest, and regular line of communication, including '2-in-a-box' accountability, is essential on all levels in order to ensure the program's success on both sides.

CONCLUSION AND COMPARING SEAR BEST PRACTICES TO LACITY ET AL. BEST PRACTICES

The Twenty Best Practices for Offshore Outsourcing compare to Captive Offshore Outsourcing at the Chicago Based Company.

After researching the literature on captive offshore IT outsourcing and offshore best practices, it is apparent there are some gaps between Sears Holdings' best practices and the literature For example Sears Holdings did not have a legal team in place to handle their offshore outsourcing as in the case of offshore to a third party arrangements. Companies studied in other case studies formed a legal team that specializes in outsourcing work.

Another major gap between literature best practices and Sears was that Sears absence of aggressive pilot projects. While they had a couple of test projects at the start of their captive offshore IT site, these projects were not strategic in testing the capability of Sears India. The literature suggests that pilot

Table 1. Comparing Sear Best Practices

	Sourcing Challenge	Best Practices to Overcome the Challenge	Equally Important for Both Domestic and Offshore	More Important for Offshore	Unique to Offshore	Best Practices by Sears
How can we swiftly move through the learning curve?	1	Create a centralized program management office (PMO) to consolidate management	X			√
	2	Hire an intermediary consulting firm to serve as a broker and guide		X		
	3	Select locations, projects, suppliers, and managers to leverage in-house sourcing expertise	X			
How can we mitigate risks	4	Use pilot projects to mitigate business risks	X			
	5	Give customers a choice of sourcing location to mitigate business risks			X	
	6	Hire a legal expert to mitigate legal risks		X		
	7	Openly communicate the sourcing strategy to all stakeholders to mitigate political risks		X		√
	8	Use secure information links or redundant lines to mitigate infrastructure risks		X		√
	9	Use fixed-price contracts to mitigate workforce risks		X		
How can we effectively work with suppliers?	10	Elevate your own organization's CMM certification to close the process gap between you and your supplier			X	
	11	Negotiate the CMM processes you will and will not pay for to avoid wasting money			X	
	12	Cross-examine or replace the supplier's employees to overcome cultural communication barriers		X		√
	13	Let the project team members meet face-to-face to foster camaraderie		X		√
	14	Consider innovative techniques, such as real time dashboards, to improve workflow verification, synchronization, and management		X		√
	15	Manage bottlenecks to relieve the substantial time zone differences			X	√
How can we ensure cost saving while protecting quality?	16	Consider both transaction and production costs to calculate overall savings realistically		X		√
	17	Size projects large enough to receive total cost savings		X		√
	18	Establish the ideal in-house/onsite/offshore ratio only after the relationship has stabilized			X	√
	19	Develop meaningful career paths for subject matter experts, project managers, governance experts, and technical experts to help ensure quality	X			√
	20	Create balanced scorecard metrics	X			√

projects should be projects with a variety of size, risk levels, and complexity to test the capability of the offshore site.

While there were gaps between best practices in literature and the Sears case study, there were also a number of similarities. One great similarity was the technique used for training employees new to the company. In both cases some form of overlap was used. The method of shadowing/ coaching to train employees in transitioning projects was used. Another similarity was the use of a Program Management Office (PMO) for the offshore IT work. The PMO oversaw the progress of the offshore site. Another major similarity was the presence of a system of measurement for success. Some companies had a statistical measurement of business success, and other companies in literature had other means of measurement. Sears used their EBIDTA and their customer feedback as a key measurement index. Both the literature and case study also emphasis the need for cultural assimilation.

REFERENCES

Adelakun, O. (2008). The Maturation of Offshore IT Outsourcing Location Readiness and Attractiveness. *Proceedings of the European and Mediterranean Conference on Information Systems. Dubai.*

Apte, S., Mccarthy, J., Ross, C., Bartolomey, F., & Thresher, A. (2007). Shattering the Offshore Captive Center Myth. Retrieved from http://www.forrester.com/Research/Document/Excerpt/0,7211,42059,00.html

Carmel, E., & Agarwal, R. (2001). Tactical approaches for alleviating distance in global software development. *Software, IEEE, 18*(2), 22–29. doi:10.1109/52.914734

Carmel, E., & Agarwal, R. (2002). The Maturation of Offshore Sourcing of Information Technology Work. *MIS Quarterly Executive, 1*(2), 65–77.

Farrell, D. (2005). Offshoring: Value creation through economic change. *Journal of Management Studies, 42*(3), 675–682. doi:10.1111/j.1467-6486.2005.00513.x

Farrell, D. (2006). Smarter Offshoring. *Harvard Business Review, 84*(6), 84–92. PMID:16770896

Jennex, M.E.and Adelakun, O. (2003) Success Factors For Offshore Information Systems development, in Journal of Information Technology Cases and Applications, 5(3), 12-31.

Kaiser, K., & Hawk, S. (2004). Evolution of Offshore Software Development: From Outsourcing to Cosourcing. *MIS Quarterly Executive, 3*(2), 69–81.

Kearney, A. T. (2004). Making Offshore Decisions: A.T. Kearney's 2004 offshore location Attractiveness index. Retrieved from http://kdi.mscmalaysia.my/static/reports/AT%20Kearney%202004%20Report.pdf

Kotlarsky, J., & Oshri, I. (2008). Country attractiveness for offshoring and offshore-outsourcing. *Journal of Information Technology, 23*(4), 228–231. doi:10.1057/jit.2008.17

Lacity, M. C., Khan, S., Yan, A., & Willcocks, L. P. (2010). A Review of the IT Outsourcing Empirical Literature and Future Research Directions. *Journal of Information Technology, 25*(4), 395–433. doi:10.1057/jit.2010.21

Lampel, J., & Bhalla, A. (2008). Embracing Realism and Recognizing Choice in IT Offshoring Initiatives. *Business Horizons*, *51*(5), 429–440. doi:10.1016/j.bushor.2008.03.007

Levina, N. (2006). In or Out in an Offshore Context: The Choice Between Captive Centers and Third-Party Vendors, Cutter IT Journal Oshri, I., Kotlarsky, J. and Willcocks, L. P. The Handbook of Global Outsourcing and Offshoring, Macmillan, 2011.

Oshri, I. (2013). Choosing an Evolutionary Path for Offshore Captive Centers. *MIS Quarterly Executive*, *12*(3), 151–165.

Oshri, I., Kotlarsky, J., & Liew, C. M. (2008). Four Strategies for 'Offshore' Captive Centers, Wall Street Journal.

Oshri, I. and van Uhm, B (2012). A historical review of the information technology and business process captive centre sector. *Journal of Information Technology, 27*(4), 270-284.

Rottman, J., & Lacity, M. C. (2006). Proven Practices for Effectively Offshoring IT Work. *Sloan Management Review*, *47*(3), 56–63.

Rottman, J. W., & Lacity, M. C. (2010). Twenty Practices for Offshore Sourcing. *MIS Quarterly Executive*, *3*(3), 35–46.

KEY TERMS AND DEFINITIONS

Best Practices: These are approaches that have been tried and tested in the industry.

Captive Offshore: Is a separate business arm of the parent company in a large enterprise.

Case Study: The use of a specific organization in a research study, for the sole purpose of the objectives of the study.

IS Strategy: Is an organizational intent to achieving goals and objectives through information systems.

IT Outsourcing: Is an IT workload that is contracted by a company to another company for the same purposes, within a specific period of time.

Offshore: Is contracting of works by a company to another company which is situated in another country.

Organisational Structure: Outlines how business entity is divided into units, to achieving the same goals and objectives.

Chapter 6
The Role of Reference, Imminent and Current Models in Enterprise Conceptual Modelling:
A Case Study of a Namibian Freight Forwarder

Thomas Schmidt
Flensburg University of Applied Sciences, Germany

Stephan Hofmann
Flensburg University of Applied Sciences, Germany

ABSTRACT

Enterprise Resource Planning (ERP) systems constitute a prerequisite for successfully managing business in many industries, including the logistics industry. Since today's standard ERP systems determine a company's business down to the smallest detail, effectively aligning a company's strategy and business processes with software-given processes is imperative for maintaining a competitive advantage. This calls for defining an Enterprise Conceptual Model based on a sound derivation of imminent processes, either directed towards current, reference or ideal processes. The case study exemplifies that an Enterprise Conceptual Model has actually helped to translate strategic goals and operational needs into business processes and, thereby, align imminent and software-given processes. The application of current, reference and ideal process models for definition imminent processes is shown. Insight is drawn from a one-case case study of a medium-sized Namibian freight forwarder and logistics service provider.

DOI: 10.4018/978-1-4666-8524-6.ch006

INTRODUCTION

Key Focus

Today, Enterprise Resource Planning (ERP) systems play a major role in managing and operating businesses in many industries. Correctly implemented and well-maintained ERP systems allow organizations to tap into, share and integrate their data and information resources and to automate business activities. By doing so, organizations can increase operational and management performance and capacity as well as drive operational and management costs down. In turn, this can lead to higher value creation for the customer and higher capacity for customer orders. The organization should end up with increased revenues, decreased costs and preferably with higher profits. This simplified derivation of benefits may give the impression the only thing organizations need to do is select the right ERP system, implement it correctly and keep it running and well maintained. This is undoubtedly correct, but at the same time anything but easy as the most important step is the balancing between the company requirements and the functions of the software (Leon, 2012).

From a business perspective, a crucial point to bear in mind is that an ERP project is a far-reaching business reorganization project. It goes from strategic considerations prior to the ERP selection, through to strategic and operational considerations during the selection and implementation and ends after transition into smooth operation (Markus & Tanis, 2000). Consequently, translating the organization's strategy into business processes and aligning business process with the ERP system's processes is key to project success.

Objectives

This paper deals with the alignment of an organization's strategy and business processes with an ERP system's processes or "software-given" processes. It investigates existing approaches and addresses the research question whether and how current, reference and ideal process models in the framework of an Enterprise Conceptual Model can improve the translation of strategic and operational goals into imminent processes. Insight is drawn from a one-case study of an ERP selection and implementation project at a Namibian freight forwarder and logistics service provider.

Research Methodology

The research is based on a one-case case study method. The underlying unit of analysis (case) of this one-case case study is a Namibian freight forwarder and logistics service provider. The analysis of this single case, in contrast to a cross-case study, allowed for an in-depth and holistic study of the prevailing mechanisms of the strategy, business process and ERP system alignment in such a project, which could otherwise hardly be achieved within a cross-case study.

The information obtained was collected, first, via qualitative interviews with a sample size of twelve managers and, second, via personal observation. In order to avoid biases the information was crosschecked and quality-assured by experienced staff of the company. The information collection phase spanned from January to October 2012.

Contribution

First, this paper will look at the link between strategy, business processes and ERP systems and set out business process modelling approaches to achieve alignment between strategy, business processes and an ERP system's processes.

Second, it will turn to the case of the Namibian freight forwarder and logistics service provider and explain how this company made use of the Enterprise Conceptual Model to achieve strategy, business process and ERP system alignment.

Terminology

The terms "current", "imminent", "reference" "software-given" process as well as "Enterprise Conceptual Model" play a key role throughout this article and therefore need to be explained:

Definition 1: Current process – Based on the fundamental definitions of a process as provided by Hammer and Champy (2006) and Davenport and Short (1990), a current process is the process the company currently has implemented and in practice.

Definition 2: Imminent process – Based on the aforementioned definitions of a process, an imminent process is a planned process, which is based on the software-given process, adapted to the company's requirements and will be implemented and practiced.

Definition 3: Reference process – Based on definitions of reference processes provided by Schwegmann and Laske (2011), here reference process models are software-specific models that describe the process structure of a particular ERP system. The software vendor or business partner provides reference process models.

Definition 4: Software-given process – Based on the aforementioned definitions of a process, a software-given process is a certain pre-defined process inherent in an ERP.

Definition 5: Enterprise Conceptual Model: An Enterprise Conceptual Model constitutes the entirety of business processes models and business data models of an enterprise.

BACKGROUND

The Route to Strategy, Business Process, and ERP System Alignment

Strategic Management determines a strategy of actions and required resources to compete successfully in the market. A prescriptive as well as an emergent strategy requires organisations to set objectives, choose options, determine actions to achieve objectives and finally to put their actions into practice. (Lynch, 2011). In addition to a shift from a prescriptive to an emergent or a combined approach, what has changed fundamentally is the way organizations approach Enterprise Conceptual Models via business process management to make use of ERP systems.

In the past, i.e. when custom-built software still coined the term ERP system, based on a strategy and chosen strategic options, they either developed a system from scratch or chose a system and adapted it to perfectly fit their business processes.

Nowadays, even though there are still many companies that fit the system to their business processes, many do it the other way round and fit their business processes to the software. This is probably due to the fact that today's standardized ERP systems allow even small- and medium-sized companies to make use of an ERP system at reasonable expense. On the one hand this is quite a positive development because more companies can reap the benefits of an integrated information system and eventually improve their business processes rapidly to a more sophisticated business process level. On the other hand this gives rise to new risks if applied business processes turn out to be inappropriate or even impeding to distinctive business processes. This is due to the fact that standardized ERP systems are, at least partly, generic solutions, which represent the industry's best practices of a software vendor, and not the company's view of doing business best. Therefore, when a company decides on a standardized ERP system, it accepts it must impose the intended way of doing business of a vendor upon itself. Although some customization settings might usually be provided, limitations are set and the intended path cannot be left without the vendor's agreement and support (Davenport, 1998; Seddon, Shanks, & Willcocks, 2003; Gronau, 2013).

However, this doesn't mean that standardized ERP systems cannot be the best choice. It rather emphasizes the importance of aligning strategy and business processes with an ERP system's processes once more.

From Strategy to Business Processes

A strategy is commonly defined on a corporate level and passed down the organizational hierarchy to the business-unit level, functional level and operational / business process level, as shown in Figure 1.

Figure 1. Strategy, Business Process, and ERP System Alignment
(Adapted from Shiang-Yen, Idrus, & Yusof, 2011)

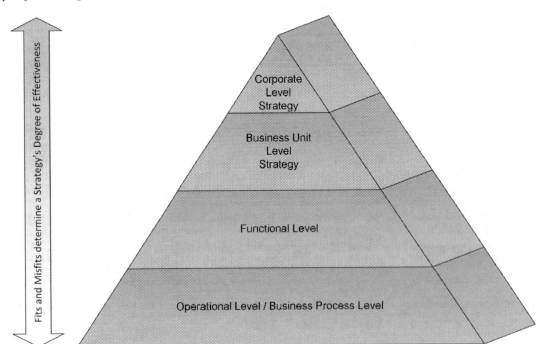

Whether selected strategies turn out to be appropriate and are put into practice well, depends on the suitability, after checking for other strategic actions, of an ERP system to the level strategies. This is because an ERP system covers many business areas and processes and thus, determines a business at the business process level (Hansmann & Neumann, 2011).

The suitability of an ERP system to the level strategies is largely determined in the selection and implementation phase where the imminent process design is established (Shiang-Yen, Idrus, & Yusof, 2011). The most sophisticated higher-level strategies are doomed to fail if a company misses passing these strategies down to the business process level and successfully translating and implementing them as business processes. This fear is not without merit as the level of detail increases dramatically on its way down to the business process level. At the business process level, this is where fits and misfits between higher level strategies and business processes become visible (Leyking, 2010).

Business Process Models

In order to design, implement, execute and control business processes, they are modelled graphically or textually in the Enterprise Conceptual Model. While textual illustration is well suited to listing activities, graphical illustration goes beyond this by representing the logical ordering between activities. Graphical illustration is usually easier to comprehend when processes are very complex, i.e. plenty of linked and hierarchical processes, and is well suited to serve as a discussion paper throughout the entire business process management life cycle (Monk & Wagner, 2012).

In an ERP project, there are several reasons to establish an Enterprise Conceptual Model via process modelling, e.g. defining ERP system selection criteria, defining and realizing design and configuration requirements or user training (Hansmann & Neumann, 2011).

For defining and realizing design and configuration requirements, i.e. aligning business processes with an ERP system, and designing imminent processes Hansmann and Neumann (2011) provide three approaches, as shown in Figure 2. These three approaches differ in the origin process.

The first alternative is to model imminent business processes solely based on reference processes. Modelling imminent processes based on reference process models allows quick modelling of imminent processes, because all adoptable processes of reference process models are supported by the ERP system. However, it does not take current processes into account. If software vendors do not provide reference process models or companies, for any reason, decide not to use offered reference process models, companies can create reference process models for themselves by modelling software-given processes and use them instead.

The second alternative is to model imminent processes regardless of reference process models or current processes. This approach emphasizes company specific process requirements and is not software-specific. Therefore, it is well suited to the software selection phase or design phase to compare the ideal process with provided reference process models or derive imminent processes. When comparing process models, it is important that both stick to some common modelling conventions, as provided by Rosemann, Schwegmann, and Delfmann (2011) and Monk and Wagner (2009).

The third alternative is to model imminent processes based on current and reference processes. Imminent processes are designed based on opportunities and requirements of current and reference process models. The more this approach is biased towards reference process models, the more it comes closer to the first alternative (Hansmann & Neumann, 2011).

Figure 2. Approaches to Process Modelling
(Adapted from Hansmann, & Neumann, 2011)

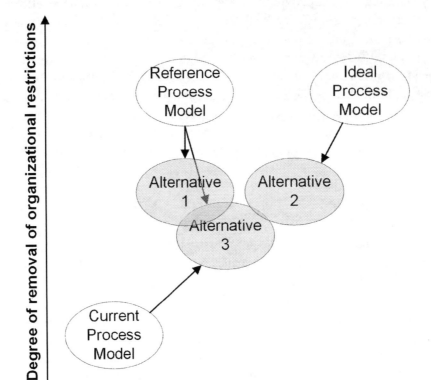

A case study of a Namibian freight forwarder shall depict these approaches to process modelling and will show the usage and advantages of using reference process models for the implementation of an ERP system.

THE USE OF AN ENTERPRISE CONCEPTUAL MODEL IN AN ENTERPRISE RESOURCE PLANNING PROJECT

The Case of the Namibian Freight Forwarder

During the last year Namibian cargo import and export has grown significantly and the logistics industry has changed rapidly. New logistics service providers have entered the Namibian market. Competition among logistics service providers has become fierce. Existing logistics service providers are in the process of streamlining and improving their operations to drive costs down and to provide enhanced services to their customers. Some do so and turn their organizations inside out by implementing an ERP system (Namibian Economist, 2012).

The Role of Reference, Imminent and Current Models in Enterprise Conceptual Modelling

One of these logistics service providers is the Namibian freight forwarder and logistics service provider, which will be dealt with in this article. The company has had several issues resulting from non-integrated, insufficient and error-prone software applications, inefficient and fragmented business processes and an inflexible and fragmented organizational structure. At the same time, the services offered, business volume and customer expectations experienced a growth. To overcome those issues and to cope with increased demands the company identified the need for an integrated information system as an enabler for improvement in software stack, business processes and organizational structure, hence the need for an ERP project.

The envisioned ERP system is going to be implemented at the company's headquarters in Windhoek as well as at its branches and affiliated companies in Namibia, Botswana, South Africa and Germany. It will cover most of the company's business areas and processes, namely air export, air import, sea export, sea import, projects export, projects import, road and courier services as well as warehousing. The process structure is shown in Figure 3.

Figure 3. Business Process Structure

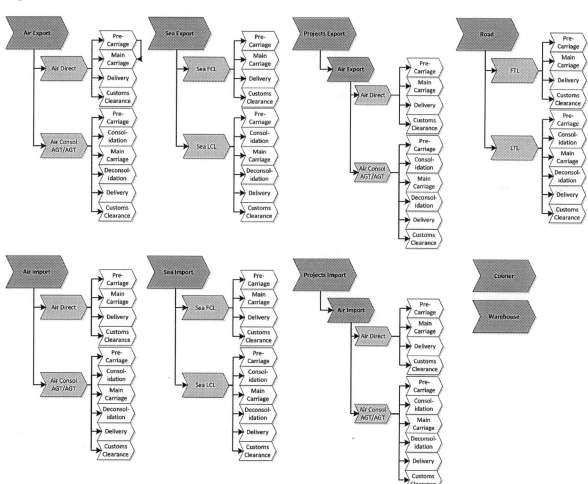

Research Design and Procedure

The company has decided to undertake software-given processes as far as possible and pursue the third alternative, model imminent processes based on current and reference processes. This implementation strategy has been chosen since the Namibian freight forwarder holds the view that freight forwarding processes are very similar company to company and branch to branch, due to national and international requirements. The selected ERP system provides many configuration options to differentiate software-given processes from competitors. Moreover, there are some processes, or activities, which are not part of the software-given processes and therefore provide room for differentiation. Further differentiation potential depends on how well the company masters the implementation and on-going maintenance.

The procedure has been divided into two steps: (1) Mapping Software-given Processes and (2) Analysis and Adaptation of Software-given Processes. Since the software vendor has not provided a reference process model, the company has decided to map generic software-given processes and use these models instead. Due to the fact that freight forwarding processes are very similar company to company and branch to branch, there is no need to create business process models for each and every company or branch. Generic software-given-process models will be used for all companies and branches. This will reduce the modelling effort enormously.

The sea Full Container Load (FCL) import process has been chosen as the sample process because the company operates in a typical import economy, recording higher imports than exports, especially from South Africa, the European Union, India, China and the United States of America and therefore, the sea FCL import process is a frequently conducted and highly important process for the company's freight forwarding business (WTO Publications, 2011).

Mapping Software-Given Processes

For the Enterprise Conceptual Model prior to the ERP system selection, the business process-modelling tool ARIS Express provided by Software AG has been used. Business processes have been mapped according to the Event-Driven-Process Chain (EPC) notation. Considering the availability of the free-of-charge process management software and the fact that the project team members, who are responsible for process modelling, have not changed since then, ARIS Express has fulfilled the company's expectations. Therefore, ARIS Express in conjunction with the EPC notation is used for the on-going process modelling as well. The key project team does the process mapping. Once the process mapping and analysing has reached a well thought-out status, secondary project team members will be involved.

Figure 4 displays an excerpt from the Enterprise Conceptual Model, the generic sea FCL import process model. It shows the creation of shipments and local transport jobs, the departure from first load port and the creation of a consolidation. The complete generic sea FCL import process is neither explained nor displayed in this paper. This is because the generic sea FCL import process is just an intermediate step. An excerpt of the imminent company-specific sea FCL import process is shown and explained later on.

The fact that only aggregated and selected process paths are considered in this mapping of generic software-given processes does not mean the ERP system does not provide more process paths or more details. It rather represents the relevance of process paths and details at that point of time. These generic business processes serve as a starting point for further analysis, communication and development and thus, represent the basis for imminent processes. Generic business processes will be converted into imminent processes in the next section "Analysis and Adaptation of Software-given Processes".

Figure 4. Excerpt from Generic Sea FCL Import Process

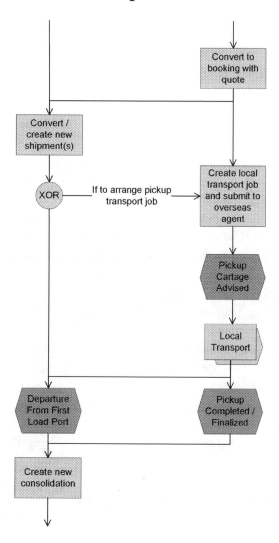

Analysis and Adaptation of Software-Given Processes

The company has selected the ERP system carefully and knows which processes and functions are not supported by the ERP system. However, during the process analysis phase it is necessary to go into much more detail to find out what the ERP system is actually capable of doing, what exactly is covered and what is not. In order to adapt its current processes to the software-given processes and determine necessary customizations or even modifications, the company's logistics specialists have analysed each software-given process in several loops with an increasing degree of detail. In particular, the following questions have been addressed:

- Does the software-given process already meet the process requirements?

- Are there any software-given process elements, which do not meet the process requirements? If so, what kind of alternatives does the ERP system provides?
- Are there any software-given process elements, which do not meet the process requirements, and the system does not provide any further alternatives, apart from omitting these process elements? If so, can the system be modified? If so, is the expected suitability and resulting value creation to the customer and company worth its external modification costs and internal effort to place an order for modification?

After getting familiar with the software-given processes, process owners and process supervisors have been called in to match the software-given processes and process requirements. Based on the Enterprise Conceptual Model the process mapping and analysing of software-given processes has shown that the ERP system comes not only with lots of process paths and several alternatives to perform a business process; moreover it provides various variables to customize processes to the company's needs. For instance, the sea FCL import process is very straight forward, but when it comes to particular processes, variables, such as organizations with different locations, different incoterms and their effects on other processes, consolidations with multiple shipments, auto-rating of pre-defined charges, interfaces to other processes and workflow templates, the system's integration and resulting interdependencies make analysing and testing procedures very complex. Here, business process models help to keep a clear perspective on the overall business process structure and on all individual business processes, which would otherwise be difficult to retain in complex structures.

Based on the previous analysing of software-given processes with process requirements, the generic software-given processes have been adapted. The results are imminent processes. Just like in the previous step "Mapping Software-given Processes", only an excerpt of the entire adapted Enterprise Conceptual Model, the adapted sea FCL import process model is displayed in Figure 5. Comparing the software-given process (left hand side) and the corresponding adapted software-given process (right hand side) reveals the same fundamental process structure as determined by the ERP system.

Deviating process paths and customizations have been taken into account where required and applicable. In addition to customizing the ERP system's functions, the system has been adapted to the company's practices. During this adaption the Enterprise Conceptual Model serves as discussion paper to identify, discuss and record necessary adaptations. In addition, the Enterprise Conceptual Model with its process models help to ensure that all project team members are speaking the same language and all "(...) are on the same page (...)" (Monk & Wagner, 2009).

The above-explained procedure has been conducted for the generic warehouse, contract warehouse, sea export, sea import, air export, air import, projects, courier, road export, road import, clearing desk and finance. This phase revealed that, besides main business processes, there are supporting processes, which have not been taken into account yet, but are essential for running other business processes. Consequently, Enterprise Conceptual Modelling goes beyond translating strategic and operational requirements into business processes. It serves at the same time as a reassessment of current business processes and can lead to previously unknown or neglected reference points for process improvements.

Lessons Learned

As a result, it can be stated that the approach to use an Enterprise Conceptual Model prior and during the implementation of the software has shown advantageous regarding the quality of the redesigned processes

Figure 5. Excerpt from Sea FCL Import Process

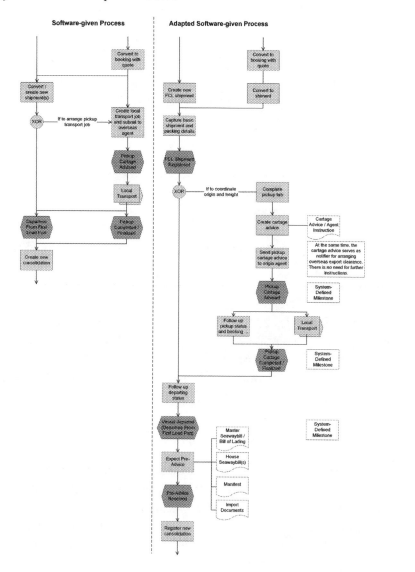

as well as the time to implement the software. Choosing the third alternative, i.e. to model imminent processes based on current and reference processes, is well suited to achieve the envisioned alignment between strategic goals, operational needs and software-given processes. "Turn-key" reference process models would have been much less time-consuming. Considering the lack of reference process models, however, the modelling of reference processes is a beneficial alternative to putting strategic goals and operational needs into practice.

Whilst the first alternative, i.e. modelling imminent processes solely based on reference processes, would work here as well, albeit leaving out current process requirements, the second alternative, i.e. modelling processes regardless of reference process models or current processes, would be of no value for the implementation phase.

SOLUTION AND RECOMMENDATION

Outline of the Results

The objective of this research was to investigate the application and value of an Enterprise Conceptual Model as an enabler for aligning an organization's strategy and business processes with an ERP system's software-given processes. The Namibian freight forwarder was able to put the theoretical framework of linking strategy, business process and an ERP system's processes into practice. The entirety of business process models has actually helped to translate strategic goals and operational needs into business processes and at the same time helped to ensure that imminent processes actually fit to the software-given processes. Most importantly, business process models served as a discussion basis for adapting the software-given process to current requirements and provided a clear perspective, even and especially for complex process structures. At the same time, modelling business processes have triggered a reassessment of current processes and provided reference points for process improvements.

Practical Implications

It can be concluded that an Enterprise Conceptual Model serves, at least, as translators and can therefore make an essential contribution to putting selected strategic goals and operational needs into practice. An Enterprise Conceptual Model should be used to align a company's strategy and business processes with an ERP system's processes. It is, however, mandatory to adapt the actual and concrete approach to company and software specifications.

Recommendations

A sound Enterprise Conceptual Model should support the implementation of ERP systems, and in general operational logistics systems. For standard ERP systems, imminent models should be modelled based on current and reference models. This facilitates the implementation of best practice processes whilst keeping company-processes that provide room for differentiation. Further potential for differentiation depends on how well the company masters the implementation and on-going maintenance of the ERP system.

Validity and Limitations

The research is based on a one-case case study method. The underlying unit of analysis (case) of this one-case case study is a Namibian freight forwarder and logistics service provider. The analysis of this single case, in contrast to a cross-case study, allowed for an in-depth and holistic study of the prevailing mechanisms of the strategy, business process and ERP system alignment in such a project, which could otherwise hardly be achieved within a cross-case study.

The information obtained was collected, first, via qualitative interviews and, second, via personal observation. In order to avoid biases the information was crosschecked and quality-assured by experienced staff of the company. The information collection phase spanned from January to October 2012.

Since this research project was based on a one-case case study, findings relate to the underlying company and circumstances. From this results that, first, the findings of this one-case case study research project should not be unconditionally generalized; however, they are transferable to similar cases as well. Cases with similar circumstances are likely to yield the same or at least similar results and are, thus, replicable. Second, the choice of the most appropriate approach for using business process models depends on the specific company and circumstances.

Taken together the choice for a one-case case study reflects the trade-off between, on the one hand, the quest for an in-depth and holistic study and, on the other hand, for representativeness.

CONCLUSION

The theory on strategy, business process and ERP system alignment is well established, yet organizations are still struggling to put available approaches into practice. This paper has shown how to make use of existing knowledge to align an organization's strategy and business processes with an ERP system process by using an Enterprise Conceptual Model. Similar to this paper, further research should deal with putting the theoretical framework into practice and thereby bridge the gap between valuable and available knowledge in science and the lack of access to this knowledge in practice.

ACKNOWLEDGMENT

The research would not have been possible without the unlimited support of the Namibian freight forwarder and its management.

The research was done under the umbrella of the Namibian-German Centre for Logistics, a joint project of the Polytechnic of Namibia and Flensburg University of Applied Sciences. It was partially funded by the African Excellence initiative of the German Academic Exchange Service (DAAD) under the Aktion Afrika of the German Foreign Ministry.

REFERENCES

Becker, J., Kugeler, M., & Rosemann, M. (2011). *Process management: A guide for the design of business processes* (2nd ed.). Berlin, London: Springer. doi:10.1007/978-3-642-15190-3

Davenport, T. H. (1998). Putting the Enterprise into the Enterprise System. *Harvard Business Review, 76*(4), 121–131. PMID:10181586

Davenport, T. H., & Short, J. E. (1990). The New Industrial Engineering: Information Technology and Business Process Redesign. *Sloan Management Review, 31*(4).

Gronau, N. (2013). *Enterprise Resource Planning*. München: Oldenbourg.

Hammer, M., & Champy, J. (2006). Reengineering the corporation: A manifesto for business revolution [paperback ed., rev. and updated]. New York: Harper Collins.

Hansmann, H., & Neumann, S. (2011). Process-Oriented Implementation of ERP-Systems. In J. Becker, M. Kugeler, & M. Rosemann (Eds.), *Process management: A guide for the design of business processes* (2nd ed., pp. 283–321). Berlin, London: Springer. doi:10.1007/978-3-642-15190-3_10

Leon, A. (2012). *Enterprise Resource Planning* (3rd ed.). New Delhi: Tata McGraw Hill.

Leyking, K. (2010). Process Follows Strategy: Plan, Execute and Control Business Process Aligned with Corporate Strategy. Information Management and Consulting, 25, 62–68.

Lynch, R. L. (2011). *Strategic management* (6th ed.). Harlow: Pearson Education Limited.

Markus, M. L., & Tanis, C. (2000). The Enterprise System Experience: From Adoption to Success. In R. W. Zmud (Ed.), *Framing the domains of IT management: Projecting the future through the past* (pp. 173–208). Cincinnati, Ohio: Pinnaflex Education Resources, Inc.

Monk, E. F., & Wagner, B. J. (2012). *Concepts in enterprise resource planning* (4th ed.). Boston, Mass, Australia: Course Technology Cengage Learning.

Rosemann, M., & Schwegmann, & A.; Delfmann, P. (2011). Preparation of Process Modeling. In J. Becker, & M. Kugeler, & M. Rosemann (Ed.), *Process management: A guide for the design of business processes* (2nd ed., pp. 41-89). Berlin, London: Springer.

Schwegmann, A., & Laske, M. (2011). As-Is Modelling and Process Analysis. In J. Becker, M. Kugeler, & M. Rosemann (Eds.), *Process management: A guide for the design of business processes* (2nd ed., pp. 133–156). Berlin, London: Springer. doi:10.1007/978-3-642-15190-3_5

Seddon, P. B., Shanks, G., & Willcocks, L. (2003). Introduction: ERP - The Quiet Revolution? In G. Shanks, P. B. Seddon, Leslie Willcocks (Eds.): Second-wave enterprise resource planning systems. Implementing for effectiveness (pp. 1–19). Cambridge, U.K., New York: Cambridge University Press

Shiang-Yen, T., Idrus, R., & Yusof, U. K. (2011). A Framework for Classifying Misfits between Enterprise Resource Planning (ERP) Systems and Business Strategies. *Asian Academy of Management Journal, 16*(2), 53–75.

The Namibian Economist. (2012). Logistics market grows tremendously. Retrieved from http://www.economist.com.na/special-focus/1120-logistics-market-grows-tremendously

Trade profiles 2011. (2011).Geneva: World Trade Organization.

KEY TERMS AND DEFINITIONS

Enterprise Conceptual Model: An Enterprise Conceptual Model constitutes the entirety of business process models of an enterprise.

ERP System: An Enterprise Resource Planning system (ERP) system can be described as a single software application with a single database that integrates business processes and functional areas, at least within the company. It processes and provides data and information in real- or near-time and is often regarded as a packaged software application.

Information Technology Strategy: Objectives, principles and measures to use the information technology within an organization efficient and effectively. This is done via alignment of a strategy, business process and an information technology system to ensure that strategic goals at the corporate and business-unit level are operationalized as information systems (here ERP-systems) supported processes.

Chapter 7
Critical Analysis of the Roles of Actors in the Deployment of Software

Tefo Sekgweleo
Tshwane University of Technology, Pretoria, South Africa

ABSTRACT

Many organizations resort to software deployment with the intention to simplify their daily activities, and for competitive advantage. The deployment consists of two main phases, development and implementation. Unfortunately, software doesn't always fulfil the organization's intentions. This is attributed to numerous factors, some of complex nature, which happen among humans, non-humans, and between humans and non-humans actors during development and implementation of software. Case study research was conducted to understand the roles of actors, and how their actions and interactions impact the development and implementation of software in the organization. Actor Network Theory (ANT) was employed in the analysis of the data. The theory focused on activities including the negotiation among actors which happened within heterogeneous network.

1. INTRODUCTION

Many companies are in competition with each other for the same group of customers, overtime and space. The challenge to attract customers leads to increased competition, and engineer innovations. According to Watson et al. (2010:24), many companies adopted information systems (IS) for innovative purposes in order to improve productivity, save costs, and increase profits. Pappa and Stergioulas (2008:38) argued that software is often developed to support particular business functions of the organization.

Companies that provide the same types of products and services are more competitively challenging than those in a niche space. The high rate of competitiveness motivates companies to develop strategy in order to make a difference. According to Hough et al. (2008:4), a company's strategy is concerned with growing the business, maintaining a competitive edge over rivals, attracting more customers, generating increased profit, and achieving targeted goals. Thus, software is intended to support and enable competitive advantage.

DOI: 10.4018/978-1-4666-8524-6.ch007

However, there are various activities such as human interactions and application of methodologies that are involved in the development and implementation of software. Avison and Fitzgerald (2006:35) argued that methodologies are vital to the development of software. In their preference for products Jain and Chandrasekaran (2009:32), argued that the types of methodologies that can be used in IS development include the waterfall model as well as spiral and evolutionary development models. Fitzgerald (2000:178) explained how methodology serves as a guideline in the software development process for organization benefit.

The development and implementation of software involve human and non-human actors. This is primarily because software comprises of various components. Each, or group of the actors have different tasks and responsibilities in the development and implementation of software. For example, Business Analysts are responsible for gathering business requirements, as well as compiling the functional design specifications (Avison and Fitzgerald, 2006:11). According to Satzinger et al. (2004:115), System Analysts design technical specifications which illustrate how the new system will function.

Both human and non-human actors work together as a collective to deliver software in accordance to organizational needs. Chen et al. (2010:240) argued that software consists of technical components and human activities and describe processes which are used to manage the organization. Actor Network Theory (ANT) focuses on the interactions between human and non-human actors within a heterogeneous network (Macome, 2008:155). Wernick et al. (2007:321) stated that irrespective of whether the actor is human or non-human they are both weighed equally as they offer the same contribution to the existence of the network.

2. RESEARCH APPROACH

The case study research method was employed in the research. According to Noor (2008:1602), a case study focuses on conducting an in-depth investigation into one or a few cases in order to gain a holistic insight about the phenomenon. The choice of the case study method was mainly because of the nature of the study, which required specific context of empirical enquiring. Parè (2004:233) defines a case study as "an empirical enquiry that investigates a contemporary phenomenon within its real-life context, especially when the boundaries between phenomenon and context are not clearly evident".

The research was carried out in a South African financial institution, Bonolo Bank. The selection of the organization was based on three factors, namely, accessibility, proximity, and evidence of specialised unit for software development and implementation. The semi-structured interview approach was used for the data collection. A total of seventeen employees were interviewed over three months in 2011. The interviewees were conducted at different levels in both IT and Business units of the organization.

The moments of translation was employed in the data analysis. This is mainly because of strength to focus on negotiation and interactions of actors within networks. Iyamu and Tatnall (2009:22) posited that actors are allowed to make decisions in the creation of the networks in which they choose to participate. The moments of translation consist of components: problemitisation, interessement, enrolment and mobilisation:

1. Problematisation. An Actor network can be formed to solve a problem or take advantage of a new opportunity. At this stage the main/focal actors are responsible for identifying problems and relevant actors to solve these problems (Greenhalgh and Stones, 2010:1287).

2. Interessement. This stage is a process whereby negotiations take place between the focal actors and other actors within the network. The roles are defined for the actors who have joined the network. Once the primary actor has negotiated with the other actors.
3. Enrolment. Actors will be expected to fulfil tasks assigned to them as agreed upon with the focal actor. According to Luoma-aho and Paloviita (2010:53), communication plays a vital role in the enrolment stage because it clarifies what is expected from the actors and what actions need to be executed.
4. Mobilisation. At this stage spokespersons are identified to represent other actors within the network (Macome, 2008:158). Good representation helps to strengthen the network.

3. SOFTWARE DEPLOYMENT

Systems software can be defined as a combination of both technical and non-technical components adopted within the organizational requirement in order to support specific needs of business (Bistričić, 2006:214; Chen et al., 2010:240). The main components of software include people, processes and technology infrastructure. Systems software is argued to have critical role in business processes and activities including competitive advantage (Tetteh and Snaith, 2006:12).

Software deployment does not always meet the objectives of organization, and it is often considered failure within this context. The challenges are traced to both development and implementation stages. Even though research has contributed significant understanding in improving software development processes, many software development projects continue to encounter challenges, such as over budget and failure to meet projected business objectives (Patnayakuni et al., 2007:286). Maguire and Redman (2007:253) posited that some of the challenges in software development include technical staff movement from one project to another. According to Wang and Liu (2006:342), systems development activity is information intensive, and decision points are frequently reached where the decision maker has insufficient information. This is caused by doubt within the systems development field. The other challenge is that sponsors may perceive the system a success whilst users see it as a failure. Mcleod and Macdonell (2011:48) stated that a system failed three years after its implementation due to continual user resistance, poor performance and financial pressures and it was finally acknowledged as a failure by its sponsors. It is very imperative for sponsors to listen to users because the users are the ones who interacts/uses the system daily.

In the last two decades, many studies such as Whittaker (1999:26), Heeks (2002:101), and Pawłowska (2004:169) have tried to address the problem of information system failure. Huff and Prybutok (2008:34) argued that software failure is caused by factors such as missed schedules, budget overspending, and the use of unproven technology, organizational changes and lack of top management involvement.

Many of the factors that have revealed and argued to be causes for software failure are connected to human' actions. Elloy (2008:802) argued that team work creates an opportunity for the sharing of ideas so that team members are motivated to learn from one another. However, and unfortunately, human interests are often not the same. People have the power to influence the outcome of software in their organizations. Giddens (1984:14) refers to power as the ability to make a difference. Along the same line, Iyamu and Roode (2010:15) argued that employees use the power bestowed on them to carry out tasks and responsibilities. As a result, organizations need to understand the interaction that takes place among employees during software deployment in order to achieve its goals and objectives.

4. ACTOR NETWORK THEORY

Actor network theory (ANT) is a theory that can be used to underpin various studies in the areas of social, science and technology. Latour (1987:4) posits that science and technology need to be studied in action and the focus must be in the dynamics of their interaction rather than on the stability of their relationships. In complementarily, Callon (1987:93) argued that "actor network is simultaneously an actor whose activity is networking heterogeneous elements and a network that is able to redefine and transform what it is made of". Therefore, ANT is more interested in inquiries, such as how networks of actors are formed, how actors and the networks fall apart, and how the actors relate with one another. Martins et al., (2009:486) argued that ANT proposes an intellectual framework that enables the analysis and balancing of the interests of the various actors in a network, whatever their nature (human, technological, organizational, political, or any other).

ANT integrates both human and non-human actors into a conceptual framework and assign equal amount of agency. As a matter of fact in ANT, both human and non-human actors are considered equal in a network (Mitev, 2009:14). Thus, actors are not superior to each other because their contribution is considered to be equal within the network. ANT helps describe how actors form alliances and involve other actors, so as to strengthen such alliances, in order to secure their interests (Huang and Hsieh, 2011:84). It provides mechanisms that hold the network together while allowing neutral treatment of the actors. Callon and Latour (1992:353) argues that ANT insists that human and non-human actors are neither hierarchized nor considered separately, but should be analysed in the same manner, and using the same language.

5. DATA ANALYSIS: ANT VIEW

The moments of translation, from the perspective of ANT was employed to investigate the social technical factors, and to gain an understanding about the disjoint between the development of software and its implementation.

5.1. Actors

From ANT perspective, actors are both human and non-human. The employees (actors) which were involved in software development and its implementation within the organization were both non-human (technical) and human (business personnel). The technical employees included the chief information officer (CIO), software developers, software testers and operation specialists. The business personnel (non-technical) employees included project managers, business managers, product owners and business analysts. One of the project managers explained that: *The various roles include the product owner, business analyst, software developers, software testers and network administrators. They are all involved in both the development and implementation of software.*

The non-human actors which were involved in the software development and implementation in the organization included various technologies such as computers, servers, networks, and software (e.g. *Zen, JBOSS* and programming languages). The technologies inclusion made it possible to develop and implement software.

The actors, both human and non-human operate within diverse networks during the development and implementation of software in the organization. The actors depend on each other and cannot be separated from the networks within which they operated.

5.2. Network

Networks were formed by both human and non-human actors. All actors (employees) were in networks, and within the networks they were directly or indirectly connected (related) through individuals and group roles and responsibilities.

In the organization, there were two units, IT and Business which were primarily responsible and accountable for software deployment. In the development of software and its implementation in the organization, there were individuals and groups, as well as technologies which were connected to one another. The groups included the Technology team, Executive Committee (Exco), and the Marketing team. One of the software development managers explained as follow: *the new business initiative gets presented to the executive committee (Exco) by the business team and Exco decides to approve or disapprove the initiative.*

The project team consisted of employees such as the project manager, product owner, business analysts, software developers and software testers. They were responsible for the software development in the organization:

In the deployment of software, different technologies were involved. Through direct or indirect connectivity or interface, the technologies depended on each other during software deployment.

In carrying out the tasks, negotiations occurred between the managers and other employees which were involved in software deployment in the organization.

5.3. Moments of Translation

The four stages of the moments of translation were used in the analysis of the data. They include problematisation, interessement, enrolment and mobilisation:

Moments of Translation: Problematisation

The Marketing Team was the initiators of software projects in the organization. The team was regarded as the internal customers to the IT unit. Competition among organizations put pressure on the business team to initiate new products or enhance the existing ones. The Marketing team initiated projects through product owners. Procedurally, the initiative was presented to the Exco for consideration. One of the employees explained as follows: *The product owners create a business case and then present it to the Exco who decides on its viability based on financial value.*

The technology team was responsible for the software development and implementation in the organization. The project managers, together with the product owners and the business analysts, were responsible for the deployment (development and implementation) of software in the organization. This was based on the roles and responsibilities of the project managers, product owners and the business analysts as defined within hierarchy structure of the organization.

However, the development and implementation of software was not as easy as it sounded. It required knowledge and skills (expertise), not just the roles and responsibilities of the employees. Therefore, it was vital to include relevant stakeholders in the software development and implementation in the organization. One of the interviewees briefly explained that: *The product owners were responsible for introducing new initiatives, managing the project and having other relations with various stakeholders such as software developers, software testers, management information system (MIS) specialists, and call centre agents.*

Software development and implementation were joint efforts of stakeholders. However, some employees were only involved for the duration of the software development whilst others continued to work with the software for as long as it existed. According to one of the senior IT managers, *we have never included the operations team from the beginning of the project but we are beginning to do so in order to improve our processes.*

Problematisation of software in the organization was through processes which involved different stakeholders at different levels. The processes were not simple or clear to many employees in the organization. This was associated to the various interests upheld by employees at individual and group levels.

Moments of Translation: Interessement

Software development and implementation in the organization attracted the attention of various stakeholders whose interests were either of a voluntary or mandatory nature or both. The stakeholders included groups and individuals such as Exco, the business team, technology team, product owners, project managers, business analysts, software developers, system analysts, software testers and database administrators. Also, the various interests were manifested by the different roles and responsibilities which the stakeholder held in the development and implementation of software. A software architect' view was that: *The top management were required to guide the technology team, which includes the software development manager, software test manager, project managers and business team.*

The stakeholders had diverse interests in the development of software and its implementation in the organization. Their interests are influenced by various factors. Some of the factors are to deliver the best software that fulfil the customers' needs, lift the organization brand higher and make a positive contribution towards the winning team.

Many of the employees had interests in the development and implementation of software primarily because they were experienced in their specialised areas. Some of them used this as an opportunity to demonstrate their wealth of knowledge and expertise to their supervisors for different reasons. Other employees were interested in the development and implementation of software because of the tasks allocated to them. It was vital for the employees to enjoy doing what they were employed to do as it increased productivity. One excited employee stated that: *I think the nice thing about software development is that it is very rewarding to see that what you have built is being used by other people.*

The interests of some individuals and groups resulted in certain actions, which were opposed to the organization's objectives. For example, some critical business requirements were overlooked by some stakeholders during the development and implementation of software. An employee sympathetically explained: *first of all, the requirement specifications lack review because by the time the requirements reach the software developer there is a lot of outstanding information. The documented requirements change too often and sometimes even without updating the original document.*

Failure to provide detailed information to various stakeholders in the development and implementation of software created setbacks in delivering certain tasks which were allocated to some employees. This affected productivity because the employees were able to do little work. This happened mainly because there was a differentiation in interests.

Other employees were interested in software development and implementation because they were bound by the performance contract they signed with their line managers on behalf of the organization. Therefore the employees were expected to perform their duties as required for the software development and implementation within the organization. According to one of the interviewees, *we conduct performance appraisals twice a year. The purpose of appraising employees was to analyse their recent successes and failures, personal strength and weaknesses.*

The various interests provided methodologies to choose from in the development and implementation of software in the organization. The methodologies were to enable the employees to follow a consistent pattern of working within the organization.

While the management made several efforts to build interest for the proposed solution to the problemitised issue, the building of interest among the employees could not be regarded as a success. Not all the stakeholders who were interested in the development and implementation of software participated in the processes and tasks. The enrolment of employees was not completely successful as some employees unwillingly accepted the tasks allocated to them and their roles and responsibilities in the development and implementation of the software.

Moments of Translation: Enrolment

Participation (Enrolment) of stakeholders was sought through different means in the organization. Enrolments of employees were reached through negotiations and agreements about the development and implementation of software within the organization. Meetings were held to update the employees about the progress of the development and implementation of software. The updates influenced some employees to participate in the processes and activities relating to the development and implementation of software in the organization.

The managers of various teams used the power bestowed on them by the organization to get the employees to participate and accept the roles and responsibilities allocated to them during the development and implementation of software. The managers also enforced the tasks allocation to individuals through the organization's compulsory performance evaluation and as such many employees were forced to participate. The performance evaluation gave little or no room for negotiation during task allocation in the development and implementation of software. One of the interviewees, a software architect explained that: *the middle management that included software development manager, project managers and business team were responsible for delivering on-time projects, and ensuring that their subordinates completed the tasks which were assigned to them.*

The outsiders' views and thoughts made the managers and others realised that communication with all stakeholders, and not only the participating actors (employees) were very significant. Therefore communication was very important in the development and implementation of software in the organization. It allowed employees to understand the details of what needed to be done in the development and implementation of software. The awareness was intended to encourage more employees' participation, one way or the other.

Processes and activities which were involved in the development and implementation of software required a team effort. The adopted formal procedure in the development and implementation of software helped the team to be more efficient and productive. However, it seemed to be the norm at times for participating stakeholders to break the rules due to frustration. But that did not help the issue. Instead it negatively impacted the systems development. One of the employees explained: *we try where possible to follow the standard components of the waterfall method that include requirements capturing, design, implementation, testing and deployment and those facets, although that doesn't always happen.*

Some employees who participated in the development and implementation of software had issues with the type of systems development methodologies being followed at the time of the study. This was because there were many methodologies and it was not clear which methodology was being followed and it caused confusion among the employees. According to one of the interviewees, *there was no formal plan really.*

Problems solving in the software development and implementation in the organization was one the factors that fascinated those employees who participated. To the participants, too many ways for solving problems were often proposed in the development and implementation of software.

There was pressure to deliver software on time or within a budget timeframe. This added more challenge at the technical level. Prior to development, proper planning was required in order to deliver the software within the proposed time frame. In dissatisfaction, one of the interviewee opined that: *the management leadership style seems to be the challenge. For example, the implementation date is dictated to us even before we start to consider the design.*

The other challenging factor was that employees were not focused in the software development and implementation because they were expected to multi task. Many employees do not often easy to find a balance when asked to multi-task. Not all participating employees were used to a multi-tasking pattern of working. Technical employees also required soft skills in order for them to manage their subordinates properly.

There was lack of consistency in resource distribution which impacted growth and experience, particularly on those employees with limited skills. For example, some of the employees who were involved in the development of software often struggled to gather requirements. This affected the quality of the software. One of the interviewees suggested that: *the business requirements should actually be put together in such a way that there is no ambiguity.*

The product owner acted as representatives for the focal actor to be able to enrol employees to the development and implementation of software. As a result, the enrolment process was a success because the employees agreed with the interests of the focal actors.

Moments of Translation: Mobilisation

In the development and implementation of software in the organization, employees acted on behalf of themselves, their teams, or the organization in entirety. The focal actor was the spokesperson who tried to convince or persuade employees to participate in the delivery of systems through its development and implementation.

In accordance to the organizational structure, the CIO was responsible for all technology related matters, including the employees who made use of the technologies. The managers of various teams within the IT unit reported to the CIO and the rest of the team members report to their respective managers. Mobilisation (pursuance) of employees was carried out along these structure and channels.

Also, the technology unit was responsible for the development and implementation of software within the organization. However, the product owners, together with the business analysts, needed to ensure that the analysis work was conducted for software to be developed. The product owners became spokespersons because they had to come up with innovative ideas concerning, e.g. introduce a new product or modify the existing one, the development and implementation of software, as well as compile the business case. A project officer explained as follows: *the product owner was accountable for ensuring that the software was implemented successfully and they make sure that what they want is actually what is implemented.*

There was joint application design (JAD) sessions which were used as a vehicle to mobilise the project stakeholders. It helped to plan the development and implementation of software within the organization. It also enabled the project stakeholders to share their ideas in order to decide on the worthiness of developing and implementing the software. According to a product owner, *only the initiatives that give us a strategic advantage in the market were considered. JAD sessions and other technical sessions were scheduled to plan software development.*

The development and implementation of software was headed by the product owners, and assisted by the project managers from monitoring perspectives in the organization. The product owners and project managers had the responsibility to coordinate project activities. In doing so, the product owners mobilises the employees to engage in the activities which were involved in the deployment of software. One of the project managers explained as follows: *it is the product owners' responsibility to make sure that everything about their product works that is, meeting the customer's expectations.*

Once the mobilisation was successful then the actor network begins to function with the objective of implementing the proposed software. The business team becomes the focal actor because the development and implementation of the software is initially instigated by them. The management was encouraged by the task of mobilisation which was linked to their performance appraisals. Mobilisation was a success and employees were enthusiastic about what they were going to contribute in the development and implementation of the software.

6. FINDINGS FROM DATA ANALYSIS

From the analysis, five significant factors were found to be critical to the development and implementation of software in the organization. The factors include prioritisation, innovation, manageability of non-technical components, procedural deficiency, process, and competitiveness at organizational level. Figure 1 depicts the factors and how they relate to each other. The factors are discussed as follows:

The requirements stage is not discussed herewith, primarily because it is considered mandatory for software development and implementation to happen. As shown in Figure 1, the activities are driven and begin with the requirements stage.

6.1. Prioritisation

The development and implementation of software is done for various reasons in different organizations. For some organizations it is to perform day-to-day duties whilst in others, it is to maximise profits.

Bonolo bank was challenged with prioritisation, which was on a key driver for financial profit. The zeal and drive for financial profitability led to less attention and priority on the employees' wellbeing. In the organization, cost reduction was the means to increasing financial gains and profits. According

Figure 1. Non-technical implications

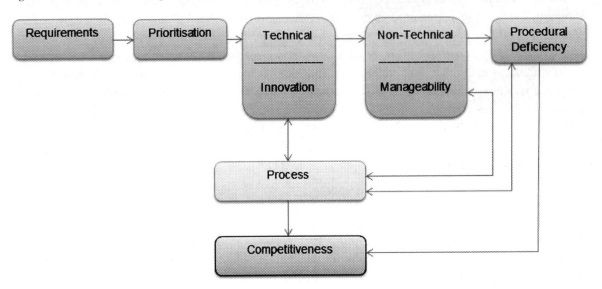

to the organization, costs could be reduced by not increasing employees' numerical strength. Due to the small number of employees in the organization, the workload of individuals increased, yet they received no financial increases.

Due to the prioritisation for financial profitability, the technology team was under resourced, numerically. Some of the employees who felt overworked for less financial reward (remuneration) resigned their appointment the organization for greener pastures elsewhere. The organization continued to hire new employees to replace those who left. Unfortunately, this did not solve the problem, nor did it benefit the organization financially as they had to retrain the new employees. It took time for new employees to adapt to a new environment and how the existing software functioned.

The prioritization helped determined, and was key driver to innovation in the organization. With particular focus and interest on innovation, software development and implementation changed with time and space, enabling competitive advantage.

6.2. Technical: Innovation

The product owners were required to be innovative at all times as they were the projects initiators leading to software development. The organization had to continuously implement new computer software or enhance existing ones in order to retain a competitive advantage. The drive for competitive advantage was the primary force for innovation. As revealed in the analysis, the employees were always willing to go the extra mile in order to complete their respective responsibilities and duties, motivation being innovation of technical resources for software development and implementation.

The organization preferred to develop software in-house for various reasons such as costs savings, intellectual property, and control over the source code. The organization also made use of free open source software in the deployment of software. The main reason was to enable the employees to be as innovative as possible, due to the extensive openness of open source software. However, the free software often required support, which also required innovative solution from the employees.

What is even more important is the process through which innovation was carried out by the employees. This required the management of non-technical factors which were involved in software development and implementation. Otherwise, innovation for potential solution gets lost in the process. As a result management was critical to the entire process of software development and implementation.

6.3. Non-Technical Factor: Manageability

One of the main challenges in the deployment of software in the organization was management. This included how planning and resources were managed. The development and implementation of software required that all levels of management to have appropriate leadership skills, meaning that the management of activities (technical and non-technical) must be balanced. Lack of balance in the management of activities was attributed to poor leadership skills. This had various effects and impacts on software development and implementation. The imbalance of manageability manifested into factors such as lack of proper planning, continuous and ambiguous requirement changes, and an imbalance of employees' workloads. The challenges sometimes resulted in software deployment failure.

Standards and processes for the development and implementation of software were in place, but they were hardly followed. It was the responsibility of the management to ensure that the standards were followed at all times. Unfortunately, it was the management themselves who often broke the rules, and did not follow the organizational process. For example, they changed system requirements as they wished during development. This was attributed to procedural deficiency.

Another issue was the balance between technical and non-technical activities. A balanced focus on both technical and non-technical aspects was required during the development and implementation of software, mainly because some of the employees who were involved specialised in particular fields.

Also, some of the managers were appointed on the basis of their years of service in the organization without little or no proper management training. This contributed to the imbalances in carrying out activities during the deployment of systems project. This type process and others as explained above led to procedural deficiency in the organization.

6.4. Procedural Deficiency

Bonolo bank had processes which were aimed at assisting employees to fulfil the tasks assigned to them. For example, to develop and implement software within the organization, the business requirements had to be documented before the project could be undertaken. However, when the requirements changed, they were often not documented. The processes to be followed and the required documents were in place, but they were hardly ever used by the employees, including the managers.

The lack of discipline in processes in the organization had a negative impact on software development as requirements kept changing. The software testers who were supposed to verify the functionalities of software against requirement specifications ended up using incomplete documents to perform their duties. This caused miscommunication between the team members. Therefore, crucial functions of the software development were omitted and discovered only after the software had been implemented.

The failure of employees to adhere to the procedural norms in the company could be attributed to a lack of understanding of the different processes that exist in the organization.

6.5. Process

From the analysis, it is clear that there were some misunderstandings among the employees concerning the processes in the organization. The misunderstanding of processes began with the entire technology team not knowing which software development methodology to follow in the organization. Some employees followed the waterfall methodology, while others employed the spiral and agile methodologies. There were some groups of employees who combined the waterfall and agile methodologies. The use of many methodologies and standards also caused confusion among the employees during development and implementation of software. As a result, it was difficult or impossible for other employees to take-over or assist in the absence of their colleagues, as they didn't understand the intricacies of the development or implementation.

Also, too many changes at the same time resulted in confusion among the employees because they were not sure what should be done. It also increased the scale of tasks to be performed which resulted in the employees being overloaded with work. This challenge created a culture whereby employees waited until the last minute before performing their duties because they were aware of the fact that the requirements could change. As a result, the employees ended up working under pressure because their carried out their tasks at the eleventh hour, causing mistakes.

The processes were meant to address the procedural deficiency and help manage innovation so as to improve upon competitive advantage in the organization. Without a process it is near impossible to competitive.

6.6. Competitiveness

Technology, through software development and implementation was considered a driver for competitive advantage in Bonolo bank. The organization invested huge amounts of money in software deployment because it was used to enable products offering services to its customers. As competition grew, processes were streamlined in order to attract more innovations.

However, procedural deficiency was a major challenge to the organization's competitiveness. This was attributed to the dependence process and management components had on procedure in the development and implementation of software in the organization.

7. INTERPRETATION AND DISCUSSION OF THE FINDINGS

As presented above, some of the factors which influence the development and implementation of software in the organization were revealed in the analysis, using the moments of translation. The factors were interpreted, making sense of why the activities happened in the way that they did during software development and implementation in the organization.

The interpretation was viewed as a higher grouping or level to the analysis of the data. In interpreting the findings, four (requirements excluded) main components as shown in Figure 2 were reached: Diffusion of Initiative, Management, Integration of Resource, and Software end Product. The components were reached based on our understanding, making sense of the findings within the context of actors' roles in the development and implementation of software in the organization.

Figure 2. Non-technical components of software deployment

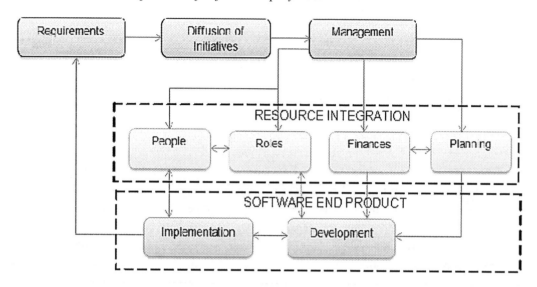

The requirements component is excluded in the discussed as did in the findings section. This was primarily because requirements were considered to be constant and norm in the development and implementation of software. Also, there weren't much of interactions and negotiations during the formulation of requirements in the organization as revealed in the analysis. The requirements were dictated to project managers and software developers.

7.1. Management

Management within the organization was accountable for enforcing roles and responsibilities of individuals and groups in order to accomplish the desired organizational goals and objectives. Managers were assigned projects, as well as the resources to accomplish them. Their roles included negotiation and coordination of employees' activities, and making decisions concerning projects. It was management responsibility to delegate duties among the team members.

Leadership skill was required in order to manage employees and their tasks. This was a challenge during software development and implementation. Some of the managers often dictated timelines prior to planning of software activities. Timelines were supposed to be negotiated with the employees who were involved in the development and implementation of software within the organization. The managers were expected to consult with the employees before making a decision that affects them.

Another challenge which required intervention was managing the mixture of technical and non-technical factors and skills. In order to balance resources and meet deadlines in the ever-increasing customer expectations, effective and efficient management was required. Thus, effective and efficient management in the deployment of software required a balance between technical and non-technical skills and capabilities for better management of software deployment.

However, a power-base which involved employees in the decision making on matters relating to software was missing. This had motivated the employees because they had felt empowered, and given the opportunity to make decisions about the project they were part of. The potentials were there that it would also encouraged and improved communication among the team members.

7.2. Diffusion of Initiatives (Innovation)

The organizations' competitiveness and sustainability depended upon fresh initiatives in order to retain current customers as well as attract new ones. The innovation of initiatives was intended to enable the organization to achieve its objectives and maximise profits in their drive for competitive advantage. However, the innovation of initiatives was not enough for competitive advantage as it was not sufficiently dispersed (diffused) amongst the stakeholders in the organization.

However, the organization preferred to carry out its software development in-house as it was considered to be cheaper than outsourcing approach. This was to allow the organization to have full control over the software development and implementation project, as well to manage the intellectual property.

Innovation begins with the innovator and spreads among individuals and groups. In the early stage of a particular innovation, growth is understandably slow as the new product establishes itself. At some point the demand grows and the product growth increases quickly as well. However, increased innovations or changes to the organization's products allowed growth to continue. Bonolo bank had the opportunity to maximise their profits before their competitors could understand their new innovation. The process was iterative in that there was continuous modification of existing products.

7.3. Resource Integration

Software development projects require human and technical resources, as has been extensively revealed. As experienced by Bonolo bank, the challenged is how to balance finance associated to both human and technical resources in the development and implementation of software. Employment of people and the purchases of equipments obviously have financial implications for the organization. As a result, having more resources than on-going projects is cost prohibitive for the organization. On the other hand, more project activities than resources could also be a problem for the employees and the organization at large. This often has impact on expected to delivering of software, as it was at Bonolo bank.

At Bonolo bank, the symptoms of employees constantly working under pressure manifested into factors such as lose of focus, panic, and manipulation of quick solutions. This was potentially of derailment to employer's objectives in the deployment of software. Also, this type of situation had impact on the development of employees.

Some of the employees were unable to handle pressure and ended up leaving the organization. The resignation of some employees created gaps, and as a result, the work load increased for the employees who remain in the organization. This had negative impacts on the development and implementation of software. Sometimes, it is easy to replace some employees who had resigned in the middle of project, but it was always difficult for new employees to adjust and integrate as quickly, and be productive in a short time.

In Bonolo Bank, there was shortage of skill when it came to utilization of the adopted open source software which was employed for development. This required the organization to seek for external help which had additional costs implications. The other alternative was to allow employees to learn and experiment with the open source software. This option affected the estimated timeline to complete certain projects' tasks.

Some of the challenges encountered by the organization emanated from the fact that there was too much focus on costs savings. The costs saving exercise had a serious impact on the successful development and implementation of quality software in the organization. The organizations struggled to find a balance between implementing quality software and saving costs.

7.4. Software End-Product

In the development and implementation of software, schedules of activities and timelines were planned by project managers. There were rarely negotiations between the employer (project managers) and employees in the deployment of software in the organization. The team members had like to be consulted, and together agree on the schedules and timelines. The scheduling of tasks and the project duration was solely done by the project manager and not the management (CEO, CIO and CFO).

As in project management practice, duration of project is supposed to be reached after schedules and activities have been agreed upon. It was different at Bonolo bank where the management had the tendency to set the project deadline at the initiative stage even before the analysis of the tasks was done. In accordance to the organization's process and procedure, management were only responsible for approval or disapproval of projects and timelines, and not set schedules and the durations.

It became the norm for business requirements to change during the development and implementation of software in the organization. Business requirements begin to arise during the development of software instead of at the planning phase. This practice was destructive to both the software developers and the business themselves.

Those who requested the development of software were not necessarily the ones who developed it. It was possible to miss some business requirements during system planning and only realise them during the development of the software. It was a very challenging practice to change business requirements instantly without following the processes which were instituted for software deployment. One of the processes was change request. This entails and requires the business to lodge a change request, have responsible individuals document the changes, and wait for the respective authorities to approve of those changes before they can be implemented.

Continuous change in the business requirements affected the team members' productivity. The team members had to wait until the last minutes before they could start with their work. This was because they knew that the business requirements were going to change. This caused the team members to be idle-with-pay for some time while waiting for the business requirements to change. However, irrespective of the waiting period, the original timeline to deliver the finished product did not change. This was another reason why the employees worked under pressure. As revealed in the analysis, working under pressure caused employees to commit mistakes, deliver some tasks unfinished and offer poor quality work.

8. CONCLUSION

Organizations continue to invest in technology, and place less emphasis on non-technical factors. Hence the same challenges non-challenges have persisted over the years. This paper presents empirical findings on the critical roles of non-technical actors in the development and implementation of software.

Many organizations know about some of the factors such as management, but they find it difficult to understand how constrain and derail processes and activities during development, as well as implementation of software. The difficulty in understanding why things happen in the way that they do comes from lack of empirical evidence. Some managers are cautious of acting upon mere speculations. This is one of the contributions of this paper.

The other contribution is the systematic approach in which the lens of ANT, moments of translation was employed in the data analysis to unveil the criticality of the interactions among stakeholders. ANT focuses on human interactions and negotiation which take place within a network. The chapter revealed how network of people were consciously and unconsciously formed heterogeneously. This will assist manager to trace activities in order to avoid pitfall, and increase competitiveness.

REFERENCES

Avison, D., & Fitzgerald, G. (2006). *Information Systems Development Methodologies, Techniques & Tools* (4th ed.). United Kingdom: McGraw-Hill.

Bistričić, A. (2006). Project information system. *Tourism and Hospitality Management, 12*(2), 213–224.

Callon, M. (1987). *In The Social Construction of Technological Systems New Directions in the Sociology and History of Technology*. Cambridge, Massachusetts: The MIT Press.

Callon, M., & Latour, B. (1992). *Don't throw the baby with the bath school a reply to Collins and yearly*. Chicago: The University of Chicago Press.

Chen, D. Q., Mocker, M., Preston, D. S., & Teubner, A. (2010). Information systems strategy: Reconceptualization, measurement, and implications. *Management Information Systems Quarterly, 34*(2), 233–259.

Combera, A., Fishera, P., & Wadsworth, R. (2003). Actor–network theory: A suitable framework to understand how land cover mapping projects develop? *Land Use Policy, 20*(4), 299–309. doi:10.1016/S0264-8377(03)00048-6

Elloy, D. F. (2008). The relationship between self-leadership behaviors and organization variables in a self-managed work team environment. *Management Research News, 31*(11), 801–810. doi:10.1108/01409170810913015

Fitzgerald, B. (2000). Systems development methodologies: The problem of tenses. *Information Technology & People, 13*(3), 174–185. doi:10.1108/09593840010377617

Giddens, A. (1984). *The Constitution of Society: Outline of the Theory of Structuration*. Cambridge, UK: John Polity Press.

Greenhalgh, T., & Stones, R. (2010). Theorising big IT programmes in healthcare: Strong structuration theory meets actor-network theory. *Social Science & Medicine, 70*(9), 1285–1294. doi:10.1016/j.socscimed.2009.12.034 PMID:20185218

Heeks, R. (2002). Information systems and developing countries: Failure, success, and local improvisations. *The Information Society, 18*(2), 101–112. doi:10.1080/01972240290075039

Hough, J., Thompson, A. A., Strickland, A. J. III, & Gamble, J. E. (2008). *Crafting and executing strategy* (South African ed). United Kingdom: McGraw-Hill.

Huang, C. C., & Hsieh, C. C. (2011). Protect Critical Information Infrastructure Systems in Financial and Healthcare Sectors: Actor Network Theory. Proceedings of *ICONS 2011: The Sixth International Conference on Systems,83-87.*

Huff, R. A., & Prybutok, V. R. (2008). Information systems project management decision making: The influence of experience and risk propensity. *Project Management Journal, 39*(2), 34–47. doi:10.1002/pmj.20050

Iyamu, T., & Roode, D. (2010). The use of structuration theory and actor network theory for analysis: Case study of a financial institution in South Africa. *International Journal of Actor-Network Theory and Technological Innovation, 2*(1), 1–26. doi:10.4018/jantti.2010071601

Iyamu, T., & Tatnall, A. (2009). An Actor-Network analysis of a case of development and implementation of IT strategy. *International Journal of Actor-Network Theory and Technological Innovation, 1*(4), 35–52. doi:10.4018/jantti.2009062303

Jain, R., & Chandrasekaran, A. (2009). Rapid system development (RSD) methodologies: Proposing a selection framework. *Engineering Management Journal, 21*(4), 30–35. doi:10.1080/10429247.2009.11431842

Latour, B. (1987). *Science in action: how to follow scientists and engineers through society.* Cambridge, MA: Harvard University Press.

Luoma-Aho, V., & Paloviita, A. (2010). Actor-networking stakeholder theory for today's corporate communications. *Corporate Communications: An International Journal, 15*(1), 49–67. doi:10.1108/13563281011016831

Macome, E. (2008). On Implementation of an information system in the Mozambican context: The EDM case viewed through ANT lenses. *Information Technology for Development, 14*(2), 154–170. doi:10.1002/itdj.20063

Maguire, S., & Redman, T. (2007). The role of human resource management in information systems development. *Management Decision, 45*(2), 252–264. doi:10.1108/00251740710727278

Martins, L., Cunha, P., Figueiredo, A., & Dias, T. (2009). IT Alignment through ANT: A Case of Sustainable Decision in the Educational Sector. *Engineering Management Conference, IEEE International,* 485-490. doi:10.1109/TIC-STH.2009.5444452

Mcleod, L., & Macdonell, S. G. (2011). Factors that Affect Software Systems Development Project Outcomes: A Survey of Research. *ACM Computing Surveys, 43*(4), 24–56. doi:10.1145/1978802.1978803

Mitev, N. (2009). In and out of actor-network theory: A necessary but insufficient journey. *Information Technology & People, 22*(1), 9–25. doi:10.1108/09593840910937463

Noor, K. B. M. (2008). Case study: A strategic research methodology. *American Journal of Applied Sciences, 5*(11), 1602–1604. doi:10.3844/ajassp.2008.1602.1604

Oates, B. J. (2008). *Researching information systems and computing.* Los Angeles: Sage Publications.

Pappa, D., & Stergioulas, L. K. (2008). The emerging role of corporate systems: An example from the era of business process-oriented learning. *International Journal of Business Science and Applied Management, 3*(2), 38–48.

Paré, G. (2004). Investigating information systems with positivist case study research. *Communications of the Association for Information Systems, 13*(1), 233–264.

Patnayakuni, R., Rai, A., & Tiwani, A. (2007). Systems Development Process Improvement: A Knowledge Integration Perspective. *IEEE Transactions on Engineering Management, 54*(2), 286–300. doi:10.1109/TEM.2007.893997

Pawłowska, A. (2004). Failures in large systems projects in Poland: Mission impossible? *Information Polity, 9*(3), 167–180.

Satzinger, J. W., Jackson, R. B., & Burd, S. D. (2004). *Systems Analysis and Design in a Changing World* (3rd ed.). USA: Thomson.

Tetteh, G. K., & Snaith, J. (2006). Information system strategy: Applying galliers and Sutherland's stages of growth model in a developing country. *The Consortium Journal, 11*(1), 5–16.

Wang, Q. Z., & Liu, J. (2006). Project Uncertainty, Management Practice and Project Performance: An Empirical Analysis on Customized Information Systems Development Projects. Proceedings of *Engineering Management Conference, IEEE International*, 341-345. doi:10.1109/IEMC.2006.4279882

Watson, R. T., Boudreau, M., & Chen, A. J. (2010). Information Systems and Environmentally Sustainable Development: Energy Informatics and New Directions for the IS Community. *Management Information Systems Quarterly, 34*(1), 23–38.

Wernick, P., Hall, T., & Nehaniv, C. L. (2008). Software evolutionary dynamics modelled as the activity of an actor-network. *The Institution of Engineering and Technology, 2*(4), 321–336.

Whittaker, B. (1999). Unsuccessful information technology projects. *Information Management & Computer Security, 7*(1), 23–29. doi:10.1108/09685229910255160

KEY TERMS AND DEFINITIONS

Actor Network Theory: It is an approach to social theory and research which originates in the field of science studies. It treats objects and humans equally as part of the social networks.

Actor-Network: It is related actors in a heterogeneous network of aligned interests.

Actors: Any material that is human beings or non-human actors.

Software Deployment: Software deployment entails all the activities that make a software system available for use.

Translation: It is how actors generate ordering effects by negotiating others' interest to one's own with the aim to mobilize support.

Chapter 8
Assessing the Influence of Actors on e-Government Policies:
Evidences from Chile and Costa Rica Experiences

Roberto Cortés-Morales
Costa Rica Institute of Technology, Costa Rica

ABSTRACT

E-government development, assumed as a public policy problem, has to consider political issues, where actors play a key role for success or failure on such policies. Several political theories admit the importance of actors in their approaches. Although there are efforts to formalize them, the model presented in this chapter looks to integrate a variety of proposals in the context of public policies. The application of the model to e-government cases on Chile and Costa Rica has shown that the characteristics of the process executed in a timeline (with their successes and failures) can be explained from actors' perspective. Issues like promoting new laws, the coordination of multiple agencies or the priority for projects on political context have to be solved with specific actors using their power resources. The explanations found could be considered for characterize future developments on e-government taking on account how critical is the actors' intervention.

INTRODUCTION

It is accepted that e-government development goes beyond of issues related on Information Technologies (IT). Such statement it is not new. Many studies have proposed that political and cultural questions have to be considered (Barros, Ruiz, Cerda & Martínez, 2012; Korteland & Bekkers, 2007; Bolgherini, 2007).

It can be supposed, for example, that using IT in order to improve efficiency and transparency on government services might provoke reactions on actors affected (such as bureaucracy reduction or a more open and easy access for a wider group of government providers).

DOI: 10.4018/978-1-4666-8524-6.ch008

Given that e-government solutions are not neutral, they shall to be assumed from public policies' perspectives. On one hand such solutions try to reach political goals like transparency, efficiency or enhanced public participation among others (Tolbert & Mossberger, 2006). On the other hand, as we pointed, actors could be affected or beneficiated from them.

Consequently, actors' importance has to be considered in order to assess success or failure of e-government policies. This approach it's not proposing to an individualistic approach. Multiples perspectives are needed to take on account regarding political, economic, social, administrative and technological variables (Cortés-Morales & Marín-Raventós, 2012a).

It is important to consider that incidences on poor e-government development are no limited just on areas like Public Administration inefficiencies or citizen dissatisfaction, but also on how enterprises could perform better their goals on productivity and/or transactions related with government. A broad analysis on institutions and how they affect economic performance is developed by North (1990).

This research has aimed to demonstrate that beside formal structures (like laws or decrees), or economic and technological capacity; how actors play is critical for e-government success. Lack of actors' adequate characterization in particular political contexts could derive on problematic experiences. Although this study is retrospective it is expected that its findings can give some notions for using the model in prospective mode.

The first section will introduce fundamentals of the model and its formal description as well the dimensions considered for e-government analysis. The second part of this chapter will describe some general characteristics of Chile and Costa Rica, countries that were selected as source of study cases. The third section presents the cases, including methodological considerations. The last part discusses the results obtained with the model application.

BACKGROUND

The importance of actors has been recognized in several fields related with political sciences like institutions (North, 1990; Tsebelis, 2001), policy networks (Klijn, 1998), governance and governability (Prats, 2001) or public policies (Subirats, Knoepfel, Larrue, & Varonne, 2008). However such importance is admitted, one can affirm that not enough efforts to characterize properties on actors have been made. Yet, some notions of concepts related to them like power, have been elaborated. For example, the capacity to avoid changes on institutions (known as veto power) is described by Tsebelis (2001). The source of such power is given by institutional results, like the number of seats that a politic party has on Deputies Chamber. Furthermore, institutional rules could construct complex models based on game theories by which actors could construct scenarios on how to play "political games" (Shepsle & Bonchek, 2005).

However, the political complexities are no limited to institutions. Since 80's decade, the reduction of the size and capacity of State and government has implied that other actors, not related directly to institutional contexts, have become more and more important for policy construction and implementation. This has been the case, for example, of policy networks (Klijn, 1998; Fleury, 2002). In this broad perspective, authors like Prats (2001) state that "strategic actors" are important for governability. Such "strategic actors" are capable to block changes on rules that govern any given society. A good governability is more that just government. Indeed it is a characteristic of a society.

In Subirats et al. (2008) it is argued the importance of actors on public policies. In their proposal it can be found a typology for actors' identification. Two main categories are defined: the public and

Assessing the Influence of Actors on e-Government Policies

the private. The public ones are those who are in legal charge of public policies. Private actors might be "beneficiaries" or "objectives". The first ones are those who are beneficed from a given policy. The second ones are the affected. Additionally a categorization of resources related to a public policy is also shown (like economic, infrastructure, human, among others). Accordingly with their argumentation, actors' importance is also relevant considering the influence of them by defending their interests as they do on any political situation.

Since e-government development is related to public policies, it should be analysed with similar approaches. However public policies analysis is often related to studies that focus on one of their phases such as problem definition, solution formulation, implementation or evaluation. The result is that no formal model has been yet proposed to examine issues concerning actors, directly related on public policies success or failure.

Given this particular theoretical need, a formal model based on actors has been developed and described. It could be assumed that it might be used for different kind of policies. Particularly this research has focused on applying it to e-government solutions.

Finally models like MACTOR and others (Godet, 2007) could be applied to multiple contexts (like business strategy) for prospective scenarios where actors' characterization is fundamental. However specific considerations, as it was pointed, on dimensions and variables for public policies applied to e-government have been proposed in order to give particular explanations (or predictions) in this area.

A MODEL FOR MEASURING ACTORS' IMPACT ON PUBLIC SOLUTIONS

The model proposed in this chapter combines many principles and concepts from the ideas presented in the Background section. Again, from Subirats et al. (2008) one can define an actor as an individual or group that defends a unique position concerning a policy. Immediately one can notice from that definition that it is not allowed the identification of actors like "Department of Treasury" because the positions of the Secretary of Treasury may differ from those of the Union who represents the workers on that Department.

Two main characteristics are defined for an actor that is involved in a given policy. First one is called "veto power". Here is wanted to characterize the potential power the actor has by measuring his resources in a specific context. Contrary to relational power definition from Max Weber (Castells, 2009; Fernández, 2002), one can say that "resources weight" is what is measured to find how he can eventually use that "weight" in a political space.

Consequently the second characteristic is indeed, the measure on how actors use their veto power to support (or not) a policy. Such characteristic is named as "support".

A basic typology of the actors' model can be defined. It is assumed that any actor has veto power and gives support in political issues of his interest. A combination of power and support sets the position of an actor as it is shown in Figure 1.

The *veto power* and *support* combinations create four possible types of actors in a given moment. Actors could be categorized as *blockers* (showing low support and high veto power), *sponsors* (both high support and veto power), *upholders* (showing high support and low veto power), or *indifferent* (both low support and low veto power).

Some basic assumptions could be formulated. For example, as more sponsor actors there are, the more feasible a policy is. Also, as more sponsor or upholder actors there are, the more legitimate a

Figure 1. Position typology for an actor concerning a public issue
(Cortés Morales & Marín Raventós, 2012a)

	Veto power	
Support	Low	High
High	UPHOLDER	SPONSOR
Low	INDIFFERENT	BLOCKER

policy is. Once veto power and support are computed, it is possible to calculate values for feasibility and legitimacy as aggregated indicators.

The resources for veto power as is explained in Cortés-Morales and Marín-Raventós (2012a) may have several origins. For example, institutional resources come from formal rules as laws, public contracts or decrees that enable particular actors within a legal frame to perform actions. Economic resources are those that can be assessed on a financial or monetary way: money, properties, equipment, etc. Table 1 summarizes actor's resources considered in the model.

On the other hand, characteristics of *support* come from two attributes. The first one is related to public *declarations* of an actor regarding a public solution. The second one are the *actions* made by an actor in the context of solving the public problem analysed.

How to assign numeric values on each attribute both for veto power and support is one of key challenges for this model. Each of those attributes may have a value between 0 and 1. The more close to 1, the more the presence of a given attribute in an actor. Table 2 shows what categories are defined to assign a value for *institutional* resource on *veto power*. For each resource described on Table 1, analogous definitions were made (Cortés-Morales, 2013; Cortés-Morales & Marín-Raventós, 2012b).

For attributes related on *support* concept, similar tables were structured as Table 3 shows, defining the action attribute.

Table 1. Power resources of actors

Resource	Definition
Institutional	Formal rules on public spaces granted to an actor by laws, decrees, political constitutions, contracts, etc.
Economic	Any resource measured on monetary basis, such as money, properties, equipment, etc.
Recognition	How an actor has influence in policies, measured by its public recognition (for example by using opinion polls)
Media	How an actor can access and use media in order to communicate its position concerning a public issue.

(Cortés-Morales & Marín-Raventós, 2012a)

Table 2. Example of assessing power resources for the institutional resource

Value	Interpretation
Highest = 1	Maximum power granted in an institutional context. For examples, in countries with dictators with absolute power, or by plebiscites (on democracies). Absolute majorities on Parliaments can be considered as well.
Very high = 0.75	The actor doesn't have absolute power but has big capacity to exercise it. For example, simple majority on Parliament, or the Presidents needing to negotiate with other State powers or groups that are mainly favourable to their regime.
High = 0,6	The actor concedes some interests to other actors in order to reach its goals. For example, supporting a law Project sponsored by some group different from actor.
Medium = 0.5	The actor should enter in negotiations with other actors even with opposite interests.
Low = 0.4	The power granted through institutions is not enough for an actor to develop actions or defend his interests. Intensive negotiations or concessions to others are required.
Very low = 0.25	The actor has little institutional support and should find other actors for defending his interests.
Lowest = 0	The actor has no institutional power.

(Cortés-Morales & Marín-Raventós, 2012a)

Note that not specific methodology limits the model. The values may be computed using qualitative methods (such as expert criteria or document analysis) or quantitative ones (like polls, surveys, data mining, among others). Finally, with basic concepts explained, it is pertinent to formalize them.

MODEL FORMALIZATION

Next paragraphs will describe the formal definitions of concepts discussed previously. The first ones are directly related on actors, specifically the veto power and the support. The second ones are applied on the totally of actors analysed (feasibility and legitimacy). Finally, a derived concept (sustainability) is described.

Veto Power Formalization

As is explained in Cortés-Morales and Marín-Raventós (2012a) it is important to consider that not every resource of veto power (listed on Table 1) has the same weight or importance in a given moment of the political context being analysed. For example, in stable circumstances, it can be affirmed that the insti-

Table 3. Characterizing the action variable for the support concept

Value	Interpretation
Full support = 1	The actor mobilizes a big amount of resources to reach policy goals as its highest priority.
High support = 0.75	The policy is one of the highest priorities of the actor by mobilizing significate resources on it.
Medium = 0.5	The actor mobilizes resources on policy but has other priorities at the same level.
Low support = 0.25	The policy has low priority for the actor, although some few resources are mobilized for it.
Total rejection = 0	No priority on the policy for the actor. No resources are mobilized.

(Cortés-Morales & Marín-Raventós, 2012a)

tutional resource may have more importance than the recognition resource, because process leaders are chosen by accepted rules like elections or presidential designations. Contrary, when institutions are in crisis and social movements are significant, we may consider that recognition could be more important because leaders are not necessarily linked to a formal institution.

Both assessing resources on actors and weighting those resources on a temporary political context is relevant for the analysis. Once performed, we can apply a formula to compute a value that serves as a reference of an actor´s veto power. The veto power of an actor in a moment or time period t, $V(t)$ is:

$$V(t) = \frac{\sum_{i=1}^{N} r(t)_i w(t)_i}{\sum_{i=1}^{N} w(t)_i} \qquad (1)$$

In (1) i is the ith resource analyzed, $r(t)_i$ is the value assessed for the resource i in the moment t for an given actor and $w(t)_i$ is the weight of the resource i in moment t. The more $V(t)$ approaches to 1, the more veto power the actor has in the period of time t.

Support Formalization

Regarding the *support* concept, here again it is important to point that in specific contexts, both *declarations* and *actions* (as attributes) could have different weights. For example, discussion about a public problem *per se* could derive on debates between actors. In such cases declarations could have more importance than actions. On the contrary, if the problem is recognized, and actors agree on solution, actions at this time are more relevant than declarations. Let $S(t)$, the actor's support for the policy in the period of time t, is formally defined as:

$$S(t) = D(t)w(t)_D + A(t)w_A(t) \qquad (2)$$

In (2) $D(t)$ is the value for declaration variable of a given actor in the period of time t, $w_D(t)$ is the weight of declaration variable in the period of time t, $A(t)$ is the value for action variable of a given actor in the period of time t, $w_A(t)$ is the weight of action variable in the period of time t. Consider that

$w_A(t) + w_D(t) = 1$.

With the veto power and the support concepts formally described, feasibility and legitimacy of public policies can be defined.

Feasibility Formalization

The *feasibility* concept is closely related on how actors use *veto power* to support (or to block) a given policy. The position of an actor (accordingly with Figure 1), could be deduced by multiplying its *veto*

Assessing the Influence of Actors on e-Government Policies

power by its *support* values. However, since veto power becomes essential to assess feasibility, it is necessary to weight it, in order to have a more accurate indicator.

Moreover, it is found that, even when same goals are pursued, the way in which actors want to implement such solutions may differ deeply. The feasibility in such cases decreases because the dispersion on supported solutions. To reflect this situation, it is proposed the following formula:

$$F(t) = \frac{\sum_{i=1}^{N} S(t)_i V(t)_i^{o(t)}}{\sum_{i=1}^{N} V(t)_i} \qquad (3)$$

In (3) for a given moment t, $F(t)$ is the feasibility for a policy considering N actors. $F(t)$ can take values from 0 to 1, meaning the less and the highest possible feasibility respectively. $S(t)_i$ is the support computed for the ith actor in moment t, $V(t)_i$ is the veto power calculated for the ith actor in moment t and $o(t)$ is the number of divergent options on solutions for the policy analysed. If $o(t)$ is greater than 1, notice that $V(t)_i$ is more affected if it tends to zero, contrary to those that are near to 1. It means that even if all values for $V(t)_i$ are expected to be affected, powerful actors are more capable to establish their position. In summary, the formula reflects how feasibility value decreases if there are divergent solutions. The state procurement case for Costa Rica is an example of this situation and it will be described later in this chapter.

Legitimacy Formalization

The legitimacy concept tries to determine the level on how actors support a policy. It is important to define the context analysed. For example, if the policy is subject of an important public debate, resources like actor's "recognition resource" are better defined by his public image. In this case, it is important to consult information such as polls, surveys, and others, that give a closer idea on how the actor is considered. On the other hand, if the project is carried inside the government with few external actors, and with no important debate, formal structures, such as administrative hierarchies, are more likely to be considered to define the actor's recognition resource.

It is found that recognition resource is important on legitimacy because it gives an idea on the weight of an actor's representation. It means, for example, if the President of a nation has a 70% of popularity and an important policy is being discussed, recognition of that actor could be closer to a 0.7 value. On the other hand, if the policy is a matter inside the government with a low level of public debate, the position of the President, as the maximum authority, could have a recognition value close to 1. Hence, the legitimacy of a public policy is expressed by the following formula:

$$L(t) = \frac{\sum_{i=1}^{N} S(t)_i wr_i(t)}{\sum_{i=1}^{N} wr_i(t)} \qquad (4)$$

In (4) $L(t)$ is the legitimacy of a policy on moment t considering N actors. $S(t)i$ is the support computed for the ith actor, $wr_i(t)$ is the weight of representation of the ith actor since his public recognition resource value. Like feasibility, $L(t)$ takes values from 0 to 1. The closer to 1 the value of $L(t)$ is, the more legitimate the policy is.

Sustainability Concept

Sustainability is a concept derived from a combined analysis of feasibility and legitimacy. Given a public policy, first is needed to establish if the policy has high feasibility. Otherwise it is useless to continue with further consideration. Logically, any policy with low feasibility impedes to make a scenario for sustainability. Simply, such policies cannot be implemented. Since most periods on successful services analysed show feasibility values close to 0.7, it is assumed that this value could be defined as a threshold for high feasibility.

Given that few but powerful actors can promote feasibility, one cannot affirm that a solution could be sustainable and in this scenario, it is pertinent taking into account what level of legitimacy is involved. Table 4 shows how the sustainability is characterized depending on its legitimacy level.

Since both legitimacy and feasibility are calculated for a particular period of time, it will be necessary to analyse different periods (if research is retrospective) to establish how sustainable a policy was. Otherwise, if the model is used in prospective mode, once the current situation is set, it is needed to determine what possible actions policy-makers have to do in order to keep or increase a policy's sustainability.

Dimensions for Analysing e-Government

The gap between model definition and empiric data is always a challenge in any factual science (Bunge, 1999). The information needed as input for the model is gathered using dimensions of analysis depending on the public problem or policy. For e-government five dimensions are used: political, economic, social, administrative and technological. Table 5 summarizes the use of such dimensions for e-government research.

Table 4. Sustainability of a policy considering high feasibility

Legitimacy	Sustainability	Description
Very High (0.80-1)	State policy	There is high consensus among actors to promote the policy. It has big chance to be executed beyond limits of government administration periods
High (0.60- 0.80)	Government policy	There are conditions for Administration on the power to implement policies of its agenda. The Administration has little opposition on Congress, or has some key allies actors who support its initiatives. Chances to consolidate the policies depend on political twists in the future (priority changes, opposite groups that gain power, etc.)
Medium (0.50 – 0.60)	Limited policy	Some interests from some groups are implemented on a policy. It may have strong opposition, but actors with power give feasibility to the policy
Low (0 less than 0.50)	Particular policy	It might exist a policy that responds to very particular interests. For example, dictators that implement a policy that is highly rejected by society

(Cortés-Morales, 2013)

Table 5. Dimensions analysis guidelines for data sources

Dimension	Example of Questions or Guides for Source Data	Related Concepts
Political	What policies have being defined on digital government?	Actors, veto power
	What actors are or not involved?	Actors
	What public positions political actors have stated?	Actor's support (declaration variable)
Economical	What resources have been assigned to e-government?	Veto power and actor's actions
	Cost-benefit studies made	Veto power (economical resource)
	Savings on using e-government	Support (actions)
Administrative	Training on public servers either in new digital services	Support (actions)
	Shared information between organizations	Support (actions)
	Implemented services	Actors (beneficiaries, objective)
Social	Policy effects on improving digital skills on citizens	Actors (beneficiaries)
	Effects on social services processes or products	Actors (beneficiaries)
Technological	Improvement on public digital infrastructure	Support (actions)
	Policies on technological issues	Support (actions)

(Cortés-Morales & Marín-Raventós, 2012a)

The previous table is an example on how questions regarding e-government are related to potential data sources and how they can be related to a specific concept of the model.

Some additional commentaries are valid on this model. For example, it could be applied to different phases of a public policy (problem recognition, formulation, implementation, etc.) and compare what differences might arise among them. Also actors could be characterized as "state actors", "market actors" or "social actors" for assessing potential gaps among sectors about some specific solution.

It has been shown, by describing this model, that policies strengths (or weaknesses) could be analysed from actors, as basic units, by characterizing them on particular or global aspects (such as institutions). Every resource may be mapped to particular attributes on actors. An application of the model was performed on e-government policies, as it is shown on following sections.

E-GOVERNMENT DEVELOPMENT ON CHILE AND COSTA RICA

Chile and Costa Rica are countries belonging to Latin America region. Both present similar characteristics on their political system as well as their economic and social development (Cortés-Morales, 2013; World Bank, 2012a, 2012b, 2012c).

At the beginning of the period of this research (2002-2010), indexes on information society development were summarized as is shown on Table 6.

However, important differences on e-government development are evidenced on the evaluations of the United Nations Public Administration (UNPAN). Table 7 shows the relative position for Chile and Costa Rica on countries ranking, according to the E-government Global Development Index (EGDI) for the period of the research.

An immediate question can arise. Why those differences with similar contexts? The EGDI has three components: On-line Services Development, Technological Infrastructure Development and Human

Table 6. Information society indexes on Chile and Costa Rica by 2002

Index	Chile	Costa Rica
GDP per capita	4 731	4 322
Human development	0.854	0.838
Fixed phones per 100 people	21.53	31.62
Mobile phones per 100 people	62.08	21.73
Personal computers per 100 people	13.87	23.87
Internet users per 100 people	27.9	23.54

(Association for Progressive Communications, 2004)

Capital. Except for the Online Services Development index, the other two are similar for both countries on 2010 (UNPAN, 2010). The political priority for adopting IT for State Modernization is a possible explanation for such service production in Chile (Barria & Araya, 2008). Consequently to look closer on how services were developed might induce critical information for e-government development.

Case Selection of E-Government Services

Two services for each country were selected. For Chile they were the State Procurement (ChileCompra) and the International Trade Single Entry services. For Costa Rica the State Procurement and Drivers License and Passports services were the ones chosen. It was the intention to pick either good or not so good experiences on both countries concerning the projects behind those services. ChileCompra and Drivers Licenses and Passports for Costa Rica were considered good experiences (Government of Chile & Interamerican Development Bank, 2008; La Nación, 2008). On the other hand, International Trade Service in Chile as well the State Procurement projects for Costa Rica have presented different difficulties to become successful (Chile Ministry of Treasury, 2005; Costa Rica General Republic Comptroller, 2012). The rational on case selection can be described as follow. With such selection it is possible:

1. To compare two projects with same goals but different results regarding success (State procurement in Chile and Costa Rica),

Table 7. EGDI ranking evolution for Chile and Costa Rica between 2003 and 2010

Year	E-Government Ranking Position	
	Chile	Costa Rica
2003	22	66
2004	22	73
2005	22	70
2008	40	59
2010	34	71

(UNPAN, 2003, 2004, 2005, 2008, 2010)

2. To compare two projects with same beneficiary group (entrepreneurs) but different results (State Procurement and International Trade Services in Chile), and
3. To analyse two successful experiences trying to find out what factors could explain such success.

The following sections will describe each service showing the results obtained from the model application.

Commentaries on Methodology

Since the model is based on actors' characterization, in order to assess their veto power and support, a variety of information sources were analysed, such as government budgets, law or normative ruling some services, media declarations, published polls and surveys, interviews, and evaluations, among others. Once data was gathered, it was mapped to some value in different dimensions, like "institutional resource". For example, if the solution was inside the Executive branch of government, President, as a maximum authority, was given a value of 1 on such resource. But if some new law was needed, Congress (as a whole) was given a value of 1 in that resource, whereas President was assigned with a minor value on that context. Detailed sources and values assigned to each actor are described in (Cortés-Morales, 2013).

For other resources, questions like: "what is the capacity of government to assign budget for E-government projects? (is there a crisis or fiscal deficit?), " is there a political situation where a specific e-government solution could be shown as a necessary measure?" (a corruption scandal, for example), "what is the capacity of an actor to access massive media?", etc. Each one of previous examples is linked to economical, recognition and media resources, respectively. From information gathered, and analysing the context, values between 0 and 1 were assigned to each actor's resource. Then, the veto power formula was applied.

Analogous process for computing the support indicator was performed. Questions like "how many times an actor refers to the policy on media?", "how much budget is assigned to a project?", "what evaluations are made?", "how human resources are trained for new services?" are used. By analysing this kind of information, it was possible to assess what public positions (or actions) were performed by actors. Again, values from 0 to 1 were assigned to each support characteristic in order to calculate the respective formula.

State Procurement in Chile

By 1997, the Chilean government promoted new procedures for State procurement in public sector. The goals established were: reaching more efficiency by creating a market of vendors and reducing cost of acquisitions for buyers and suppliers. Additionally, transparency was also an expected value on those procedures. IT was intended to create a platform to be used by vendors and buyers while the public could observe on the system with no restrictions, the cost of contracts, the suppliers invited and contracted, and other information coming from the procurement process. The original intention was the mandatory use of the procedures and the IT platform in the whole public sector, including local governments. For such goal, a new law was required. By 1999, President Frei sent to Congress the law proposal. However, he was near of the end of his presidential period, and the election process for new president and Congress was also running. Therefore, the proposal had little chance to be discussed and voted. By 2000, Mr. Ricardo Lagos was elected President of Chile. Nevertheless he showed support for the State procure-

Table 8. Feasibility and legitimacy for State procurement in Chile

Period	Feasibility	Legitimacy
1997-2000	0.64	0.74
2000-2002	0.67	0.71
2002-2003	0.91	0.89
2003-2006	0.93	0.91
2006-2010	0.88	0.88

ment project (as well others related with E-government), discussion in Congress of new law was too slow. Some temporary measures were adopted inside the Executive Power to promote the use of new procedures, although their use was not mandatory.

However, by 2002, public scandals on corruption were known in Chile. Lagos's government attempted to confront that situation by promoting an agreed agenda with the political opposition, where E-government projects had obtained more priority, including the one related to State Procurement. Between October 2002 and May 2003, the new law was discussed and voted, creating a new public service named ChileCompra. Since then, resources have been allocated continuously and ChileCompra has become one example of best practices for State procurement solutions (RedGEALC, 2007).

The model was applied on five different periods, generating the results listed in Table 8.

Results reflect the situation described above. Efforts in the first two periods are limited by the inexistence of an institutional framework that could maximize the solution. The Congress was the key actor on those two periods as well in the third one because that critical resource (the creation of the institution by a new law) was in its scope (the Congress in both cameras voted by unanimity every approval step on the process of the law related with State Procurement, so as a whole, Congress was considered as a one actor).

In the key period 2002-2003, both feasibility and legitimacy increase their values, coincidentally with the big political support granted by actors to the project and the law.

Further periods keep those values high, even with government changes (2006-2010). Additionally with the project exclusively on hands of Executive Branch, an important effort on resource allocation and support are well reflected on success of the service.

From sustainability concept described in Table 4, clearly the policy implemented with the service ChileCompra, is close to be a "State policy".

Chilean International Trade Single Entry Service

The goal of this service has been to provide to enterprises an IT platform where all official procedures related to international trade in Chile can be coordinated by giving a single entry for users (Benavides, 2011). First formulations on such a project can be found on the document of vision for the use of IT in Chilean society (Chile Presidential Commission on New Information Technologies, 1999). On 2001, project ISIDORA was launched in order to build that service.

However by 2005, Chile´s Budget Office discovered several problems on project's execution, despite it had an important economic funding near to USD 2.4 million (Chile Ministry of Treasury, 2005). Project management was located on IT department of Customs Service, diminishing the political capacity

Table 9. Feasibility and legitimacy for International Trade Service in Chile

Period	Feasibility	Legitimacy
2001-2006	0.40	0.39
2006-2010	0.50	0.52

required. Specifically, the necessary coordination hadn't been accomplished given that in the International Trade process involves 18 different agencies. Additionally, the project was characterized for being too ambitious for the short period of time assigned.

By 2006 and 2007 new management tried to simplify projects' outputs with very specific procedures using IT. However, the coordination continued to be located at National Customs Service and political coordination issues still have not been resolved. By 2010, after a government change, new efforts were taken seeking to resolve project's needs by giving it a higher political priority. Applying the model in two different periods has generated the results that Table 9 lists.

These results closely reflect the above description for that service. Although Chile has needed an efficient IT platform to support international trade, the project has been executed in an IT organizational context and could not reach to have a big political support. Otherwise, issues on coordination could have been solved more easily. Low values on feasibility and legitimacy reflect how actor priorities were assigned to this particular project: there has been no special attention from powerful actors. Differently from State Procurement, no action from Congress was needed. This gave the whole responsibility to Executive Branch members. This scenario institutionally more propitious could not be exploited for better results. Finally, because there is low feasibility, no sustainability analysis could be done.

State Procurement in Costa Rica

Costa Rican efforts on developing an IT-based solution for State procurement service had started by 2000. President Rodríguez launched a government program for improving State capacities to serve the productive sector. A variety of e-government solutions were promoted including "CompraRed", the name of the State procurement service. A first version of an informative platform began to operate in 2001.

By 2002, the new administration of President Pacheco continued improving the platform. The service was located on the Department of Treasury. By 2005, a new version with transactional capacities was delivered. The use of CompraRed was declared mandatory for all Executive Power agencies, but not for decentralized public institutions, other State Powers or local governments.

By 2006, President Arias installed the Digital Government Office, who served to a Commission of Ministers on Digital Government, coordinated by Vice-president Kevin Casas. Mr. Casas gave strong political support to Costa Rican e-government policy. Even with Vice-president Casas resignation and with some good results on e-government projects, the Digital Government Office had continued with projects formulations, including a new State procurement system. In 2008, the Digital Government Office announced a new platform named "Mer-link" with no relation with "CompraRed" either as a product or with government agency responsible (the Department of Treasury has not been taken into account for "Mer-link"). By 2010, strategies differ with no unique solution for public sector and for entrepreneurs. Two periods were analysed with the results shown in Table 10.

Table 10. Feasibility and legitimacy for state procurement in Costa Rica

Period	Feasibility	Legitimacy
2002-2006	0.58	0.55
2006-2010	0.43	0.73

As values show in Table 10, no solution was consolidated by 2010. Even if efforts have been taken, the fact that no actions to provide an institutional framework for the use of unique procurement procedures, decreases the capacity of any solution. Moreover, the existence of two divergent options (CompraRed and Mer-link) has the effect to undermine the feasibility value (as formula (3) predicts due of the existence of divergent solutions), even if legitimacy had increased in the second period. Consider that, if there were just one option, feasibility value could be increased to 0.74. This is a good example, in which feasibility and legitimacy evolve in different directions.

Drivers Licenses and Passport Services in Costa Rica

By 2006, Vice-president Kevin Casas, during President Arias government, promoted the e-government policy in Costa Rica. A presidential decree at the very beginning of Arias Administration, installed the institutional structure for the development of e-government (Costa Rica Presidency of the Republic, 2006). The Digital Government Secretary Alicia Avendaño began a search for projects with low risk both on costs and on political coordination. Two services were selected: the provision of driving permissions (licenses) and passports for citizens.

To that moment, these services were offered in very few points of attention in Costa Rica territory (with just 3 offices for each one) and lines were always crowded. The Costa Rican government made an alliance with a local public bank, the "Banco de Costa Rica" (BCR). This bank was committed to install, in its regional and metropolitan offices, the necessary systems and human resources to provide both services. Once the platform was launched, improved impact on citizen's life was noticed: it was no longer required to travel to far government offices to obtain those documents. The attention time was reduced from 4 hours (in the best of cases) to 15 minutes.

By September 2007, Vice-president Casas resigned from office after the service was consolidated. Since then, just one more service had been added to that platform. Synergies between agencies were lost with the resignation of Vice-president Casas. With model application, the results shown in Table 11 were found.

As is shown in Table 11, very high feasibility and legitimacy values were found for the first period. It shows as well that actors involved were committed to move their resources with high priority. Complexities could be found by coordinating agencies (Migration, Transport, Digital government and Vice-president

Table 11. Feasibility and legitimacy for Drivers licenses and Passports Services in Costa Rica

Period	Feasibility	Legitimacy
2006-2007	0.98	0.98
2007-2010	0.68	0.75

Offices, BCR and others) that only good political leadership could accomplish successfully. During the next period, the project still has a good level of feasibility (near to 0.70), but descending value reflects the poor expansion of new services. As a consolidated platform that helps to promote e-government in Costa Rica, most actors show declarative support, keeping high (but less) legitimacy. Finally, sustainability can be considered as a "government policy" near to reach "state policy" level.

SOLUTIONS AND RECOMMENDATIONS

The model presented on this chapter has aimed to demonstrate how important are actors considering a variety of resources that they can use in order to promote e-government development. The approach made has shown how the project history and results is directly related with actors' performance.

Nevertheless large investments both on economic and IT resources might be done (as State Procurement case in Costa Rica), is now evident that lack of political definitions and leadership (among other considerations analysed) can compromise project success.

In perspective of public policies for e-government development, high political decision-makers have to assess a variety of resources such as the institutional one (both for project development and service operation), recognition (what actors need for having enough empowerment and ability to lead, solve and coordinate political needs of projects), beyond just IT and economic issues.

Designing an e-government project, beside the political objectives definition, needs to define as well how resources could be handled and assigned to actors, in order to reach potential high feasibility and legitimacy.

FUTURE RESEARCH DIRECTIONS

The model presented is an effort to generate indicators that evidence how actors affect policies. In this particular case e-government, viewed as strategic projects to modernize public administration, should impact the good performance on services directed both to people and business.

The application of the model can be strengthen by analysing other services in different national and political contexts. Additionally, its use in prospective mode could bring some strategic predictions in order to make more accurate decisions for future projects.

Some particularities of the model, for example if other resources are added for veto power could be justified depending on the context or policy analysed. Yet, the basis of the model, illustrated on Figure 1, can remain without alteration.

As well, some methodologies applied to specific resources may improve model application. For example, the analysis of information retrieved in social networks by using advanced computer techniques could assess important parameters as "declarations" of an actor. It would be important to identify some components of the model where massive information analysis and other computer sciences methods could help for obtain more accurate data.

In conclusion, to review some characteristics of the model and to apply it in prospective mode as well to deepening its use on social aspects, such as responding questions like "why some societies are more likely to develop e-government policies?" are in the horizon of new researches.

CONCLUSION

More than ten years have been passed since authors like Porter (2001) or Carr (2003) argued that IT resources weren't sufficient for good and sustainable strategies in business. Analogously, public sector experiences showed that strategic use of IT should be contextualized on politic goals that are capable to attract actors' support. Indeed, the model application on four cases selected showed how the actors' involvement, characterized as support from their power resources, could effect on success or failure on developing e-government services.

Beyond typologies made on e-government, like those proposed by Fountain (2001) or Layne and Lee (2001) that were used on specific analysis such as elaborated by UNPAN, political and policy constraints shall to be understood in order to assess what critical factors are important for that kind of projects.

Characteristics such as solving leadership on complex projects with the participation of multiple agencies (International Trade Services on Chile), institutional requirements (ChileCompra), choosing and implementing a unique solution (State Procurement on Costa Rica) or granting political priority (Platform Services on Costa Rica and ChileCompra) is clear evidence on how actors' could affect policies on e-government.

Some guidelines can be drawn from this research. Empowering actors by using resources on multiple dimensions could help in policy design. Beyond leadership, to gain political support in any phase of public policies supported by e-government strategies, shall impact on success.

REFERENCES

Association for Progressive Communications. (2004). *Monitor Políticas TIC y Derechos en Internet en América Latina y el Caribe*. Retrieved October 5 2008 from http://lac.derechos.apc.org/

Barria, D., & Araya, E. (2008). Modernización del Estado y Gobierno Electrónico en Chile 1990-2006. *Buen Gobierno*, 80-130.

Barros, A., Ruiz, C., Cerda, A., & Martínez, H. (2012). *polisDigital*. Santiago de Chile: Centro de Sistemas Públicos, Ingeniería Industrial, Universidad de Chile.

Benavides, P. (2011). *La Ventanilla Única de Comercio Exterior: Factores claves de éxito* [Unpublished master's dissertation]. Universidad de Chile. Santiago de Chile.

BID / Government of Chile. (2008). Chile: Evaluación del Sistema Nacional de Compras y Contrataciones Públicas. Santiago de Chile: Gobierno de Chile.

Bolgherini, S. (2007). The Technological Trap and the Rol of Political and Cultural Variables: A Critical Analysis of E-Government Policies. *Review of Political Research*, 24(3), 259–275. doi:10.1111/j.1541-1338.2007.00280.x

Bunge, M. (1999). *Buscar la filosofía en las ciencias sociales*. México: Siglo XXI.

Carr, N. (2003, May). IT Doesn't Matter. *Harvard Bussiness Review*, 5-12.

Castells, M. (2009). *Comunicación y Poder*. Madrid: Alianza Editorial.

Chile Ministry of Treasury. (2005). *Informe Final Programa Proyecto Isidora.* Santiago de Chile: Ministerio de Hacienda.

Chile Presidential Comission on New Information Technologies. (1999). *Chile: hacia la sociedad de la información.* Santiago de Chile: Presidencia de la República de Chile.

Cortés-Morales, R. (2013). *Análisis comparado de las políticas públicas de gobierno digital en Costa Rica y Chile entre los años 2002 y 2010* [Unpublished doctoral dissertation]. Universidad de Costa Rica. San José, Costa Rica.

Cortés-Morales, R., & Marín-Raventós, G. (2012a). *An analytical model to measure feasibility on e-government policies. Internet Technologies & Society 2012* (pp. 69–76). Perth, Australia: IADIS Press.

Cortés-Morales, R., & Marín-Raventós, G. (2012b). *El desarrollo del gobierno digital: la perspectiva basada en actores para el caso de las compras del Estado en Costa Rica. XXXVIII Conferencia Latinoamericana en Computación e Informática 2012* (p. 91). Medellín, Colombia: CLEI.

Costa Rica General Republic Comptroller. (2012). *Informe sobre las iniciativas que impulsan el gobierno digital y una sociedad basada en la información y el conocimiento.* San José de Costa Rica: CGR.

Costa Rica Presidency of the Republic. (2006). *Gobierno Fácil.* Retrieved from http://www.gobiernofacil.go.cr/e-gob/gobiernodigital/ebooks/Decreto_Comision_de_Gobierno_Digital.pdf

Fernández, O. (2002). Weber y Foucault. *Reflexiones, 2*(81).

Fleury, S. (2002). El desafío de la gestión de las redes de políticas. *Revista Instituciones y Desarrollo,* (12-13), 221-247.

Fountain, J. (2001). The Virtual State: Transforming American Government? *National Civic Review, 90*(3), 241–251. doi:10.1002/ncr.90305

Godet, M. (2007). *Prospectiva Estratégica: problemas y métodos.* San Sebastián, España: Cuadernos de Liptor.

Klijn, E. (1998). Redes de Políticas Públicas: una visión general. In W. Kickert & J. F. Koppenjan (Eds.), *Managing Complex Networks* (M. Petrizzo, Trans.). London: Sage.

Korteland, E., & Bekkers, V. (2007). Diffusion of E-government innovations in the Dutch public sector: The case of digital community policing. *Information Polity, 12,* 139–150.

La Nación. (2008, July 18). Pasaportes y licencias. *La Nación.* Retrieved from http://www.nacion.com/opinion/Pasaportes-licencias_0_989301101.html

Layne, K., & Lee, J. (2001). Developing fully functional E-government: A four stage model. *Government Information Quarterly, 18*(2), 122–136. doi:10.1016/S0740-624X(01)00066-1

North, D. C. (1990). *Institutions, Institutional Change and Economic Performance.* Cambridge, MA: Cambridge University Press. doi:10.1017/CBO9780511808678

Porter, M. E. (2001, March). Strategy and Internet. *Harvard Bussiness Review.*

Prats, J. (2001). Gobernabilidad democrática para el desarrollo humano. Marco conceptual y analítico. *Revista Instituciones y Desarrollo*, 103-148.

Shepsle, K. A., & Bonchek, M. S. (2005). *Las Fórmulas de la Política*. México: Taurus.

Subirats, J., Knoepfel, P., Larrue, C., & Varonne, F. (2008). *Análisis y Gestión de Políticas Públicas*. Barcelona: Ariel.

Tolbert, C. J., & Mossberger, K. (2006, May-June). The Effects of E-Government on Trust and Confidence in Government. *Public Administration Review, 66*(3), 354–369. doi:10.1111/j.1540-6210.2006.00594.x

Tsebelis, G. (2001). *Veto Players: How Political Institutions Work*. Princenton, NJ: Princeton University Press.

UNPAN. (2003). *UN Global E-Government Survey 2003*. New York: United Nations.

UNPAN. (2004). *Global E-Readiness Report 2004*. New York: United Nations.

UNPAN. (2005). *Global E-Government Readiness Report 2005: from E-Government to E-Inclusion*. New York: United Nations.

UNPAN. (2008). *UN E-Government Survey 2008: From E-Government to Connected Governance*. New York: United Nations.

UNPAN. (2010). *United Nations E-Government Survey 2010: leveragin e-goverment at a time of financial and economic crisis*. New York: United Nations.

World Bank. (2012a). *Exportaciones de productos de TIC (% de las exportaciones de productos)*. Retrieved from http://datos.bancomundial.org/indicador/TX.VAL.ICTG.ZS.UN

World Bank. (2012b). *Data*. Retrieved from http://datos.bancomundial.org/indicador/GC.XPN.TOTL.GD.ZS

World Bank. (2012c). *Data*. Retrieved from http://datos.bancomundial.org/income-level/UMC

KEY TERMS AND DEFINITIONS

Actor: An individual or group that has a unique interest in a policy context (Subirats et al., 2008).
Feasibility: Measure based on actors' veto power that indicates how feasible a public policy could be.
Legitimacy: Measure based on actors' support that indicates how legitimate a public policy could be.
Support: How actor supports a given policy by declarations or performing actions.
Sustainability: Characteristic of any public policy with high feasibility based on the legitimacy computed for such policy.
Veto Power: The capacity of an actor to maintain the political status quo (Tsebelis, 2001). In the case of this research different resources are used to measure actor's veto power.

Chapter 9
Enterprise Architecture for Business Objectives:
Understanding the Influencing Factors

Leshoto Mphahlele
Tshwane University of Technology, Pretoria, South Africa

Tiko Iyamu
Cape Peninsula University of Technology, South Africa

ABSTRACT

The demand for better services by customers and citizens keeps increasing at a rapid rate, enabling organizations the leverage towards competitive advantage. The enterprise architecture (EA) has merged as a possible solution for addressing organizational challenges, as well as for competitiveness and sustainability. The EA deployment involves agents, which are both human and non-human. The agents, based on their interest, influences and determines how the EA is deployed. During the deployment of EA, agents transform themselves in accordance to their interest at the time and space, making the process challenging in achieving the organisational needs. As examined and presented by this chapter, understanding of agents' interests is significant if the challenges that they pose are to be managed for successful deployment of EA. The chapter presents the impact of agents on the deployment of EA in organizations, through the lens of structuration theory.

1. INTRODUCTION

Many organizations, including government agencies, have realized the significance of the EA. There is a growing interest in organizations to adopt the EA, to assist mitigating the challenges of constant and complex changes (Strohmaier & Deng, 2006). Some of the factors that pose challenges to competitive advantage of organizations are adaptiveness, uniformity and scalability. EA is a tool that enhances the organization in terms of the objectives pursued at the time. This is argued to be done through its capability to improve the business processes, applications, data and infrastructure through standardization (Van de Raadt & Vliet, 2008).

DOI: 10.4018/978-1-4666-8524-6.ch009

The EA consists of different domains, which include business, information, application, technology, infrastructure and service oriented architecture. According to Iyamu (2010), the focus and deliverables of the EA domains manifests in the relationship and connectivity among the domains during the implementation phase of the EA. Thus, the completion of each domain contributes towards the success of developing and implementing the EA in the organization. However, organizations continue to fail to define the individual domains and their connectivity, thereby increasing complexity in the deployment of EA (Glissmann & Sanz, 2011).

Each of the domains of EA has its distinct roles and boundaries. According to Hafner and Winter (2008), the business architecture represents the enterprise model, which includes service exchanges and financial flows in value networks and strategies. The domain of information architecture covers data and information of all types, and their usage, interrelationships and demographics, as well as their definitions, ownership, distribution, and composition (Iyer & Gottlieb, 2004). The application domain provides a foundation and guidance to the organization, on how to develop and implement application for business competitive advantage (Pereira & Sousa, 2004). According to Pulkkinen (2006), the "Technical dimension covers the technologies and technological structures used to build the information and communication systems in the enterprise".

EA is developed and implemented sequentially, in accordance to the domains: from business to technical architectures. This is to enable logical flow and manage the dependence of the domains. During the development and implementation interactions happen among technical and non-technical agents (factors). Some of the factors include people, process and technology. According to Wang and Zhao (2004), the development of the EA means adopting approaches that incorporate the people, processes, business and technology to achieve the organizational goals and objectives. The interaction that takes place during development and implementation makes the processes and technologies to be understood and interpreted differently by individuals and groups. This is often to assert individual power. Iyamu (2009) argued that during the implementation, power is exercised to protect individual's interests, which shapes the outcome of information technology strategies in the organization.

The primary aim of the chapter was to understand the impact of social dynamics as embedded into organizational structure, on the deployment of the EA in organizations. Based on this goal, interpretive case study was employed, and structuration theory (ST) was selected as the theory that underpinned the chapter.

Structuration theory involves and focuses on processes and interactions that take place between actors and structural features within social context. The key tenets of structuration theory are agent (or agency) and structure. Agents are both technical and non-technical. To be categorized as an agent, individuals or technical artifacts need to have the capability to make a difference (Giddens, 1984).

2. ENTERPRISE ARCHITECTURE

The scope of enterprise architecture (EA) includes various domains such as information, business, and technical within an organization. The domains constitute both technical and non-technical artifacts, such as people, process and technology. The scope of EA emphasizes processes, people, information and technology, and their relationship (Orlikowski, 1992). The EA is intended for various objectives, such as transformation, from one organization to another. As organization transform, both human and non-human agents also transform. According to Aier and Weiss (2002), the Enterprise Architecture Management is intended to support and coordinate enterprise transformation. Jonkers et al (2006) argued the significance of the EA in organizations, and that it can assist in the development of strategies which can be incorporated into different areas such as: (1) existing processes, (2) ICT infrastructure and (3) other modules of the organizations.

Despite the increasing interest and the growing need for EA, there remain many challenging factors, which include process, people and technology. According to Kaisler et al (2005), there exist many challenges and problems continue in the development and implementation of EA. These challenges are rarely technical, but arise from process and people, which are often connected to political. According to Chuang and Lobberenberg (2010), some of the critical elements to consider when adopting the EA are processes, communication, organization politics, and ownership.

3. RESEARCH METHODOLOGY

The case study research method was adopted. The strengths of the case study approach is in its flexibility to allow the researcher to freely use his or her ability to attain a variety of information within context. A South African company, Bakgaga Network Services (BNS) was used as the case study. The company selection was based on two main factors, accessibility and evidence of EA deployment. According to Yin (2009), the most commonly used techniques for collecting data in a case study includes interviews.

The semi-structured interview technique was employed, which enable the research to probe (in depth) why things happened in the way that they did in the environment. Iyamu (2011) emphasises the critique of knowing why, where and how to collect data. In Gray (2009), the ability of probing further questions in the semi-structured interview allows the exploration of paths that have not yet been considered. A total of 14 employees were interviewed. The employees were from both business and IT departments, and at different levels of the organizational structure. The data was interpretively analyzed, using the duality of structure of the structuration theory.

As shown in Figure 1, the duality of structure covers structure, modality and interaction. In structuration theory, human actions are enabled and constrained by structures, yet that these structures are the result of previous actions (Gray, 2009).

Interaction happens between agents in a recursive characteristic manner within structure which they are a part. As depicted in Figure 1, interaction with structure is through modality, which is categorized into interpretative scheme, facility and norms. The dependency of agents and structure on each other to produce and reproduce actions overtime is referred to as duality of structure.

Figure 1. Duality of Structure
(Giddens, 1984)

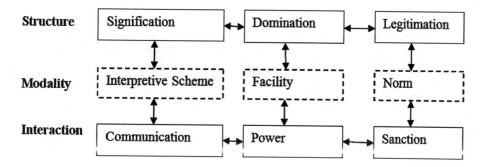

4. DATA ANALYSIS: STRUCTURATION VIEW

The objective of the chapter is to investigate and understand the social dynamics embedded within the organizational structure, and their role and impact on the deployment (development and implementation) of the EA. The ST was adopted to facilitate the investigation and analyse the data. In the chapter, data was collected from one organization, using the interview technique. The analysis of the data is presented as follows:

A. Agent

In structuration, agents are both human and non-human. The deployment (development and implementation) of the EA in the organization involves employees (human agents) such as the Chief Information Officer (CIO), IT architects, business analysts, IT managers, and project managers.

The development of the EA was carried out by the IT architects, under the leadership of the Chief Architect in conjunction with the CIO. The employees that were involved in or responsible for the deployment were not necessarily the ones who were involved in the implementation of the EA in the organization. The implementers of the EA include employees such as IT managers, IT architects, and other technologists. According to one of the employees, *"The offices of the CIO in conjunction with the Chief Architect are responsible for the development, as well as the implementation of the EA in the organization"*. In the deployment of the EA, the employees are confined and act within structure (rules and resources). They were perceived to have some form of degree of influence during the deployment of the EA in the organization.

B. Structure

The deployment of the EA in the organization was carried out through adherence to rules and regulations, using available resources. The rules and regulations, including governance and standards were formulated within the organizational requirements as mandated by the organization.

The resources required in the deployment were vitally critical in determining the deployment of the EA in the organization. The resources included human (skills), finance and technology (software and hardware). One of the interviewees stated: *"the resources used in the deployment of the EA are driven by the organizational strategy and requirements"*. Agents and structures depend on each other. Agents operate with structures, and structures exist or are created by agents. In the process, they both produce and reproduce actions in duality.

C. Duality of Structure

The duality of Structure enacts the interaction between human and the structural properties (rules and resources) during the deployment (development and implementation) of the EA in the organization. The structures and interactions that took place during the deployment of the EA were of socio-technical nature. In Table 1 below, the structuration theory analysis of the deployment of the EA is summarised. The discussion that follows after the table should be read together with the table to get a full appreciation of the analysis with duality of structure in the deployment of the EA in the organisation.

Table 1. Enterprise Architecture Deployment

Significance	Domination	Legitimation
The EA was essentially important in the organisation. Hence its accountability was with the CIO, at the highest level in accordance with the organisational hierarchy.	Under the auspices of the CIO, the IT architects and managers were responsible for the deployment of the EA in the organisation.	The EA is deployed within rules and regulations, as mandated by the organisation.
Interpretative Scheme	**Facility**	**Norms**
The EA documents the current state and defines the strategic direction of technology, as well as business processes in the organisation.	The organisation uses different technologies, individuals' roles, responsibilities and skills during the deployment of the EA.	The EA was deployed in accordance with organisational definition of business processes, standards, rules and regulations. The deployment was carried out along on EA domains' perspectives.
Communication	**Power**	**Sanction**
There was interaction between the CIO and the Chief Architect. There was little communication between the CIO and the domain architects who carry out the actual deployment of the EA.	The CIO uses the organisational mandate to instruct the deployment of the EA. IT architects and managers used authority bestowed on them to protect their individual interests during the deployment of the EA.	The deployment of the EA was approved by the CIO, chief architect, the domain Architects and other stakeholders.

Duality of Structure: Signification and Communication

In the organization, the deployment of the EA was critical for both IT and business strategies. In the organization, the EA was generally considered important mainly for competitive advantage, through its technological and business processes. A senior manager expressed his view as follows:

... the EA plays a very critical role, mainly because it bridges business strategies with information technology capabilities in achieving the organizational strategies.

The EA was carried out by different individuals and groups (units) within the organizational structure. The individuals' roles and responsibilities were critical in the deployment of the EA, and as such, needed to be clearly defined. The deployment of the EA requires collaboration among all stakeholders. As such, employees who were involved in the process needed to fully understand their roles, responsibilities and accountabilities. Understanding was vested in the communication among the stakeholders and their interpretation of the events, processes and activities. Many of the employees in the organization seemed to understand the significance of their individual roles, as one of the interviewees put it:

If the individual's roles and responsibilities are not clearly defined, you can delay the deployment of the EA in the organization, and this could put the company at risk.

The deployment of the EA was based on the organizational strategy, technology and business requirements. The IT architects and business analysts gathered the requirements from the business managers and users. The requirements were interpreted and translated into architectural requirements, thereafter, documented. The tasks of coordinating the gathering of both technology and business requirements and translation to architectural requirements were performed by the IT architects.

The organization had a procedural approach, which was used to allocate tasks for the deployment of the EA in the organization. The tasks were allocated and communicated to teams and units based on their accountability, specialties and area of focus. Both the IT and business units shared the tasks depending on the domain. The tasks were drilled down from units to individual level. One of the managers explained in detail:

Normally tasks are assigned by the project owner. These tasks correspond with individual skills, experience and responsibilities, for example, a business analyst will be responsible for gathering and analyzing the business requirements.

Unfortunately, the communication channel as defined by the organizational structure was not strictly or often followed. Employees seem to be divided into groups and networks of friends as opposed to the organizational structures and channels. The employees associated themselves in accordance with where and with whom they find comfort. According to one of the employees, a senior manager,

… we are one team in IT, but there are different groups within the team. The reason for the formation of the groups is because some people want to shine and share information among their groups.

Due to the lack of structured communication among the stakeholders, the processes and efforts in the deployment of the EA was a challenge and became difficult to manage in the organization. Implications of the lack of structured communication included lack of collaboration, which often derailed the deployment of the EA through certain factors such as personalization of events and reluctance to cooperate. It also manifests to lack of synergy between business and IT stakeholders in the deployment of EA in the organization.

The deployment of the EA was influenced by certain factors, which were both human and non-human. These factors led to some individuals and groups being dominant and powerful during the deployment of the EA in the organization.

Duality of Structure: Domination and Power

Under the auspices of the CIO and sectional heads of departments, the IT unit was instructed and made accountable for the deployment of the EA in the organization. One of the senior managers explained:

… the CIO and senior personnel in the organization within IT are obliged to ensure that EA is deployed to deliver on the business objectives.

All technology including the EA matters were made the sole responsibility and accountability of the IT unit. However, the participation of the business was critical, because EA was driven by the organizational strategies and objectives. Unfortunately, the business division participation was a challenge. This challenge was a derailing factor in the deployment of the EA. The challenge was a derailing factor mainly because the IT unit depended on the business for funding of its activities, processes and events. As has been established so far in this analysis, the deployment of the EA involved many people (employees) from different units of the organization, which includes varieties of specialized skills and based on requirements as defined by the organizational structure. Some of these employees were responsible for enabling and managing the processes and activities during the deployment of the EA.

Enterprise Architecture for Business Objectives

However, the organization didn't seem to have sufficient skills and knowledgeable employees to facilitate and carry out the activities that were involved in the deployment of the EA. The deployment of the EA was done through its domains, which included information, business, application and technology architectures. The insufficient skills posed a serious challenge during the deployment of the EA in the organization. Some of the interviewees as echoed by their colleagues commented:

I used to work with the EA team, and I realised that most of the people where wearing big shoes "they are not fit to hold the positions as Architects.

The roles and responsibilities played a vital role during the EA deployment. The roles and responsibilities of the individuals were influenced by the relationship many of them had with their colleagues. The relationships were built on working together over the years and between employees with good (acclaimed better) knowledge of the subject. Some of the employees used the relationship that they had with their colleagues to influence decisions during the deployment of the EA. One of the interviewee's observed:

Sometimes when you propose something relating to enterprise architecture, it feels like you stepped on someone's domain. This is because some people believe they own certain things in the organization, so they become negative towards change and they could dictate the activities of the EA.

Influences as controlled and managed by certain individuals were caused mainly because there was no proper performance contract and appraiser system in place. Managers could use their prerogative and the mandate bestowed on them to make decisions as they wished.

Unfortunately, some employees used their knowledge and expertise of the technologies to pursue reasons other than the organization's interest in EA deployment. These employees used their knowledge as a source of control and manipulation in the decisions that were made during the deployment of the EA in the organization. These employees used their expertise and stock of knowledge of the technologies as mechanism to control and demonstrate authority over their colleagues when it came to carrying out technological tasks during EA deployment. Such practices had an impact on the deployment of the EA in the organization. An interviewee explained:

People guide their domains, guide their intellectual property (IP), and don't want to move or change. It is about job security.

Some employees in the organization overlooked the importance of the EA deployment, instead focused on personal gains or interests. These groups of employees resisted and reluctantly accepted tasks that were allocated to them, whenever they felt that events and activities in the deployment of the EA were not in their interest. Such practices had an impact on the deployment of the EA as it discouraged some employees from participating in activities and processes of the EA. One of the senior managers explained that:

You find that there are people who run their own regimes, and if the EA is not going to benefit them and it's of no use to participate in the process.

The organization formulated a mandate to ensure the deployment of the EA. Different employees carried out the mandate using various technologies at various times. The employees' roles and responsibilities, including the stock of knowledge they acquired over time were instrumental during the deployment of the EA. The manifestation of individual's interests and agendas was a huge challenge that threatened the efforts of the organization in achieving the benefits of the EA.

Duality of Structure: Legitimation and Sanction

The deployment of the EA followed and adhered to the organizational rules and regulations; thereby making it required approval from various authorities along the organizational structure. The rules and regulations including available resources ensured that the deliverables of the EA fulfill the business requirements and needs for competitive advantage. A manager expressed her view as:

The business rules are what drive the EA deployment. If there is a rule that specifies what to do or not to, this decision is critical to assist the configuration of the different domains of the EA.

The managers and team leaders were responsible for ensuring that the deployment of the EA was carried out within the rules and regulations of the organization. They also enforced and ensured that their staff adhered to those rules and regulations in carrying out their individual and group tasks.

Even though the managers did all they could to ensure that employees carried out their tasks as allocated and adhered to the rules and regulations, some of the employees were reluctant to abide. The rules and regulations were difficult to enforce mainly because the culture of the organization allowed individual independence and there was no performance contract and appraiser within which employees' activities could be managed. One of the team leaders explained:

In our case, corporate governance is a set of rules, regulations and guidelines. We expect you to adhere to them, but if you don't adhere to them, you won't be penalized.

As a result of such a culture of individual independence and flexibility, many standards and principles existed in the environment. Some of these standards and principles were not documented, they were individualized. This resulted to duplications of processes and activities in the deployment of the EA in the organization. This implication defeated some of the benefits and intended deliverables of the EA. One of the interviewees explained:

Because we followed different standards, the work was not consistent, because we were all from IT but when we went to business we provided different things.

The executive committee in the organization approved the deployment of the EA. The decision was primarily based on the available resources including the organizational rules and regulations. In summary, rules, regulations and resources were vital and critical; hence it was significant how they were applied in the deployment of the EA. This makes the organizational structure very important, mainly because different degrees of power are associated with and assigned to various levels in the organizational structure.

5. FINDINGS AND DISCUSSION

From the analysis, using the duality of structure from the perspective of the structuration, some factors were found to be critical in the deployment of the EA in the organization. The factors as depicted in Figure 2 were viewed as critical, because they could play a multifunctional role, as enablers and with the same constraints. The factors include communication channel, task allocation, and awareness, stock of knowledge, skills transfer, and value measurement. These factors are discussed below:

D. Communication Channel

Communication is critical. Through it, awareness is gained; knowledge is transferred; understanding is achieved; and much more. It is even more important that communication is carried out through the channel; otherwise, the purposes and intentions as highlighted above would be defeated.

A communication channel was critical to the EA deployment in the organization. It was intended to enable synergy between the EA stakeholders. This was not the case in terms of the relationship between the IT and business units. Not only was the communication lacking between the IT and business units, but due to the individual and group practices, communication within the IT unit itself was hampered, resulting in factors such as personalized interests being more functional.

As revealed by the analysis of the data, the business unit had lost confidence and trust in the organization's IT unit. This was a manifestation of the lack of information and communication among the stakeholders including the business unit. The lack of information sharing and communication through structured channels continuously hamper the deployment of the EA. The business unit, which was the primary sponsor, thought that the IT unit was not delivering on its strategic mandate. As such they began to withdraw their support for the EA deployment.

Even when the information was shared and communicated, the content was perceived and interpreted differently by the EA stakeholders in the organization. Some employees relied on their individual stock of knowledge to convey and interpret the deployment of EA and the tasks they were assigned to perform.

Figure 2. Factors influencing EA deployment

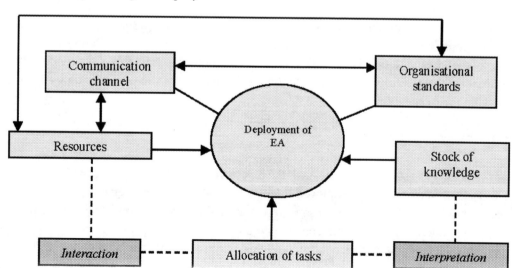

E. Stock of Knowledge

In terms of stock of knowledge, two things are fundamental, how knowledge is stored, and how it is applied. Knowledge is often filtered before it is stored, otherwise, it would be of little or no value. On the other hand, if knowledge is applied appropriately, it would defeat its intended aim, as well as lose value.

It was critical for the organization to ensure that the tasks allocated to individuals, complemented and were aligned to their skills, knowledge and experience. This is mainly because the EA deployment relies intensively on best practices and skills. This has proved to be a challenge as most of the participating stakeholders, particularly, newly appointed IT architects seemed to lack the necessary skills and knowledge required for EA deployment. Those who had experience and knowledge of the EA held on to it, and used it as their sources of power to dominate and negotiate things of personal interests such as promotion and remuneration increases.

The analysis of the data also revealed that the inexperience and the lack of stock of knowledge had implications and an impact on the deliverables of the EA in the organization. This limitation provided some people with leverage over others. The majority of the people used it to command the space they occupied. The chief architect had the authority to dictate the approaches and methods through which the EA could be deployed. Certainly, the knowledge and skills for the EA deployment was lacking in the organization. The deployment of the EA was challenged because a lack of knowledge hampered people's capabilities to perform tasks and utilize EA technologies, approaches and methods.

F. Task Allocation

The tasks were an important aspect of the deployment of the EA. They represented the work that needed to be done. It was clear that the organization needed to clearly define its tasks, ensuring that employees were aware of the accountability and expected contributions of the EA deployment.

Unfortunately, many of the employees found fault on how tasks were allocated in the deployment of the EA in the organization. As a result, some employees did not, and other reluctantly accepted the tasks that were allocated to them. The fault was related to the claim that some of the tasks allocated to them did not align with their skills and experiences, and that some of their colleagues were favored.

Due to the lack of satisfaction among the employees, some of them did not take full responsibility for their lack of participation during the deployment of EA. Also, the allocation of tasks enabled the organization to assess the required technology, its usage and distribution to different teams. This was not the case with Bakgaga Networking Services, because evidence showed that people who have been in service longer had the authority to choose who they wanted to work with, and also how resources were to be utilized in the organization.

G. Organizational Standards

The organization mandated the deployment of the EA to be carried out within specified requirements and standards. The standards were employed to ensure that the EA delivered on its mandate to serve, enable and support the business requirements, processes and activities, using available resources. The standards enabled and at the same time constrained employees' actions during the deployment of the EA. It was important to establish such control measures, because employees' actions tend to be driven by individual beliefs and interests as opposed to organizational objectives. The standards were sometimes constraining factors, as some of them (standards) were not compatible or easy to integrate. But it was clear that some employees in the organization didn't adhere to the organizational standards. This had impact on the EA deployment. For example, some technologies were duplicated.

The analysis revealed that the standards were often not enforced by the employees. This was attributed to the fact that employees' actions were not monitored during the deployment of the EA. The culture was that some employees defined their own standards that had an impact on the EA, causing their actions to derail processes and activities.

Some of the employees explained that although there were organizational standards in place, some of the employees did not adhere to them as a form of protest. This resulted from a claim that some senior personnel promoted individuals to the architect positions based on their relationship, instead of their competency to perform the work. This culture is a legitimised practice in the organization, based on the power and mandate bestowed on the managers, that they could apply their prerogative to make final decisions. As a result, the process of advancing employees to positions as defined by the organization was often not adhered to.

H. Resources

Resources that included technology, people and processes were crucial during the deployment of the EA in the organization. The different technologies, which were necessary to facilitate the EA deployment, were always at the disposal of certain individuals and teams. The use and distribution of these technologies was intended to be managed through organizational standards. Unfortunately, these technologies were used as mediums for championing personal agendas, accumulating control and authority. Some of the employees in the organization withheld what was bestowed to them to nourish their self-interests.

The analysis highlighted that the significance of resources to them confirms their importance, authority and commanding capabilities; hence they constantly protect the resources because without them, they would be perceived as redundant and powerless in the organization. As a result of such human practices, the EA deployment could suffer setbacks. It is important that the use and distribution of such resources is enforced and instructed by the organizational standards at all times.

The findings from the analysis help to understand some of the factors that influence the deployment (development and implementation) of the EA in organizations. The factors as presented above were further examined (interpreted). The interpretations of the findings are discussed in the section that follows.

6. INTERPRETATION OF THE FINDINGS

As the chapter seeks to understand the roles and impact of organisational structure on the deployment of the EA, the findings above are interpreted to further elaborate upon why organisations deployed the EA is in the way they do. The interpretations are aimed at understanding how and why things (factors from the findings) happened the way they did in the deployment of the EA in the organisation. The above findings were interpreted into factors namely, awareness, skills alignment, requirements alignment and governance. These factors as depicted in Figure 3 are dependent and are simultaneously significant to the value of the EA in the organisation. The factors are discussed below.

Figure 3. EA deployment in the organisation

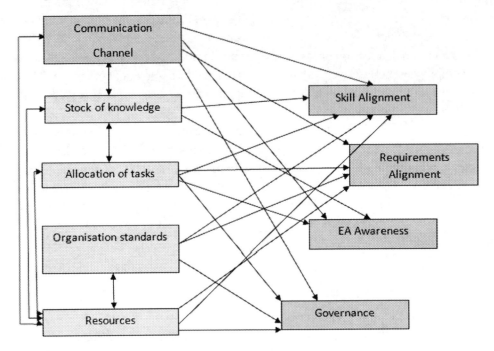

The EA Deployment in the Organisation

The deployment of EA in organisations is characterised by factors presented herewith. The factors are interpretation from the findings which were gathered from the analysis. This generalisation is based on this empirical study. The communication channel was intended to be used as a medium for communicating the significance of the EA deployment in the organisation. This includes vital factors such as skills alignment, requirements alignment, awareness and governance, which has an impact on or influences the deployment of the EA. Through the application of stock of knowledge and using the other available resources (such as technology), the employees in the organisation interpreted and carried out their tasks in the development and implementation (deployment) of the EA. In the deployment of the EA, stock of knowledge was also used as a source of power and influence during the allocation of tasks as it draws on skills and awareness.

The allocation of tasks was influenced by and depended on available skills (other resources included), organisational requirements, awareness of the employees, and the governing of activities and events. Another influencing factor is the channel through which the tasks are communicated to the employees and the general stakeholders. The organisational standards relating to the EA was formulated based on the organisational requirements. It is intended to be enforced using individual and group skills. The organisational standards require monitoring, measurement and management within the organisational governance. The resources required for the deployment of the EA are influenced by and managed through and by skills, requirements alignment and governance, on the one hand.

On the other hand, they require stock of knowledge, understanding of how tasks are allocated, and a communication channel to make proper use of the resources and improve upon desirability. Governance is of significant value in the deployment of the EA. The governance includes standards, principles and policies. The principles and policies guide the selection, use and management of technologies and processes, and the activities involved in them. In the deployment of the EA, the organisation depended on the defined standards to enable and facilitate the allocation of tasks and communication channels. The standards provided some form of guidelines to the employees on the rules and regulations for the deployment. Some of the employees felt compelled to follow them, but others refused; there was a great sense that the organisation had standards but failed to enforce them on the employees. Unfortunately, there were negative results, as evidenced. For example, some resources that were utilised in the deployment of the EA were not guided by the organisation's standards. This was because some employees in the organisation had the capabilities to control resources to protect their own territories. This was derailing the deployment of the EA in the organisation. Resources are important and they need to be assigned to competent employees, based on their stock of knowledge and capabilities; otherwise they run the risk of being redundant to the tasks allocated.

i. Skill Alignment

In the organisation, the EA deployment includes a basket of people from different organisations' units. These people represented a container of different skills and expertise that were critical towards the EA deployment. It was important that the organisation assess the current resources (people, technology and processes) available, to ensure that they are integrated into the EA deployment. The integration was intended to ensure that available skills were aligned according to the EA deployment tasks and the technology utilised. Unfortunately, the organisation was faced with manifolds of challenges including the EA skills shortage.

Such challenges impeded the EA deployment in terms of delayed processes, failure to implement some technologies. There were other factors that impeded the skills alignment in the organisation, such as the senior personnel being protective of their resources and incompetent individuals promoted to architects. Some of the managers refrained from committing their staff to the EA deployment because they prioritised their activities as more important. As a result of individual prioritisation practices in the organisation, the EA deployment was given less consideration in terms of budget, time and human capital; and this also challenged the alignment between IT and business.

Other factors contributing to the skills alignment in the organisation include promotion tactics in the organisation. Some of the employees were promoted based on their affiliation to senior personnel or key decision-makers in the organisation. The decision to promote individuals to architectural positions should be on merit and their capability, instead of personal relationships. As a result of such promotion tactics, the organisation had architects who failed to interpret and carry out processes and implement some of the technologies required in the EA deployment; this had a huge impact on the EA deployment in the organisation. The factors that are identified above as challenging to skills alignment when it came to the EA deployment were manifestations of the effect of organisational structure. The organisational structure plays a vital and critical role as it influences and dictates rules and regulations within which events produce and reproduce themselves in the organisation.

ii. Requirements Alignment

The organisational environment included different working spaces in terms of IT and business needs. The business was responsible for defining the strategies and objectives, while the IT was mandated to support and enable the strategies and objectives through technological artefacts, as well as manage all technology-related matters in the organisation. Hence, IT had the sole responsibility to develop and implement the EA in the organisation. However, the EA should be a collaborative effort between the two units (IT and business) but business distanced itself in terms of partaking in the actual deployment process. Hence, the technological interpretation of the business objectives and strategies that were required for the EA deployment became difficult. There were some issues, which included personalisation, and individualisation, which led to some employees' failure to commit to alignment. Even though the organisational structure was opposed to these acts, the same organisational structure fortified the power of the individuals to enact the actions. This culture was gradually normalised in the organisation, and it hampered the EA deployment as employees increasingly became reluctant to cooperate or commit to requirements gathering and alignment.

The formation of groups and societies within the organisation also contributed to the lack of cooperation among other employees when it came to aligning both business and IT alignments. These groups were formed within the organisational structure without the executives having full knowledge of the effect. The groupings as enforced through the organisational structure thereby allowed certain individuals to strengthen their authority and drive political agendas. The diversity of stakeholders rationalised the importance of continuous participation and commitment throughout the EA deployment. Such participation should be enabled and managed by governance in the organisation. Unfortunately, as observed in the skills alignment, governance is continuously challenged in all spheres, including the requirement alignment and lack of commitment in the EA deployment. The intention was to use the organisational structure to outline individual roles and responsibilities. Although this was not often the case, some of the employees found it difficult to carry out processes and such difficulties were due to their lack of experience and skills. This lack related to issues including the misinterpretation of requirements. Some of the employees found it difficult to relate the business requirements with different domains of the EA. The lack of vision also led to some of the senior personnel viewing the EA deployment as a foreign entity, thus refraining from participating in the process. This entitled the issues of institutionalising the EA deployment in the organisation. Thus, the institutionalisation of the EA should be enabled and managed by governance.

iii. EA Awareness

The deployment of the EA is as important as its awareness. It helps the stakeholders, particularly employees from the business unit, to understand the concept and intentions in the organisation. The awareness helps the stakeholders to make decisions on whether to be interested and participate; hence the content of the awareness is critical. Awareness could be carried out in various channels and mediums. Although the organisation has taken the initiative to deploy and practice the EA, some of the employees were not aware of the activities, processes and events. One of the employees indicated that the person responsible for managing the architects was still a manager for another department.

It was clear that the roles and responsibilities in the organisational structure or organogram were not clearly defined and communicated. All these deficiencies indicated that the EA deployment was not strongly communicated, and also indicated the critical role of the organisational structure on the EA in the organisation. The organisation had external expertise assisting with the deployment. Unfortunately some employees were reluctant to participate or receive the EA. This is mainly because the efforts of the EA do not align with the organisational structure. This resulted in the deployment of the EA not being fully supported by many employees in the organisation and such resistance manifested the misinterpretation and lack of awareness of the EA in the organisation.

iv. Governance

The governance was an important element in the EA deployment. It provided a set of artefacts necessary to enable and manage the EA deployment process. Some of its capabilities included defining the decision-making processes, rules and regulations, policies and principles. Unfortunately, due to the difficult circumstances surrounding the EA deployment, the governance in the organisation was questionable. The EA deployment should be guided and legitimised by the organisations' rules, regulations and using available resources. Unfortunately, some of the employees refused to sanction (approve) certain requirements, it was not at their favour. Their actions and behaviour contradicted organisational requirements, especially the senior personnel, because they preferred defining their own individual regulatory elements and refuted the ones defined within the organisational structure. When it came to the deployment of the EA, it was evident that the distribution and allocation of resources was problematic. This was due to the fact that some of the senior personnel did not realise that key (skilled) employees under their auspices were involved in the EA deployment process. This and other acts were manifestations of a lack of emphasis on governance. Otherwise, for example, resource allocation should have been governed by the rules and regulations of the organisation, instead of individuals protecting their interests.

The individualisation and personalisation of interests that became a normalised structure in the organisation derailed the deployment of the EA. The governance is intended to facilitate and channel those structures towards the organisation's goals and objectives. As a result, the decision-making process was challenged due to individuals trying to dominate this space, while communication channels were not properly followed because some of the employees chose when and how they would participate. Clearly, EA deployment requires governance to be enforced from the management level within the organisational structure, filtered down to the rest of the employees in the organisation. The next section presents the data analysis including the findings from the analysis, of the other organisation (case) that was used in the chapter.

7. CONCLUSION

Without EA, organisations could fail to have a holistic view, monitor and manage its business processes, information flow, technology selection and deployment. Business and IT units' alignment and organisational structure often have an impact on and influence the deployment of the EA. How these factors impact and influence the deployment of the EA in organisations are not known. The outcome of the chapter helps managers of EA to gain a better understanding of the critical factors that have an impact on and influence the deployment of the EA in their respective organisations. Some of the factors were not known to them, and those that they seem to be aware of were not empirically proven. The empirical nature of the chapter will give the managers more confidence and prove in their actions and responses. The chapter contributes to existing academic literature. Currently, there are not many academic studies on the topic of EA. Also, there are no subjects and courses on EA in institutions of higher learning in South Africa and many other countries.

This chapter helps managers of EA to gain a better understanding of the critical factors that have an impact on and influence the deployment of the EA in their respective organizations. Some of the factors were not known to them, and those that they seem to be aware of were not empirically proven. The empirical nature of the chapter will give the managers more confidence and prove in their actions and responses. Also, the chapter contributes to existing academic literature. Currently, there are not many academic studies on the topic of EA.

REFERENCES

Aier, S., & Weiss, S. (2002). An institutional Framework for the Analyzing Organisational responses to the Establishment of Architectural Transformation. *In the Proceedings of the European Conference on Information Systems.*

Burton, B., Gail, N., Newman, D., Burke, B., Allega, P & Lapkin, A. (2007). Predict 2008: Emerging trends force a clearer and deeper focus on enterprise architecture.

Chaung, C. J., & Lobberenberg, J. (2010). Challenges facing enterprise architects: a South African perspective. *In the Proceeding of the 43rd Hawaii International Conference on System Science.*

Giddens, A. (1984). The constitution of society: Outline of the theory of structuration. Cambridge, UK.

Glissmann, S. M., & Sanz, J. (2011). An Approach to Building Effective Enterprise Architectures. *In the Proceeding of the 44th Hawaii International Conference on System Sciences.*

Gray, D. E. (2009). *Doing Research in the real world.* Sage Publication Ltd.

Hafner, M., & Winter, R. (2008). Process for Enterprise Application Architecture management. *In the Proceedings of the 41st Annual Hawaii International Conference on System Sciences.*

Iyamu, T. (2009). The Factors Affecting Institutionalisation of Enterprise Architecture in the Organisation. *In the Proceeding of the 11th IEEE Conference on Commerce and Enterprise Computing.* Vienna.

Iyamu, T. (2010). Theoretical analysis of Strategic implementation of Enterprise Architecture. *International Journal of Actor-Network Theory and Technological Innovation, 2*(3), 17–32. doi:10.4018/jantti.2010070102

Iyamu, T. (2011). Institutionalisation of the enterprise architecture. *International Journal of Actor-Network Theory and Technological Innovation, 3*(1), 1–27. doi:10.4018/jantti.2011010103

Iyer, B., & Gottlieb, R. (2004). The Four-Domain Architecture: An approach to support enterprise architecture design. *IBM Systems Journal, 43*(3), 587–597. doi:10.1147/sj.433.0587

Jonkers, H., Lankhorst, M., Ter Doest, T., Arbab, F., Bosma, H., & Wieringa, R. (2006). Enterprise architecture: Management tool and blueprint for the organization. *Information Systems Frontiers, 8*(2), 63–66. doi:10.1007/s10796-006-7970-2

Kaisler, S., Armour, F., & Valivullah, M. (2005). Enterprise Architecting: Critical Problems. *In the Proceedings of the 38th Annual Hawaii International Conference on System Sciences.*

Orlikowski, W. J. (1992). The duality of Technology: Rethinking the concept of technology in organizations. *Organization Science, 3*(3), 398–427. doi:10.1287/orsc.3.3.398

Pereira, C. M., & Sousa, P. (2004). A method to define an enterprise architecture using the Zachman framework. *In the Proceedings of the 2004 ACM symposium on applied computing.*

Pulkkinen, M. (2006). Systemic Management of Architectural Decisions in Enterprise Architecture Planning. Four Dimensions and Three Abstraction Levels. *In the Proceedings of the 39th Annual Hawaii International Conference on System Science.*

van der Raadt, B., & van Vliet, H. (2008). Van der Raadt, B. & Van Vliet, H. (2008) Designing the enterprise architecture function. *Lecture Notes in Computer Science, 5281*, 103–118. doi:10.1007/978-3-540-87879-7_7

Wang, X., & Zhao, Y. (2009). An Enterprise Architecture development method in Chinese Manufacturing Industry. *IEEE Journals, 3*, 226–230.

Yin, R. K. (2009). Case study research, design and methods. California, Newberry Park: Sage publications.

Yu, E., Strohmaier, M., & Deng, X. (2006). Exploring intentional modelling and analysis for Enterprise Architecture. *In the Proceedings of the Enterprise Distributed Object Computing conference workshop.*

KEY TERMS AND DEFINITIONS

Architecture: Is a design of structure including artefacts, for future flexibility.

Business: Is a legal entity, set with vision and mission the means by which an organization sets out to achieve its desired goals and objectives.

Enterprise: A legally registered business, with its sets goals and objectives. It has divisions and units that are geographically spread.

Governance: Is a structured methodical approach, consisting of rules and regulations for managing processes and technological artefacts within an organisation.

IS Strategy: Is an organizational perspective on the investment in, deployment, use, and management of information systems.

Organisational Structure: Outlines how processes and activities including task allocation and distribution are organised and managed, to achieving objectives.

Structuration Theory: Is a theory that defines duality of structure. It claims that events can be enabled and at the same time constrained in the process production and reproduction.

Chapter 10
IT Governance Practices of SMEs in South Africa and the Factors Influencing Their Effectiveness

Charles Boamah-Abu
University of Cape Town, South Africa

Mike Tyobe
University of Cape Town, South Africa

ABSTRACT

The higher failure rate in SMEs is attributable factors including poor leadership, management and governance. Although IT adoption is prevalent in SMEs, not much is known about its governance. This research investigated IT governance practices in 67 SMEs in selected industries and provinces in South Africa. The findings revealed both sound and poor practices. SMEs with centralised IT departments had better practices, e. g., IT strategic investments; closer interactions among IT and business managers; and training of employees. The other SMEs managed IT opportunities poorly, e. g., irrationally IT investment decision-making; poorly defined IT roles and responsibilities; and noncompliance with IT legislations. It was also found that firm size, industry type and location influenced IT governance practices. Larger SMEs had more effective practices and there were differences in IT resource management among provinces. However, age of a firm and years of IT usage did not have much influence.

INTRODUCTION

The importance of SMEs cannot be over-emphasised. Various authors have highlighted their contribution to job creation, poverty alleviation, socio-economic growth and in promoting flexibility and innovation (UNDP-APDIP, 2007). However, compared to larger firms, SMEs have a higher failure rate. Bowler, Dawood, and Page (2007) report high failure rates of SMEs in South Africa. Similar problems have been reported elsewhere in Africa. According to Kazooba (2006), while Uganda continues to have a high Total Early Stage Entrepreneurial Activity (TEA), the discontinuation rate of these SMEs is also high compared to other African countries. Many of these researchers attribute these failures to poor leadership, poor management and governance.

DOI: 10.4018/978-1-4666-8524-6.ch010

Interest in governance and survival of small enterprises has developed over the years (Steger, 2004; Kazooba, 2006; Ekeledo & Bewayo, 2009). It is widely established that successful development of the SME sector in Africa and other developing countries requires strategies aimed at developing a combination of entrepreneurial, technological and managerial competencies (Beyene, 2001; Ekeledo & Bewayo, 2009). According to the OECD (2004), IT can improve resource management, communication and business operations within SMEs. Although conducive policies and decreasing cost have contributed to a significant increase in IT adoption in SMEs, IT investments are still poorly governed and have not resulted in the anticipated increased performance. This highlights the need for governance mechanisms to protect investments in IT and the interests of shareholders or stakeholders providing the resources (King, 2002; King 2009; Calder, 2005).

The ITGI (2006) contends that SMEs can derive the same benefits from IT governance as larger organizations. Jain (2009) argues that in the current global crisis, SMEs can achieve long-term growth by optimising IT, governance, and risk and compliance measures. Notwithstanding the potential benefits, developments in the field have concentrated almost exclusively on larger firms. Little is still known about how IT is governed in SMEs or how SMEs can be assisted to improve these practices. The findings from large firms may not be generalised over SMEs as SMEs have different IT requirements. They tend to adopt a more operational than strategic view of business and are more reactive to immediate demands than longer term goals (Kyobe 2008). Furthermore, Csaszar and Clemons (2006) observe that IT governance studies are predominantly qualitative and anecdotal, making it difficult to generalise findings and to advance normative judgement. Buckby, Best and Stewart (2009) also maintain there is a noticeable paucity of empirical and quantitative research in IT governance in general, and in SMEs in particular. The purpose of this research was to investigate the factors which contribute to effective IT governance practices in this sector in South Africa. In the following sections present a review of literature on IT governance, IT governance research in SMEs and the factors which influence IT governance.

LITERATURE REVIEW

Since the advent of IT, researchers and practitioners have been preoccupied with its governance and contribution to business performance. The objective of any form of governance is to set and control strategies to ensure that business goals are accomplished. This involves developing overall strategies, establishing structures through which decision authority may be delegated to management, and ensuring that managerial activities are consistent with achieving these strategies.

Domains of IT Governance

There is no universally accepted definition of IT governance. Due to the complex nature of the discipline, different definitions emphasise different aspects, and this divergence has permeated both research and practice (Webb, Pollard & Ridley, 2006). The overarching objective of IT governance is to manage risk and maximise IT value (ITGI, 2003; Jordan & Silcock, 2005), which may be accomplished through strategic alignment, resource management and performance management (Webb *et al.*, 2006). According to ITGI (2003), IT governance consists of the following domains: strategic alignment, risk management, resource management, performance management and value delivery.

Strategic alignment measures the extent to which a firm's IT strategy is aligned to its long-term business strategy (Luftman, Papp & Brier 1999). Although there are counter-arguments, there is consensus that firms which achieve strategic alignment outperform those which do not. Chan and Reich (2007) identified factors, e.g., size, industry and level of IT use, which impact on alignment and reported that smaller firms were well-aligned because of the high-level of communication.

IT resource management is concerned with the appropriate investment in, and the effective allocation and use of, IT resources to achieve business strategy (Calder, 2005; ITGI, 2003). IT resources include people, physical infrastructure, intellectual property, information, and IT relationships (ITGI, 2003; Weill & Ross, 2004). Appropriate investments include procurement of IT products and services, and the recruitment, development and retention of staff (ITGI, 2003). IT structure and decision-making authority (Ein-Dor & Segev, 1982), relational mechanisms (Peterson, 2004), IT capabilities (Prasad, Heales & Green, 2009) and measurements against predefined metrics (Calder, 2005; ITGI, 2003) have been identified as important to IT resource management. Outsourcing and partnerships are also being used to meet the day-to-day operational needs of firms.

The main objective IT risk management is to protect IT assets, mitigate risk and optimise opportunities for pursuing business strategies (Calder, 2005). Attendant to the growing dependence of firms on IT is the risk from investment and use. A firm's vulnerability to threats may be accentuated by IT project failure; loss or exploitation of information assets; ineffective policies and procedures and IT outsourcing issues, e.g., incapable vendors and inappropriate contracts (Jordan & Silcock, 2005).

IT performance management measures IT benefits (or IT value) and the processes which achieved these benefit (ITGI, 2003). It is linked to strategic alignment, risk management, resource management and value delivery (Buckby et al., 2009). Current approaches emphasis both qualitative (e.g., financial) and qualitative (e.g., customer satisfaction, and learning) benefits (Calder, 2005). Measuring benefits is complex and fraught with poor methodologies, which make it difficult to determine IT value (Tallon & Kraemer, 2003).

IT value delivery measures the extent to which IT contributes to business performance. IT value includes risk reduction, revenue increases, employee productivity and customer satisfaction. It is generally agreed that not all IT investments yield the perceived value. This may be ascribed to factors such as application of inappropriate techniques and failure to evaluate IT benefits before or after investment (Ward & Peppard, 2005). It is reported that IT value takes about two to three years to show (Devaraj & Kohli, 2003); vary across industries and firms (Weill & Ross, 2004); and depends on management support and allocation of responsibility (Ward & Peppard, 2005;).

IT Governance Research

It is generally agreed that IT governance is complex and multifaceted. However, both research and practice isolate and concentrate on distinct aspects (Buckby et al., 2009). There are three main research streams, viz. locus of control, contingency and a combination thereof (Brown & Grant, 2005). Locus of control refers to the location of IT decision-making in a firm (Peterson, 2004), and primarily focuses on the relationship between organizational structure and IT benefits, e.g. what structure leads to improved IT benefits (Ein-Dor & Segev, 1982). The three main types of loci of control are: centralized, decentralized and federal.

Table 1. Factors influencing IT governance

Characteristic	Source	Factor
Management expertise in IT governance	Weill and Ross (2004)	Managerial
Top management support in IT governance	Ali & Green (2005), Ward and Peppard (2005); Weill and Ross (2004)	
Size	Weill & Ross (2004)	Organisational
Organisational and IT structures	Ein-Dor and Segev (1982); Weill and Ross (2004)	
Business strategy	Weill and Ross (2004)	
Relationships	De Haes and Van Grembergen (2005); Peterson (2004)	
Shared understanding	De Haes and Van Grembergen (2005)	
Communication between IT and business managers	De Haes and Van Grembergen (2005	
Processes	De Haes and Van Grembergen (2005); Peterson (2004)	
IT Intensity	Ali & Green (2005); Sohal and Fitzpatrick (2002)	
Industry type	Weill and Ross (2004)	External
Outsourcing	Prasad *et al.* (2009)	
Regulation	Korac-Kakabadse and Korac-Kakabadse (2001)	

The contingency stream, on the other hand, acknowledges that IT governance "exists" within an organisational context and, thus, is influenced by managerial; organisational; and external factors (Brown & Grant, 2005). These studies have evolved from individual to include multiple contingencies, and various factors have been identified and investigated, e.g., firm type, firm size, regional difference, organisational and decision-making structures, and business strategy(Weill & Ross, 2004); top management support (Ali & Green, 2005); and IT intensity (Ali & Green, 2005; Sohal & Fitzpatrick 2002).

Some researchers advocate for an integrated approach. Consequently, contemporary studies combine the streams above. For example, Weill and Ross (2004) provide a framework which combines structures, decision-making and stakeholder participation. Table 1 shows some of the managerial, organisational and external characteristics of firms in the literature relevant to IT governance research.

In accordance with the working definition of IT governance adopted for this research, IT governance practices may be defined as "the repeated effort aimed at strategic alignment, and the management of risk, resources, and performance to ensure IT delivers value". Figure 1 illustrates the relationship between IT governance practices and IT value.

Figure 1. Relationship between IT governance and IT value

IT Governance in SME

Smallbone (2004) examines governance issues among SMEs in the new Accession States and notes that governance relates to the rules, procedures and practices affecting how power is exercised. Governance in the context of SMEs relates to good management, e.g. of human resources, information, quality and compliance with regulations. It also relates to respect for the environment, social and community responsibility, participation in the political process.

In general, SMEs are defined according to the number of employees, annual income and total assets (Burgess, 2002; Ghobadian & O'Regan, 2006). In South Africa, the National Small Business Act (NSBA, 1996) and the National Small Business Amendment Act (NSBAA, 2003) define SMEs by industry type, in terms of the number of full time employees, total annual turnover or total asset value. The definition by number of full time employees was adopted for the present research.

It is agreed that the SME sector is heterogeneous, composed of firms with diverse characteristic, e.g., size, resources and industry type. According to Burgess (2002), the firms have different IT requirements, intensity and processes and, therefore, IT research needs to target selected niches and differentiate between groups. Southern and Tilley (2000) contend that managerial practices, organisational demographics and external factors influence what, and how, IT is used. Table 2 summarises managerial, organisational and external characteristics of SMEs which impact on the use of IT, and likely to influence IT governance, in the sector.

Table 2. Factors affecting use of IT in SMEs

Characteristic	Source	Factor
Position in organisation	Seyal, Rahim and Rahman (2000)	Managerial
IT expertise and experience (from professional and educational background, etc.)	Burgess (2002)	
Management involvement and support (including decision-making, training, etc.)	Burgess (2002)	
Gender	Martin and Matlay (2001)	
Size	De Lone (1988); Ein-Dor and Segev (1982)	Organisational
Age	De Lone (1988)	
Years using computers	De Lone (1988)	
IT Capabilities (infrastructure, employees IT skills, processes)	Caldeira and Ward (2003)	
Organisational and IT structures	Ein-Dor & Segev (1982)	
Relationships (communication, learning, training, etc.)	Burgess (2002)	
Location	Burgess (2002); Martin and Matlay (2001)	External
Sector	Burgess (2002); Martin and Matlay (2001)	
External agencies (e.g. government agencies, vendors)	Premkumar (2003)	
Government legislation and support	Burgess (2002)	

Managerial Factors

Most SMEs are owned and managed by individuals or small groups of individuals. The qualitative characteristics of the owners, managers or their equivalent (hereafter referred to as management) are, therefore, important to firm performance. Management is central to setting and monitoring strategy; decision-making; organisation and use of resources and, therefore, influences what and how IT is applied to business processes. It may be concluded that management characteristics, e.g., professional background, knowledge and experience, influence IT governance practices and, thereby, impact on IT value in SMEs. Empirical studies link managerial characteristics such as attitude, IT expertise, involvement in activities of the firm, readiness to train employees, and managerial approach to improved IT value (Burgess, 2002). Seyal *et al.* (2000) investigated the relationship between position and IT usage. Martin and Matlay (2001) report differences in the perception of IT value by gender.

Organisational Factors

Various authors identify age, size, resources and organisational structures as some of the factors which impact on the growth of SMEs. The size of a firm determines its characteristics, e.g., size of business operations, infrastructure, expertise, and organisational structures and, consequently, what and how IT may be used. The older a firm, the more likely it would have acquired requisite resources. It can, therefore, be concluded that these factors influence IT governance. Larger SMEs are more likely to acquire IT infrastructure and expertise due to the size of their operations. Gregor *et al.* (2004), however, found no relationship between firm size and IT value. De Lone (1988) reports age of a firm and the number of years it has been using IT are likely to affect what and how IT is used. Huang, Zmud and Price (2009) report centralised IT structure improves IT governance SMEs.

External Factors

The growth of a firm depends on the extent to which its management is able to deal with external environment (Lighthelm & Cant, 2002). Factors such as government legislation and support; industry type and location affect SMEs and, therefore, influence what and how IT may be used. For example, firms derive benefits, e.g., collaboration, learning and specialised expertise, from industrial clusters. It can be posited that external factors influence IT governance in SMEs. Burgess (2002) claims geographical differences in resources and culture affect the use of IT in SMEs. Martin and Matlay (2001) contend SMEs in urban areas are likely to possess the requisite infrastructure, internal IT expertise, and external support than those in rural areas. Burgess (2002) states there is a relationship between industry type and the type of IT used. Seyal *et al.* (2000) notes firms in the financial sector are more likely to have higher IT intensity than those in the manufacturing sector.

Figure 2 shows the logical relationship between the factors which affect the use of IT in SMEs, IT governance practices and IT value. This conceptual framework was used to guide the present research. The next section describes the research methodology adopted in this study.

Figure 2. Conceptual framework

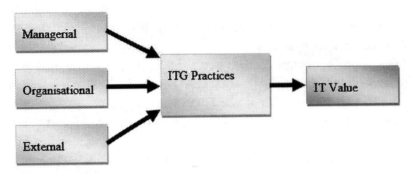

RESEARCH METHODOLOGY

A survey was conducted to gather data. First a target population was identified. This consisted of firms with less than 200 full time employees, in accordance with the definition of SMEs (NBSA, 2003). Only firms in IT, finance, transport and retail industries in the Western Cape, Eastern Cape and Gauteng provinces of South Africa were studied. These industries were considered to have high IT intensity. Ali and Green (2005) and Sohal and Fitzpatrick (2002) found a relationship between IT intensity and IT governance. It may be concluded that the selected industries exhibited the characteristics to be investigated. The different niches also allowed for comparison. The provinces selected were also representative for two reasons. First, 46 and 18 (a total of 64) percent of SMEs in South Africa are in Gauteng and Western Cape respectively (RIA!, 2006). Thus, between them, the three provinces account for about two-thirds of SMEs in South Africa. Second, the differences in resources allowed for comparisons: Gauteng and Western Cape are well-resourced whereas Eastern Cape less-resourced.

An appropriate sample frame was constructed from business directories which contained up-to-date mailing lists of SMEs. Stratified purposive sampling technique (Teddlie & Yu, 2007) was used to draw a representative sample of 600 (50 SMEs per industry, per province; i.e., 200 firms per province). In general a sample size of about 400 is adequate for a large population (Leedy & Ormrod, 2005). A questionnaire was designed, based on the literature review and conceptual framework, to collect data from respondents in management position. This was an appropriate data source, as management are responsible for strategy (Ghobadian & O'Regan, 2006) and IT decision-making (Southern & Tilley, 2000). To improve validity and reliability, operational definitions of variables were adopted from extant literature and adapted where appropriate. The questionnaire was pretested, piloted, reviewed and subsequently administered by e-mail and in-person. To increase response rate, a follow-up strategy was implemented to remind participants who had not returned responses to do so.

The questionnaire consisted of two parts: *Section 1* focused on managerial, organisational and external characteristics. The type and location of firm were identified and coded by the researchers to reduce length. *Section 2* focused on IT governance variables (Strategic Alignment, IT Resource Management, IT Risk Management, IT Performance Management and IT Value). Only 67 usable responses were received, a response rate of 11.2 percent. Low response is typical of research which involves SMEs (Bergeron, Raymond & Rivard, 2004), top management (Ghobadian & O'Regan, 2006) or IT gover-

Figure 3. Distribution of firms by industry and province

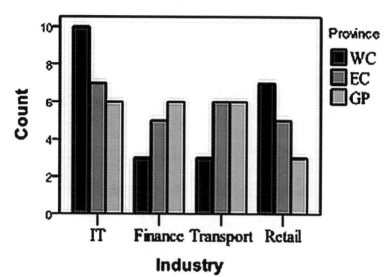

nance in SMEs (O'Donohue, Pye, Warren, 2009). Lucas (1991) claims a sample of 50 is acceptable for quantitative analysis. Ali and Green (2007) used statistical analysis for 54 responses. Therefore, 67 may be considered acceptable. Responses were coded, inspected, captured into a statistical packages and cleaned for data analysis.

Findings and Analysis

Figures 3-5 show the distribution of firms. About one third belonged to the IT industry. Responses were almost equally distributed among provinces- about one-third each. On the average (mean and median) the firms were about 11 years old and had used computers for about 10. It may be concluded that the firms were mature, had acquired the necessary IT capabilities and established effective IT governance practices. About 40 percent had centralised IT structures.

Figure 5. Distribution of firms by years using computers

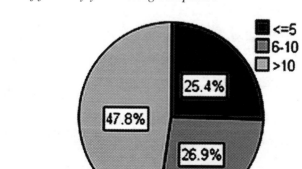

Table 3. Distribution of respondents by position, background and gender

	Characteristic	Frequency	%
Position	Owner-Manager	34	50.7
	CEO	7	10.4
	IT Manager	19	28.4
	Other	7	10.4
Background	Business	33	49.3
	IT	24	35.8
	Other	10	14.9
Gender	Male	46	68.7
	Female	21	31.3

Tables 3 and 4 show the distribution of respondents. About half were owner-managers; about half had business background, over two-thirds were males; and about three-quarters and three-fifths had more than five years' experience in business and IT management respectively. A small group of non-respondents firms were followed up and compared with respondents (Leedy & Ormrod, 2005). No significant differences were found. It may be concluded that the sample was representative of the population.

Descriptive statistics were used to summarise responses for individual item. Less than half (46.3 percent) of respondents agreed (i.e., agreed or strongly agreed) that their firms were familiar with the ECT Act. However, a further analysis revealed that of the 41 firms which had data policies, only 27 were aware of the ECT Act. The firms also demonstrated IT strategy and investment planning, and risk and resource management.

About 60 percent had aligned business and IT strategies. In about half, IT benefits drove IT investments. There was evidence of resource management: more than 60 percent had acquired the requisite IT infrastructure and expertise for business operations; kept inventory of such resources; trained employees and used outsourcing for shortfall in resources.

Over 60 percent identified information risks, implemented data policies and reported security breaches. It was also revealed that over half of respondents had formal agreements with their service providers. This suggests risk management. There was also evidence of interaction among IT and business managers, which suggests these managers understand IT goals.

Table 4. Distribution of respondents by experience in general and IT management

	Years				Distribution	
	Mean	Median	SD	Category	Frequency	%
Management	8.7	8.0	5.4	<= 5	18	26.9
				6 - 10	27	40.3
				>10	22	32.8
IT Management	6.2	6.0	4.7	<= 5	29	43.3
				6 - 10	26	38.8
				>10	12	17.9

IT Governance Practices of SMEs in South Africa

Table 5. Descriptive Statistics (IT governance practices and IT value)

Variable	No. of Items	A	Mean	SD
IT and Business Alignment	4	0.82	3.57	1.04
IT Resource Management	5	0.61	3.54	0.73
IT Risk Management	5	0.84	3.39	0.95
IT Performance Management	8	0.80	3.04	0.74
IT Value	5	0.57	3.49	0.60

On a five-point Likert scale, only four items had less than the average score (i.e., 3). This suggests that, in general, respondents agreed with or were ambivalent about the opinions expressed by the items, which corroborates the foregoing findings. However, the values for skewness and kurtosis showed responses were not normally distributed.

Differences in IT governance, according to managerial; organisational; and external characteristics, were examined using average score for variables. Table 5 shows the reliability coefficients (α), means and standard deviations. All variables had α values above 0.6, except IT value. It may be concluded that the instrument was generally reliable for the present exploratory research (Hair, Black, Babin, Anderson & Tatham, 2009). It may also be observed (from mean and standard deviation) that, on a five-point Likert scale, the firms rated average across all aspects of IT governance. This also confirms the evidence of effective IT governance practices in the firms.

Non-parametric statistics were used to analyse differences in practice, as the sample size was small and responses were not normally distributed. Kruskal-Wallis tests were used for more than two categories and Mann-Whitney for two categories (Cavana, Delahaye, & Sekaran, 2001; Leedy & Ormrod, 2005). The research was exploratory so differences were analysed at 10 percent significance level (p) and 95 percent confidence interval (Cavana *et al.*, 2001). Tables 6 and 7 show results of the Kruskal-Wallis tests. The highlighted cells indicate significant differences at p<0.1 and at the respective Chi-Square (χ^2) and degrees of freedom (df) values.

Tables 8 and 9 present results of the Mann-Whitney tests. It can be observed that there were significant differences across all practices, between firms with and without IT centralised. However, there was no significant differences in practices, according to gender.

Table 6. Differences among respondents by position, background and experience

	Position (df=3)		Background (df=3)		Yrs in Current Position (df=2)		Yrs in IT Mgt (df=2)	
	χ^2	Sig.	χ^2	Sig	χ^2	Sig	χ^2	Sig
Strategic Alignment	19.09	0.00	8.86	0.01	0.41	0.81	2.30	0.32
IT Resource Mgt	13.99	0.00	3.13	0.21	1.53	0.47	1.20	0.55
IT Risk Mgt	14.51	0.00	11.56	0.00	0.89	0.64	4.22	0.12
IT Performance Mgt	21.32	0.00	5.53	0.06	1.90	0.39	0.82	0.66
IT Value	6.74	0.09	5.12	0.08	1.07	0.59	0.10	0.95
df=Degrees of Freedom; χ^2=Chi-Square; Sig = Asymptotic Significance								

Table 7. Differences among firms in practices by province, industry and firm size, age and years of using computers

	Size (df=5)		Age (df=2)		Using Computer (df=2)		Province (df=2)		Industry (df=3)	
	χ^2	Sig	χ^2	Sig	χ^2	Sig	χ^2	Sig.	χ^2	Sig
Strategic Alignment	10.37	0.02	0.89	0.64	1.45	0.49	3.53	0.17	11.45	0.01
IT Resource Mgt	7.67	0.05	0.75	0.69	1.33	0.51	5.77	0.06	2.36	0.50
IT Risk Mgt	13.27	0.00	0.26	0.88	0.09	0.96	2.53	0.28	7.13	0.07
IT Performance Mgt	10.15	0.02	2.83	0.24	2.58	0.28	4.07	0.13	9.62	0.02
df=Degrees of Freedom; χ^2=Chi-Square; Sig = Asymptotic Significance										

Table 8. Differences among firms by IT structure

	Alignment	Resource Mgt	Risk Mgt	Performance Mgt
Mann-Whitney U	236.00	325.50	226.50	255.00
Z	-3.83	-2.68	-3.96	-3.58
Asymp. Sig. (2-tailed)	0.00	0.01	0.00	0.00

Table 9. Differences between respondents by gender

	Alignment	Resource Mgt	Risk Mgt	Performance Mgt
Mann-Whitney U	446.00	399.50	370.50	448.00
Z	-0.50	-1.14	-1.53	-0.47
Asymp. Sig. (2-tailed)	0.62	0.26	0.13	0.64

Table 10. Relationship between IT governance practices and IT value

	Alignment	Resource Mgt	Risk Mgt	Performance Mgt	IT Value
Alignment	1.000				
Resource Mgt	0.54**	1.00			
Risk Mgt	0.67**	0.55**	1.00		
Performance Mgt	0.66**	0.52**	0.59**	1.00	
IT Value	0.34**	0.35**	0.50**	0.39**	1.00
**. Correlation is significant at the 0.01 level (2-tailed). N =67					

Kendall's-Tau, a non-parametric test effective for ordinal variables, was used to examine bivariate relationships among practices, and also among practices and IT value. Table 10 shows the results. It may be concluded, from the correlations, that there were significant relationships among the practices, and also among the practices and IT value. The low correlations could be attributed to over-simplifying a complex phenomenon for investigation (Ein-Dor & Segev, 1982).

The research purpose was to determine some of the factors which influence IT governance practices in SMEs. The next section presents the findings in the context of extant literature.

Discussion of Findings

The analysis of individual items showed evidence of IT strategic alignment as well as investment, resource and risk management. This was corroborated by the average scores. Specifically, evidence of centralized IT structures, interaction among IT and business managers and training of employees were also discovered. Centralized IT structures facilitate alignment by ensuring close interaction between IT and business managers ITGI (2006), efficient allocation of resources, and operational efficiency (Huang et al., 2009). It is probable the firms leverage centralised IT structures to achieve strategic alignment, and consequently, investment, resource and risk management practices (ITGI, 2006). However, most firms were unaware of legislation but had implemented data policies. These firms may have policies inconsistent with legislation. Harindranath, Dryerson and Barnes (2008) found lack of awareness of IT-related policies developed to assist SMEs and Kyobe (2009) reported lack of compliance with IT regulation.

There were significant differences among respondents in all IT governance variables, according to position, and by background, except IT resource management and IT value. It may be concluded that management position and professional background influenced these variables. These were expected. Different parts of a firm may have different strategies and underlying practices to achieve IT value (Tallon & Kraemer, 2003). Similarly, differences in background mean differences in expertise, which may shape IT strategy, practices and, therefore, value. These may explains the foregoing differences.

On the contrary, there were no significant differences according to number of years in general business or IT management position as well as gender. Management gains experience through ongoing involvement (Weill & Ross, 2004). While it is expected tenure in these positions will result in cumulated experience and, therefore, effective IT governance it appears mere tenure has no effect. The distribution of respondents may explain why there were no differences in tenure and gender. As shown in Tables 3 and 4, most respondents had more than five years of tenure in general and IT management and over two-thirds were male. Lastly, the non-significant differences in IT resource management and IT value according to background may be explained by the large percentage (about 78 percent) of business and IT managers.

There were significant differences among firms across all practices, according to firm size and IT structure. It may be concluded that the size and type of IT structure influence IT practices. A Kendall-Tau test linked centralised IT structure to larger SMEs. These were expected. Compared to smaller firms, larger firms may have adequate resources dedicated to IT governance, including centralised IT structure. Further analyses revealed firms with centralised IT structure ranked higher across all practices. Although the direction of association is inconclusive, it may be speculated that larger firms with centralised IT department are more likely to have effective IT governance practices. Centralised IT structure facilitates alignment as it ensures a close relationship between IT and business managers (ITGI, 2006), efficient allocation of resources, and operational efficiency (Huang et al., 2009). It may be concluded that the larger firms set up centralised IT structures for effective IT governance.

The firms differed according to type of industry in all practices except IT resource management and according to location in only IT resource management. These were anticipated. It may be concluded that these the type and location of industry influence these practices. Different industries have different IT strategies, risks and benefits, which may explain the differences in IT strategy, risk and performance management. However, it appears the sampled sectors had the appropriate IT infrastructure and manage-

Figure 4. Distribution of firms by age

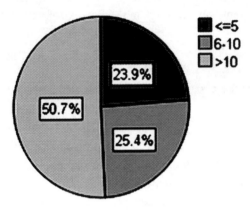

ment expertise. Similarly, expertise in IT resource management may differ according to geographical locations. For example, Martin and Matlay (2001) point out SMEs in urban areas are likely to acquire requisite IT resources, expertise and support. Further analysis showed Gauteng, with well-developed infrastructure and expertise had the highest mean rank in IT resource management. However, it appears the firms across all provinces (geographical location) had similar strategic, risk and performance management practices.

It was expected that the older a firm or the longer it had used IT, the more likely it would have established its IT capabilities, built the requisite expertise and implemented effective practices (Prasad et al., 2009). To the contrary, there were no significant differences across all practices, according to age of firm and the years they had used computers. This may be attributable to the distribution of participating firms (Figures 4 and 5). The average age of the firms was about 11 years (SD=6.66); most were over five years old; and had used computers for over 10 years. It may be that the firms were mature (both in age and use of computers), and may have acquired the necessary experience in IT governance over time.

Lastly, it may be concluded, from the correlation among the IT governance variables, that changes in one variable may causes corresponding changes in other variables. That is, improving one practice may result in improvement in other practices and also in IT value. This is consistent with the literature (ITGI, 2006).

CONCLUSION AND RECOMMENDATIONS

The research purpose was to identify some of the characteristics of SMEs which influence IT governance. The findings lead to three overarching conclusions. There were some evidence of effective IT governance practices: strategic and investment planning as well, resource and risk management. However, most firms were unfamiliar with IT legislation. Some managerial (position and background of a manager), organisational (size of firm and IT structure) and external (location and industry type) influence IT governance practices in SMEs. Lastly, there are relationships among IT governance practices and IT value. The conclusions below are also drawn from the findings.

Involving managers of different positions and background can improve IT governance and, and thereby, IT value in SMEs. Huang *et al.* (2009) notes that top management involvement results in appropriate behaviour, improved relationship and cumulated expertise. For example, operational management expertise can be harnessed to develop a shared business and IT strategy and consistent organisational practices to achieve IT value.

The size of firm and type of IT structure influence IT governance practices. It also appears larger firms with centralised IT structures performed better. Larger SMEs can, therefore, use centralised IT structures to improve IT governance practices. Ward and Peppard (2005) claim a designated role for IT governance could facilitate relationships, and thereby, contribute to IT value. Smaller SMEs which do not have the resources to set up IT structures can, therefore, use designate authority to improve practices.

The type and location of a firm influence IT governance. SMEs derive benefits from industry clusters and can take advantage of collaborations and alliances with other firms, both large and small, to improve IT infrastructure as well as technical and managerial expertise. As stated elsewhere, different industries have different IT requirements, based on business operations. Thus, some practices may be essential to an industry, e.g., information security (i.e., risk management) to the financial sector (Kankanhalli *et al.*, 2003). Firms can exploit clusters to focus on practices essential to their industries to achieve IT value. For example, industries may develop sets of best practices for achieving IT value.

Improving an IT governance practice can improve other practices and IT value. In addition, an improvement in the latter may also contribute to improved practices. However, due to lack of expertise and financial resources, an overarching IT governance framework may be costly to implement in SMEs (O'Donohue *et al.*, 2009). Therefore, firms can identify a primary value to achieve with IT (e.g., IT security) and leverage organisational structures (e.g., centralised IT structure) and practice (e.g., IT risk management) towards achieving this value, and thereby, improve other IT governance practices (ITGI, 2006).

In sum, the findings above have implications for both practice and research: there is no "one-size fits all" approach to IT governance. Policy makers and agencies responsible for promoting IT in SMEs need to focus on IT governance practices to improve IT value, taking into cognisance the diversity of the sector. A designated IT structure is essential to creating the necessary relationships for IT governance to be effective. Furthermore, operational and other managers must be involved to harness their expertise.

CONTRIBUTION, LIMITATIONS, AND FUTURE RESEARCH

The research makes contributions to both theory and practice. It has provides empirical evidence of some of the managerial, organisational and external factors which influence IT governance practices in SMEs and the relationship among these practices and IT value. In addition, it makes recommendations for practice. Notwithstanding the foregoing, it is recognised that, as with all research, there are limitations. The nature of the phenomenon, practical research design decisions and the inherent weaknesses in methods may have affected the reliability of findings and conclusions.

IT governance is a complex phenomenon, aspects of which were isolated and investigated. Therefore, this research cannot claim to have considered the plethora of factors that impact on IT governance in SMEs. Many factors (e.g., participation of employees, incentives, relationships with larger firms) were not considered for investigation. Consequently, the findings may be treated with caution. Governance is an ongoing process. While a cross-sectional approach has established factors of influence and relationships, it could not establish causality. Therefore, for most part, the explanations of the results were based on plausible interpretation. Longitudinal research could address causality, and, thereby, assure an empirical basis for interpretations.

The data collection relied on self-reporting, which is prone to bias. IT governance is a sensitive subject and respondents may have given socially desirable answers, which may have affected the validity of findings (Leedy & Ormrod, 2005). Also Love *et al.* (2005) state that strategic benefits of IT are subjective, and therefore difficult to quantify. The questionnaire solicited perceptions on strategic issues, which may have caused respondents to give inaccurate responses. Method triangulation could be used to corroborate findings. The final sample size of 67, although representative of the sample frame and acceptable for statistical analysis, was small and could have affected the accuracy of the analysis, findings and conclusions. The sample was drawn from four industries in three provinces. While it may be relevant to other SMEs, the findings and conclusions may be applicable only to firms in the selected sectors and provinces.

The research lays a foundation for future investigation. A longitudinal research approach could address the issues of causality, and thereby, provide deeper insight into IT governance in SMEs. Lastly, this research has provided evidence of IT governance practices in SMEs. It may be instructive to know how these practices are undertaken. A research strategy which employs qualitative methods may provide this insight.

REFERENCES

Ali, S., & Green, P. (2005). Determinants of Effective Information Technology Governance: A Study of Intensity. In *Proceedings of International IT Governance Conference*. Auckland, New Zealand.

Ali, S., & Green, P. (2007). IT Governance Mechanisms in Public Sector Organisations: An Australian Context. *Journal of International Management, 15*(4), 41–63.

Bergeron, F., Raymond, L., & Rivard, S. (2004). Ideal Patterns of Strategic Alignment and Business Performance. *Information & Management, 41*(5), 1003–1020. doi:10.1016/j.im.2003.10.004

Beyene, A. (2002). Enhancing the Competitiveness and Productivity of Small and Medium Scale Enterprises (SMEs) in Africa: An Analysis of Differential Roles of National Governments through Improved Support Services. *Africa Development. Afrique et Developpement, 27*(3), 130–156.

Bowler, A., Dawood, M. S., & Page, S. (2007). *Entrepreneurship and Small business Management*. Pretoria: Juta and Co. Ltd.

Brown, A. E., & Grant, G. G. (2005). Framing the Frameworks: A Review of IT Governance Research. *Communications of the Association for Information Systems, 15*, 698–712.

Buckby, S., Best, P., & Stewart, J. (2009). The Current State of Information Technology Governance Literature. In A. Cater-Steel (Ed.), *Information Technology Governance and Service Management: Frameworks and Adaptations* (pp. 1–42). UK: Information Science Reference. doi:10.4018/978-1-60566-008-0.ch001

Burgess, S. (2002). Information Systems in Small Business. In S. Burgess (Ed.), *Managing Information Technology in Small Business: Challenges & Solutions* (pp. 1–17). Australia: Idea Book Publishing. doi:10.4018/978-1-930708-35-8.ch001

Caldeira, M. M., & Ward, J. M. (2003, June 27-29). Using Resourced-Based Theory to Interpret the Successful Adoption and use of Information Systems and Technology in the Manufacturing Small and Medium Sized Enterprises. *Proceedings of The 9th European Conference on Information Systems Bled.* Slovenia.

Calder, A. (2005). *IT Governance: Guidelines for Directors.* United Kingdom: IT Governance Publishing.

Cavana, R. Y., Delahaye, B. L., & Sekaran, U. (2001). *Applied Business Research: Qualitative and Quantitative Methods.* Australia: John Wiley & Sons Ltd.

Chan, Y. E., & Reich, B. H. (2007). IT Alignment: What Have We Learned? *Journal of Information Technology, 22*(4), 297–315. doi:10.1057/palgrave.jit.2000109

Csaszar, F., & Clemons, E. (2006). Governance of the IT Function: Valuing Agility and Quality of Training, Cooperation and Communications. *Proceedings of the 39th Hawaii International Conference on Systems Sciences.* doi:10.1109/HICSS.2006.197

De Haes, S., & Van Grembergen, W. (2005). IT Governance Structures, Processes and Relational Mechanisms: Achieving IT/Business Alignment in a Major Belgian Financial Group. *Proceedings of the 38th Hawaii International Conference on Systems Sciences.* doi:10.1109/HICSS.2005.362

De Lone, W. L. (1988). Determinants of Success for Computer Usage in Small Business. *Management Information Systems Quarterly, 12*(1), 51–61. doi:10.2307/248803

Devaraj, S., & Kohli, R. (2003). Performance Impact of Information Technology: Is Actual Usage the Missing Link? *Management Science, 49*(3), 273–289. doi:10.1287/mnsc.49.3.273.12736

ECTA (2002). Electronic and Communication Act, No. 25 of 2002.

Ein-Dor, P., & Segev, E. (1982). Organisational Context and MIS Structure: Some Empirical Evidence. *Management Information Systems Quarterly, 6*(3), 1064–1077. doi:10.2307/248656

Ekeledo, I. and Bewayo, E. (2009). Challenges and Opportunities Facing African

Entrepreneurs and their Small Firms. (n. d.). *International Journal of Business Research*, 9, 3, 52-59

Ghobadian, A., & O'Regan, N. (2006). The Impact of Ownership on Small Firm Behaviour and Performance. *International Small Business Journal, 24*(6), 555–585. doi:10.1177/0266242606069267

Gregor, S., Fernandez, W., Holtham, D., Martin, M., Stern, S., Vitale, M., & Pratt, G. (2004). *Achieving Value From ICT: Key Management Strategies.* Canberra: Department of Communications, Information Technology and the Arts.

Hair, J. F., Black, W. C., Babin, B. J., Anderson, R. E., & Tatham, R. L. (2009). *Multivariate Data Analysis.* New Jersey: Pearson Education, Inc.

Harindranath, G., Dryerson, R., & Barnes, D. (2008). ICT Adoption and use in UK SMEs: A Failure of Initiatives? *Electronic Journal Information Systems Evaluation, 11*(2), 91–96.

Huang, R., Zmud, R. W., & Price, R. L. (2009). IT Governance Practices in Small and Medium-Sized Enterprises: Recommendations from an Empirical Study. *IFIP Advances in Information and Communication Technology, 301*, 158–199. doi:10.1007/978-3-642-02388-0_12

IT Governance Institute (ITGI). (2003). *Board Briefing on IT Governance, (2nd ed.)*. Retrieved from: http://www.itgi.org

IT Governance Institute (ITGI). (2006). IT Governance in Practice: Insight From Leading CIOs. Retrieved from: http://www.pwchk.com/home/eng/it_governance_cios.html

Jain, P. (2009). *Strategies to Survive the Slowdown*. Retrieved from www.financialexpress.com/news/strategies-to-survive-the-slowdown/459764/0

Jordan, E., & Silcock, L. (2005). *Beating the Risk*. England: John Wiley & Sons.

Kankanhalli, A., Teo, H., Tan, B. C. Y., & Wei, K. (2003). An Integrative Study of Information Systems Security Effectiveness. *International Journal of Information Management, 23*(2), 139–154. doi:10.1016/S0268-4012(02)00105-6

Kazooba, C. (2006). Causes of Small Business failure in Uganda: A Case Study from Bushenyi and Mbarara Towns. *African Studies Quarterly, 8*, 4, http://web.africa.ufl.edu/asq/v8/v8i4a3.htm

King, M. (2002). *King II Report on Corporate Governance*. Retrieved from: www.iodsa.co.za

King, M. (2009). *King III Report on Corporate Governance*. Retrieved from: www.iodsa.co.za

Korac-Kakabadse, N., & Korac-Kakabadse, A. (2001). IS/IT Governance: Need for an Integrated Model. *Corporate Governance, 1*(4), 9–11. doi:10.1108/EUM0000000005974

Kyobe, M. (2009). Factors Influencing SME Compliance with Government Regulations on Use of IT: The Case of South Africa. *Journal of Global Information Management, 17*(12), 30–59. doi:10.4018/jgim.2009040102

Kyobe, M. E. (2008). The impact of entrepreneur behaviours on the quality of e-commerce security in Urban SMEs: A comparison of Urban and Rural findings. *Journal of Global Information Technology Management, 11*(2), 58–79. doi:10.1080/1097198X.2008.10856467

Leedy, P. D., & Ormrod, J. E. (2005). *Practical Research: Planning and Design*. New Jersey: Pearson Education.

Lighthelm, A. A., & Cant, M. C. (2002). *Business Success Factors of SMEs in Gauteng*. Pretoria: University of South Africa.

Love, P. E. D., Irani, Z., Standing, C., Lin, C., & Burn, J. M. (2005). The Enigma of Evaluation: Benefits, Costs and Risks of IT in Australian Small-Medium-Sized Enterprises. *Information & Management, 42*(7), 947–964. doi:10.1016/j.im.2004.10.004

Lucas, H. C. (1991). Methodological Issues in Information Systems Survey Research. In K. L. Kraemer (Ed.), *The Information Systems Research Challenges: Survey Research Methods* (pp. 273–285). Boston, MA: Harvard Business School Press.

Luftman, J., Papp, R., & Brier, T. (1999). Enablers and Inhibitors of Business-IT Alignment through a Unified Framework. *Communications of the Association for Information Systems, 1*, 1–32.

Martin, L. M., & Matlay, H. (2001). "Blanket" Approaches to Promoting ICT in Small Firms: Some Lessons from the DTI Ladder Adoption Model in the UK. *Internet Research: Electronic Networking Applications and Policy, 11*(5), 399–410. doi:10.1108/EUM0000000006118

NBSA (National Small Business Act). (1996). National Small Business Act, No. 106 of 1996.

NBSAA (National Small Business Amendment Act). (2003). National Small Business Amendment Act, No. 26 of 2003.

O'Donohue, B., Pye, G., & Warren, M. J. (2009). The Impact of ICT Governance within Australian Companies. In A. Cater-Steel (Ed.), *Information Technology Governance and Service Management: Frameworks and Adaptations* (pp. 163–177). UK: Information Science Reference. doi:10.4018/978-1-60566-008-0.ch008

Oates, B. J. (2006). *Researching Information Systems and Computing*. London: Sage.

OECD. (2004). ICT, E-Business and SMEs. Paris: Head of Publications Service, OECD.

Peterson, R. (2004). Crafting Information Technology Governance. *Information Systems Management, 21*(4), 7–22. doi:10.1201/1078/44705.21.4.20040901/84183.2

Prasad, A., Heales, J., & Green, P. (2009). Towards a Deeper Understanding of Information Technology Governance Effectiveness: A Capabilities-Based Approach. *Proceedings of the International Conference on Information Systems (ICIS)*. Retrieved from: http://aisel.aisnet.org/icis2009/122

Premkumar, G. (2003). A Meta-Analysis of Research on Information Systems Implementation in Small Business. *Journal of Organizational Computing and Electronic Commerce, 13*(2), 91–121. doi:10.1207/S15327744JOCE1302_2

RIA! (Research ICT Africa!). (2006). Towards an African e-Index: SMEs e-Access and Usage Across 14 African Countries. Retrieved from: www.researchictafrica.net

Seyal, A.H., Rahim, M. M. & Rahman, M. N. (2000). An empirical investigation of use of information technology among small and medium business organisations: a Bruneian scenario. *Electronic Journal Information Systems in Developing Countries, 2* (2000).

Smallbone, D. (2004). *'Institutions, governance and SME development in transition economies' Paper 5. Working Party on Industry and Enterprise Development, Expert meeting on Good Governance for SMEs, April*. European Commission for Europe.

Sohal, A. S., & Fitzpatrick, P. (2002). IT Governance and Management in Large Australian Organisations. *International Journal of Production Economics, 75*(1), 97–112. doi:10.1016/S0925-5273(01)00184-0

Southern, A., & Tilley, F. (2000). Small Firms and Information Systems Technologies (ICTs): Toward a Typology of ICT Usage. *New Technology, Work and Employment, 15*(2), 138–154. doi:10.1111/1468-005X.00070

Steger, T. (2004 April, 1-2). Corporate Governance of German SMEs – A review with special regards to the situation in East Germany [Economic Commission For Europe Paper No. 6], Committee For Trade, Industry and Enterprise Development. Proceedings of Expert meeting on Good Governance for SMEs.

Tallon, P., & Kraemer, K. L. (2003). Investigating the Relationship between Strategic alignment and IT Business Value: The Discovery of a Paradox. In N. Shin (Ed.), *Creating Business Value with Information Technology: Challenges and Solutions* (pp. 1–22). USA: Idea Group Publishing. doi:10.4018/978-1-59140-038-7.ch001

Teddlie, C., & Yu, F. (2007). Mixed Methods Sampling: A Typology With Examples. *Journal of Mixed Methods, 1*(1), 77–100. doi:10.1177/2345678906292430

UNDP-APDIP (United Nations Development Program-Asia Pacific Development Information Program). (2007). The Role of Government in Promoting ICT Access and use by SMEs: Consideration for Public Policy. Retrieved from: www.apdip.net/apdipenote/12.pdf

Ward, J., & Peppard, J. (2005). *Strategic Planning for Information Systems*. England: John Wiley & Sons Ltd.

Webb, P., Pollard, C., & Ridley, G. (2006). Attempting to Define IT Governance: Wisdom or Folly? *Proceedings of the 39th Hawaii International Conference on Systems Science*. doi:10.1109/HICSS.2006.68

Weill, P., & Ross, J. W. (2004). *IT Governance: How Top Performers Manage IT Decision Rights for Superior Results*. Massachusetts: Harvard Business School Press.

KEY TERMS AND DEFINITIONS

Governance: Setting strategies and creating structures and mechanisms to ensure intended outcomes can be achieved.

IT Governance Practices: How IT governance is actually conducted in organizations; i.e., how IT strategic alignment and management of resources, risk, and performance is conducted to ensure IT delivers value).

IT Governance: Alignment of IT and business strategies as well as management of IT resources and risks to ensure IT delivers intended business value.

IT Performance Management: Tracking and measurement of IT value (i.e., extent to which IT has contributed to achievement of business strategy) and the processes by which this was achieved.

IT Resource Management: Appropriate investment in IT resources and effective allocation and use of such resources to achieve business strategy.

IT Risk Management: Protection of IT resources and mitigation of risk in pursuance of business strategies.

IT Strategic Alignment: Alignment of IT and business strategies to ensure the former supports business processes and engenders new and superior strategies.

IT Value/Performance/Benefit: The contribution of IT to business performance; i.e., the extent to which IT contributes to achievement of business strategy.

Practice: How work is actually done in an organization; it involves organized activities (doings and sayings).

Small and Medium Enterprises (SMEs): Firms in South Africa which employ less than 200 full time employees.

Chapter 11
The Interplay of Agents in Improvising Telecommunication Infrastructures' Services to Rural Community of South Africa

Sharol Mkhomazi
Tshwane University of Technology, South Africa

ABSTRACT

The deployment of telecommunication infrastructures is a challenge in many parts of South Africa particularly in the rural areas. The challenge has impact of communities' members as they do not have network coverage for Internet in some areas. The challenge gets worse with individual telecommunication service provider. Hence there is technological proposal for sharing of infrastructure by the service providers. However, the sharing of infrastructure is not as easy as notion by many individuals and groups institutions included. The article presents findings from a study on how a South African telecommunication network service provider could deploy shared infrastructures in the country's rural communities. The sharing of infrastructure is described by the structure and actions of agents within the infrastructure sharing process. Structuration theory was employed as a lens in the data analysis. The key findings include insufficient distribution of infrastructure, ownership responsibility, competitiveness, infrastructure deployment cost, and signification of regulation.

1. INTRODUCTION

The deployment of telecommunication infrastructures is considered by policy makers and regulators, as a basic telecommunications service in many countries (Roman, 2009). Broadband is described as one of the telecommunications innovations that is growing fast in developed countries (OECD, 2009). Globally the market for broadband is expanding and many countries are faced with the challenge of pro-

DOI: 10.4018/978-1-4666-8524-6.ch011

viding broadband coverage and services to its population particularly, in rural areas. Statistics released by (OECD, 2009), show that these affected countries continue to slide further behind the rest of the world in terms of the broadband penetration rate and the speed of local fixed line broadband offerings. Developing countries, including South Africa, seem to experience challenges in terms of deploying telecommunication infrastructures across the geographical locations of the country. In addition, access to the infrastructure is also a challenge especially in the rural areas. The challenges in reaching and serving rural communities include costs of investments, population and geographical landscapes (Muente-Kunigami & Navas-Sabater, 2009). The geographical location should however not be a limitation on access to telecommunication infrastructures' services, due to differences in countries' economic and political landscapes (Herselman, 2003).

Owing to the challenges of telecommunication infrastructures accessibility and deployment, rural areas tend to fall behind regarding access and use of telecommunication infrastructures, thus suffering the risk of being ill-equipped in a world that is gradually becoming digital. This unequal access to communications increases the existing digital divide between rural and urban areas (Bhawan & Marg, 2007).

Relying on telecommunications operators to provide networks to all citizens in the country, including rural areas, sharing infrastructure is more likely to ensure that network infrastructures are built and operated efficiently in these areas. Thus, infrastructure sharing can be considered a tool to addressing rapid deployment of telecommunication infrastructures in the country.

2. OBJECTIVE

The objective of the study was to examine the account of agents in improvising telecommunication infrastructures' services to rural community of South African. The data collection and analysis were guided by the duality of structure from the perspective of Structuration Theory, a lens used to understanding the roles of the different agents in the deployment of telecommunication infrastructures. in the country's rural communities.

The remainder of this paper is divided into six sections. The first section is the literature review, which covered infrastructure components, and the underpinning theory, structuration theory. In the second section, the methodology that was followed in the study is discussed. The data analysis is presented in the third section. Findings and interpretation of the findings are presented in the fourth and fifth sections, respectively. Finally, a conclusion was drawn.

3. LITERATURE REVIEW

Due to the roles of the influencing factors, the development and deployment of telecommunication infrastructure has increasingly become very complex. The influences factors in the deployment of telecommunications infrastructures include technology, process and people as presented in Figure 1.

Figure 1. Components of IT strategy
(Iyamu & Adelakun, 2008)

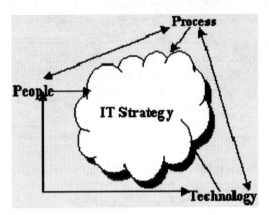

3.1 People

The development and implementation of telecommunications network infrastructure are conducted through processes which are formulated by people (Iyamu & Adelakun, 2008). People have an integral and essential role in a process. Any worthwhile endeavour involves having the right people doing the right things the right way at the right time (Heiring & Phillips, 2005). Thus, people should be involved from different disciplines as they are crucial in translating their insights into the technology innovation process. Different people bring different skill sets and view points to any project (Heiring & Phillips, 2005).

According to Iyamu and Adelakun (2008), people act on the basis of their interpretations and these drive and determine the capabilities of the technology, the process of using the technology and the outcomes of the technology. Wixom (2001) further point out that while people can make a given project succeed the same people can make a project fail. Therefore, people and the roles they play, are key to the success to innovation and, innovation is a process and dependent on people to drive it forward (Heiring & Phillips, 2005). Therefore, the crucial job of telecommunication infrastructures deployment and negotiating the sharing is thereof performed by people through processes.

3.2 Process

Shtub and Kami (2010) defined process as a *"specific ordering of work activities across time and place, with a beginning, an end, and clearly identified inputs and outputs"* (. Within the context of this article, process is responsible for the non-technical aspects of shared telecommunication infrastructures development from requirements to deployment and sharing stages. The importance of process is to reduce time and improve quality when developing and deploying technology infrastructure (Mooney, Gurbaxani & Kraemer, 2001). The failure of most technology infrastructure deployment is the lack of well-defined processes. The first insights into the infrastructure process are community interactions, stakeholder goals and concerns (Jensen & Scacchi, 2005).

The deployment of telecommunications infrastructure is done through processes at different locations throughout the country, in both rural and urban areas. The processes are applied differently based on context and requirements of each geographical area. The processes through which organisation's telecommunication infrastructures were deployed, were initiated, developed and carried out by people. Some of the people (stakeholders) involved in the deployment processes, include CEOs, CIOs, IT managers and IT technicians. These people are guided by organisational and regulatory process.

3.3 Technology

Technology infrastructure consists of physical technology which includes technological artefacts. According to Nyrhinen (2006), technology infrastructure consists of various components such as hardware and software, used to produce services. In Markard (2009), technology infrastructure is referred to as socio-technical in nature.

In providing telecommunications services, firstly, the service providers deploys different technology infrastructures to meet their goals, and for competitive advantage. The infrastructure includes all technologies that enable the high speed transfer of multi-media and high bandwidth information (Papacharissi & Zaks, 2006). However not all technologies are appropriate for all areas of the country owing to the variety of landscapes across the geographical locations of the country. For example, some areas are mountainous, which has an impact on the frequency spectrum and network coverage by the base station.

Iyamu and Adelakun (2008) argue that there are underlying relations between these three components. Their existence is enacted by their interactions. Structuration theory focuses on the relationship and interaction between human and non-human agents.

3.4 Structuration Theory

The two main tenets of the Structuration Theory (ST) are Agent and Structure. In ST, agents are both human and non-human (Iyamu, 2013). The theory is concerned with the influence on human interaction of institutional (structural) aspects of social life such as rules, communication and power structures and, the reproduction of these structural aspects through human interaction (Giddens, 1984). He developed the theory with the aim of understanding how social practices are ordered across time and space.

The theory looks at the recursive interplay of action and structure in social practice (Giddens, 1979). These actions are carried out by agents within the structure, thus social structure is drawn upon by agents in their day to day actions and is thus produced and reproduced by these actions. Social structure is therefore seen as being drawn on by human agents in their action, while the actions of human in social contexts serve to produce and reproduce the social structure. It is therefore the process whereby the duality of structure evolves and is reproduced over time and space in social systems (Gao & Lyytinen, 2003). The duality of structure suggests that action is guided by structure and that structure is created by action (Giddens, 1984). In other words, people's actions create structure and without action, structures disappear. The social system can be understood by its structure, modality and interaction. Thus rules and resources governing the social systems are translated into action by actors' interactions within the social system.

4. METHODOLOGY

Research methodology highlights the methods and tools that are used during the research process Babbie & Mouton, 2006). To understand how the telecommunication infrastructures can be consolidated and shared among current telecommunications network providers in South Africa, a qualitative research approach was adopted. This is primarily because the approach's strength and its explicitly emphasises on real World and natural seatings in understanding why and how certain things happen the way they do (Mkhomazi & Iyamu, 2013). This research approach regards reality as subjective therefore allows the researcher to discover reality from the participants' point of view, as participants may have different interpretations regarding the phenomena in question (Denzin & Lincoln, 2005).

Within the qualitative paradigm, the case study method was adopted, mainly to contribute specific knowledge about the processes and activities involved in the deployment of shared telecommunication infrastructures in the rural areas of South Africa. It offered an opportunity to formulate a detailed description of the social or organisational aspects of the social-technical interplay when deploying shared telecommunication infrastructures in rural areas.

Leo telecommunications was selected for the study. This was mainly because of the objectives and goals of the organisation, which focuses on the deployment of telecommunications infrastructures in the country. A total of twelve employees were interviewed within the organisation. The interviewees included five senior and seven junior employees of the organisation. Of the twelves interviewees, eight were at technologists, and others were at management levels. Each of the interviewees has spent at least five years in the organisation, as at the time of this study.

ST as a lens was used to analyse data. The use of ST allowed the study a more complete analysis of how telecommunication infrastructures sharing and implementation were affected by technical and non-technical factors, which manifest from the reproduction of actions of the agents.

ST is a social-technical theory which focuses on interaction between human and non-human agents. From the perspective of ST, Giddens (1984) offers three modalities that link human action to social structure. The modalities (interpretive schemes, facility and norms) link human actions (communication, power and sanction) with the structurural components (signification, domination and legitimation). According to Iyamu (2013:228), "Structuration offers a subtle and detailed view of the constitution of social life. Its analytical dimensions through the duality of structure and its associated modalities could be very detailed and helps in an empirical analysis in some instances. Human action is composed of structures of meaning, power and moral frameworks". The theory has been extensively applied in information systems studies, owing to its strength to examine agents relationship (Jones and Karsten, 2008).

5. STRUCTURATION VIEW OF SHARED TELECOMMUNICATION INFRASTRUCTURE DEPLOYMENT

The duality of structure, was used as lens in the analysis of data. Following the duality of structure, Table 1 presents the interactions that happened between agents during the deployment of telecommunications infrastructure in South Africa.

The Interplay of Agents in Improvising Telecommunication Infrastructures' Services

Table 1. Deployment of telecommunication infrastructure

Signification	Domination	Legitimation
The deployment of telecommunications infrastructure is considered strategic and operational in the organisation. The infrastructure is used to provide services which are the main focus of the organisation.	The CEO is responsible and accountable for the deployment of telecommunications infrastructure by the organisation.	Telecommunications infrastructure is deployed within the rules and regulations of the organisation, as well as that of the country.
Interpretative Scheme	**Facility**	**Norms**
The telecommunications infrastructure deployment is intended to provide services to audiences as widely as possible. This ensures competitive advantage and return on investment (ROI).	The deployment of telecommunications infrastructure involves both technical and non-technical components, such as technology, people and processes.	The organisation deploys infrastructure to provide telecommunications services such as the Internet to the communities.
Communication	**Power**	**Sanction**
The deployment of telecommunications infrastructure involves procedural activities, which are shared among the stakeholders, through defined channels.	The organisation provide telecommunications infrastructure and as such they have the authority to deploy infrastructure in geographical locations throughout the country as they deem fit.	The employees, including technicians and managers, approve of the deployment of infrastructure in different geographical locations throughout the country.

Duality of Structure: Signification and Communication

The deployment of telecommunication infrastructures was important to Leo Telecommunications, primarily because it was the core of its businesses. The business strategy of the organisation was based on their infrastructures that they deployed to ensure, enable and support telecommunication services such as the Internet and mobile telephone communication. The strategy focuses on a competitive advantage. A manager clarifies one of the purposes of the organisation by stating as follows, *"the core business of the organisation is to provide mobile telecommunications services. Therefore the deployment of infrastructure is crucial for the organisation's competitive strategy in the telecommunications market"*. The organisation focuses on the type of infrastructures they deployed, as well as on the location, and how they were deployed. The rationale for the deployment of infrastructures in selected and certain areas was primarily aimed at the realisation of objectives, such as ROI and competitive advantage.

Due to the fact that the telecommunication infrastructures were deployed for competitive advantage, the type, how and where the deployment takes place was vital. However, the availability of the infrastructures was not only critical to Leo Telecommunications, it was also considered to be an important factor to citizens, businesses and government entities, for development and economic growth of the country. One of the managers did emphasis, *the organisation provides access to telecommunications network infrastructure by leasing the transmission links to businesses such as banks and companies as a commercial agreement "*

Leo Telecommunications followed certain processes in the deployment of their infrastructures. These processes included the organisational rules and regulations. The rules and regulations were communicated through various channels to the stakeholders that were involved in the deployment of the infrastructures. The rules and regulations were considered very important as these were the main means through which stakeholders, particularly the technicians, were controlled and managed during the deployment of infrastructures.

As revealed earlier, there were external rules and regulations that influenced the deployment of telecommunication infrastructures. These rules and regulations were communicated to the organisation as part of the requirements which they had to consider in the deployment of their telecommunication infrastructures. The rules were therefore often incorporated into to the organisation's deployment process as guidelines to be followed when deploying telecommunications infrastructure. One of the managers explained that, *"during the planning phase of the project the municipal bylaws and regulatory requirements are taken into account to be able to project how much time is needed to build the infrastructure"*

Unfortunately for Leo Telecommunications, the Government's (Municipal bylaws) rules and regulations were not the same across the country. They have an impact on how and where telecommunications infrastructure can be deployed. This made the rules and regulations significant factors in the deployment of telecommunication infrastructures in the different geographical areas. One of the managers explained as follow: *"Sometimes the application process takes longer because of the slow process of site approval from municipalities. The problem in our country is that our municipalities do not follow the same procedures in certain areas when it comes to the deployment of telecommunications infrastructure"*.

When it came to communication of processes and activities, the organisation adopted the top-bottom approach in the deployment of its telecommunication infrastructures. For example, the CEO share with his immediate reporting-line (Managers) where, when and how certain infrastructure should be deployed. The Managers further share the information with their subordinates. In general the employees and managers of Leo Telecommunications understand the significance of communication in the deployment of telecommunications infrastructure. The communication helped to clarify the roles and responsibilities to stakeholders that were involved in each of the activities of infrastructure deployment.

The communication that takes place in the deployment of telecommunication infrastructures aids in the understanding of the individual and groups' roles and responsibilities. The communication also helps to understand why specific infrastructures were deployed in certain areas. The factors of communications, interaction and understanding manifested themselves into how certain individual and groups dominated and, certain facilities (infrastructures) were preferred. The next section covers domination and power within the frame of duality of structure.

Duality of Structure: Domination and Power

Different stakeholders are involved in the infrastructure deployment process. The executive manager of the Engineering department in Leo Telecommunication was responsible and accountable for where, how and when telecommunications infrastructure was deployed. The manager was mandated by the executive committee based on the organisational objectives and strategy. One of the managers explained, *the executive manager presents the mandate to deploy infrastructure to all managers in the Engineering division. He based his ideas on the readings of the current telecommunications infrastructure and technology deployment globally"*

This deployment of the telecommunication infrastructures included processes, people (stakeholders) and technology. The stakeholders applied the processes and facilities (technology infrastructures) in the way they understood or suited them. For example, some of the technicians and engineers deployed the telecommunication infrastructures in an area where they were more comfortable to do so. The technicians could make certain critical decisions mainly because their managers relied on their unique and specialised technical know-how. They used this as their sources of power, and used it to dominate when it came to certain technical exploration and decisions in the deployment of infrastructures. This often happened in the consideration to deploy telecommunication infrastructures in the rural areas, where many factors such as base station deployment and connectivity were involved. The decisions were often of a collective nature. One of the employees explained, *there are stakeholders' meetings every quarter to discuss areas where the organisation has no coverage and areas where we need to upgrade network infrastructure".*

The technicians enforced their power, even though the initial decisions were made by the Executive committee. The outcome of the executive committee was normally communicated to the field workers (technicians and engineers) to deploy the telecommunications infrastructure as prescribed. Upon the decision to deploy infrastructure and when the site and environmental assessments are done, the organisation presents its proposal to deploy network infrastructure to the local municipality and regulatory authority for approval. One of the participants expressed his understanding as follows: *"once the site is identified and the organisation's legal team has signed for any legal issues that might arise after the site has been deployed, the organisation starts negotiations with the local municipality and gets approval from the regulatory authority to deploy network infrastructure".*

The organisation understood that they could share telecommunication infrastructure with other service providers if they wanted to do so. The challenge was how to address the control and management of the shared infrastructure. Each of the organisations strives to have maximum power over their infrastructure. It was seen as a contributing factor to their competitiveness. Another important factor was that Leo Telecommunications and other service providers did not know how the infrastructures could be shared in order to achieve mutual benefits. However, many of the employees in the organisation do understand that there would be benefits if infrastructures are shared with other telecommunication companies. One of the interviewees shared her view as follows: *"the organisation deploys infrastructure solely instead of sharing with other organisations because the telecommunications market is saturated and competition is very high".*

There was also the factor of land property which was owned by the Government (Municipality). The Municipality often defines what and how infrastructure should be deployed on its property. In some cases, the number of infrastructures deployment was limited in certain areas. According to some of the employees of the organisation, *"Municipalities don't allow everybody trenching for fibre deployment. Network operators are forced to share the base station and the price of trenching in some areas". "There are many cases where the municipalities wouldn't like to see more network sites built especially in the city areas and we have to respect that".*

Cost was a critical factor in the deployment of telecommunication infrastructure, particularly when it came to return on investment and sustainability. It was understood by some employees, including managers, that if infrastructures are shared with other telecommunication companies, there could be cost savings. On behalf of the organisation, one of the managers briefly explained: *"The primary driver of Leo Telecommunications is embracing infrastructure sharing in its operational efficiency to actually reduce the cost".* However, there are different views on the sharing of infrastructure within the organisation. Sharing of telecommunications infrastructure has a major impact on the organisation's competitive advantage. Many of organisations including Leo Telecommunications vest their power on their competitive advantage. Some individuals who participated in the study expressed their views: *"Infrastructure sharing can stifle or kill competition because once there are commercial inter-company agreements, those companies are no longer in competition in that area. They are splitting up the market so that they can turn a profit", "There is no competitive advantage for organisations sharing infrastructure because they are providing the same services which makes it difficult to distinguish yourself in the market".*

The Government requests and urges the telecommunication companies to deploy telecommunication infrastructures across the country, at a 99.9 percent rate by the year 2013. This is to empower all areas of the country with a facility to get involved in economic and social activities. Even though the Government urges companies to reach a certain (99.9 percent) percentage, the final decision do rest with them. Leo Telecommunication has the power to decide how much infrastructure they deploy, and where they deploy them. The organisation's deployment strategy was the reason why Leo Telecommunication infrastructures, such as base stations are insufficiently deployed in certain areas. The selection of areas for network deployment was based on the organisation's investment strategy. The organisation's network does not cover all the geographical areas within the country, hence the struggle and challenge for network for internet connectivity. This decision could be attributed to the population size of the community. As a result of the limited infrastructure, the facilities to make use of the Internet were prohibitive. According to one of the managers, *"The organisation has over the years systematically deployed network infrastructure in areas where there is a large population of people that do not have any telecommunications services"*.

The deployment of telecommunications infrastructure in geographical locations was based on certain criteria, such as population density and average income group. Even though the Government does not consider the use of income group as legitimate, Leo Telecommunications continue to consider it as a criterion. Some of the managers in the organisations confirmed as follows: *"The organisation is not focusing on deploying telecommunication infrastructures in rural areas, but in bigger towns". Population density and average salary is taken into consideration before we can deploy infrastructure in certain areas"*. Most of the advanced facilities (technologies) such as 3G and HSPA+ were deployed in urban areas. This was mainly because the organisation considered urban areas as a source for higher revenue. This strategy was to achieve advantage over competitors. According to some of the managers, *"It will be a waste of money and resources to deploy 3G technologies in rural areas, because it is not used by the majority of the people"*. *"It is expensive to deploy advanced technology infrastructure in a community of few people if you are not sure they will use it"*.

There are contradictory views and opinions in the organisation. Some of the employees believe the lack of technology deployment in less populated areas, was not a cost factor, but rather a people problem. The people problem was caused by lack of understanding and technical know-how. Unfortunately, the decision of the Executive Committee was final. One of the managers who was dissatisfied with the strategy (decision) explained as follows: *"We don't have a technology problem; there is no reason why technology cannot cover everybody in South Africa. Cheaper technology can be deployed, however it is the people involved in the network roll-out plan to make a decision"*. In addition to the technologies, there were other factors that influenced and sometimes hampered the deployment and sharing of infrastructures in the rural areas. The factors included ownership and maintenance of infrastructures. For example, spectrum was owned by the Government, and thus not readily available to the organisation as it is required. As such, spectrum availability was seen as a barrier to penetrating rural areas. Some of the managers pointed out: *"It is difficult to deploy infrastructure in rural areas because of insufficient spectrum. The organisation is hoping that the availability of the digital dividend spectrum which will be available in two to three years when the analogue TV technology is switched off will be able to cover the rural areas with broadband technologies"*.

Maintenance of infrastructure is another factor that was a challenge for Leo Telecommunications when deploying network infrastructure. It was regarded as expensive and difficult to maintain the network in rural areas. According to one of participants, *"The maintenance of the transmission sites in rural areas is a challenge. Unavailability of electricity results in the maintenance of transmission sites to be expensive because the organisation has to deploy generators to maintain the sites"*.

Leo Telecommunications ensured that the infrastructures that they deployed were solely under their control and management. The infrastructures were then used as a source of power when it came to a competitive advantage and sustainability. However, this led to their services to the community being prohibitive. It could have been avoided if infrastructure was shared with other telecommunications organisations to reduce costs of resources and management.

Even though the telecommunication infrastructures that were deployed made services scarce and prohibitive, they were provided within the rules and regulations of the organisation and the Government. The next section presents the analysis on how the infrastructures were legitimised, how they became the norm and, got approval (sanctioned) for their deployment.

Duality of Structure: Legitimation and Sanctions

Leo Telecommunications holds a license to supply mobile communications services to customers in South Africa. As such, the organisation provides a technology platform for delivering telecommunications services. This covers services such as Internet to the communities, rural areas included. One of the participants in the study explained: *"The organisation rolls out network infrastructure with the intention to achieve the goal of putting the power of Internet in people's hands"*.

As already revealed, the technology investment was a crucial component in the deployment of telecommunications infrastructure. Apart from the rules and regulations, the varying environmental factors also determined the legitimisation of the choice of technology. Some participants in the study shared views on behalf of the organisation: *"With certain areas (rural) having hills, mountains and rivers it has been a challenge for the organisation to find the technology which is less expensive that can cover the footprint of at least five kilometres"*. *"The majority of rural communities are utilising the GPRS and EDGE services to provide broadband data needs"*.

The deployment of telecommunication infrastructures is accepted within the organisation as a business strategy. As a result, the types of infrastructures, where and how they were deployed were fundamental to the organisation's objectives. These aspects attributed to why certain areas like rural areas, where the community is sparsely populated and people struggle with affordability, receives limited network coverage.

The organisation adopts processes which were considered suitable, in the deployment of telecommunications infrastructure across the country. The two processes adopted were technical oriented process and management strategy. The technical process was a bottom-up approach, while the management strategy process was a top-down approach. The top-bottom approach was the process which allowed the management (Executives) to make strategic decision on behalf of the organisation. The strategy was then drilled down to other employees for implementation. However, before the strategy was formulated, data which forms part of the requirements were collected from technicians and the engineering field works. This was the bottom-up approach. One of the managers explained as follows: *"The organisation follows the top-down approach for deploying telecommunications infrastructure and this strategy has been accepted by all stakeholders as the operational process of doing things in the organisation"*.

Results from technicians and engineering field works were approved at various levels of the organisational structure before they were presented to the management team. Some of the considerations of the field works included population areas, landscape of different locations and infrastructure fit. In addition to the engineers' field works, the Government's policies and regulations were also taken into consideration and adhered to when it came to the development of the organisation's strategy document. The strategy document was presented at all levels in the organisation for buy-in and understanding before they could embark on implementation.

Based on the Government's policies and regulations, the regulatory body specified service level requirements in the license that they granted to Leo Telecommunications. The service level requirements included Municipal by-laws. A complete implementation or adherence to the service level requirements was not an easy task to achieve, particularly, when they considered their financial profitability interest. On behalf of the organisation, some of the managers expressed their views as follows: *"The municipal bylaws requirements make the process of deploying infrastructure difficult and slow". "The major obstacle to have 100 per cent telecommunication infrastructures penetration in the country is the regulatory requirements in the sense that they cannot expect the same service levels everywhere and the company to turn profits"*.

The telecommunication infrastructures deployments followed legitimised processes and were approved by involved stakeholders. However, the processes gave little or no room for negotiation. Even though the processes were challenging, they were accepted as the norm in the organisation. The management continued to base their decisions of financial implications and competitive advantage.

Based on the above analysis, some factors were found to be of influence to the rationale why telecommunication infrastructures and deployment thereof could or could not be shared amongst the companies. The findings are discussed in the following section.

6. FACTORS INFLUENCING TELECOMMUNICATION INFRASTRUCTURE DEPLOYMENT

As mentioned above, from the analysis, some factors were found to be influencing and critical to the deployment of telecommunication infrastructure sharing. The factors include insufficient distribution of infrastructure, ownership responsibility, competitiveness, infrastructure deployment cost, and signification of regulation. The factors interconnect and depend on each other as illustrated in Figure 2, and discussed below.

- **Insufficient Distribution of Infrastructure:** Telecommunication Infrastructures support and provide services such as the Internet and Mobile telephone system. Telecommunication infrastructures are therefore critically important to almost everyone in the country, particularly to those who know and understand the usefulness. As a result, it is essential to deploy the infrastructure in every location of the country. Unfortunately, that is not the case as at the time of this study. Leo Telecommunications, the company used as the case study, deployed telecommunication infrastructures based on their core business and competitive advantage strategy.

Based on the strategy of the organisation, telecommunication infrastructures were selectively deployed to achieve its goals and objectives, which were primarily cost factors (return on investment). In an attempt to manage cost and be more profitable, infrastructures were scarcely acquired and distributed. Areas with low population density received limited coverage as a result of insufficient infrastructures.

The insufficient distribution of telecommunication infrastructures manifested from geographical prioritisation in accordance to the organisation's strategy. As revealed in the analysis, lack of business interest in certain geographical locations (rural), was influenced by a cost factor, a return on investment strategy. Sharing of infrastructure with other telecommunication companies will help resolve this challenge. In this case, financial implications and commitments in the purchase and management of the infrastructures will be shared amongst the parties.

Figure 2. Factors influencing telecommunication infrastructure deployment

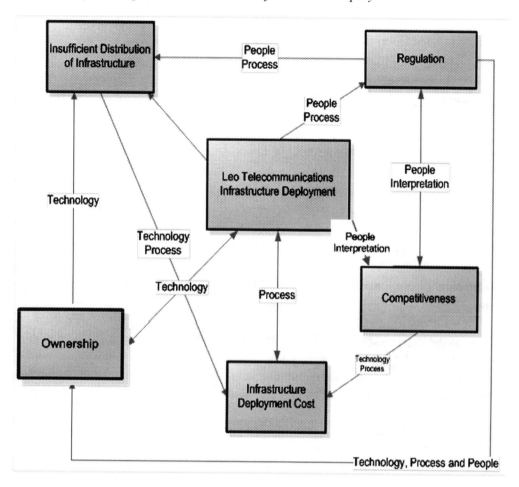

- **Regulation:** Regulation provides guidance, administrative processes and procedures in the operationalisation of services. The importance of regulation is that it provides operators with know-how acts and behaviour (in terms of services and competition) in the telecommunication industry. Regulation has a major influence on the deployment of telecommunication infrastructure, as it defines the product types and where and how deployment should be carried out. Regulation helps to manage and keep control of governance. For example, based on regulation, spectrum technology is not owned by telecommunication companies.

The Government's regulation forces the telecommunication companies, Leo Telecommunications included, to provide all areas of the country with some telecommunication infrastructures. Otherwise, limited access which is currently provided to rural areas would have been reduced to zero. The reason is that such area is not financially viable, as revealed in the analysis.

Leo Telecommunications incorporates the regulations in their deployment of infrastructure strategies and decision making and this aids in the projection of return on investment. However, the organisation is challenged with the deployment of shared infrastructure owing to the fact that regulatory policies and standards governing the telecommunication industry are not consistent throughout the different municipalities.

Regulation will foster and facilitate sharing of infrastructure in the country. Sharing of infrastructure will improve sufficient distribution among the geographical locations. However, the same regulation constrained telecommunication from sharing some infrastructures such as spectrum

- **Competitiveness:** Competition contributes to the reduction of costs (pricing of services), affordability and innovation in a market environment. It is said to be a key aspect of telecommunication services accessibility and affordability. The role of competition is believed to encourage more rapid telecommunication infrastructure deployment and improvement.

Owing to competitiveness, the organisation was challenged with the rapid and specific technology deployment in some rural areas. The organisation adopts different approaches in deploying infrastructure, which was influenced by the competitive advantage with respect to where and how to deploy telecommunication infrastructures. Infrastructures were not shared. This had an impact on the telecommunication services in different geographical areas, thus making services prohibitive.

Owing to the dimensions of the geographical locations, the competition among the network service providers increases with regards to their drive to achieve return on infrastructure investment. The technologies which were deployed were based on return on investment and had a major impact on the sharing of infrastructures. Enhancing competition was one of Leo Telecommunications' goals. However, at the time of this study, the organisation considered infrastructure sharing as defeating the purpose of competitiveness. The impact of competitiveness on the telecommunications environment leads to an increase in the deployment of infrastructures. Many of these infrastructures were duplicated. Unfortunately, the end users, which are the communities, indirectly bear the cost.

- **Infrastructure Deployment Cost:** The control and reduction of expenses are every business' strategic goals. Both capital and operational costs are fundamental to the operationalisation, sustainability and growth of the business. The costs form part of the total cost of infrastructure deployment and, it influences the organisation's net profit. Cost of infrastructure deployment was influenced by the geographical locations.

The cost of infrastructure deployment in the rural areas was considered to be higher as compared to the urban areas. Hence, Leo Telecommunications was challenged when it came to deploying infrastructures in rural communities. The costs associated to deployment of telecommunication infrastructures were attributed to transportation and capacity.

The proximity of many of the rural areas and where infrastructures are located, controlled and managed from the organisation's Head Offices were not close. Leo Telecommunications deploys infrastructures in accordance to population size and landscape. This meant that capacity of the infrastructures which were deployed in rural areas were less utilised. This forces the organisation to deploy less, which was not enough to cover the community. If the telecommunication infrastructures are shared, the cost could be reduced, ultimately making affordability easier for the community members.

- **Ownership:** Some of the technologies, such as spectrum, used by Telecommunication companies (Leo Telecommunications included) in South Africa were not owned by them. Spectrum refers to radio frequencies on which all telecommunications signals travel and which supports bandwidth capabilities. It is a critical element in the deployment of telecommunication infrastructures.

The Interplay of Agents in Improvising Telecommunication Infrastructures' Services

Ownership of spectrum was fundamental on how, where and when technologies were accessed, deployed, managed and controlled. As a result of the lack of ownership, there was limitation on the technology's availability. The limited technology was therefore channelled to areas where return on investment was more guaranteed. This had an impact on the organisation's strategic objectives such as infrastructure sharing.

The findings from this case (Leo Telecommunications) as discussed above were caused and influenced by certain factors. On these bases, they were interpreted..

7. INTERPRETATION AND DISCUSSION

The interpretation of the factors influencing telecommunications infrastructure deployment discussed above unveiled the existence of the causes and influences and these factors are mapped as shown in Figure 3. The core of those causes and factors of influence in the deployment of telecommunication infrastructures include deployment strategy, scarcity of technological resources and regulatory standards. The factors are depicted in the Figure 3 and discussed below.

Deployment Strategy

Activities that were carried out by Leo Telecommunications were guided by strategy. In alignment, the telecommunication infrastructures that were deployed by the organisation were within its strategy. Although the organisation's deployment strategy was influenced by other two factors (scarcity of technological resources and regulatory standards), the organisation primarily focused on return on investment and competitive advantage. As revealed from the analysis and findings, some of the items and elements which constitute the deployment strategy are discussed in the remainder of this section.

Figure 3. Sharing telecommunications infrastructure deployment

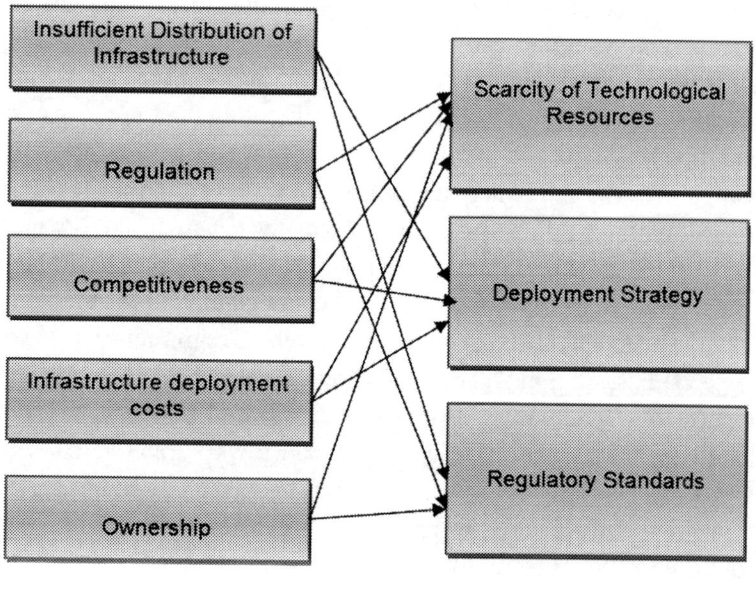

Community population and geographical landscape has a major influence on the deployment strategy. These factors have an impact on the deployment of sufficient infrastructure across all geographical locations. It ultimately resulted in inequality in the infrastructure distribution process and the way in which the organisation prioritises geographical areas. Some areas, especially rural areas, are not considered to be priorities, which results in a lack of sufficient infrastructure such as base stations. The organisation regards these areas as not being economically viable in terms of returns on their investment. The rural areas are considered to be low-income markets and the organisation is therefore less interested in deploying shared telecommunication infrastructure. Since urban areas yield more income, infrastructure investment is primarily defined for urban areas.

In accordance with the organisation's standard process, they solely use most of their infrastructure, rather than sharing with other operators because of the saturated telecommunications market. However, in certain areas, particularly in urban areas, they do explore shared infrastructure deployment. In some cases the organisation has to comply with requirements of the land owners (municipalities). Because of the competitive advantage in the industry, particularly in rural areas, it is not a preferred deployment process for the company.

A strategy that encompasses shared infrastructure can still be of value for the organisation's profitability and sustainability. Infrastructure sharing could however be instrumental in increasing the coverage of telecommunications services in the country. The penetration in rural areas will not only support the growth of telecommunications service providers, but will also boost the demand for telecommunication services through its infrastructures.

Scarcity of Technological Resources

Similarly, the scarcity of technological resources factor was influenced by deployment strategy and regulatory standards factors. In the deployment of telecommunication infrastructures and technological choices, management play a key role in the deployment strategy. Deployment of telecommunications infrastructure is meaningless without the technology infrastructure that makes it operational. Leo Telecommunications deploys different technologies, but these technologies are not suitable for all geographical areas.

The deployment of infrastructures required technological resources, which the deployment strategy and regulatory standards should support and enable. Unfortunately, there was scarcity of technological resources in the deployment infrastructures of Leo Telecommunications. This impacts infrastructure sharing. Some of the rationales that led to this factor (scarcity of technological resources) are discussed further in this section.

Available technologies for the implementation of telecommunication infrastructures are expensive and depending on the geographical dimensions their footprints have a limited range. These limitations have become a barrier to sufficient infrastructure deployment in the country. In some rural communities, which are characterised by hills and mountains, it has been a challenge for the organisation to deploy less expensive technology with adequate coverage for the whole community. For example, some communities only have one 2G base station and one radio network controller for 3G sites. The base station has five cell sites connected to it and each site covers a footprint of five kilometres of the area.

Some rural areas do not have network coverage and those who are covered with the network, are partially covered with some portions out of the network coverage. The majority of the areas covered are limited to 2G technologies which are insufficient for telecommunication infrastructures' services. Even though the foot print of the transmission site technologies covers five kilometres of the area, the majority of the coverage is outside the ratio of the community. This was influenced by the strategy of the organisation, which focuses on return on investment. Another primary factor which drives the decision to deploy the infrastructures in the way they did was the scarcity of technological resources.

Technologies such as spectrum have a major impact on the deployment of shared telecommunications infrastructure. The scarcity of spectrum is a major concern and it also contributes to how and where the organisation (Leo telecommunications) chooses to deploy telecommunication infrastructures. However, spectrum availability is a regulatory issue and it could take years to actually see further telecommunication infrastructures penetration in the country. However if spectrum could be shared it would expand the network service coverage in rural communities and, in areas where telecommunication infrastructures is non-existent.

Regulatory Standards

The deployment of telecommunication infrastructures was influenced and guided by regulatory standards. The regulatory standards were from both the Government and within the organisation. The regulations were aimed at maintaining uniformity, control and competitive leverage.

The regulatory standards were expected to ease support and management of telecommunication infrastructures. Also, adherence to the same standards would ensure and facilitate infrastructure synergy and consolidation. More importantly, standardisation would engineer sharing of infrastructures among the telecommunication companies. Otherwise, the telecommunication companies will continue to have different definitions for the various infrastructures, and how they deploy them. Different definitions and standards lead and contribute to slow deployment, expensive resources and, increases competition and cost of services to the community.

Even though standardisation was crucial to the Government, some of the Municipalities had different standards in their operations. The lack of standardised procedures from Municipalities for defining the regulatory requirements has a major impact on the deployment of telecommunication infrastructures. While it was necessary to meet the requirements of the environmental impact assessments in the interest of the communities, delays in granting permission had an impact on the deployment time of telecommunication infrastructures. However, some regulatory standards which were intended to support and guide deployment of infrastructures were constraining in certain areas. This was primarily because of the lack of unification of standardisation.

There was an urgent need to streamline the procedures within different Municipalities throughout the country. This was to formulate a single standardised policy, so as to achieve faster deployment of infrastructures. There were no proper guidelines promulgated on how a Municipality's bylaws should be communicated to telecommunications organisations. This indicates that a consultation process with Municipalities was necessary to draft a standard policy on infrastructure deployment requirements in order to guide service providers in the deployment of infrastructure particularly base stations.

8. CONCLUSION

This article empirically unveils the criticality and signification of telecommunication infrastructures sharing in rural areas of South African communities. The study therefore argued that infrastructures sharing in developing countries such as South Africa can only be achieved through collective responsibility by actors, which include the telecommunication companies, regulatory boards and the communities. Therefore, deployment of telecommunication infrastructure constitutes social and political, as well as technological factors and processes. Thus the approach of sharing can be considered as a tool to addressing rapid deployment of telecommunication infrastructures.

The findings from the study are intended to assist the stakeholders to accelerate deployment and sharing of telecommunication infrastructures in the rural areas of the country. The consolidation of telecommunication infrastructures could help reduce cost and promote economic growth, and in so doing, or in effect, alleviate poverty in rural areas. The processes and influencing factors of shared telecommunication infrastructures involve socio-technical factors and the interplay between human action and social systems.

REFERENCES

Babbie, E., & Mouton, J. (2006). *The Practice of Social Research*. Cape Town: Oxford University Press.

Bhawan, M. D., & Marg, J. L. (2007). Telecom Regulatory Authority of India (TRAI): recommendations on infrastructure sharing. Delhi-110002.

Denzin, N. K., & Lincoln, Y. S. (2005). The SAGE handbook of qualitative research (3rd ed.). London: Thousand Oaks: Sage Publications.

Gao, P., & Lyytinen, K. J. (2003). *China telecommunications transformation in globalization context: a structuration perspective*. Paper presented in the IFIP/TC8.2 and 9.4 Working Conference on IS Perspectives and Challenges in the Context of Globalization. Athens, Greece. doi:10.1007/978-0-387-35695-2_14

Giddens, A. (1979). *Central problems in social theory*. Basingstoke, UK: Macmillan.

Giddens, A. (1984). *The Constitution of society: Outline of the theory of Structuration*. Berkely, CA: University of California Press.

Heiring, D., & Phillips, J. (2005). Innovation Roles: The people you need for successful innovation [White Paper].

Herselman, M. (2003). *ICT in rural areas in South Africa: Various case studies*. Paper presented at the InSITE Conference. Pori, Finland.

Iyamu, T. (2013). Underpinning Theories: Order-of-Use in Information Systems Research. *Journal of Systems and Information Technology*, *15*(3), 1–13. doi:10.1108/JSIT-11-2012-0064

Iyamu, T., & Adelakun, O. (2008). *The impact of non-technical factors on Information Technology Strategy and E-business*. Paper presented at the PACIS Conference, Suzhou, China

Jensen, C., & Scacchi, W. (2005). Process Modeling of the Web Information Infrastructure. *Software Process Improvement and Practice*, *10*(3), 255–272. doi:10.1002/spip.228

Jones, M. R., & Karsten, H. (2008). Giddens's structuration theory and information systems research. *Society for Information Management and The Management Information Systems Research*, *32*(1), 127–157.

Markard, J. (2009, October 29). Characteristics of infrastructure sectors and implications for innovation processes. *Discussion paper for the workshop on environmental innovation in infrastructure sectors*. Karisruhe.

Mkhomazi, S. S., & Iyamu, T. (2013). A Guide to Selecting Theory to Underpin Information Systems Studies. In Y. Dwivedi, H. Henrksen, D. Wastell, & R. De (Eds.), *Grand Successes and Failures in IT* (pp. 525–538). doi:10.1007/978-3-642-38862-0_33

Mooney, J. G., Gurbaxani, V., & Kraemer, K. L. (2001). A Process oriented framework for assessing the business value of Information Technology. *ACM SIGMIS Database, 27*(2), 68–81. doi:10.1145/243350.243363

Muente-Kunigami, A., & Navas-Sabater, J. (2009). *Options to increase access to telecommunications services in rural and low income areas*. Washington DC, USA: World Bank working paper.

Nyrhinen, M. (2006). *IT Infrastructure: Structure, properties and processes* [Working paper, W-403]. HSE Print Organisation for Economic Cooperation and Development.

Papacharissi, Z., & Zaks, A. (2006). Is Broadband the future? An analysis of broadband technology potential and diffusion. *Telecommunications Policy, 30*(1), 64–75. doi:10.1016/j.telpol.2005.08.001

Roman, E. S. (2009). *Bringing broadband access to rural areas: A step-by-step approach for regulators, policy makers and universal access program administrators*. Paper presented at the Nineth Global Symposium for Regulators. Beirut, Lebanon.

Shtub, A., & Kami, R. (2010). *ERP: The Dynamic of Suppuly Chain and Process Management*. New York: Springer. doi:10.1007/978-0-387-74526-8

The role of communication infrastructure investment in economic recovery: Working party on communication infrastructure and services policy. (2009). OECD. Retrieved from http://www.oecd.org/dataoecd/4/43/42799709.pdf

Wixom, B. H., & Watson, H. J. (2001). An Empirical Investigation on the factors affecting Data Warehouse success. *MIS Quaterly, 2*(1), 17–41. doi:10.2307/3250957

Chapter 12
Engineering the Services of the Library through Mobile Technology

Eunice Mtshali
Tshwane University of Technology, South Africa

ABSTRACT

Many universities are struggling to response the needs of its users. This is attributed to the rapid change in technological innovations. The growing interest on mobile technology in organisations is at a fast pace, particularly in institutions of higher learning. Mobile technology could be used in academic libraries to provide a better service to their clients or improve the service that they currently provide. Case study research was conducted at Capital University to understand the factors that could influence and impact the adoption of mobile technology in academic library services.

1. INTRODUCTION

The adoption of mobile technology in organisation including institution of higher learning is rapidly increasing, more than ever in the last few years (Castells et al., 2007).The increase in adoption and usage of mobile technology has expanded challenges and opportunities for business, social and educational services. This rapid diffusion, particularly among students and teenagers presents numerous opportunities for business, social and educational services (Bicen & Cavus, 2010; Brown et al., 2003; Roblyer et al., 2010).

The development and use of ICT in libraries has slowly emerge on which, there has been many successes and failures over the past years (Igben & Akobo, 2007). Developments in ICT have impacted all sectors of society, including the education system. In institutions of higher learning, the application of ICT is changing how teaching and learning are carried out in many ways. This includes academic and non-academic activities and processes.

DOI: 10.4018/978-1-4666-8524-6.ch012

Before the advent of ICT, academic libraries were the sole custodians of information, which was predominantly in print. ICT brought changes necessitated by new information repackaging. Academic libraries are faced with managing hybrid resources (print and electronic) and are challenged to acquire the necessary skills (Poole & Denny, 2002).

In the past several years, both public and academic libraries have begun implementing mobile versions of at least some elements of their web sites including catalogues; online journal articles (Bridges et al. 2010).Rapid developments in ICT and evolving learner behaviours require learning institutions to continuously re-evaluate their approaches to deliver service to their clients. The increasing availability of low-cost mobile and wireless devices and associated infrastructure usher in both opportunities and challenges for educational institutions and their teachers and learners. Mobile learning and mobile technologies brings the rewards of placing institutions at the forefront and addresses student requirements for flexibility and ubiquity, that is, 'anywhere, anytime (Clyde, 2004; Gay et al., 2001; Hill & Roldan, 2005; Liu et al., 2003), and any device' learner engagement.

The use of mobile technologies for service delivery is rapidly increasing. Many organisations including institutions of higher learning have in the recent years employed mobile technologies such as cellular phone, specifically, the short messages service (SMS), and multimedia messaging services (MMS) to deliver various services. Many institutions of high learning have adopted the E-Learning and M-Learning approaches to enhance flexibility and improve on students and research outputs. When considering the use of mobile technologies in academic library services it is not sufficient to recognize that a large number of library patrons use mobile phones. The particular type of device they use and the degree to which they are web-enabled must also be considered. The range of device available can greatly impact the use and acceptance of mobile technologies in libraries (Bridges et al. 2010).Paying attention to the types of devices the users have can also help to design mobile services that best meet the user's needs.

2. RESEARCH APPROACH

Qualitative research approach was selected mainly because of rationale such as its probing and close interaction nature. The qualitative research approach allows for clarification from respondents to questions from the researcher. Also, it allows for close interaction with interviewees, enabling the researcher to develop a deeper understanding of the situation. Also, the researcher can observe events and actions as they happen, without removing them from their context (Babbie & Mouton, 2001).

The study adopted the case study method as its research design Creswell (2009) define case studies as a strategy of inquiry in which the researcher explores in depth a program, event, activity, process, or one or more individuals. Yin (2009) recommended case study inquiries for "how" and "why" types of research questions, where the researcher has little or no control, and the purpose is to investigate real-life contexts, phenomena, and situations . Capital University was used as the study. The focus of the study was on the university's library.

The user of the university's (Capital University) library includes students and academic employees. The users have various backgrounds, and come from different academic disciplines in accordance with the university structure. The university was structured into seven faculties. The library provides services, which include books, electronic thesis and dissertation & DVD requests, printed and electronic journal articles to the faculties. The services were provided through information systems and technology, and manually.

Data was collected using semi-structured interviews and library documentations. The interpretive approach was employed in the data analysis, using Technology Acceptance Model (TAM). The analysis exploited the social context in the adoption and use of mobile technology to enhance library services at the Capital University.

TAM was used in the analysis of the data from the case study. TAM is a behavioural model based on Ajzen and Fishbein's (1980) theory of reasoned action (TRA). Davis (1989) developed the technology acceptance model to explain and predict user acceptance of information systems. The Davis' (1989) research model was aimed at determining what causes people to accept or reject information technology. TAM is intended "to provide an explanation of the determinants of computer acceptance that is general, capable of explaining user behaviour across a broad range of end-user computing technologies and user populations, while at the same time being both parsimonious and theoretically justified" (Davis et al., 1989).

TAM attempts to address why users accept or reject technology and how users' acceptance is influenced by system characteristics. TAM assumes that people tend to use or not to use technology to the extent that they believe it will help them perform their jobs better. TAM consists of four main components, namely perceived ease of use, perceived usefulness, behavioural intention and actual system use. TAM components help to gain better understanding of the factors which influence and impact the adoption of mobile technology in the delivery of the library services.

3. DATA ANALYSIS: TAM VIEW

TAM is intended "to provide an explanation of the determinants of computer acceptance that is general, capable of explaining user behaviour across a broad range of end-user computing technologies and user populations, while at the same time being both parsimonious and theoretically justified" (Davis et al., 1989). TAM establishes a theoretical basis for explaining causal links between the two key constructs, Perceived Usefulness (PU) and Perceived Ease of Use (PEoU) of an information system, behavioural intentions (BI) and actual system usage.

Perceived Ease of Use

In TAM, Perceived ease of use is regarded as process expectancy primarily because it focuses on a person's subjective perception about the level of effort which is needed to use a computer system.

As at the time of this study in 2012, the academic library of the Capital University provided services to the students and academia. Some of the services that the library provided included availing materials for teaching, learning and research. The availability of the materials is determined by its accessibility.

The materials of the University library were accessed by students and academia through different means and channels. Some of these mean included the physical presence at the library premises, telephonic and email inquiries, and online via the library's website through the electronic resource portal.

Academia had the option to search for books electronically from their offices but some of them often didn't. This was because they thought that the electronic system was complicated and they claimed that it was easy for them to physically seek for assistance from librarians. As expressed by one of the interviewees:

Several at times when I attempt to make use of the systems in my office, I find it challenging. But when I physically access the services, especially through the librarian assistance is quicker and easier because the librarians know where to find the information quicker.

The users who preferred computer based systems had different background and knowledge pertaining to information systems and technologies. Their background and knowledge influenced their ability and interest on how they used current and new technologies which were deployed in the environment to provide them with the services that they required. One of the interviewees expressed herself as follow:

When I search for books I first check them on an online public access catalogue (OPAC), OPAC is a computer system we use to check for books, journals, and DVD.

The users who prefer the manual system of service were also divided in terms of how they wanted to be assisted with the services that they requested for. Some of them, particularly the academia, find it frustrating, time consuming and wasting to stand on the queue. Others find benefit to it as they could have the opportunity to interact with the librarians and request for more help other than what they originally wanted. One of the academia explained,

… my physical presence at the library, helps me to understand more about the services they offer, and build a friendly personal relationship with the librarians.

Many of the users intended to make use of the services of the library as much as they can from wherever they were and as flexibly as possible. This obviously required deployment of technological innovation. An example is using emerging mobile technology artefacts such as iPhone, iPad and kindle. Unfortunately, the library was not responding to technological innovation as much as it should. According to one of the interviewees, "most of the students do not have laptops, they have mobile phones."

There were some conservative people who struggled to learn to use newer technologies. The interest was influenced by fear and intimidation of the technologies, which was a manifestation of practical unconscious biasness that they were difficult to learn and understand. As a result, this group of users preferred the other systems through which services were manually carried out, or where a librarian has to use the systems on their behalf.

The current systems, both manual (physical) and information systems pose various types of challenges for the different users. Even though there were challenges, the systems still had to be used. This was because of the usefulness of the services offered by the library. The usefulness was however the end. The means was considered useful by various people in different ways, in accordance with the users' view and perspectives.

Perceived Usefulness

Perceived usefulness is defined as the extent to which a person believes that using a system will improve his or her processes, activities, as well as job performance within a context. Usefulness in this context is the extent to which individuals and groups of users perceive the systems to be useful in getting required services from the library of Capital University.

The library provided infrastructure to enable the users carry out the search. This was often done through an electronic catalogue system installed in personal computers (PCs). Some of them thought it was useful for them to use the system at the premises of the library primarily because they could get the assistance of the librarians whenever they encounter problems with the system. Even though some of the users thought that it was useful to connect at any time and from anywhere, it was unfortunately not the case as there was often no connectivity when they were outside Capital University's campus.

Due to the manual and fixed nature of the current systems that were used by the library to provide services, there were numerous challenges, as has been revealed above so far. The systems did not support mobility and flexibility in terms of time-of-usage, making it difficult to use the system to achieve the objectives. It would be more useful for both students and academia to access the library services from anywhere and at anytime. A common view among the users was expressed by one of the interviewees as follows:

I would like to have access to the library services from anywhere and at anytime without connectivity difficulty or hindrance.

Mobile technology was thought to be of better assistance in an attempt to increase the library's productivity and improve effectiveness in its academic obligations and activities. This is mainly because many of the students and academia believe that some of the services were of significant usefulness to them. The services included search for library catalogue for books, and online journal articles on databases, using different mobile devices that they own. As such, it was of critical importance for those services to be available at all times, online, and seamlessly.

The services which were provided by the library were considered to be either useful or useless by different individuals and groups. Such considerations or conclusions were based on their various interests, which are influenced by their individual intentions and behaviours.

Behavioural Intentions

In using the services, many of the users preconceived expectations and predictions about the systems or the responses of the library's employees. This formed their behavioural response and approach towards whether to use or not to use, and how they use the systems for the services that they required. The behaviours were influenced by certain factors which were of conscious or unconscious acts, which were both positive and negative in nature.

Some of the users seem to have given up exploring the systems to get the best out of the services. This was because of their mind-set and attitude. According to Giddens (1984), the mind that makes up the sentiments of the selfhood could be attributed to the behaviour of unconsciousness. Letseka and Iyamu (2011) argued that an individual's consciousness is the layer upon which an individual may either know or claim to process knowledge.

Time was the main factor which influences the behaviour of the users in attempts to use the services of the library. Most of the library users made use of the system off campus more often than they do on campus for various reasons. This was because some users did not have enough time during University operating hours to use the system. They had other commitments such as lectures and teaching. Also, there was more human mobility than ever before. As response to change, technologies are required to enable the human mobility. Unfortunately, the intention to use the services outside campus was often hampered by lack of access to the systems.

Some of users, particularly the younger generation, were prepared to learn how to use mobile technology such as the blackberry to access the services offered by the University library through the internet at convenient times. The thought and notion of the use of emerging technologies influenced some of the users to have a negative attitude towards the use of the current systems which they considered to be obsolete or outdated. According to one of the users,

I own a blackberry phone; I used it for my internet access. It would be preferable to access the library services from my mobile phone.

Library users could be encouraged and motivated to adopt a new system and use it if they perceive that their organisation is providing the necessary resources and organisational support. Organisational infrastructure support is a determinant of perceived usefulness while technical support is a determinant of perceived ease of use.

Actual Usage of the System

Actual system use refers to users' utilization of the system functionalities. Any information system that is not used has a little or no value in it. It is therefore important to find out why individuals choose to use or not to use an information system through which the library provides its services. This depended on how individuals valued the system for the required services. Usefulness and ease of use predict the system usage through attitude and behavioural intentions. Actual use is a behavioural response measured by the individual's actions.

There were many users who made use of the system to access the library services such as the library computer catalogue system as search engine for materials which included books, DVD, and electronic journal articles. As expressed by one of the interviewees:

… when I need books, I first search for its availability on OPAC, which is a computer system used at the library.

However, some of the users did not use the system because they thought that it was complicated. As a result, they always asked for assistance from the librarians.

In terms of system usage, location was critical. More students and academia used the system to access library services while on campus because that was when they could have access to the system. As a result, many of them were forced to be on campus even when they did not intend to do so. According to an interviewee, as

… a fulltime postgraduate student, it is convenient for me because I am always on campus. I don't have a personal PC with internet connectivity.

Some of the users, particularly the postgraduate students and academics preferred to use the system while outside the University campus. This was primarily because of the nature of their work. Unfortunately, they could not do so because there was no connectivity to the library's system from off campus. Some of the journal articles in the databases could only be accessed through the university network, which was only possible while within the campus.

Another deficiency was the limited resources at the library. There seems to be a shortage of staff resulting in a slow response to users' requests for assistance. For example, only two librarians were dedicated to a Faculty with different departments, a total of seven thousand students and a large number of academics.

The users had different interests and zeal to use the systems. The way or manner in which some of them used the systems also differed. Many of the users had preferred a flexible and scalable usage of the system. There were many factors which impacted and influenced the results and output of the current systems that were used deployed at Capital University's library. Those factors were extracted from the analysis, using the lens of Technology Acceptance Model. The findings are now presented in the next section.

4. FINDINGS

Based on the analysis as discussed above, factors which influenced and impacted the current systems used by the library services at Capital University were identified. The factors include technology obsolesce, lack of training, information sharing, technology innovation, lack of resources and organisational structure. As shown in Figure 1, the factors are interconnected, meaning they require holistic attention rather than isolate each of them. The factors could also have a negative impact on any new systems if they are not well managed or addressed. The discussion below should be read with the figure to gain better understanding.

Technology Obsolesce

The Capital University library was challenged in striving to meet its user's needs. This was attributed to the state of the technologies which were currently deployed in the library. The majority of the technologies were obsolete and had reached the end-of-life. Technology end-of-life means its parts and accessories are prohibitive or no longer exist. The life span of technology infrastructure such as personal computer (PC) and laptop is between three and five years. This is in accordance to the definition of manufacturers such as IBM and Intel.

Figure 1. System Critical Factors

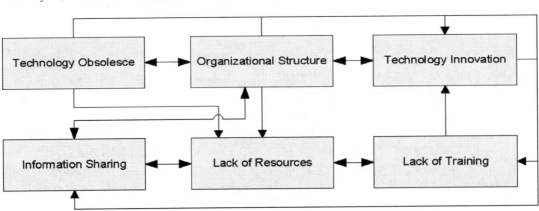

As a result of obsolesce or end-of-life nature of the technologies, they were either incompatible or difficulty to integrate with the emerging technologies such as the mobile technologies. For example, it was difficult or impossible to connect to the current system from outside the University campus network. The users had different backgrounds; their needs were demanding and dynamic. Therefore they required appropriate responses. The current technologies which were deployed were not able to fulfil these requests and desires. The Library needs to make contributions as information disseminators, they need to understand and exploit ICT infrastructures and emerging technologies in delivering their services to the users. The library could embrace advances in technology changes so that they could be on path with the changing technology and be able to provide better services to the users.

Systems' Training

Capital University's library offers training to users of it facilities primarily to be able to use their system independently when accessing some of the services such as electronic journal articles. Some of the users did attend the training but others did not because they did not perceived it to be useful. The non-attendance of the training sessions was attributed to lack of awareness. The training schedules were poorly communicated to the users. In addition, there was no clear indication or plan which was circulated in advance for users' preparation. Users were therefore not encouraged to attend the training sessions. This has contributed to their difficulty in using and accessing library services with the current system which is deployed in the library.

The training sessions which were provided by the library was of vital importance mainly because some of the library staff members do not possess the necessary skill that was required to carry out their expected duties in assisting the users on their request. The training was aimed to enable the users for self-help. Another factor that made the training vital was the shortage of staff in the library. There was only one staff in each section (per Faculty) of Capital University's library.

Lack of Resources

The success of any organisation depends on its ability to provide and maintain products, facilities and services that answer the needs of its users. The library was responsible for fulfilling information needs of its users. The proper performance of the library's functions requires well organised services which would be supported by infrastructure comprising of an administrative authority in the form of legislation, organisational structure, adequate finance, facilities, manpower and collection of documents.

The challenge most users, particularly students, experience was the limited number of computers (PC). The number of available computers (PC) in the library was not enough in ratio to its users. Students had to queue in order to get an opportunity to use the computers (PC) to access the library's system. The facilities were important because not all students owned personal computers. The limited number of computers led to students' inability to access the system, making them perceived that complexity in the system. Also, subject librarians were not enough in number. There were only two librarians per faculty responsible for academics as well as both undergraduate and postgraduate students. The shortage of staff affected the turnaround time of the services they provide to users.

Information Sharing

With the rapid increase in demand, it would always be difficult to acquire all the materials which are needed by users. No single library could be self-sufficient. As such, networking and resource sharing with other libraries is essential. Partnership and cooperation in local, national and international libraries has become unavoidable for Capital University library in order to improve and enhance on their services. Networking is one of the most effective ways of serving users' needs comprehensively. Capital university library was able to provide information material such as books and journal articles that the university does not have from other libraries.

Capital University achieves cooperation through the establishment of consortiums. The agreement between academic and special libraries to assist each other with books and journal articles through interlibrary library loan helps libraries to provide quality service to their users. Resource sharing is aimed at extending the resources and services of libraries to a wider category of users and to improve the ability of participating libraries to perform their basic function of matching users' needs and information sources.

Organisational Structure

The library structure consists of different sections that collaborate to achieve a common goal which was to deliver service to users (students and academics). The employees include top management, subject librarians, trainee librarian and library assistants in different sections such as the lending counter and interlibrary loan. The structure limited employment in certain areas. For example, there were only two subject librarians per faculty. This created a challenge and frustration for the users. The users would sometimes wait longer for response. This situation influences the users to assume that the subject librarians were either incompetent or do not manage their time well when it came to actual use of the system.

Technology Innovation

Information technology, as it has emerged in recent decades, constitutes an ongoing process of innovation. Innovation requires an investment in resources. Therefore responsibility lies with senior management to ensure that investments are made wisely and add value to the organisation at large. The continuous changes in technology influence users' perceptions as well as competitiveness in many organisations. With regard to library and information services, the technological changes are high. Research tools are making it more user-friendly for new ideas to be disseminated and shared very quickly, easily and at real-time.

As revealed in the analysis, the current technological infrastructure limits the users from applying certain technologies. This influenced users' perceptions and intentions when it came to using the services which the University's library offers. Latest technologies such as mobile technology have reshaped the way users' thinks and behaves. Understanding the rapid change of new technology is central to the future of the library in improving the library services.

To make more sense of the findings, and putting things in perspectives, the most prevalence factors were identified and interpreted.

5. INTERPRETATION OF THE FINDINGS

The interpretation entails going forward, and it is therefore generalised for the learning benefits of other academic libraries. The factors identified for further discussion include connectivity, technology strategy, governance, communication and operationalization:

1. **Connectivity:** Connectivity between the users and the library is important to enable them to communicate, as well carry out transactions. Electronic connectivity has over the years improved how individuals and groups carries out transactions and communicate. The internet plays a vital role in improving what the university library provides. It has reduced the distance barrier in the communication between the library and its users, by making it possible for academia and students to find the materials that they need from the library without physical presence. In order to remain economically viable when students and academia change geographical locations, it is necessary and essential for the University to extend its library access offerings beyond the physical boundaries of its campus. However, there seems to be little or no correlation between how innovatively the institution delivers library services to its stakeholders when they are off campus or outside the Capital University network (LAN) and when they are on campus.

2. **Technology Strategy:** The technology strategy is intended to define the strategic direction for technology related matters over time. This includes technological artefacts, methods and approaches which are employed for the deployment of technology within a period, a three to five year is recommended. This is primarily because of the rapid and frequent change of technologies. To ensure complementarily, compatibility and alignment, technology strategy requires constant review on an annual basis. The technology strategy encompasses the mission, vision and values of the organisation. The library of Capital University requires a technology strategy in order to respond to rapid technological change as well as meet the increasing needs of its users. The obsolete nature of technology in the library is due to a lack of technology strategy. The lack of a technology strategy has hampered some of the services which the library could offer to its users such as; they are not able to respond to new innovations. The current technologies which are deployed in the library to provide services are outdated. As a result, they slow the processing of requests (by users) for delivering of library services and hinder the use (application) of technology innovation.

3. **Governance:** Governance helps to address the rules and responsibilities for technical and non-technical resources. This is carried out within the organisational structure. It cannot function well if roles and responsibilities are not well defined and understood by users and employees of the library. The library employees including the users need to know their roles and responsibilities on accessing and providing library services. If library employees understood the roles and regulations on how training is approved, who gets to be trained and when users have to be trained, it would eliminate the challenges they (library) face in training their users on how to use the library system to access services. It is important that the library structure ensures the ability to deliver services in terms of the expectations of its stakeholders. The capacity to do so depend on the structures created to ensure that services are delivered to users. There is a need to ensure that all library employees are ready towards achieving the efficient and effective rendering of services to the users. Limited resources dictate that the library needs to identify, as accurately as possible, the needs of its users and deliver service in an efficient and effective manner in relation to the numerous needs that exist. Continuous review of the manner in which the library provides service to its users is necessary to

ensure efficiency and effectiveness. Organisational structure and governance of the library needs to be compatible with the culture and tradition of the University and community (users) that the library serves.

4. **Communication:** Communication is a scheme through which awareness is created, clarification is sought, and understanding is gained among the interested and involved actors. It could be employed through various ways including technological artefacts, hence the adoption of Mobile technology. Currently, the communication and information sharing that exists in the library is too limited to fulfil the university's goals and objectives in ensuring the users are well supported to carry out their academic obligations and responsibilities. The communication challenges are attributed to time, physical barriers and technology constraints. Library employees and consumers need to communicate and share information at all times in order to have a good understanding of each other's needs and expectations thereby providing and enhancing the services. Communication and information sharing can be done through, and by technology on real-time basis, and without geographical boundaries and barriers. This entails and means that the communication scheme should facilitate instant and virtual services in the mobility of actors.

5. **Operationalization:** In the context of this study, operationalization constitutes development, implementation and practice of information systems and technologies. The library's processes and activities require operationalization in a way that would enhance and provide efficient and effective services to its consumers. Efficiency and effectiveness entail availability at all times, from anywhere, and through using different flexible devices. Challenges in the current operations of the library services, hinder its goals and objectives. The challenges include constraints to availability and lack of flexibility such as physical barriers and incompatibility of technology devices. Mobile technology is intended to address these challenges operationally.

Mobile technology application provides the stakeholders with more freedom for organisations and users to perform various tasks without the limitation of time and location (available anytime from anywhere). It creates an impact on the business operations. Mobile technology would facilitate communication among users and employees of the library through the enhancement of communicating efficiency and information timeliness. Mobile technology would revitalize business process through changing data access pattern; the library would be able to use mobile technology to provide timely services to the users.

5.1 Adoption of Mobile Technology for Library Services

Based on the analysis, the findings and interpretations of the case study as presented above, a Framework was developed, as depicted in Figure 2. The framework is aimed to guide and facilitate the adoption of Mobile Technology to enhance the library services in the Capital university library, and learning for other academic libraries. As illustrated in the Figure23, the services which are provided by the library will be better enabled by technology (Mobile) which allows for mobility (anywhere), flexibility and available at all times. The deployed technology requires management to review its services otherwise, the purposes would be defeated. Manageability involves critical factors such as governance, process and people. Both the technology and management efforts and factors ensure the communicative scheme, which facilitates communication and information sharing in the services provided by the library of the university (CU).

Figure 2. Framework for Adoption of Mobile Technology

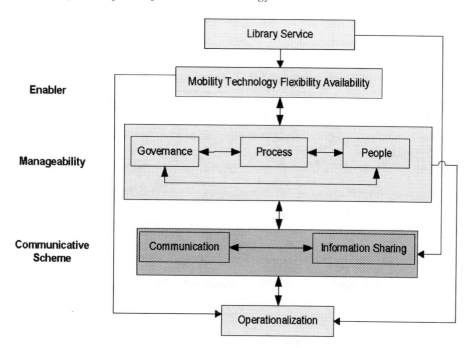

The discussion that follows should be read in conjunction with Figure 2 to gain a better understanding of how some factors could influence and impact the adoption of Mobile Technology in an academic library.

i. Library Services

The effectiveness and efficiency of the operationalization of the library's activities is essential and significant to the university's (CU) academic performance. The library is a focal point for teaching, learning and research. It is expected to provide information and resources to students and academics of the university, for their academic obligations and responsibilities such as teaching, assignments, projects and research.

The adoption of Mobile technology is intended to enhance the library's services. This is to provide access to information and resource material (such as e-book) online, at anytime and from anywhere. The technology is as good as its manageability to enhance the intended services. Also critical is the communicative scheme which must contribute to improved services.

ii. Technology

The goals and objectives which inform and drive the services of the University library require enabling and management. As a result, the technology which is adopted to enable the services is critical. As revealed in the analysis and interpretation sections, the current information systems deployed in the library are challenged with fulfilling and achieving the goals and objectives of users of Capital University.

The adoption of Mobile technology is intended to create and support information systems which are integrated with people and processes in order to provide service in an effective and efficient manner. Mobile technology is adopted for employees in the library to communicate with each other, to avail the services they provide online, and for the users to access the services in a flexible manner. The adoption of Mobile technology is intended to modernise and improve the services the University's library provides.

The manageability of the adoption of Mobile technology includes critical factors such as governance, process and people. The governance defines principles, standards and policies within which, and how the Mobile technology is used to carry out the services of the library at greater height. The Process factor ensures the procedural approach through which, and how employers and users carries out their roles and responsibilities. Critically, People (employers and users) use and interpret technology in their own way to make a difference.

iii. Governance

Governance defines standards, principles and policies. It is driven by the organisational (library) requirements, goals and objectives pursued at the time. As such, it is not static, it requires continued review. The governance is used to guide the selection, deployment and use of the technology. It constitutes and at the same time provides a guide to both technical and non-technical factors.

The adoption of the Mobile technology requires governance. This includes the standard of the Mobile technology, the principles on how the technology is deployed and the policy on usage. The governance also guides the manageability such as upgrading of the technology. Also, the governance defines the roles and responsibilities within timeframe, based on the tasks and activities which are involved in the adoption of Mobile technology in the library.

Governance is not always straight forward in practices and reality. Hence manageability of the focal actors such as people and process are critical.

iv. Process and People

It is impossible or difficult to separate process and people in a social context. A social context consists and constitutes people, artefacts and events within a legitimised entity. Process is a guideline for the events and activities which people are involved-in, or carries out. People exist within process, and process is formulated by people.

Process is an action taken or established, usually a routine set of procedure to convert it from one form to another. Process involves steps and decision in the way work is accomplished, and may involve a sequence of events. On one hand, the library uses technology to enable and support its processes. On another hand, People need to be technologically inclined to use different mobile devices that is used to access library services.

Irrespective of the potential of the technology, people decide on how to make a difference. The use of technology is conscious, and can be of practical unconsciousness. Hence the consciousness and training of employees and users of the library services is significantly critical.

v. Communication and Information Sharing

Communication and information sharing are constituted in the concept of the communicative scheme. The communicative scheme facilitates interactions and information flow between individuals and groups for the same or similar purposes in a network. Communication in the library is carried out within the library (between employees and users) and in some cases between libraries. Effective communication is essential in an organisation because it creates mutual understanding between people. Library is geared towards serving the users of the library in order to achieve desired results.

Information sharing is vital in an organisation because it help employees to share with each other their responsibilities. This helps employees of the library to provide a better service, individually and collectively. Information sharing is enabled through communication, once they understand the processes and the technology on how to deliver services to their users, leads to operationalization of new technology.

The communicative scheme is enabled by mobile technology, to ensure that communication and information are delivered in real-time, virtualised and available through various devices at real-time. The adoption of Mobile technology helps to communicate and share information intensively and extensively without time limitation, geographical barriers, and information sharing is enforced.

vi. Operationalization

Operationalization entails the applicability and use of the library services by the employees and consumers (users). Based on the analysis and interpretation of the analysis, the adoption of Mobile technology would enhance the effectiveness and efficiency of the library's activities.

Mobile technology allows library users to access library services from anywhere and at anytime. Mobile technology also enables and supports the library website. Mobile technology enforces authentication, so users their identification to get access to the electronic resources of the library.

6. CONCLUSION

Based on the findings from the analysis, a new system is required to improve the services that the library of the university offers. Otherwise, it would be business as usual; the users would continue to be on dissolute state. Thus, somehow this has an impact on academic (including research) outputs. The adoption of mobile technology as a new system is required.

The adoption of mobile technology would take cognisance of the factors that have been identified from the analysis. These factors would guide the adoption of the mobile technology to efficient and effective use.

However, without the appropriate infrastructure facilities, equipment and staff expertise it will be impossible to adopt mobile technology in academic libraries. Mobile devices through mobile technology will enhance and improve students and academics performances and productivities. This makes this study very important to libraries, students and academics.

REFERENCES

Ajzen, I., & Fishbein, M. (1980). *Understanding attitudes and predicting social behaviour*. Englewood Cliffs, NJ: Prentice-Hall.

Babbie, E., & Mouton, J. (2001). *The practice of social research*. Cape Town: Oxford University Press.

BICEN, H. & CAVUS. (2010). The most preferred social network sites by students. *Procedia: Social and Behavioral Sciences, 2*(1), 5864–5869.

Bridges, L., Rempel, H. G., & Griggs, K. (2010). Making the case for a fully mobile library website from floor maps to the catalogue. *RSR. Reference Services Review, 38*(2), 309–320. doi:10.1108/00907321011045061

Brown, I., Cajee, Z., Davies, D., & Stroebel, S. (2003). Cell phone banking: Predictors of adoption in South Africa - an exploratory study. *International Journal of Information Management, 23*(1), 381–394. doi:10.1016/S0268-4012(03)00065-3

Castells, M., Fernandez-Ardevo, M., Linchuan Qiu, J., & Sey, A. (2007). *Mobile Communication and Society: A Global Perspective*. Cambridge, MA: MIT Press.

Clyde, L. A. (2004). M-learning. *Teacher Librarian, 32*(1), 45–60.

Cresswell, J. W. (2009). *Research design: qualitative, quantitative and mixed methods approach* (3rd ed.). Thousand Oaks, CA: Sage Publications.

Davis, F. D. (1989). Perceived usefulness, perceived ease of use, and user acceptance of information technology. *Management Information Systems Quarterly, 13*(3), 319–340. doi:10.2307/249008

Davis, F. D., Bagozzi, R. P., & Warshaw, P. R. (1989). User acceptance of computer technology: A comparison of two theoretical models. *Management Science, 35*(1), 982–1003. doi:10.1287/mnsc.35.8.982

Gay, G., Stefanone, M., Grace-Martin, M., & Hembrooke, H. (2001). The effects of wireless computing in collaborative learning. *International Journal of Human-Computer Interaction, 13*(2), 257–276. doi:10.1207/S15327590IJHC1302_10

Giddens, A. (1984) The constitution of society: Outline of the theory of structure. Berkley, CA university of California Press.

Hill, T. R., & Roldan, M. (2005). Toward third generation threaded discussions for mobile learning: Opportunities and challenges for ubiquitous collaborative environments. *Information Systems Frontiers, 7*(1), 55–70. doi:10.1007/s10796-005-5338-7

Igben, M. J., & Akobo, D. I. (2007). State of Information and Communication Technology (ICT) in Libraries in Rivers State, Nigeria. *African Journal of Library and Information Science, 17*(2), 150–34.

Letseka, M., & Iyamu, T. (2011) The Dualism of the Information Technology Project, in the *Proceedings of the 2011 Annual Conference of the South African Institute of Computer Scientists and Information Technologists*. Cape Town. doi:10.1145/2072221.2072261

Liu, J., Chun-Sheng, Y., Chang, L., & Yao, J. E. (2003). Technology acceptance model for wireless internet. *Internet Research: Electronic Networking Applications and Policy, 13*(13), 206–222. doi:10.1108/10662240310478222

Poole, C. E., & Denny, E. (2001). Technological change in the workplace: A state wide survey of community college library and learning personnel. *College & Research Libraries, 62*(6), 503–515. doi:10.5860/crl.62.6.503

Roblyer, M. D., McDaniel, M., Webb, M., Herman, J., & Witty, J. V. (2010). Findings on Facebook in higher education: A comparison of college faculty and student uses and perception of social networking sites. *The Internet and Higher Education, 13*(1), 134–140. doi:10.1016/j.iheduc.2010.03.002

Yin, R. K. (2009). *Case study research: design and methods* (4th ed.). Los Angeles: Sage.

KEY TERMS AND DEFINITIONS

Engineering: This is the process of providing alternative for better or solution for the same goals and objectives.

Information and Communication Technologies (ICT): This term refers to diverse technologies and systems, consisting of hardware, software and the communication equipment.

Information System: It consists of technologies, processes and people, to enable and support the management of information for organisational purposes.

Mobile Devices: Refers to all technological artefacts that moveable.

Mobile Technology: Refers to all technological artefacts that moveable, this includes software.

Services: Is the University's library offering to assist the students and staff in their academic pursuits.

Technology Acceptance Mode: Is a theory to understand how why, how and when people make use of technological artefacts in their environment.

Chapter 13
E-Competences for Organisational Sustainability Information Systems

Zoran Mitrovic
Mitrovic Development and Research Institute, South Africa

ABSTRACT

The present patterns of economic development are deemed to be 'unsustainable'. It is believed that the concept of sustainability, assisted by the use of information and communication technologies (ICT) through organisational sustainability information systems (OSIS), is a 'cure' for current extraordinary environmental changes. However, the effective use of these systems requires an ICT competent (e-competent) workforce. E-competences, a combination of ICT-related knowledge, skills and attitudes are discussed in a number of studies but the European e-Competence Framework 3.0 is the only known framework that includes a single sustainability related e-competence. This study, however, reveals that, although the E-eCF3.0 sustainability e-competence is relevant, it is not sufficient for the effective use of OSIS as it transpired that the users should also possess other e-competences if these systems are to be exploited effectively.

INTRODUCTION

The present pattern of economic development, characterised by extraordinary environmental changes resulting *inter alia* from human economic activities, is deemed to be unsustainable as it escalates a number of complex societal and environmental problems (Holland, 2003; De Moor &Kleef, 2005; Gough, 2013). An alternative environment is advised that is supported by economic viability, healthy ecosystems and a more equitable social framework (e.g. UNDP, 1994; Holland, 2003; Elliot, 2007). Although this alternative thinking has its origin in the concept first explored at the UN Confernce on the Human Environment in Stockholm (Sweden) in 1972, the sustainability idea gained prominence only in 1987 when the Brundtlandt Report defined sustainability as *"development that meets the needs of the present withouth compromising the ability of future generations to meet their own needs"* (WCED, 1987, p.8).

DOI: 10.4018/978-1-4666-8524-6.ch013

This report alerted the to path of alternatives as opposed to the more confrontational discourse that existed between the proponents of economic development and those concerned with the environment.

The sustainability challenges are numerous: climate change, energy and water supply, biodiversity and land use, chemicals, toxics, and heavy metals, air pollution, waste management, ozone layer depletion, oceans and fisheries, deforestation (e.g. Esty& Winston, 2006, p. 33). Addressing them is a complex task but there are at least four main reasons for organisations to urgently attend to sustainability development (Epstein, 2008, pp. 21-22): (i) disregarding government and industry sustainability related codes of conduct can incur penalties and fines, legal costs, lost productivity due to additional inspections, potential closure of operations, and damage to corporate reputations; (ii) the consequences of poor sustainability performance and mismanagement of stakeholders can incur reputational damage and potential loss in market share as the general public and non-government organisations (NGOs) are increasingly advocating for adherence to sustainability issues; (iii) sustainability conducted business can create financial value by lowering costs (e.g. due to a decrease in regulatory fines) and increase revenue (e.g. due to improved corporate reputation); (iv) social and moral obligations towards communities in which businesses operate as corporations make a significant impact on society and the environment.

The complexity around sustainability development requires a holistic framework (Sachs, 2015) and the involvement of new methods and tools (De Moor &Kleef, 2005; UN, 2012). Information and communication technologies (ICT) are seen as such tools (Dompke et al, 2004; Yi and Thomas, 2007; Hilty, 2008) as these technologies *"can change the behaviour of businesses and consumers, and through these changes, ICT can help the environment without scarifying economic output"* (GIIC, 2008, p. 2). The development of the personal computer and the Internet are regarded as key milestones of the *"sustainabuity revolution"* (Edwards, 2005; Elliot, 2007; MacLean, Souter & Creech, 2012) as ICT and sustainability are *"at long last"* seen to belong together (Hilty, 2008, p. 9). Computers and information systems, for example, make it easier to: (i) track organisational resource use and productivity, (ii) benchmark across facilities, products, and production lines, and (iii) make a comparative analysis of raw material consumption, energy required, and waste generation (Esty& Winston, 2006, p. 109). Contemporary reports estimate the market for ICT for sustainability will tremendously increase. For example German SAP estimated in 2011 that the market for 'sustainability software' will reach $7 billion within five years (SAP, 2011) while the Verdantix report, focused on the US market, estimated that that sustainable business spend will grow from $34.6 billion in 2012 to $43.6 billion in 2017 (Verdantix, 2013).

However, the use of ICT for sustainability also has a downside as it has become one of the major contributors to environmental contamination throughout its lifecycle phases: production, use and in its disposal (Elliot, 2007). For example, e-waste from computers, televisions, telephones and other devices is one of the fastest growing problems in both developed and developing countries (Hasan, 2002; UNEP, 2005, pp. 17-18; Sarapuu, 2015). Increasing provision of ICT services which increases levels of energy consumption by ICT equipment can contribute to global warming, particularly if this energy is mostly produced by coal-burning power stations. To make the situation worse, it seems that the use of ICT in developed countries is a *fait accompli*, yet continues to operate outside an endurable sustainability framework. For example, some leading developed countries have refused to sign some important international sustainability-related documents such as the 'Kyoto protocol' (Kyoto, 1998). The use of ICT will continue to grow in both developed and developing countries and, if not used in the sustainability manner, might add to global ecological ruin.

The negative sustainability effects coming from ICT use, however, can be balanced by promoting positive effects and alleviating negative ones proactively (Yi and Thomas, 2007, p. 1). This will depend on the way these technologies are used by the organisational workforce as only ICT competent (e-competent) employees can be equipped to derive benefits (including sustainability ones) from ICT-based organisational information systems (Romani, 2009; e-skills UK, 2010; Mitrovic, 2010). ICT competence or e-competence refers to a demonstrated ability to apply skills, knowledge and attitudes to achieve observable results (Ee-CF, 2014). It is, however, important to explain that this term is often used interchangeably with the term 'e-skills', which broadly refers to the ability to develop and use ICT within the context of a knowledge environment and associated competences that enable the individual to participate in a world in which ICT is a requirement for advancement in business, government and civil society. As both terms include 'competences' and 'skills' in their definitions, which can instil some confusion of terms, this study is based on the above Ee-CF (2014) definition of e-competences; e-skills are here considered as an element of e-competences. It is also important to note that the possession of e-competencies is a necessary but not sufficient prerequisite for the effective and efficient development and use of sustainability information systems. The soft skills (such as critical and creativity thinking, a habit of life-long learning) and the discipline-related and trade-specific hard skills are just as important as e-competences for the development and use of sustainability information systems. However, due to the limited scope of this chapter, these important factors will not be further discussed.

PROBLEM AND OBJECTIVES

Currently, e-competent personnel are in very short supply in developing countries such as South Africa, the host country of this research (eSEW, 2010; eSN, 2010; ITWeb 2008; Accenture, 2008; NeSPA, 2013). As these people are seen as vital in addressing poverty, sustainable livelihoods, the fight against crime, the building of cohesive communities, international cooperation, and the building of a developmental state, the South African National e-Skills Plans of Action 2010 and 2013 (NeSPA, 2010 & NeSPA 2013), make provision for development and application of e-competences – including sustainability ones.

The problem arises from the fact that the development and application of sustainability e-competences is still not well understood either in South Africa or internationally. The notion of sustainability e-competences is briefly explained in the document 'European e-Competence Framework 3.0' (Ee-CF2.0), which suggests that a single e-competence is sufficient for the effective use of the organisational sustainability information systems. Is this single e-competence indeed sufficient? This framework does not, up to date, offer adequate evidence. Thus, this research was set to: (i) obtain an initial understanding regarding the sufficiency of the sustainability e-competence proposed by the European e-Competence Framework 3.0, (ii) possible identify the need for other e-competences needed for the effective use of organisational sustainability information systems, thus (iii) to provide a theoretical basis for further development of e-competences.

The overall aim of this chapter is (i) to promote researchers' and practitioners' awareness of challenges related to the sustainability e-competences and (ii) to identify critical areas of intervention as a better understanding of these issues can be potentially useful for:

- **Academics:** To research and derive models and theories for the practical application and teaching;
- **Practitioners:** (IS/IT, managers, business managers and the HR function) To determine what particular e-competences would be needed for the effective use of organisational sustainability information systems;
- **Policy-Makers:** To create research evidence based e-competences related policies since more effective bridges between knowledge, policy and practice are needed (Hearn & White, 2009);

APPROACH TO THE STUDY AND THE CONTENTS OF THIS PAPER

In order to meet the study's objectives, it would be useful to review the literature on the intersection between sustainability information systems and sustainability e-competences but such works could not be readily obtained. Thus, this study has taken an approach that included:

- Exploration of the literature dedicated to the sustainability information systems in order to identify the possible need for sustainability e-competences;
- Comparison of the needed e-competences with the Ee-CF3.0 Sustainability Development e-competence (which will be explained hereafter) in order to: (i) establish sufficiency of these e-competences for addressing sustainability issues through the use of organisational information systems; (ii) identify other e-competences possibly required by organisational sustainability information systems.

This approach was taken since the best way to understand any phenomenon is to view it in its context (Kraus, 2005). Thus, epistemologically, this research was based on the notion of *"internal reality"* (Dervin, 1977; Olson, 1995; Kraus, 2005), which denotes subjective information defined as:

- **Ideas:** those found in the reviewed literature and also this researcher's ideas regarding sustainability and e-competences,
- **Structures:** represented by the frameworks used in this study (Ee-CF3.0, sustainability information systems and the South African National e-Skills Plans of Action since this research was conducted in this country),
- Which are *imputed to reality by people* (by the authors cited in this study and this researcher);

This paper is further organised in the following way: the next section is dedicated to the sustainability information systems and the basic (minimum of) organisational sustainability processes that these systems support. This is followed by the sections dedicated to the description of e-competences - with the emphasis on the sustainability e-competence and its sufficiency for the effective use of the sustainability information systems. The paper ends with the discussion about the need for other sustainability related e-competences, followed by the concluding remarks.

SUSTAINABILITY INFORMATION SYSTEMS AND PROCESSES

The idea that ICT can, through organisational information systems, play a role in achieving sustainability is supported by a number of authors (e.g. Avouris& Page, 1995; Shaft et al., 1997; Schlenzig, 1999; Daugherty et a al., 2002). For this research, however, the most significant was the work done by researchers at the Swiss Federal Laboratories for Materials Testing and Research (EMPA) and the scientific community of Environmental Informatics, organised in the expert committee 'Informatics for Environmental Protection' of the German Informatics Society. Their work was done systematically throughout the last two decades and has taken a balanced approach by exploring positive and negative aspects of impact by ICT on sustainability. That approach helped in the understanding of: (i) different types of sustainability information systems (for public and private organisations) and (ii) the basic (minimum of) organisational sustainability processes supported by these systems. Analysis of these processes has elicited ICT-related knowledge and skills (e-skills) required for the effective use of organisational sustainability information systems, which was important for the identification of needed sustainability-related e-competences.

Hilty and Ruddy (2000) and Hilty (2008, pp. 25-33) make the main distinction between Environmental Information Processing (EIP) (e.g. monitoring and control, information management, data analysis, decision support) and Information Society Technologies (IST). EIP encompass two kinds of information systems: Environmental Information System (EIS), used by public sector organisations, and Environmental Management Information System (EMIS), used by private sector organisations (Table 1).

Environmental Information System (EIS)

Environmental Information Systems (EIS), which were in use from the 1970s, fulfilled at least the following three important functions: (i) *Public awareness about the condition of public goods*, (ii) *Political decisions* and (iii) *Executing instruments of environmental policy* (Hilty, 2008, pp. 17-28). Analysis of the processes embedded in these functions elicited knowledge and skills needed to appositely manage these processes – this is shown in Table 2.

Table 1. Categories of interaction between ICT and the environmental dimension of sustainability

Environmental Information Processing (EIP)	Public sector: Environmental Information Systems (EIS) operated by public authorities	Public awareness about condition of public goods
		Prerequisites for political decisions
		Existing instruments of environmental policy
	Private sector: Environmental Management Information Systems (EMIS)	Legal compliance
		Environmental reporting to stakeholders
		Eco-efficiency and material flow management
Information Society Technologies (IST)	Direct impact on material intensity of economy	Material intensity of ISTs' production life cycles
	Indirect impact on material intensity of economy	Substitution potential
		Optimisation potential
		Induction Potential

(Source: Hilty, 2008, p. 25)

Table 2. EIS basic sustainability processes, skills and knowledge

Environmental Information Processing (EIP)	Sustainability Processes	Needed Knowledge	Needed e-Competences (For Use EIS For)
Public Sector Environmental Information Systems operated by public authorities (EIS)	Raising public awareness about condition of public goods	Environmental norms	Managing environmental information: e-competences to use appropriate software (e.g. reporting software)
	Environmental political decision-making	• Understanding environmental status quo • Making prediction (using EIS)	E-competences to use of tools for modelling and simulation (e.g. differentiation of the climate change anthropogenic portion)
	Executing instruments of environmental policy	• Understanding legal compliance regulations (e.g. Kyoto protocol, national laws) • Understanding need for emergence actions	Managing environmental information (e-competences to use tools for): • Crate and maintaining appropriate database • Continual info provision • Tracking pollution to the source

(Source: Author based on: Hilty, 2008, p.25)

Environmental Management Information Systems

Environmental Management Information Systems (EMIS) emerged only in the 1990s and were designed to support the environmental management of the private sector, which nowadays increasingly requires thinking in strategic corporate networks (Hilty et al., 2000). Use of EMIS is associated with the following functions (Hilty, 2008, pp. 30-33): (i) *Legal compliance*, (ii) *Environmental/sustainability reporting to stakeholders*, and (iii) *Eco-efficiency and material flow management*. Analysis of the fairly complex processes (particularly those of eco-efficiency and the material flow management) embedded in these functions elicited knowledge and skills needed to appropriately manage these processes – this is shown in Table 3.

Table 3. EMIS basic sustainability processes, skills and knowledge

Environmental Information Processing (EIP)	Sustainability Processes	Needed Knowledge	Needed e-Competences (For Use EMIS for)
Private Sector Environmental Management Information Systems (EMIS)	Legal compliance	• Eco development inside company • Eco modelling	• Discovering eco development inside company • System modelling
	Environmental/sustainability reporting to stakeholders	Stakeholders sustainability requirements	Managing environmental information: reporting of environmental impact and risks (e.g. using HTML- or XML-based software)
	Eco-efficiency and material flow management	• Improving eco-efficiency: strategic and operational • Life Cycle Assessment (LCA) • Effect of application on the LCA of products and services • Design For the Environment (DFE) • Building up strategic corporate networks (especially recycling networks) • Real-time process control for minimizing emissions or increasing energy efficiency	• ICT-supported Real Time process control (e.g. pollution, energy use) • Building up strategic corporate networks • Life Cycle Assessment (LCA) and Design For the Environment (DFE) • Real-time process control for minimizing emissions or increasing energy efficiency

(Source: Author based on: Hilty, 2008, p. 25)

The next step in this study was to explore the possible sustainability impact of the information and communication technologies used for building these information systems since these technologies can add to sustainability or otherwise.

ICT FOR ENVIRONMENTAL INFORMATION SYSTEMS

Information and communication technologies needed for building EIS/EMIS were until recently called Information Society Technologies (IST, as shown in Table 1) but today it is more appropriate to talk about specific types of ICT with the potential for deep sustainability change, such as 'ambient intelligence', 'ubiquitous computing' or the 'Internet of things'. Regardless of the name, the most important aspect of ICT is its capacity to reduce the *material intensity* of production, consumption, and disposal of products, as well as the capability of connecting logistic processes (e.g. transportation, storing). This refers to the transformations of mass or energy that are involved in providing a product or service, which is considered as increasing eco-efficiency and is named '*dematerialisation*'. Another similar term '*immaterialisation*' denotes a substitution of a physical function with a pure information service (Hilty, 2008; 2000). In the context of this study, it is important that in both cases use of ICT can contribute to eco-efficiency. The impact of ICT on sustainability is given in Figure 1.

The direct impacts of ICT on sustainability (*first-order effects*) can be seen through the life cycle of ICT hardware: production, use and disposal (seen as e-waste) while indirect impact (*second-order effects*) is seen through four effects: two positive (*substitution* and *optimisation*) and two negative (*induction* and *rebound effect*) (Hilty et al., 2005) - as seen in Figure 2.

Since the scope of this chapter does not allow for a more detailed description of the above-mentioned concepts, the tabular view of information technology related basic sustainability processes, skills and knowledge are given in Table 4.

Figure 1. Direct and indirect impacts of ICT on the material aspect of sustainability
(Source: Hilty, 2008, p. 39)

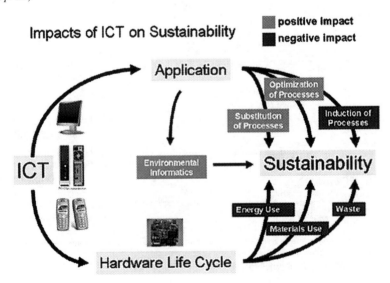

E-Competences for Organisational Sustainability Information Systems

Table 4. Information technology related basic sustainability processes, skills and knowledge

	Sustainability Processes	Needed Knowledge	Needed e-Competences (For Use EIS/EMIS for)
Information Society Technology (ICT)	Managing direct impact	• Material intensity of IST's product life cycle • Dependences on ICT infrastructure • Risk from 'Unmastered complexity' of ICT (the Precautionary Principle – PP) • LCA of ICT Hardware	Design ICT hardware having in mind its LCA (production, exploitation, disposal): • energy use • material use • -waste
	Managing indirect impact (Effect of application of ICT on the LCA of products and services)	Substitution potential of ICT (functional equivalent): • Dematerialisation • Immaterialisation • Organisation of innovative services that contribute to production processes and/or products	Achieving Substitution effects, i.e. ability use of EIS/EMIS for: dematerialisation/immaterialisation and innovation services
		Optimisation potential of ICT: • Dematerialisation through optimisation of processes and products with respect to material and energy efficiency (perform existing processes more efficiently in order to raise productivity) • Efficiency vs. Sufficiency • Organisation of innovative services (e.g. to make possible something new that has not been previously feasible) • Contribution of information services to the net product • Use of algorithms to accelerate processes (in building software)	Achieving Optimisation effects, i.e. ability to use of EIS/EMIS for: • Users: dematerialisation, efficiency/sufficiency, innovative services, product-related information management. • Software developers: programming skills of using algorithms to accelerate business sustainability information-related processes
		Induction potential of ICT	Avoiding or minimising Induction effects
		Rebound effect of ICT: • Software design and implementation (Featurism and Software bloat) • Hardware (Miniaturization paradox) • User-related (Goal displacement by users) • Organisation Level (information work rebound effect: 'explosion' of number of electronic transactions and documents)	Avoiding or minimising of ICT Rebound effects by using EIS/EMIS in the way that would avoid using only necessary features for the business processes and avoid goal displacement. Also ability to avoid unnecessary ICT-related transaction by using information systems efficiently.

(Source: Author, based on: Hilty, 2008)

Figure 2. A conceptual framework for ICT effects relevant in the context of sustainability
(Source: Hilty, 2015)

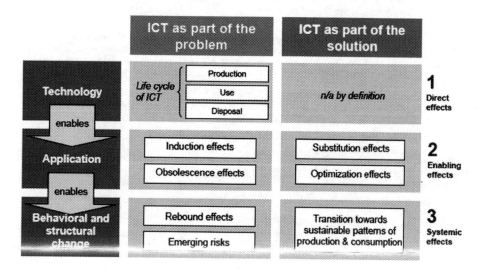

In order to establish what e-competences employees should possess in order to effectively use EIS or EMIS, it was necessary to: (i) explore the sufficiency of the Sustainable Development e-competency proposed by Ee-CF3.0 and (ii) possibly identify the need for other e-competences for the effective use of sustainability information systems. The latter was done by 'mapping' the knowledge and skills identified in the EIS and EMIS processes (given in the previous tables) with knowledge and processes described as elements of the Ee-CF3.0 e-competences, which is depicted in the following section.

EE-CF AND SUSTAINABILITY DEVELOPMENT E-COMPETENCE

ICT competence or e-competence, as explained in the European e-Competence Framework is a holistic concept directly related to workplace activities and denotes a demonstrated ability to apply knowledge, skills and attitudes for achieving observable results. This is incorporating complex human behaviours expressed as embedded attitudes (Ee-CF, 2014).

The notion of e-competences is fairly new and it was not surprising that the reviewed literature exposed only one framework - the European e-Competence Framework (Ee-CF) - that includes a sustainability related competence. In general, this framework focuses on e-competences needed to: (i) develop, operate and manage ICT projects and processes, (ii) exploit and use ICT, (iii) make decisions and develop strategies, and (iv) foresee new scenarios.

This framework considers end users, business managers and ICT (IT/IS) practitioners but does not include competences related to basic/scientific research in the ICT field. The Ee-CF, which focuses on competences that are needed and applied in the ICT business related workplace, is aimed at aligning

Figure 3. Sustainability Development e-competence
(Source: Ee-CF, 2014)

Dimension 1 e-Comp. area	A. PLAN				
Dimension 2 e-Competence: Title + generic description	A.8. Sustainable Development Estimates the impact of ICT solutions in terms of eco responsibilities including energy consumption. Advises business and ICT stakeholders on sustainable alternatives that are consistent with the business strategy. Applies an ICT purchasing and sales policy which fulfills eco-responsibilities.				
Dimension 3	Level 1	Level 2	Level 3	Level 4	Level 5
e-Competence proficiency levels e-1 to e-5, related to EQF levels 3 to 8	–	–	Promotes awareness, training and commitment for the deployment of sustainable development and applies the necessary tools for piloting this approach.	Defines objective and strategy of sustainable IS development in accordance with the organisation's sustainability policy.	–
Dimension 4 Knowledge examples Knows/aware of/familiar with	K1 metrics and indicators related to sustainable development K2 corporate social responsibility (CSR) of stakeholders within the IS infrastructure				
Skills examples Is able to	S1 monitor and measure the ICT energy consumption S2 apply recommendations in projects to support latest sustainable development strategies S3 master regulatory constraints and international standards related to ICT sustainability				

Table 5. Relevant dimensions of European e-Competence Framework - Ee-CF 3.0

Dimension 1	Dimension 2
Plan	A.1. IS and Business Strategy Alignment A.2. Service Level Management A.3. Business Plan Development A.4. Specification Creation A.5. Systems Architecture A.6. Application Design A.7. Technology Watching A.8 Sustainable Development A.9. Innovating
Build	B.1. Design and Development B.2. Systems Integration B.3. Testing B.4. Solution Deployment B.5. Technical Publications Development B.6. Systems Engineering
Run	C.1. User Support C.2. Change Support C.3. Service Delivery C.4. Problem Management
Enable	D.1. Information Security Strategy Development D.2. ICT Quality Strategy Development D.3. Education and Training Provision D.4. Purchasing D.5. Sales Proposal Development D.6. Channel Management D.7. Sales Management D.8. Contract Management D.9. Personnel Development D.10. Information and Knowledge Management D.11. Needs Identification D.12. Digital Marketing
Manage	E.1. Forecast Development E.2. Project and Portfolio Management E.3. Risk Management E.4. Relationship Management E.5. Process Improvement E.6. ICT Quality Management E.7. Business Change Management E.8. Information Security Management E.9. IS Governance

(Source: Ee-CF, 2014)

company's needs and views, reflecting company requirements, and relating to specific skills and job profiles (UGe-CF, 2008). E-competence is, by this framework, defined as a demonstrated ability to apply *knowledge* (set of know-what), *skills* (ability to carry out managerial or technical tasks), and *attitudes* (cognitive and relational capacity – e.g. analysis capacity, synthesis capacity, flexibility, pragmatism) for achieving observable results. The Ee-CF is structured in four dimensions, which reflect different levels of business and human resource planning requirements (for more details see UGe-CF, 2008; Ee-CF, 2014). Table 5 shows two main dimensions of all e-competences while Figure 3 portrays all relevant elements of the Sustainability Development e-competence.

From the viewpoint of this study, Ee-CF was important as its version 3.0 introduced an e-competence named 'Sustainable Development'. This e-competence is positioned within Dimension 1 'Plan' (Ee-CFM, 2010), as shown in a self-descriptive Figure 3.

The 'attitudes' element of e-competences is not included in this study as the analysis of the literature regarding sustainability information systems could not offer sufficient discussion related to this notion.

(IN)SUFFICIENCY OF EE-CF SUSTAINABILITY DEVELOPMENT E-COMPETENCE

The comparison of the description of knowledge and skills described by the dimensions and levels of the Sustainability Development e-competence with the knowledge and skills identified through the analysis of EIS, EMIS and also the direct and indirect impact of ICT, has disclosed that the Sustainability Development e-competence can be related to the majority of sustainability processes related to EIS or EMIS. However, it appeared that sufficiency of this e-competence did not address all identified EIS and EMIS sustainability processes. This is attributed to the limited scope of the Ee-CF 3.0 e-competence as it only refers to the *Plan* component of *Dimension 1*. Thus, in addition to planning, achieving organisational sustainability also requires execution, monitoring and evaluation, which is reflected in other e-competence groups of this Dimension: *Build, Run, Enable,* and *Manage*.

It was, therefore, concluded that other e-competences defined by Ee-CF 3.0, should also be considered when capacitating employees for the effective use of EIS or EMIS. For example, the analysis of the process of raising sustainability public awareness showed that the effective management of this process requires employees to possess more than the *Sustainability Development* e-competence. The personal development skills and (some) knowledge of information and knowledge management (*Enable*, D.9 & D.10 - Table 5) are also relevant in this regard as well as the *User support competence* (*Run*, component C.1) of *Dimension1*. This, for example, suggests the importance of the users' reporting training. It can be further argued that this process also requires some e-competences from the *Manage* group of *Dimension 1*: *E.1 Forecast development* and *E.4 Relationship Management*. Similar argument will apply to the *Environmental/sustainability reporting to stakeholders* related to EMIS.

The process of the *Executing instruments of environmental policy* by using EIS also requires e-competences that belong to the components of: *Run* (*C.1 User support*) and *Enable* (*D. 3 Education and training provision/reception*; *D.9 Personal development*; *D.10 Information and knowledge management*). The sustainability process of the *Legal compliance* (EIS) requires, for example, the e-competences that belong to the components of *Build* (*B.1 Design and Development*: understand and build the legal requirements in EIS); the *Run, C.1 User support* (in order for EIS users to comply to the legal requirements); *Enable,* (*D.4 Purchasing, D.7 Sales management, D.8 Contract management, D.9 Personal development*) as all these activities should be performed in accordance with the sustainability legal requirements.

The EMIS eco-efficiency and material flow management processes require e-competences from all groups belonging to the *Dimension 1*. This also applies to the processes of managing the indirect impact of ICT in an organisation, while the process of managing the direct impact of ICT requires (at least) e-competences from the groups of *Plan, Enable,* and *Manage*.

In summary, as identified in this study, the *Sustainability Development* e-competence of Ee-CF 3.0 is not sufficient to address EIS and EMIS related sustainability processes. It appeared that employees should also possess other e-competences described in Ee-CF 3.0 if effective ICT-supported sustainability development in an organisation (public of private) is to be achieved (Table 6).

Table 6. Possible positioning of Sustainability Development e-competence

Environmental Information Processing (EIP)	Processes	e-Skills	Knowledge	e- Competence
Public Sector Environmental Information Systems operated by public authorities (EIS)	Public awareness about condition of public goods	Ability to use Reporting software	Understanding environmental norms	PLAN: A.8 RUN: C.1 ENABLE: D.9; D.10 MANAGE: E.1; E.4
	Prerequisites for political decision	Ability to use of tools for modelling and simulation (e.g. differentiation of the climate change anthropogenic portion)	• Understanding status quo • Making prediction using EIS	PLAN: A.1; A.3; A.8 BUILD: B.1; B.2; B.3; B.4; B.5 RUN: C.1 ENABLE: D.9; D.10 MANAGE: E.1; E.4; E.7
	Executing instruments of environmental policy	• Ability to use tools for: • Crate and maintaining appropriate database • Continual info provision • Tracking pollution to the source	• Legal compliance regulations (e.g. Kyoto protocol, national laws) • Need for emergence actions	PLAN: A.7; A.8 RUN: C.1 ENABLE: D.3; D.9; D.10 MANAGE: E.1; E.4; E.7
Private Sector Environmental Management Information Systems (EMIS)	Legal compliance	Ability to use appropriate software for: • Discovering eco development inside company • ICT system modelling	• Understand eco development inside company • Understand eco modelling	PLAN: A.3; A.4; A.8 BUILD: B.1 RUN: C.1 ENABLE: D.4; D.7; D.8; D.9 MANAGE: E.1; E.4; E.7
	Environmental/ sustainability reporting to stakeholders	Ability to use appropriate software for managing and reporting environmental risk	Understanding stakeholders requirements	PLAN: A.3; A.8 BUILD: B.1 RUN: C.1 ENABLE: D.9; D.10 MANAGE: E.1; E.4; E.7
	Eco-efficiency and material flow management	Ability to use: • ICT-supported Real Time process control (e.g. pollution, energy use) software • -Use of LAC & DFE software	• Improving eco-efficiency:): strategic and operational • Life Cycle Assessment (LCA • Design For the Environment (DFE) • Effect of application on the LCA of products and services	PLAN: A.3; A.4; A.8 BUILD: B.1; B.2; B.3; B.4; B.5 RUN: C.1 ENABLE: D.2; D.9; D.10 MANAGE: E.1; E.2; E.5; E.6; E.7

continued on following page

CONCLUSION

This research was set to: (i) obtain an initial understanding regarding the sufficiency of the sustainability e-competences (*Sustainability Development*) as proposed by the European e-Competence Framework 3.0, for addressing sustainability issues in an organisation and (ii) identify the possible need for other e-competences for addressing sustainability issues in an organisation.

The first objective was achieved by reviewing the pertinent literature, which elicited (i) environmental sustainability processes in an organisation, (ii) kinds of information systems (EIS and EMIS) that are capable of supporting these processes, and (iii) the environmental sustainability knowledge and e-skills needed to utilise these information systems effectively. The comparison of these knowledge and skills with the knowledge and skills described by the *Sustainability Development* e-competence of Ee-CF3.0

Table 6. Continued

Environmental Information Processing (EIP)	Processes	e-Skills	Knowledge	e- Competence
Technology (ICT)	Managing direct impact	Ability to produce and manage ICT hardware LCA (production, exploitation, disposal) in order to control: • energy use • material use • waste	• Material intensity of IST's product life cycle • Dependences on infrastructure and companies who dominate the market • Risk from 'Unmastered Complexity' of ICT (the Precautionary Principle – PP) • LCA of ICT Hardware	PLAN: A.3; A.4; A.8 ENABLE: D.4; D.8; D.9 MANAGE: E.2; E.6; E.7; E.9
	Managing indirect impact (Effect of application of ICT on the LCA of products and services)	Ability to use ICT in Substitution processes	Substitution potential of ICT (functional equivalent): • Dematerialisation • Immaterialisation • Organisation of innovative services that contribute to production processes and/or products	PLAN: A.4; A.8 BUILD: B.1; B.2; B.3; B.4; B.5 RUN: C.1 ENABLE: D.5; D.6; D.7; D.9; D. 10 MANAGE: E.2; E.5; E.6; E.7
		Ability to use ICT in Optimisation processes	Optimisation potential of ICT: • Dematerialisation through optimisation of processes and products with respect to material and energy efficiency (perform existing processes more efficiently in order to rise productivity) • Efficiency vs. Sufficiency • Organisation of innovative services (e.g. to make possible something new that has not been previously feasible) • Contribution of information services to the net product • Use of algorithms to accelerate processes (in building software)	PLAN: A.3; A.4; A.8 BUILD:B.1; B.3; B.4; B.5 RUN: C.1 ENABLEB: D.5; D.6; D.7; D.9; D. 10 MANAGE: E.2; E.5; E.6; E.7
		Ability to use ICT for controlling Induction processes	Induction potential of ICT	PLAN: A.3; A.4; A.8 RUN: C.1 ENABLE: D.9; D. 10
		Ability to use ICT for controlling Rebound processes	Rebound effect of ICT: • Software design and implementation (Featurism and Software bloat) • Hardware (Miniaturization paradox) • User-related (Goal displacement by users) • Organisation Level (information work rebound effect: 'explosion' of number of electronic transactions and documents)	PLAN:A.8 RUN: C.1 ENABLE: D.9; D. 10

(Source: Author)

(belonging to the *Plan* group of e-competences) has established insufficiency of this e-competence for the appropriate use of EIS or EMIS - this is related to the second objective of this study. The findings suggest that effective use of EIS or EMIS also depends on the possession of other Ee-CF3.0 e-competences belonging to the groups *Build*, *Run*, *Enable*, and *Manage*. This implies that not only organisational planners are responsible for tackling sustainability issues but also all other employees since even the best-conceived eco-advantage strategy fails if not connected with the managers and workers who must implement it (Easty& Winston, 2006, pp. 248-249).

Mapping of Ee-CF3.0 e-competences' components of knowledge and skills to the knowledge and skills needed for operating EIS or EMIS, as shown in Table 6, can be considered as an initial theoretical framework for sustainability e-competences. At this moment, though, it is not clear whether the other e-competences shown in this embryonic framework should be named sustainability competences or if the *Sustainability Development* competence should be 'extended' by these other competences. This would help in clearly defining sustainability e-competences as often unclear terminology combined with the existence of a multiplicity of definitions means that concepts might change depending on the framework of use (OECD, 2005) and thus make operationalisation difficult.

It is also relevant to acknowledge certain limitations of this study. The analysis of sustainability processes, knowledge and skills needed for the effective use of EIS or EMIS was mainly based on the work of the group of authors (Hilty and others) associated with EMPA (Switzerland) and the German Informatics Society (GI). Although the work of other authors might reveal different sustainability processes or types of sustainability information systems, the work analysed here was deemed sufficient for meeting the objectives of this study. Other limitations of this study include the non-exhaustive analysis of the EIS and EMIS processes and, consequently, non-exhaustive mapping of e-competences to these processes. Exclusion from the discussion regarding (i) the social component of the notion of sustainability and (ii) the e-competences' component of *Attitudes* are also seen as limitations of this research.

Due to the limited scope of this chapter, a discussion regarding the workforce, which are expected to possess these e-competencies, is also omitted. However, it is important to state that the various organisational role players will need different sets of e-competences. For example, the line managers would require a different set of e-competencies compared to the e-competences needed by the assembly line workers. Similarly, the software engineers in the ICT sector will need e-competences quite different from those needed by organisational ICT users in corporate or public organisations.

The above mentioned circumscriptions, however, did not significantly influence reaching the objectives of this study. It is now up to the researchers and practitioners to proactively respond to this study, thus helping to enrich our understanding regarding ICT-supported sustainability development, in general, and sustainability e-competences, in particular. Sustainability is "*a future oriented social process of learning, searching and structuring, characterised by considerable ignorance, uncertainty and a variety of conflicts, a 'regulative idea'*" (Minsch et al., 1998 in Hilty, 2008, p. 23). In this regard, it would be useful to explore the development and use of e-competences in organisations that are currently exploiting EIS or EMIS as new theories should be devised from the real world in conjunction with the existing theories in the literature. Following the framework set out in this paper, it would also be worthwhile to develop a framework of mapping the sustainability e-competencies with the various groups of employees in an organisation requiring these competencies.

REFERENCES

Avouris, N., & Page, B. (Eds.). (1995). *Environmental Informatics – Methodology and applications of environmental information processing*. Dordrecht: Kluwer Academic Publishers.

Daugherty, P. J., Myers, M. B., & Richey, R. G. (2002). Information support for reverse logistics: The influence of relationship commitment. *Journal of Business Logistics, 23*(1), 85–106. doi:10.1002/j.2158-1592.2002.tb00017.x

De Moor, A., & Kleef, R. (2005). A social context model for discussion process analysis. In Hilty, L. M., Seifert, E.K., & Treibert, R. (Eds) (2005) Information systems for sustainable development. Hershey: Idea Group Publishing.

Dervin, B. (1977). Useful theory for librarianship: Communication not information. *Drexel Library Quarterly, 13*(5), 16–32.

Dompke, M., von Geibler, J., Göhring, W., Herget, M., Hilty, L. M., Isenmann, R., et al. (2004).Memorandum Nachhaltige Informationsgesellschaft. *Stuttgart: Fraunhofer IRB Verlag*.

e-skills UK. (2010). Technology for growth [overview report]. *e-skills UK's 'IT and Telecoms Insights*. Retrieved from www.e-skills.com/Research-and-policy/Insights-2010/2671

Easty, D., & Winston, A. (2006). *Green to gold*. New Haven: Yale University Press.

Edwards, A. R. (2005). *The sustainability revolution: portrait of a paradigm shift. Gabriola Island*. New Society Publishers.

Ee-CF. (2014). European e-Competence Framework 3.0: A common European framework for ICT professionals in all industry sectors. *European Commission*. Retrieved from http://profiletool.ecompetences.eu/

Elliot, S. (2007). Environmentally Sustainable ICT: A critical topic for IS research? *Retrieved from* http://aisel.aisnet.org/pacis2007/114

Epstein, M. (2008). *Making sustainability work: best practices in managing and measuring corporate social, environmental, and economic impact*. Sheffield: Greenleaf Publishing.

eSEW. (2010). *E-skills: European Week 2010 underlines e-skills' potential to help Europe's economic recovery*. Brussels. Retrieved from http://europa.eu/rapid/pressReleasesAction.do?reference=IP/10/220&format=HTML&aged=0&language=EN&guiLanguage=en

eSN. (e-skills News) (2010).The e-skills Manifesto - Employers call for action on e-skills. Retrieved from www.e-skills.com/cgi-in/go.pl/newscentre/news/news.html?uid=1067

GIIC – Global Information Infrastructure Commission. (2008). The GIIC Tokyo Declaration. *Retrieved from* www.giic.org

Gough, I. (2013 July, 8-10). The challenge of climate change for social policy. *Proceedings of Social Policy Association Annual Conference*. Sheffield, UK.

Hearn, S., & White, N. (2009). Communities of practice: linking knowledge, policy and practice. Retrieved from http://www.odi.org.uk/resources/download/1129.pdf

Hilty, L. (2008). *Information technology and sustainability: Essays on the relationship between ICT and sustainable development*. Norderstedt: Herstellung und Verlag: Books on Demand Gmbh.

Hilty, L. M., & Aebischer, B. (2015). ICT for Sustainability: An Emerging Research Field. In L. M. Hilty & B. Aebischer (Eds.), *ICT Innovations for Sustainability. Advances in Intelligent Systems and Computing 310*. Heidelberg: Springer International Publishing. doi:10.1007/978-3-319-09228-7_1

Hilty, L. M., Binswanger, M., Bruinink, A., Erdmann, L., Froehlich, J., Köhler, A., et al. (2005).The Precautionary principle in the Information Society – Effects of pervasive computing on health and environment (*2nd ed.*). *Swiss Center for Technology Assessment (TA-SWISS). Retrieved from* www.empa.ch/ssis

Hilty, L. M. & Ruddy, T. F. (2000). Towards a sustainable Information Society. *Informatik/Informatique 4 (2000), 2-9*.

Hilty, L. M., Schulthess, D., & Ruddy, T. F. (Eds.). (2000). *Strategische und betriebsübergreifendeAnwendungenbetrieblicherUmweltinformationssysteme*. Marburg: Metropolis.

Holland, A. (2003). Sustainability. In D. Jamieson (Ed.), *A Companion to Environmental Philosophy*. Oxford: Blackwell Publishing.

ITWeb (2008, September). ITWeb - JCSE ICT skills survey [DVD of Powerpoint presentation].

Kraus, S. E. (2005). Research paradigms and meaning making: A Primer. *Qualitative Report, 10*(4), 758–770.

Kyoto Protocol to the United Nations Framework Convention on Climate Change. (1998). *New York: United Nations*.

MacLean, D., Souter, D., & Creech, H. (2012). ICTs, the Internet, and Sustainability. *International Institute for Sustainable Development*. Retrieved from https://www.iisd.org/pdf/2012/changing_our_understanding_of_sustainability.pdf

Minsch, J., Feindt, P.-H., Meister, H.-P., Schneidewind, U., & Schulz, T. (1998). *InstitutionelleReformenfüreinePolitik der Nachhaltigkeit*. Marburg: Metropolis.

Mitrovic, Z. (2010). Positioning e-skills within an organisation: An information systems management viewpoint. *SA Journal of Information Management, 12*(1), 427–434. doi:10.4102/sajim.v12i1.427

National e-Skills Plan of Action. (2010). e-Skills Institute. Pretorian Department of Communications: e-Skills Institute.

National e-Skills Plan of Action. (2013). *Pretorian Department of Communications: e-Skills Institute*. Retrieved from www.doc.gov.za/documents-publications/category/14-e-skills-documents.html

New Perspectives on ICT skills and employment. (2005). *Directorate for Science, Technology and Industry*. Retrieved from www.oecd.org/dataoecd/26/35/34769393.pdf

Olson, H. (1995). Quantitative 'versus' qualitative research: The wrong question. Retrieved from www.ualberta.ca/dept/slis/cais/olson.htm

Romani, J. C. C. (2009). 21 century literacies and OECD. *IV Congress of CyberSociety*. Retrieved from http://www.cibersociedad.net/congres2009/en/coms/21-century-literacies-and-oecd/114/

Sachs, J. (2015). *The Age of Sustainable Development*. New York: Columbia University Press.

SAP's plan to make money by cutting carbon. (2011). *Technology Review, Business*. Retrieved from www.technologyreview.com/business/27001/?nlid=3977

Sarapuu, K. (2015). Dangerous e-Waste is the World's Fastest Growing Municipal Waste Stream. *Let us do it World*. Retrieved from http://www.letsdoitworld.org/news/dangerous-e-waste-worlds-fastest-growing-municipal-waste-stream

Schlenzig, C. (1999). Energy planning and environmental management with the information and decision support system MESAP. *International Journal of Global Energy*, *12*(1–6), 81–91. doi:10.1504/IJGEI.1999.000840

Shaft, T. M., Ellington, R. T., Meo, M., & Sharfman, M. P. (1997). A framework for information systems in life-cycle oriented environmental management. *Journal of Industrial Ecology*, *1*(2), 135–148. doi:10.1162/jiec.1997.1.2.135

UGe-CF. (2008). User guidelines for the application of the European e-Competence Framework. *European Commission*. Retrieved from www.ecompetences.eu

UN. (2012, July 27). *The future we want. Resolution adopted by the General Assembly*. UN General Assembly.

Verdantix. (2013, June 4). US Sustainable Business Spending 2012-2017. Retrieved from http://www.verdantix.com/index.cfm/papers/Products.Details/product_id/544/us-sustainable-business-spending-2012-2017/-

WCED - World Commission on Environment and Development. (1987). Our common future [Brundtland Report]. Oxford University Press.

Yi, L., & Thomas, H. R. (2007). A review of research on the environmental impact of e-Business and ICT. *Environment International*, *33*(6), 841–849. doi:10.1016/j.envint.2007.03.015 PMID:17490745

KEY TERMS AND DEFINITIONS

E-Competences: This term refers to ICT competencies, which are defined as a demonstrated ability to apply knowledge, skills and attitudes for achieving observable results.

Environmental Information System: This system is defined as ICT-based system that supports environmental management in the public sector organisations.

Environmental Management Information System: This system is defined as ICT-based system that supports environmental management in the private sector organisations.

Information and Communication Technologies (ICT): This term refers to diverse technologies generally consisting of hardware, software and the communication equipment.

E-Competences for Organisational Sustainability Information Systems

Information System: It is a system composed of ICT and people that produces information needed for decision-making processes in an organisation.

Sustainability e-Competences: These are e-competencies used to estimate, plan, implement eco-friendly ICT solutions and monitor the impact of these solutions on the natural environment.

Sustainability: It is defined as an ability or capacity of something to be maintained or to sustain itself. In this chapter it refers to economic and social development as well as the environmental protection.

Chapter 14
Information Systems Innovations Using Competitive Intelligence

Phathutshedzo Nemutanzhela
Tshwane University of Technology, South Africa

ABSTRACT

The chapter outlines Information System's (IS) innovations using Competitive Intelligence (CI). The theoretical foundation supporting this chapter was reviewed and Information System framework was implemented. Recommendations as to how the framework for Information Systems innovation was implemented have been addressed in this chapter. Knowledge is used as a focal factor for competitive advantage, through effective and efficient performances by employees in many organisations. As a result, knowledgeable employees are expected to share their knowledge with others to increase innovation within the organisation. Unfortunately, this is not always the case. Generally, employees behave differently within an organisation. The main challenge is that no organisation has total control of its employees' behaviour and actions. The behaviour and action has an impact on how Information Systems are deployed for innovation, in creating competitive advantage. As a result, many systems have been deployed by different organisations in attempt to address this challenge for the interest.

1. INTRODUCTION

Through Information Systems, an organisation executes its business strategy and attempts to realize its business goals. Lederer & Gardiner, 1992 refer to this as 'a portfolio of computer-based applications'. The Information Systems component is largely responsible for meeting the goals and objectives of the organisation. According to Iyamu & Olummide, (2010) the Information Systems component consists of systems through which the business carries out its processes and logic. They are directly used by the end user (those who act on behalf of the business). Many organisations use Information Systems as a tool for their various innovations to support and enable processes and activities. Innovation is an on-going process to create, enable and support improvement for competitive advantage by the organisa-

DOI: 10.4018/978-1-4666-8524-6.ch014

tion (Mariano & Pavesi, 2010). William & Baumol, (2010) argued that large firm's use innovation as a competitive weapon, a compound of systematic innovative activity within the firm. However, innovation carries with it significant risks.

Companies keep competing against each other using products and services, making Competitive Intelligence (CI) an important tool in the development of strategy in the organisations. The importance of Competitive Intelligence is attributed to its contribution to technological knowledge and intelligence, and it use for the analysis of Information Systems innovation in organisations. It should be pointed out early that innovation and technology are often taken in a similar light as asserted by Rogers (2003) that 'we often use the word "innovation" and "technology" as synonyms.' And as such CI is primarily intended to be used for the state of art, technological trends and challenges, with a strategic vision on competitiveness and customers (Ashton & Klavans, 1997; Fleisher, 2003). Competitive Intelligence therefore can be considered as a tool for innovation process, observation of market, analysis of strategic behaviors of both competitors and customers, including their values, expectations and needs (Krücken-Pereira, Debiasi, & Abreu, 2003).

An innovation according to Rogers, (2003) is considered as 'an idea, practice, or object that is perceived as new by an individual or other unit of adoption.' A unit of adoption in this case could be the organisation, a society and also a target market. Technological Innovation in products and processes constitutes a crucial factor for national economic growth (Manual De, 2008; Lacerda & et,.al, 2001). According to Fang (2005) Innovation can be divided into three categories: Radical innovations, Incremental innovations, and Product innovation. Martins & Terblanche, 2003) define innovation as "the implementation of a new and possible problem-solving idea, practice or material artefact (e.g. a product) which is regarded as new by the relevant unit of adoption and through which change is brought about".

Competitive Intelligence offers a real strategic advantage for many businesses (Stephen, 2006) Gilad, (2000) argues that some of the largest corporate organizations have a dedicated CI department, while smaller businesses often practice CI on an ad hoc basis. This they do so by informally collecting information from a variety of internal and external sources, such as the Internet, trade shows conferences and networking meetings. Competitive Intelligence is of importance to many businesses mainly because it helps to formulate strategy, as well as make informed decisions.

The CI is deployed with the intention to better, coordinate internal processes and activities of organizations, primarily, to reach market more effectively. Gathering people, the logic and the physical architecture around common purposes provide individuals with the information they need to expand their own knowledge (Malhotra, 2000; Hoven & Van, 2001). This approach help to build high performance teams in the organisation. This indeed, is the foundation of the integrated organisation, where the information technology is capacitating technological innovation.

Competitive Intelligence has the main function of processing and refining information and knowledge, whether it is within an organisation or in a network of organisations. Martre & Jean-Louis, (1994) argues that complex modes of competition in organisations are increasing and are characterized by cooperation-competition relationships to which companies must adapt. Competitive Intelligence should be applied to adjust strategy to the new paradigm of competition. McCord, (2002) view, competition leads to collaboration and Competitive Intelligence.

Competitive Intelligence and Information Systems seem to have a common focus, to meet the needs of the users. Information Systems in many ways enable the gathering of information that later becomes Competitive Intelligence. And Competitive Intelligence facilitates the creation of information system innovations in the way it is used during the process of improving products and services.

2. RESEARCH METHODOLOGY

The main focus of the chapter was to investigate and understand the impact of Competitive Intelligence on Information Systems innovation products and services in organisations. The approaches and methods employed in the chapter include the case chapter, qualitative research method, and semi-structured interview approach. The data was analysed, using the Innovation-decision process from the perspective of DoI theory.

The case chapter was adopted primarily because it is an approach that assists to achieve a deep understanding of a specific phenomenon. According to Cooper & Schindler, (2006) the case chapter is an approach which combines individual and (sometimes) group interviews with record analysis and observation; used to understand events and their ramifications and processes. Hofstee, (2006) argued that the case chapter approach is useful when detailed knowledge is required of any particular case. A pseudonym name, "Divhetsheleni" was used to represent the case, the organisation used in the chapter. The participants were codified from DV_LA001 to DV_LA012 to adhere to the ethical consideration as agreed with the organisation and the university.

The qualitative research method was selected for the chapter. This was because of the nature of the chapter, which required variety and wide spread of view and option about the phenomenon. According to Cooper & Schindler, (2006), qualitative research includes 'an array of interpretive techniques which seek to describe, decode, translate, and otherwise come to terms with meaning, not frequency'. The qualitative chapter allows data to be gathered from multiple sources Yin, (2009). In other words it is not limited to one source of information.

The research employed the interview and documentation approaches in the data collection. The interview approach allows the researcher to put questions to a respondent face-to-face (Welman & Kruger, 2001). The research followed the semi-structured interview technique of the interview research approach so that the process does not lose focus, at the same time allows probing of responses. According to Kvale, (1996) the most useful interview format for conducting qualitative research is often "semi-structured" (sometimes called "moderately scheduled"). This means the interview is not highly structured, as is the case of an interview that consists of all closed-ended questions, nor is it unstructured, so that the interviewee is simply given a license to talk freely about the topic. This was advantageous for data collection because it made it possible to explain the questions that were not understood by the respondent and there was chance to further probe responses.

2.1 Diffusion of Innovation (DoI)

The Innovation-decision process from the perspective of DoI theory was employed in the data analysis. In DoI theory, technological Innovation is communicated through particular channels, over time, among the members of a social system (Rogers, 2003). The theory is concerned with the manner in which a new technological idea, artefact or technique, or a new use of an old one, migrates from creation to use.

According to (Rogers, 2003), the Innovation-decision process involves five steps. As shown in Figure 1, the process include: (1) knowledge, (2) persuasion, (3) decision, (4) implementation, and (5) confirmation. These stages typically follow each other in a time-ordered manner. The stages are briefly described below.

Figure 1. Diffusion of Innovations
(Rogers, 2003)

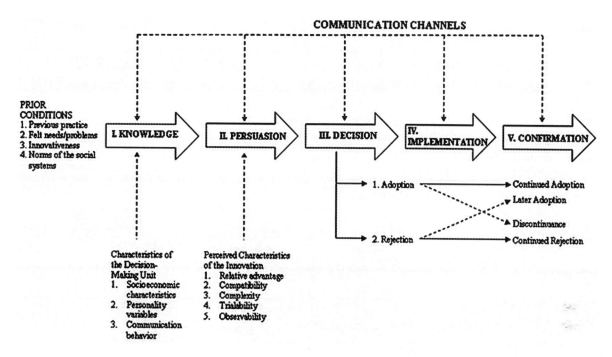

The Innovation decision process characterized as a process that occurs while individuals participate in a series of actions related to decisions (Rogers, 1995). *Knowledge* occurs when individuals are aware of the Innovation and gain understanding of its functions. *Persuasion* is when individuals or decision-making units exhibit favourable or unfavourable behaviour toward the Innovation. *Decision* indicates when the individual or unit decides to adopt or reject the Innovation. *Implementation* occurs when the individual or unit decides to use the Innovation. *Confirmation* occurs when decision makers confirm or reject their decision to adopt the Innovation (Rogers, 1995).

3. DATA ANALYSIS

Using the Innovation-Decision Process (Rogers, 2003), the analysis of the data is presented as follows:

3.1 Knowledge

Knowledge involves management efforts - from identifying needs to delivering intelligence products and services to consumers and clients. Similarly, innovations are evaluated, monitored and controlled using knowledge. In the organisation, knowledge was applied in the development of innovation, which was supported by policy, and generated new requirements. Through knowledge the organisation could innovate, as well as plan how to utilise the products and services from innovation. According to DV_LA003 (p4:30-31),

Knowledge in the organisation is assessed by questions, and, they are categorised into needs, such as intelligence problem, decisions, risk metrics (risk tolerance level) and measurement methods. The organisation was challenged by the knowledge to innovate, primarily, for competitive advantage.

The organisation focuses on the innovations of security tools and approaches. DV_LA004 (p13:100-101) explained that there is a growing use of Competitive Intelligence in the financial services sector and mentioned that

... the organisation has spent considerable resources to protect their businesses from infiltration of their systems by other forces.

According to DV_LA003 (p7:45-46),

Knowledge is a vital tool, as such, and the organisation conducts surveys to assess employees' knowledge on the deployment of CI. The organisation worked hard on communicating with staff, ensuring strategies were clear, addressing performance and remuneration issues and motivating people.

A number of employees, within the organisation, did not have the knowledge regarding some of their Information Systems innovation Product and Service offerings. This was attributed to factors such as inadequate skills; no clear consequences of not meeting performance standards; lack of alignment with strategy and a reward system that fails to motivate properly.

If employees are not informed, or are knowledgeable about products and services it creates risk to both individuals and the organisation. DV_L003 (p7:62-63) explained that

... everyone in the organisation are aware of the strategy and possesses knowledge of the products and services which are deployed in the organisation.

3.2 Persuasion

At the Persuasion stage, a person's main type of thinking is affected by, or related to, feelings. Some employees in the organisation develop an attitude towards certain Innovation and are psychologically involved with Information Systems Products and Services. According to DV_LA002 (p5:55-56), *there is a marketing team which responsible innovation, and persuades the Board of Directors for approval.* Post approval, the rest of the employees is persuaded on implementation and use of the innovation.

Organisations use incentives and bonuses as tools to persuade employees to perform their tasks, and align with the organisational innovative strategy. An employee stated that

... when I am working on any project, I know that I should do my ultimate best to make sure the project becomes a success. The lack of some knowledge, on my part, in being able to deliver successfully on the project, affects my incentives and can, sometimes, also affect everyone involved on the project. DV_LA006 (p16:172-173).

Some employees felt that only using the marketing team is exploitative because of the rest of the team's limited perception of the innovation, and reality. Not having a say in the matter may serve as an indicator of the message's influence on this stage. However, DV_LA001 (p2:14-15)

... believes that, by having one team focusing on finding new ideas to innovate, it eliminates time waste and also cuts cost; inevitably speeding up the delivery process.

DV_LA004 (p8:83-84), commented that there is a perception that

people who work in the field might have first information of latest innovation, but often choose to remain silent because it's not their place to come up with new ideas. The employee added that it then becomes more difficult or easier to persuade these people to adopt innovation in the organisation, as they already know more about it. This depended on the type of findings they have about the innovation, as a result of their interaction with clients.

Another interviewee, DV_LA005 (p9:148-149) commented that

Key Performance Indicators (KPIs) is good approach to periodically assess the performance of the individuals, business units and the organisation at large.

The employees further explained that

... in the organisation, KPIs is defined in a way that is understandable, meaningful, and measurable. They are rarely defined in such a way such that their fulfilment would be hampered by factors seen as non-controllable by the organisations or individuals responsible. The KPI ensure that each employee knows the organisation's expectations, as well as the output required by the customers.

3.3 Decision

Many of the individuals in an organisation do not adopt innovated Information Systems Products and Services without proper testing and evaluation. The latter was carried out in relation to the usefulness and fit in the organisation's environment. Some individuals used partial trial to gain better understanding of innovation and deployment of products and services in the organisations.

One of the interviewees, DV_LA008 (p6:17-18) provided the following explanation;

... some employees in the organisation are policy decision-makers and initiate requirements for CI products and services. These decision-makers are the recipients of the end Products and Services of CI through Information Systems Innovation. The decisions are based on information and knowledge, and sometimes lead to the levying of more requirements; thus triggering the Intelligence Cycle. After finishing a cycle, a new set, or improved set, of template will be produced that will be used in monitoring and identifying risk.

According to a Director, DV_LA002 (p5:43-44),

It is common to find deployments filled with projects that have attractive returns on investment but do not move the needle on performance parameters that matter in the marketplace. In selecting Products and Services to innovate and build a portfolio of improvement initiatives, clear linkage to strategic priorities needs to be established; not just at the outset, but on an on-going basis.

When making decisions, one of the most seductive pitfalls is to become comfortable with embracing innovations that are, in themselves, attractive without paying sufficient attention to overall optimization.

Although finance could be viewed as the artery of a firm and an important indicator of management direction, management mindset encompasses more variables than only financial decisions.

The organisation's brand, strategy, employees and customers play a major role when making a decision to innovate. The brand has to define the organisation through the innovation. The innovation has to align with strategy, the employees' need for knowledge and skills to deploy the CI innovation, and the customer has to get the best Product and Services that will help solve their problems. DV_LA001 (p3:19-20).

3.4 Implementation

Each division at Divhetsheleni has its own strategic team that deals with implementing the strategy of the division, making sure it aligns with the organisational strategy. All CI implementation is defined by the same vision and goals in order to improve innovation, as well as to create a competitive brand. The *strategy team ensures that Information Systems Innovation aligns with the organisation's strategy. However, the organisation had a Marketing Department, which was responsible for innovations that needed to be implemented in all the various divisions of the organisation. According to one of the employees, (DV_LA001 p2:18-19), Implementation of a new innovation was about being prepared to measure the organisation's performance consistently, constantly, to recognise weaknesses and, indeed, be willing to address those weaknesses. This begins with initial measurement, which serves as an indication of where the organisation is, so that it can determine where it wants to be. The o*rganisation still follows old traditional ways of implementation, while Information Systems Innovation challenges the employees to acquire more knowledge, and understanding, of the products and services they deploy. The organisation readiness to implement becomes a challenge during the innovative process.

A forward–looking organisation seeks to provide value-added offerings, through Information Systems Innovation, at every stage of its life in order to improve the culture of the organisation. The organisation's *high-performance culture was characterised by openness and trust, with clear accountability for execution, and the freedom to take calculated risks; thereby constantly raising individual and organisational performance. This was expressed by DV_LA005 (p15:204-205).*

According to DV_LA002 (p6:64-65),

… most of the organisation's successful implementations of a remuneration strategy, and the alignment of benefits across all staff, are based on job function rather than grades.

The employee further expressed that,

Performance scorecards reflect an integrated approach to sustainability and are balanced across economic, environmental, social, transformational and cultural elements. Our commitment to driving high performance is evident in our new organisational structure, with the separation of support structures from the client-facing clusters to ensure that the business is able to focus on improving economic performance regardless of economic conditions.

3.5 Confirmation

Confirmation was the recognition, by the organisation, of the benefits of using Information Systems Innovation; its integration into the organisation's on-going routine, or promotion of the innovation to others; as well as the identification of Products and Services to be deployed. This gives the organisation an opportunity to provide feedback immediately when decisions for tomorrow's solutions are being made. According to one of the employees,

... we establish a team work with our clients from the beginning of the deployment, DV_LA006 (p18:248-249). This team work between the organisation and the customers made it possible to test and confirm the proposed innovation.

In addition, another employer, DV_LA001 (p3:29-30) commented that *in cases whereby many solutions required testing, the customer gave the organisation access to people who were experts on the applications.* The collaboration between hardware and software providers, at this early stage, eliminated the risk normally associated with new technology deployment.

4. FINDINGS

The findings from the analysis are presented in this section as follows:

I. Culture

When an organisation is operating globally, culture always becomes a challenge. The organisation high-performance culture is characterised by openness and trust, with clear accountability for execution, and the freedom to take calculated risks; thereby constantly raising individual and organisational performance. For the organisation to deliver on its high performance culture, it must have created an environment where information is shared openly, whereby its' people are reward for their skills. In addition, trust must be created to ensure that employees do not feel used.

Each innovation has performance scorecards that reflect an integrated approach to sustainability. These are balanced across economic, environmental, social, transformational and cultural elements. In addition, these innovation performance scorecards assist in building a new organisational structure; separating support structures from client-facing clusters. This ensures that the business is able to focus on improving economic performance, regardless of economic conditions, and innovation oversees the different conditions affecting the organisation. In addition, being an international company will not make any difference as far as the organisation's innovation is concerned. Its culture will address all organisational branches, ensuring that each innovation aligns with the culture of that particular environment. Cultural barriers are addressed, directly, by strategy where most factors have already been identified.

II. Knowledge Sharing

One of the challenges of an organisation is that of getting people to share their knowledge. In the organisation, so much depends on teamwork and collective knowledge sharing. It was only a handful of employees who had the kind of knowledge with which they could hold their peers (and bosses) to ransom. Such individuals were Directors or Managers of the organisation not wanting to lose trade secrets. Also, there were specialists who have been in the organisation for many years and have built up their own unique way of achieving success without perhaps even understanding the deep tacit knowledge of how they do it. All these pose threats to the organisation, when they wanted to innovate, such individuals held on to the expertise that they have. Employees took pride in not having to seek advice from colleagues, and wanted to discover new ways for themselves. Other employees lacked trust in their employer so they refrained from sharing the knowledge that they have gathered over the years.

The organisation needed to create a commitment of culture, to address change, challenge, for competitive advantage. If, as is often the case, time pressure leads to poor knowledge sharing, then there must be a commitment to allow time for it to happen. Commitment to knowledge sharing must be demonstrated throughout the organisation. It was apparent through what the leaders of the organisation say and do. It was shown by commitment in the organisations' processes, reward systems and development of programmes.

Above all, commitment to knowledge sharing was shown by individuals, throughout the organisation being committed to sharing their knowledge with others; even if it is not formally part of their 'daily deliverables', employees were not prone to share by overtly being rewarded. It was not only about financial reward. Stimulus-response does not work in complex systems, as human beings are motivated by more than just financial reward. One can ensure appropriate rewards are in place, but the better option is to remove any disincentives to sharing that exist and helping employee see for themselves that knowledge sharing is in their personal interest. The old paradigm was 'knowledge is power'; today it needs to be explicitly understood that 'sharing knowledge is power'.

III. Repositioning

The organisation shifted its focus from repositioning its brand to building the brand and the brand promise. When the organisation innovates, the brand needs to sell the idea. Therefore, the customer has to start seeing the innovation from the brand perspective.

Core to building the organisation's profile is the achievement of the two defined aspirations of being the 'most respected and inspirational brand' and being a 'great place to work'; while overcoming perceptions that the brand is elitist. The organisation continues to inspire, motivate and challenge people to make a difference, whilst striving to become a leader in client-employee understanding and care; across all market segments. The introduction of a new brand expression, 'Make Things Happen', accentuates the intensified, and increased, nationwide above and below-the-line advertising campaigns to position the organisation's brand in a more relevant and approachable manner. As an organisation, this demonstrates a deeper understanding and caring in relation to the financial needs of communities and the country, as a whole. As a result, brand measures show significant improvements in an organisation's positioning in the market; in both awareness and acceptance.

IV. Education and Awareness

Education and Awareness in the organisation encouraged and enhanced employees' participation in activities aimed at conservation, protection and management of the environment. This was essential for achieving sustainable development. The organisation seems to ignore the importance of educating their staff about information systems product and services and the path taken by the organisation to deploy competitive intelligence. There appears to be the assumption that seems that all employees are aware of the deployment process. Employees who were not aware of the organisation in which they operate they are more of an expense, than an asset, to the company. Their inability to transfer, or acquire skills, from one other is evident since they are not cognisant of the innovation taking place within their organisation. Spending the necessary time to educate employees, and making them aware of CI, will cut organisation costs and reduce time spent doing feasibility studies on the process of adopting and implementing innovation by an outside partner.

On the other hand, the organisation was doing itself great justice each time it innovate on marketing strategy, that inform and educate their customers about the innovation, that were conducted. The strategy allowed for the involvement of the employees, who respond to customers numerous questions having sought the appropriate answers with regards to the introduced innovation. Unfortunately those employees within the organisation, who were not involved in the marketing strategy, remained uninformed and lacked the knowledge to carry certain tasks effectively.

V. Continuity

The organisation improved on innovations across all business clusters in order to create a single view of its client base. It enables a closer relationship with clients, and facilitates better co-ordination of its activities. The organisation strives to provide more transactional service offerings, and the driving of primary investor status, by focusing on further enhancements of the Electronic Banking Channel Project for corporate clients.

Some divisions, however, are planning on introducing a number of new products, services and business ventures. A dedicated unit, which focused on driving innovative products, was established. The organisation intended to build on the innovative products that they launch each year; aiming to have improved its innovation delivery capability significantly. Particular focus will be on driving down the cost of Information Technology (IT), project delivery and improving time to market. The organisation continues to improve the process of determining, prioritising and selecting the right innovation projects to optimise the return on investment.

Innovation goes beyond mere project delivery efficiency and relates to the innovative capacity of the entire business of the organisation. The organisation might, therefore, adopt Service Orientated Architecture (SOA) as a strategy; whereby SOA enables enhanced agility and improves innovation capability through multiple utilisation, standardisation, simplification and rationalisation of components in the IT landscape for competitive advantage.

VI. Inclusiveness

Some of the innovation for process improvement lies with the process owners. This is not a new concept, but it bears emphasising: as the organisations did not take this aspect serious during innovation.

Frequently, process owners are frontline people who do not have the chance to participate in improvement efforts. While they may not be formally trained on how to use some quality tools, their closeness to the process is a vantage point which could be second to none. The organisation uses their marketing team to come up with innovation. The same team runs the marketing campaigns and interacts with the customer, and paid less attention to the employees who actually deploy the process.

Every project or deployment needs to ask the question: "Who knows the process or sub process best, and in what manner are the process owners gaining access to their unique knowledge and insight?". Some of innovations are led from the current deployment of an innovation. When people involved in the deployment process are not included in the initial innovative process, the organisation loses some of those excluded employees' valid and potential input with regards to the innovation. Improvement efforts were often staffed by technical experts from mid- to senior management levels. This was in order to avoid missing key opportunities that frontline people could identify, instinctively; project leaders need to make participation broad and inclusive. This can be done in a variety of ways, some of which are interviews and group brainstorming sessions, or requesting that process owners be included as part of the team.

At a minimum, project leaders need facilitation skills training, coaching and practice in order for them to effectively elicit insights from a diverse array of down-the-line personnel.

VII. Prioritization

One of the most seductive pitfalls is for an organisation to become comfortable with doing information systems innovation projects that are in themselves attractive, without paying sufficient attention to overall optimisation. It was common to find deployments filled with information systems innovation projects that have attractive returns on investment, but do not move the needle on performance parameters that matter in the marketplace. In selecting information systems innovation projects and building a portfolio of improvement initiatives, clear linkage to strategic priorities needs to be established, not just at the outset but on an on-going basis.

Creativity is not generally associated with defining the portfolio of information systems innovation projects; however, on-going re-evaluation can uncover opportunities for innovation. The sum, or where time and attention is placed, defines an organisation's strategic direction. The organisation spends much time building their brand. Brand distinguishes them from their competitors. Brand sells the innovative idea that the organisation is trying to achieve. It is vital for an organisation to always align their innovation with the brand and strategy of the company. Lack of time to actually plan the project thoroughly can have a huge impact on how the project is carried out. Innovation requires strategic thinking and the employee's initiative to implement and make it a success.

The next section presents the interpretation of the findings from the case chapter.

4.1 Interpretation of the Findings

The findings from the analysis are regarded as the factors which influence the Innovation of Competitive Intelligence (CI) within the Information Systems environment. The Products and Services of CI manifest into many other components, as depicted in Figure 2. The discussion that follows explains each of the components.

Figure 2. Factors influencing Competitive Intelligence on Information Systems innovation

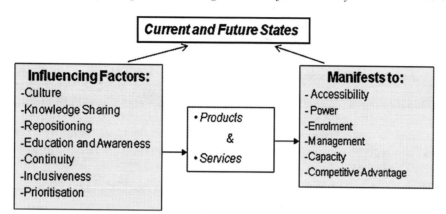

- **Accessibility:** This refers to the organisational ability to access information needed for the making of public decisions as well as its ability to share the economical status of the organisation with its employees. It also speaks of the sharing of knowledge and expertise by employees, with their peers, without hiding any information for fear of any threat that might arise. Some of these include the following; "If I share some of my knowledge, will you use it out of context, misapply it (and then blame me!), or pass it off as your own without giving any acknowledgement or recognition to me as the source?"
- **Power:** This is often a cop out by managers, or change agents, who are not adequately addressing the human factors or motivational aspects. In the organisation, so much depends on teamwork and collective knowledge; it is only a handful of people who have knowledge on which they can hold their peers (and bosses) to ransom. There are some specialists who has been in the organisation for many years, and built stock of knowledge, which they use as a source of power. However, knowledge is power but is, typically, not the primary reason for lack of knowledge sharing.
- **Enrolment:** Based on different interests, many employees decide either to enrol (participate) on the innovations process or not. Also, those who enrol might do so reluctantly, depending on the interest. Personal interest takes priority above the organisation's interest.
- **Management:** There is pressure on productivity, on deadlines, and it's a general rule that the more knowledgeable you are, the more people there are waiting to collar you for the next task. Management ensures that lessons learnt by individuals and groups are captured into the knowledge database for sharing.
  - Another aspect of management is the use of aligning rewards and recognition to support appropriate behaviours, efficiency and productivity by employees. This minimizes, and eventually eradicates, the schemes that are based on seniority or individual expertise, rather than team effectiveness.
- **Capacity:** At regular team meetings, time must be allocated to understand and improve internal processes. Too many meetings are task and output focused, but fail to address the means of achieving successful outcomes.
- **Competitive Advantage:** This is the strategic advantage one organisation entity has over its rival entities within its competitive industry. Achieving Competitive Advantage strengthens and positions an organisation better within the business environment.

In order for an organisation to develop a competitive advantage it must have resources and capabilities that are superior to those of its competitors. Without this superiority the competitors can simply replicate what the organisation was doing, and any advantage disappears quickly.

Framework for Information Systems Innovation

From the analysis and findings, the case chapter provides insight to the different characteristics of Competitive Intelligence (CI) Products and Services Innovations within the Information Systems environment. This is illustrated in Figure 3. To have a full understanding, the discussion that follows should be read with the Figure 3.

Organisations that are strong in Adaptability and Involvement have an edge in innovation and creativity, while organisations excelling in Mission and Consistency have a high measure of stability, return on investment and return on sales. Organisations measuring high in all components have a dramatic financial advantage over organisations that are weak in these areas. Organisations at the bottom perform just as one would expect: They are sluggish, wasteful and out of touch with their customers.

A differentiated corporate culture can build sustainable long-term competitive advantage and help to attract and retain talented staff. The various management and leadership development programmes are key enablers. Organisation needs to become the employer of choice, recognising that market competition for talent continues to increase. Continued focus remains on making organisations a great place to work and able to attract, develop and retain the best people.

The economic capital, risk appetite and risk adjusted performance management methodologies of the organisation get to be embedded across the group, and fully integrated into strategy and reporting; in parallel with the historical return on ordinary shareholder's equity (ROE). The risk management structure is maintained for the continuous build of a strong risk culture, including firmly establishing risk as an enabler for growth; a competitive advantage and a key source for innovation.

Figure 3. Competitive Intelligence products and services innovations within the Information Systems environment

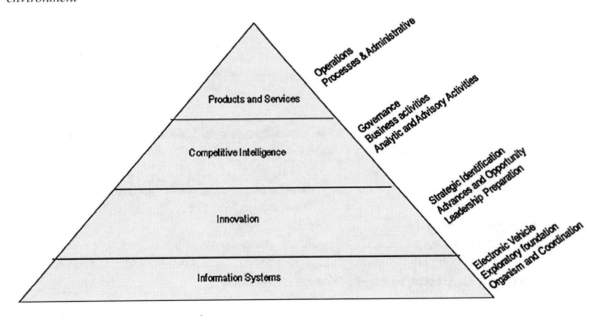

There is reliance, by the organisation, on the Key Performance Indicators (KPI's) to identify or measure the acceptance of innovation by a client. KPI, for an organisation, is a tool that persuades decision makers as a result of the reaction of the customer towards the organisation's innovation. It also measures an employee's performance on certain tasks related to the innovation.

The organisation and its executives are grappling with several concerns relating to the management and institutionalisation of knowledge sharing. They see the most pressing need as developing a structured and systematic approach to what is known as knowledge sharing. Knowledge sharing has gained increasing attention in recent years and has become more relevant in the fast changing, IT-driven world; primarily due to the fact that organisations always want to stay ahead of their competitors.

Information Systems innovation begins with the organisational environment, whereby there is top-down support for project management practices and investment, by the organisation, in the innovation process. In rolling out Products and Services, implementation by the organisation focuses on doing so correctly, rather than simply doing what it takes to complete the Competitive Intelligence deployment as quickly as possible, at a minimum cost.

If successful implementation of products and services contributes directly to strategic objectives, then the bottom line Information Systems and innovation should lead to organisational success. Innovation requires an investment in resources, therefore responsibility lies with senior management to ensure that investments are made wisely and add value to the organisation as a whole. Unsuccessful Competitive Intelligence deployments translate into poor investment and, ultimately, senior management is accountable for projects not reaching the objectives of the organisation.

In conclusion, the brand of an organisation brand is a key intangible attribute by which they compete. Its main objective is to support differentiators; and reposition the company as being significantly different from any other financial organisation. In so doing, potential clients are drawn to the brand which, ultimately, encourages them to choose their organisation above that of their competitors.

For a company to deploy Competitive Intelligence successfully, appropriate organisational awareness of the culture of competitiveness must be cultivated. While decision makers should call the shots on what intelligence is required, information gathering should be on everyone's mind. Through the findings and interpretation of the two case studies on the impact of Competitive Intelligence Information Systems products and services innovations in organisations, a Framework was developed to illustrate stages that organisations have to following during Information Systems innovation.

From the findings and interpretation of the case chapter on the impact of Competitive Intelligence on Information Systems products and services innovations in organisations, a Framework was developed, Figure 4. The Framework is aimed at providing direction for organisations during Information Systems innovation, the stages on the Framework encompasses the activities involved in Information Systems innovation.

The Information Systems it's composed of five different stages that organisations need to follow for deployment of CI products and services. Each Stage has columns that are categories by different aspects of innovation on a row level. All innovation stages or phases actives, roles and responsibilities, requirements and Information Systems inputs for the deployment of a successful Competitive Intelligence products and services has been illustrated in this framework.

Figure 4. Framework for Information Systems innovation

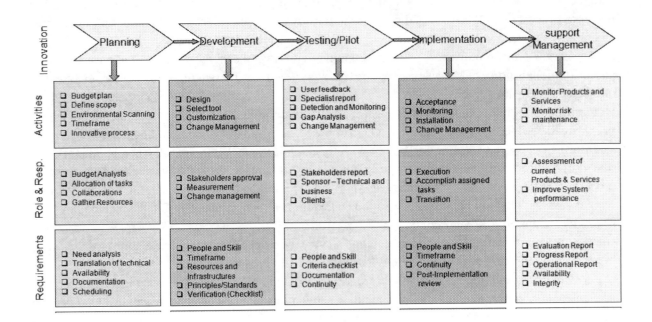

5. CHAPTER RECOMMENDATIONS

Analysis and interpretations assisted the researcher in achieving the objectives of this chapter. However, some gaps were identified. Based on the identified gaps, recommendations are made in two distinct areas. They are as follows:

5.1 Culture

Aligning organisational culture with the strategy of the organisation in order to improve information systems products and services innovation is one of the gaps that were identified in this chapter. Organisational culture is the personality of the organisation. Culture is comprised of the assumptions, values, norms and tangible signs (artifacts) of organisation members and their behaviours.

Organisation has some factors which are not addressed; this factors impacts on employee's willingness to share information. Such factors are lack of performance contract, organisation perform on a centralised environment, and fear of losing their jobs if they share knowledge and skills they have. Their environment limits or forces the employees to restrain from sharing knowledge, as they lack measure to use for persuasion. Employees who have information that is worth to the organisation to be shared refrain from sharing because of fear. Fear that they will lose their jobs. They fear that their junior will oppress them, and also fear of losing power they have through that knowledge, skills, expertise or information. Not being in position to innovate, can also be another reason why employees don't share information that can help change the scope of the business.

Organisations need to create a commitment to culture, to change, to challenge, to compete and co-operate. If, as is often the case, time pressure leads to poor knowledge sharing, then there must be a commitment to allow time for it to happen. Commitment to knowledge sharing must be demonstrated throughout the organisation. It is apparent through what the leaders of the organisation say and do. It is shown by commitment in the organisations' processes, reward systems, development programmes etc.

Culture means that each information systems innovation that the organisation deploys will have to align with the vision, mission, strategy; norms and the environment in with the business operate. It is recommended that the strategy of the organisation should be re-structured every time before any competitive intelligence deployment to make sure it aligns with the culture of the organisation. Employees will know the products and services that best suit their organisation and customers and they can work with confidence. They will place trust in their environment and the Information systems and from there it will be easy to bring out individual experiences and share them.

Organisation should create an openness culture that will allow each employee to share their views, fears and be able to address the factors that impacts them not to share information with their peers.

5.2 Knowledge Sharing

Employees' not willing to share information, knowledge and expertise with their peer is the second gaps that were identified in the chapter. Knowledge sharing is an activity through which knowledge (i.e. information, skills, or expertise) is exchanged among people, friends, or members of a family, a community or an organisation.

One of the challenges organisation is facing is that of getting people to share their knowledge. People have pride in not having to seek advice from others and in wanting to discover new ways for themselves. Not realising how useful particular knowledge is to others. An individual may have knowledge used in one situation but be unaware that other people at other times and places might face similar situations. Additionally, knowledge derived for one need may be helpful in totally different contexts; or it may be a trigger for innovation - many innovative developments come from making knowledge connections across different disciplines and organisational boundaries.

Knowledge sharing activities are generally supported by knowledge management systems. However, technology constitutes only one of the many factors that affect the sharing of knowledge in organisations, such as organisational culture, trust, and incentives (Nemutanzhela & Iyamu, 2011). The sharing of knowledge constitutes a major challenge in the field of knowledge management because some employees tend to resist sharing their knowledge with the rest of the organisation.

Sharing knowledge also needs to be rewarded. Knowledgeable people do like to share their expertise. It's just something about their work environment that discourages this natural inclination. Understanding these barriers and individual motivations is the first step towards implementing changes in the work setting. Human beings are motivated by more than just money. Organisation need to ensure that appropriate rewards are in place to increase on the number of employees to share knowledge.

For the organisation to have an effective knowledge sharing organisation have to first start to practice it at lower level. The higher up the organisation the more effective they will be in changing the culture but even if they are low down the hierarchy, they will have an influence. Second, they should put in place the knowledge sharing technology and train and educate people in its effective use. The two together – people with the appropriate knowledge sharing mind-set and the appropriate knowledge sharing technology to support them will rapidly bring about a knowledge sharing culture that helps organisation better meet their business objectives.

Analysis confirms that employees are not educate and also not aware of the information systems products and services that need to be innovated. In both cases CI is deployed without any monitoring system. Therefore activities become difficult to measure and manage. Employees are not committed to achieving organisational objectives, because they retain their knowledge. An evaluation system will assist managers to rate the contribution of individuals to how knowledge is shared; how knowledge is retained; how knowledge is managed and the type of resources needed to support knowledge sharing.

This chapter has sought to contribute further to the knowledge concerning Competitive intelligence products and services and Information Systems by applying the established factors found from this analysis a framework was developed which will shed light on how Competitive Intelligence of Information Systems innovation is deployed. However, in Furtherance to the realisation of set factors, the following are recommendations for further research:

1. Management must consistently motivate its strategic team so that it will analyse the customer's needs, seek to satisfy them, and try to adapt the products and services to these needs, react to competitors, actions and responses.
2. Management should work in collaboration with other workers in the organisation and share knowledge and information about products and services, customers and competitors with these workers.
3. Research efforts in the future should consider themes and issues that have emerged from this paper.
4. A research of the relationship that exists between market leadership and Competitive Intelligence products and services.
5. A research on how organisation can improve Information Systems Innovation in order to deploy a successful CI Products and Services.
6. A chapter of the direct impact of Competitive Intelligence and strategic management.

In line with this, attention could be devoted to examine the affiliation of these constructs in other environments other than Financial and Information and Communication technology.

6. BENEFIT FROM THE ANALYSIS

The benefit in this chapter is in twofold. It contributes to the body of knowledge and to the Organisation, particularly the cases used in this chapter: The benefits are presented as follows:

i. Body of Knowledge

The chapter contributes to the body of knowledge from both theoretical and practical perspectives.

This chapter significantly refines the body of knowledge concerning the impact of competitive intelligence on Information Systems products and services innovation in organisation context. This chapter will contribute to the body of existing literature on competitive intelligence, Information Systems and Innovation.

This chapter contributes to the organisation particularly, Financial and Information and communication technology organisations. It also contributes to the Society of Competitive Intelligence practices (SCIP) in South Africa for further recommended research topics.

ii. Organisation

The framework from this chapter can be used to understand and develop an Information Systems Innovation process (Nemutanzhela & Iyamu, 2011). The frameworks explains how Information Systems Innovation can be implemented through different system development life cycle stages, who are involved on the deployment, what are the inputs and outputs as the results of the whole deployment. It also explains how Information Systems Innovation can manifest in Competitive Intelligence products and services.

The chapter can assist leaders and managers in organisations to better understanding the factors which are involved in deploying Competitive Intelligence in an organisation.

7. CONCLUSION

This chapter was holistically and comprehensively carried out within the scope as demarcated. The findings and the analysis of the chapter indicate that further research relating to Competitive Intelligence can be conducted. Some of the suggestions are:

1. **Organisational Culture:** It would be in the interest of academic organisations to investigate and gain a better understanding of how organisational culture impacts on Competitive Intelligence products and services in organisations.
2. **Underpinning Theories:** It would be a significant contribution to apply different theories such as Organisational information processing theory (OIPT) and Technology-Organisation-Environment Framework (TOT framework) in a similar chapter. Organisation need to be knowledgeable about the Competitive Intelligence products and services they deploy so that they can make better decisions to innovate. Organisational information processing theory is applied to Organisations that need quality information to cope with environmental uncertainty and improve their decision making. (Premkumar, Ramamurthy, & Saunders, 2005). Another theory that can also be applied in a similar chapter is TOT framework because the chapter establishes organisational culture as being one of the main concerns when deploying CI products and services. TOT framework emphasises the process by which an organisation adopts and implements technological innovations which are influenced by the technological context, the organisational context, and the environmental context (Tornatzky & Fleischer, 1990).The environmental context includes the size and structure of the industry, the organisation's competitors, the macroeconomic context, and the regulatory environment (Tornatzky & Fleischer, 1990). Both these theories have been applied in the Information Systems fields but not in organisational culture and Competitive Intelligence fields.

Knowledge sharing is critical to Information System Innovation in the organisation that deploys it, making it very useful for competitive advantage. The chapter helps managers to gain better understanding of how knowledge sharing influences products and services in the organisations.

Sometimes the effect of Competitive Intelligence on the innovative process is not obvious, but it does exist because the companies compete, and are challenged with customers' needs. Therefore it is strategically important to equip as many as possible employees with enough knowledge to carry out the customers' demands. Regardless of how knowledge is acquired, Competitive Intelligence deployment relies on the knowledge individuals and group have about the Information Systems products and services.

REFERENCES

Ashton, W. B., & Klavans, R. A. (1997). *Keeping abreast of science and technology: technical intelligence for business*. United States: Battelle Press.

Cooper, D., & Schindler, P. (2006). *Business Research Methods*. New York: McGraw-Hill.

Fang, Z. (2005). Exploring the synergy between entrepreneurship and innovation. *International Journal of Entrepreneurial Behaviour & Research, 11*(1), 25–41. doi:10.1108/13552550510580825

Fleisher, C. S. (2003, March/April). Competitive Intelligence Education: Competencies, Sources and Trends. *Information Management Journal*, 56-62.

Gilad, B. (2000). An Ad Hoc, Entrepreneurial CI Model. *Competitive Intelligence Magazine, 3*(4), 33–39.

Hofstee, E. (2006). *Constructing a Good Dissertation: A Practical Guide to Finishing a Master's, MBA or PhD on Schedule*. South Africa: EPE Publishers.

Hoven, D., & Van, J. (2001). *Information Resource Management: Foundation for knowledge management*.

Iyamu, T., & Olummide, O. O. (2010). Components of the computing environment. *GESJ: Computer Science and Telecommunications, 3*(26), 144.

Krücken-Pereira, L., Debiasi, F., & Abreu, A. F. (2003). Technological innovation and Competitive Intelligence: an interactive process. *READ - Electronic Journal of Directors, v.7*. Retrieved from http://read.adm.ufrgs.br/read21/artigo/artigo5.pdf

Kvale, S. (1996). *Interviews: An introduction to qualitative research*. London: Sage.

Lacerda, A. C., & et al. (2001). *Strategic technology for competitiveness: Technology in inserting the variable strategic planning*. São Paulo: Nobel.

Lederer, A. L., & Gardiner, V. (1992). The process of strategic information planning. *Journal of Strategic Information Systems (1:2)*, 76-83.

Malhotra, Y. (2000). Knowledge Management & New Organization Forms: A framework for Business Model Innovation. *Information Resources Management Journal, 13*(1), 5–14. doi:10.4018/irmj.2000010101

Mariano, C., & Pavesi, S. (2010). *How management can foster continuous product Innovation*. Integrated Manufacturing Systems. Retrieved from http://www.emerald-library.com

Martins, E., & Terblanche, F. (2003). Building organizational culture that stimulates creativity and innovation. *European Journal of Innovation Management, 6*(1), 64–75. doi:10.1108/14601060310456337

Martre, H. L., & Jean-Louis, C. P. (1994). *Intelligence and strategy business publication in the French Documentation*.

McCord, S. (2002). *Competitive Intelligence in the academic environment*. Washington State University.

Nemutanzhela, P., & Iyamu, T. (2011). A Framework for Enhancing the Information Systems Innovation: Using Competitive Intelligence. [EJISE]. *The Electronic Journal Information Systems Evaluation, 14*(2), 242–253.

Oslo Manual - Proposed guidelines for collecting and interpreting data on technological innovation [Translation of the Financier of Studies and Projects]. (2008). Retrieved from http://www.oecd.org/science/inno/2367580.pdf

Premkumar, G., Ramamurthy, K., & Saunders, C. S. (2005). Information processing view of organisations: An exploratory examination of fit in the context of interorganisational relationships. *Journal of Management Information Systems*, 257–294.

Rogers, E. M. (1995). *Diffusion of Innovations* (4th ed.). New York: Free Press.

Rogers, E. M. (2003). *Diffusion of Innovations* (5th ed.). New York: Free Press.

Stephen, H. (2006). *Management Information Systems for the Information Age* (3rd ed.). McGraw-Hill Ryerson.

Tornatzky, L. G., & Fleischer, M. (1990). *The Processes of Technological Innovation*. Lexington, Massachusetts: Lexington Books.

Welman, J. C., & Kruger, S. J. (2001). *Research Methodology: for the Business and Administrative Sciences* (2nd ed.). South Africa: Oxford University Press.

William, J., & Baumol. (2010). *The Free-Market Innovation Machine: Analyzing the Growth Miracle of Capitalism*.

Yin, R. K. (2009). Case Chapter Research: Design and Methods (4th ed.). SAGE Publications Inc.

KEY TERMS AND DEFINITIONS

Competitive Intelligence (CI): Is the action of defining, gathering, analysing, and distributing intelligence about products, customers, competitors, and any aspect of the environment needed to support executives and managers making strategic decisions for an organization.

Diffusion of Innovation (DoI): Is a theory that seeks to explain how, why, and at what rate new ideas and technology spread through cultures.

Information Systems (IS): Is a system composed of people and computers that processes or interprets information. The term is also sometimes used in more restricted senses to refer to only the software used to run a computerized database or to refer to only a computer system.

Innovation: Is a new idea, more effective device or process. Innovation can be viewed as the application of better solutions that meet new requirements, in articulated needs, or existing market.

Product: A product is the item offered for sale. A product can be a service or an item. It can be physical or in virtual or cyber form.

Services: The action of helping or doing work for someone.

Technology: Machinery and devices developed from scientific knowledge.

Chapter 15
Competitive Intelligence for Business Enhancement:
Deployment Framework

Relebohile Moloi
Johannesburg, South Africa

ABSTRACT

Many organisations employ Competitive Intelligence (CI) to enable and support their goals and objectives, periodically. The CI is deployed by many organisations mainly to collect and analyse relevant data for decision making and competitive advantage. CI products are deployed in various ways in different contexts. CI products differ in many ways such as in terms of compatibility and the functionalities that they offer. The functions of a CI product are considered to be of significant to the organisation that deploys it. Otherwise, it would be short of enabling and supporting its objectives. The compatibility is critical mainly because each environment is unique. Many organisations have acquired CI products which they could not use because of compatibility challenges they encountered during implementation. This is one of the reasons why the criteria for selection and deployment of CI products are very important in many organisations as explored and presented in this chapter.

1. INTRODUCTION

Competitive Intelligence (CI) is an information system which many organisations make use of to determine their competitiveness. CI is a system that performs various functions such as management and dissemination of information; and collection and analysing of data. Van Brakel (2005:1) defines Competitive Intelligence as, "a business discipline that is used by companies and countries alike as a means to improve competitiveness by making better use of information".

CI as a system, is often used by some organisations as a decision making tool in their businesses. Guimaraes (2000) argues that an organisation can improve its competitive edge and its overall performance by applying an effective CI programme. According to Brouard (2006) organisations should scan the environment in which they operate to ensure that they are ahead of the changes that are happening in their industry, and they are aware of what their competitors are doing in order for them to react quickly if and when necessary.

Primarily, organisations make use of CI products to improve their competitiveness. According to Dou et al. (2005: 209) some CI products make use of patents in their design and development. Xu et al. (2011) argue that it is imperative for organisations to ensure that they identify possible risk that they may be faced with pertaining to products as well as any plans that their competitors may have. Viviers and Muller (2004) posit that organisations use CI to enhance their competitiveness and that it is regarded as a legitimate business activity.

Due to factors such as rapid change in business requirements, as well as increasing competition amongst organisations, there is more demand for CI products. According to McGonagle and Vella (2004), CI is becoming more and more vital to firm's survival in today's dynamic markets. Myburgh (2004) stated that the objectives of CI are to manage and reduce risk, make knowledge profitable, avoid information overload, ensure privacy and security of information, and use corporate information strategically.

Information Systems such as CI is intended to bridge the gap between business initiatives. It is implemented mainly to assist organisations in improving their effectiveness and efficiency. There are a number of CI products that are currently deployed by organisations. Some of them are transaction processing systems, decision support systems, knowledge management systems and database management systems. In order for an organisation to gain its own competitive advantage using information systems such as CI, it has to ensure that its focus is on its structural capabilities (Song and Li-Hua, 2005).

The primary goal of this article is to provide a framework which could guide the deployment of CI products in organisations. This was done by critically analysing current studies, imploring experiential learning of many years in different organisations. Also, the framework is intended to assist employees in organisations to understand the influencing factors in the deployment of CI products.

2. COMPETITIVE INTELLIGENCE

Competitive intelligence (CI) has become a very important source of information for business planning and other activities and is considered to be a set of legal and ethical methods used to gather information about competitors' activities from public and private sources (Jaworski et al., 2002). If organisations understand CI factors and the factors that enhance their effectiveness, they will be more concerned with the utility of their competitive intelligence output, according to Jaworski et al. (2002).

CI is both a product and a process (Myburgh, 2004). The product is information on the competitors in the market and it is used as the basis for specific action. The process is the systematic acquisition, analysis and evaluation of information for competitive advantage over known and potential competitors.

However, gaining access to this information is not enough. It is important to gain the information quickly before the competitor gets hold of it (Johns and Van Doren, 2009). It is therefore important to understand the competition in order for an organisation to be able to adapt to changing market and environmental trends. On one hand, it is argued that CI has the capability to set organisations apart from one another, and that it can also be used to inform an organisation about emerging trends within the business. On the other hand, it can be used to identify threats that potential competition may bring about.

The deployment framework examines four main components: explored business requirements; established the functionalities; interpreted the service offering; took cognisance of the various products listed by Dugal (1998); and understand the human factor:

2.1 Business Requirements

Irrespective of the rationale for the deployment of CI in organisations, requirements is critical. The requirements set the direction and helps determine value, as well return on investment. According to Dugal (1998:24) requirements are important in order for organisations to ensure that the CI function fulfills their specific needs, whether for internal customers or external clientele. The requirements for selecting and implementing CI products are different from both business and technical perspectives. Further, the requirements differ from one organisation to the other.

For many organisations, CI is often intended to be a differentiating factor within the market, as it is able to stand in a better position within the market place. According to De Pelsmacker *et al.* (2005:607) 'CI as a strategic business tool has long been proposed in an effort to increase a company's competitiveness". Cohesive marketing enables an organisation to provide information which enables it to build a consistent and cohesive marketing message that is based on the changing market. According to Buchda (2007), organisations have experienced changes in their market environments and in the industries that they operate in.

CI is a vital component of an organisation's strategic planning and management process and it is therefore important for it to pull together the data and information from a strategic view and to allow an organisation to predict what is going to happen in its competitive environment (Bose, 2008). The people that are responsible for CI within an organisation are the ones that identify the key information that is passed onto the key decision makers in the organisation. The use of CI products can be the differentiating aspect in the industry. Some benefits of using Competitive intelligence include differentiation, cohesive marketing communication plans, pre-selling as an idea to the target audience and having the ability to build credibility with customers.

2.2 Competitive Intelligence Functions

According to Bernhardt (1993), CI "is a business tool that can make a significant contribution to the strategic management process in modern business organisations, driving business performance and change by increasing knowledge, internal relationships and the quality of strategic plans".

Competitive intelligence is growing in organisations and decision makers are beginning to recognise its role and importance. According to Ignatov (2004:27), "the role of CI could be specified as a method of making information the instrument for stable business development". However, very few publications indicate *how* this function should be installed and positioned in an organisation in order to benefit decision-making and ultimately support the innovation process (Havenga and Botha, 2003).

CI gives some direction to the research and development. Organisations may identify potential opportunities for investing in new technology and help incorporate new technologies into their own products. By so doing, they identify potential technology-based threats to market, share and identify possible partners for collaborative research and development (Vedder and Guynes, 2002). According to Vedder and Guynes (2002: 50), "CI can also play a role in the development and operation of Strategic Information Systems (SIS)".

Business managers as well as executives make the intelligence gathering process easier if they are specific about their intelligence needs such as the strategic alliances and acquisitions, technology planning and decisions in relation to certain competitors (Herring, 1999).

The functionalities of CIs are not necessarily the services that they offer. This could be attributed to human actions and interaction with the organisational structure, as well as with the technology.

2.3 Competitive Intelligence Services

CI products are deployed to offer varieties of services in organisation. Primarily, they are intended to improved quality of information, improved threat and opportunity identification, and improved awareness. According to Johns and Van Doren (2009:552), "there seems to be greater recent need for CI because organisations are constantly changing their services and marketing messages to stay successful". CI is rapidly becoming one of the most significant components information systems services to business (Ignatov, 2004).

As has been established, CI products are deployed for different reasons, primarily for an organisation to have good competitive service and solutions it has to benchmark the services that it offers to its customers. This is intended for organisations to ensure that they stay ahead of their competition and to understand what their competitors are doing and what services they are offering in the market. According to Bose (2008:511), "CI has attracted plenty of attention lately because of the explosion of information now publicly available through blogs, wiki's text messages, e-mail and other electronic communications, which form the basis for building meaningful CI".

An organisation's competitive strategy is also important in order for an organisation to be able to determine the direction in which it wishes to take its business relative to its competition. According to Johns and Van Doren (2009:563) "knowing the competition better prepares the sales team, customer service reps, the product development team, operations and marketing teams to incorporate the information in their jobs so that they may make strategic decisions for the firm".

2.4 Competitive Intelligence Products

CI products are used for different reasons within organisations. Organisations realise the importance of Competitive Intelligence and in order for them to remain competitive they have to improve their strategic decisions. By so doing, they are able to perform better than their competitors (Bose, 2008).

It is important for clients to understand what kind of intelligence they require as different intelligence modes can be offered. Dugal (1998:17) also observes that "the products in the product line are significantly unique in terms of their generation and application". According to Herring (1999:5) the critical success factor in any intelligence operation is meeting the user's real needs. The different products, according to Dugal (1998) are as follows:

a. Current intelligence: a perishable product designed to provide users with first exposure to new developments. It is often used in decision-making and provides legitimacy to the CI function.
b. Basic intelligence: is designed to help managers make informed decisions and to substantiate recommendations to top management. Current and potential competitors are monitored and industry trends are also monitored.

c. Technical intelligence: is designed for engineers and scientists as they have special technical skills and backgrounds.
d. Early warning intelligence: provides an inkling of emerging opportunities or threats in advance.
e. Estimated intelligence: offers likely scenarios based on the qualitative views of the analysts.
f. Work group intelligence: the CI analyst gets a comprehensive picture of the groups requirements and can provide the right intelligence.
g. Targeted intelligence: deals with narrow specific requirements of internal clients.
h. Crisis intelligence: is generated and delivered by CI support teams formed specifically to alleviate or negate the effects of crisis.
i. Foreign intelligence: sieved through "culture screens "which might otherwise be misinterpreted.
j. Counterintelligence: is a non-product. It is effective when the organisation remains secure and its secrets well kept.

Based on the availability of numerous CI products, and the different needs and rationales, it is important to have a framework through which any of the products could be deployed in organisations. Also, human involvement in the makes deployment even more complex. Without a framework, the deployment of CI will continue to be challenging to organisations.

2.5 Human Influence on Competitive Intelligence

The roles of individuals and groups are significant and critical to the deployment of any CI products in organisations. Human actions determine and influences how CI products are deployed and used, overtime. According to Callow et al (2002), in some organisations the adoption of Competitive Intelligence is dependent on senior management's commitment and alignment to the organisations strategy as they are the ones that provide direction and guidance to the organisations employees. Bradford and Powell (2000:181) argued that management should at all times take into consideration resource-based strategy and core competence thinking cautiously as they require correct assumptions to be made about the environment as well as competitor capabilities.

Creating an environment that supports two-way communication between intelligence users and CI professionals is vital. In addition, a supportive environment should promote a two-way communication system that both identifies and defines the organisation's intelligence needs (Herring, 1999).

Organisations can use this information to improve their businesses and the service they offer to their customers. According to Hesford (2008:17), "CI involves the systematic collection and analysis of information about competitors". CI helps strategists to understand the forces (humans included) that influence the business environment (McGonagle and Vella, 2002).

It is important to ensure that the correct business requirements are gathered. According to Herring (1999:5), it requires a cooperative effort by both management (users) and CI professionals to create the environment necessary to support the two-way communications required to identify and define the organisation's real intelligence needs. Once senior management understand their role in the creation of intelligence, the design process can then begin.

An organisation's intelligence needs results in the production of intelligence that management feels compelled to act upon. This is one of the most elusive goals of CI products. Organisations make use of CI products for various reasons. According to Herring (1999:4) the use of a systematized or formal

Figure 3. Competitive intelligence deployment framework

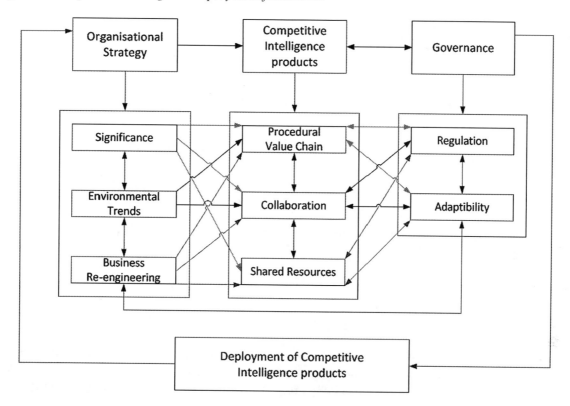

"management-needs identification process" is a proven way to accomplish that task. According to Jaworski et al. (2002:280) "understanding and improving the CI generation process also has considerable practical significance".

3. COMPETITIVE INTELLIGENCE DEPLOYMENT FRAMEWORK FOR BUSINESS ENHANCEMENT

Based on the critical review above, and experiential involvement, a set of Strategic Components and Influencing Factors were exhumed. As shown in Figure 3, both Strategic Components and Influencing Factors formed, and were mapped in the development of the CI Deployment Framework (CDDF).

The Strategic Components are not necessarily influential vice versa in the deployment of CI products in organisations. However, both Strategic Components and Influencing Factors are significant and critical if the deployment of CI is to have return on investment, and enhance the business of the organisation that deploys it.

3.1. Strategic Components

As depicted in Figure 1, the strategic components in the deployment of CI products include 5 components Collaboration, Procedural Value-Chains, Environmental Trends, Regulation, and Adaptability.

Figure 1. Strategic components in competitive intelligence deployment

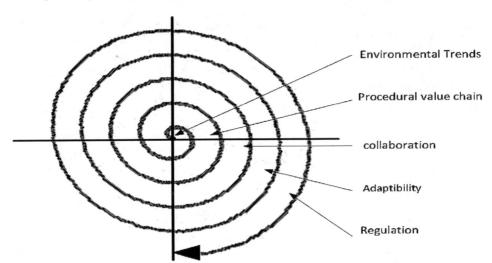

3.1.1 Collaboration

It is required to have an on-going collaboration among organisational units, particularly business and information technology (IT). The collaboration changes as the functions of the business and the stakeholders that are involved in the deployment of CI products change. The procedural value chain changes constantly as the business changes and environmental trends change. It is important for the organisation to continuously adapt as the environment changes and evolves. The environmental trends analysis is on-going as markets change and factors that influence them change all the time as environments change. Regulation is an on-going process in the deployment of CI products in the organisations.

Lack of collaboration between the two (business and IT) units could have a negative impact on the deployment of CI products. For example, if either of the two units does not participate in the development of the business as well as its technological requirements, the deployment of CI products in the organisation could be terminated. Also, lack of collaboration could lead to an imposition of technology on the business. IT might also feel that the business unit decided on a tool on their own without them knowing whether the tool would fit in the organisation's architecture or whether there was still capacity to support and maintain the tool.

Collaboration leads to shared accountability and responsibility between the business unit and IT. This also helps to reduce any potential issues that could be experienced during the deployment of the CI products. Collaboration helps each of the business units to understand what the requirements of the other unit are, as well as the reasoning behind their decisions. Thus, both units depend on the other for enablement and support of the process and activities for the organisation's competitive advantage.

3.1.2 Procedural Value-Chain

The communication and technology procedures which are often employed to enable and support processes and activities are aimed at adding value to the organisation. This entails applying different methods and techniques such as technology in providing valuable communication to stakeholders and interested parties. For example, information on the processes followed for the deployment of CI products is readily available on the organisations intranet for easy accessibility. These processes outline what needs to be done by the business units before CI products can be deployed in the organisation.

The channels and structures that are involved in the deployment of CI products ensures that processes and procedures are followed. This assisted the business units in ensuring that they did things correctly so that they did not encounter problems when audits were done. This also encouraged them to follow proper processes and not take short cuts lest they had to re-do some of their work. The organisational structure guided the process as well as the channels that could be followed for the deployment of CI products.

3.1.3 Environmental Trends

The environmental trends are a necessitated vital influence in the deployment of CI products in organisations. The trends naturally manifests from human relationships, costs, maturity of products, and availability of local skill-sets.

Relationships are vital in the deployment of CI products in the organisation. It is vital for harmony and stability among stakeholders. The relationship among the stakeholders influences the selection of and deployment of technology in organisations. The relationships also influence the cost of the technology. The worldwide trends as well as organisational trends play a role in the relationships that the organisation built.

The competition in the environment influences the cost of IT systems such as the CI products, as well skill-set. The organisation had to take the cost of the technology and well as the skill - set into account. This is to ensure that the costs of services are not exorbitant as the skills required to assist with the deployment of the CI products would be readily available.

The organisation also considered the cost of getting new technology that was not used in the organisation. This would have been costly for them as the users of the CI products would not have been familiar with the technology and in the end this would have been far too costly for them as they would have to get support for the technology, probably from the international arena.

3.2. Influencing Factors

The influencing Factors, which are illustrated in Figure 2, constitute of Communication, Collaboration, Processes and Business (Case) Development. The factors are discussed as follows:

3.2.1 Shared Resources

In many organisations, departments and units work in silos, and a result, resources are not shared. Sharing of resources assists organisations to work a lot more efficiently and effectively. For example, it enables them to be able to share ideas and also to assist with clarification of some information that might not be clear.

Also, sharing of resources is of beneficial for the business and IT departments to come together before procurement of CI products. With shared resources, roles and responsibilities of the department that are involved in the deployment of CI products are clearly defined. It also assist in the identification of the resources that would play a role in the deployment of CI products, be it technical or non-technical resources.

Figure 2. Factors influencing competitive intelligence deployment

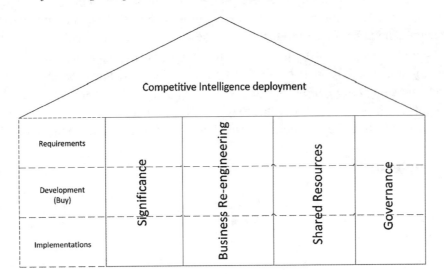

3.2.2 Governance

It is important in any organisation for all its employees to understand the rules of engagement which governs the organisation. The organisation should have clearly defined standards that are communicated to the employees. Also, there should be consistency in the application of the standards within the organisation and between the divisions and departments. Over and above all, there should be a structure in place that informs the manner in which things should be done in the organisation, the processes and procedures that should be followed for the deployment of CI products.

By not adhering to the processes and procedures that govern the organisation, each department will follow their own process for the acquisition of CI products and this could prove to be costly for the organisation. The CI products that are introduced in the environment could potentially not fit into the architecture of the organisation and they could also struggle finding resources with the appropriate skills.

3.2.3 Significance

It is important to understand why the organisation decided to deploy CI products in the organisation. Understanding the business requirements is critical for the justification of the business initiative. The employees of the organisation should understand the business requirements in order for them to see the value and the importance of deploying CI products in the organisation.

If it is not clear why the business is embarking on the deployment of CI products, the employees will not see their value and will as a result not buy into the idea. The significance of the requirements needs to be clear to all the people that will be involved directly or indirectly with the deployment of the CI products in the organisation. This will ensure that their implementation is carried out more effectively.

3.2.4 Business Re-Engineering

Having clearly defined goals and objectives is very important in any organisation. This will assist the organisation with the analysis and design of workflows as well as the processes that they need to follow in the organisation. This will also help the employees understand and clearly identify the tasks that they need to perform in order for them to realise the business goals and objectives. It is important that it is clear what the business and strategic goals of the business are for the deployment of CI products.

If the employees as well as the vendors do not understand what the business goals are they will not be able to deliver solutions that will enable the organisation to achieve its goals. The requirements that will drive the business re-engineering have to be defined as these will influence the development of the business re-engineering. The business re-engineering will shape the implementation.

3.3. Deployment Framework

The factors in the two groups above are mapped together develop a Framework, Figure 3. The Framework is aimed at providing an in-depth understanding of the socio-technical factors which influences and guides the deployment of CI products in organisations. The Framework is further discussed below.

The organisational strategy consists of the goals and objectives of the organisation. The strategy dictates and drives the selection and deployment of CI products in the organisations. As depicted in Figure 3 above, three factors were identified as critical in the organisational strategy. The factors include signification (significance) that is the importance of processes and activities to the organisational strategy; environmental trends, which take into consideration factors which are external to the organisation, but relevant for competitive advantage; and business re-engineering, which evolves over time as the organisation strives to meet its goals and objectives.

The selection of CI products is based on the organisation's strategy. CI products are intended to facilitate and support strategic objectives such as the procedural value chain; collaboration among the processes and activities; and sharing of resources for competitive advantage. To ensure that the selection and deployment of CI products meet the organisational strategy, governance is formulated.

The Governance constitutes standards, principles and policies, which are made of processes. These standards, principles and policies are used to guide the deployment of CI products in the organisations. The aim is to ensure consistency, flexibility and adaptability of CI products within the organisation. The processes as defined by the governance need to be understood, visible and adhered to by employees to ensure that the deployment of CI products in the organisation achieves the strategic objectives.

The significance of the CI products and its business re-engineering is driven by the organisational strategy. The environmental trends from the perspective of CI products are highly considered in the organisational strategy. The organisational strategy is very significant and this influences many factors including the procedural value chain pursuit at the time. The significance of the goals and objectives defines the collaboration which occurs amongst the stakeholders, (internal and external stakeholders), including the processes which are involved in the selection and deployment of CI in the organisation. The collaboration also influences how resources (technical and non-technical) are shared within the organisation.

The business re-engineering also influences the manner in which the organisation responds and reacts to environmental trends. The internal as well as external environmental trends impact on the procedural value chain and the processes which guide the selection and deployment of CI products in the organisations. In addition, the collaboration which occurs has an impact on how resources are shared, as well as how business re-engineering is carried in the organisations.

Governance is critical when defining the adaptability of the environment and the CI products that are deployed. An adaptable environment influences how resources are shared. Sharing of resources makes collaboration effective and efficient.

The regulations of governance define and shape the environment in terms of adaptability and flexibility. This ensures the correct fit of the selection and deployment of CI products in the organisation.

The management and process orientation of the components as depicted in Framework Figure 3 above assists the organisation in achieving its goals and objectives in the pursuit of competitive advantage. The Framework is aimed at understanding the socio-technical factors; thereby enhance the selection and deployment of CI products in the organisations.

4. CONCLUSION

The article is of significant contribution in that it is important for organisations to have a good understanding, and assess the service offering, functionalities, suitability and requirements of CI products which they intend to deploy.

Another contribution of the article is the practicality it brings on the socio-technical nature of the deployment of CI products. It makes a huge contribution as it helps the business and IT managers to understand the influencing factors. How these influencing factors manifested themselves into the pitfalls which impacted and sometimes derailed the selection and deployment of CI products is of great importance. These pitfalls influence the deployment of CI products and it is important for organisations to be aware of them and to address them in their organisations.

The article exhumes factors which are critical but are never understood, or are often taken for granted during the selection and deployment of CI products by some of the stakeholders. For example, the managers would now understand the importance of roles, responsibilities and governance in the selection and deployment of CI products. There is a high likelihood that this would help the organisation improve its competitive advantage.

REFERENCES

Bernhardt, D. (1993). *Perfectly Legal Competitor Intelligence. How to Get It, Use It, and Profit It from It*. London: Pitman Publishing.

Bose, R. (2008). Competitive Intelligence process and tools for Intelligence Analysis. *Industrial Management & Data Systems, 108*(4), 510–528. doi:10.1108/02635570810868362

Brouard, F. (2006). Development of an expert system on environmental scanning practices in SME: Tools as a research program. *Journal of Competitive Intelligence and Management, 3*(4), 13–29.

Buchda. (2007). Rulers for business intelligence and competitive intelligence: an overview and evaluations of measurement approaches. *Journal of Competitive Intelligence and Management,* 4(2) 18-30.

De Pelsmacker, P., Muller, M., Viviers, W., Saayman, A., Cuyvers, L., & Jegers, M. (2005). Competitive intelligence practices of South African and Belgian exporters. *Marketing Intelligence & Planning,* 23(6), 606–620. doi:10.1108/02634500510624156

Dou, H., Leveille, V., Manullang, S., & Dou, J. M. Jr. (2005). Patent analysis for competitive technical intelligence and innovative thinking. *Data Science Journal,* 4(3), 26–38.

Dugal, M. (1998). CI product line: A tool for enhancing user acceptance of CI. *Competitive Intelligence Review,* 9(2), 17–25. doi:10.1002/(SICI)1520-6386(199804/06)9:2<17::AID-CIR5>3.0.CO;2-0

Guimaraes, T. (2000). The impact of competitive intelligence and IS support in changing small business organisations. *Logistics Information Management,* 13(3), 117–125. doi:10.1108/09576050010326510

Havenga, J. & Botha, D. (2004) *Developing Competitive Intelligence in the knowledge-based Organisation,* 7(1), 8-17.

Herring, J. P. (1999). Key intelligence topics: A process to identify and define intelligence need. *Competitive Intelligence Review,* 10(2), 4–14. doi:10.1002/(SICI)1520-6386(199932)10:2<4::AID-CIR3>3.0.CO;2-C

Hesford, J. W. (2008). An empirical investigation of accounting information use in competitive intelligence. *Journal of Competitive Intelligence and Management,* 4(3), 17–49.

Ignatov, A. A. (2004). Competitive Intelligence in Russia. *Journal of Competitive Intelligence and Management,* 2(2), 26–44.

Jaworski, B. J., Macinnis, D. J., & Kohli, A. K. (2004). Generating Competitive Intelligence in Organizations. *Journal of Market-Focused Management,* 1(5), 279–307.

Johns, P., & Van Doren, D. C. (2010). Competitive Intelligence in service marketing: A new approach with practical application. *Marketing & Planning,* 28(5), 551–570. doi:10.1108/02634501011066492

Song, Z., & Li-Hua, H. (2005). *Comparative Study of Obtaining Competitive Advantage from Information.* IEEE.

Van Brakel, P. (2005). Innovation and Competitiveness in South Africa: the case for competitive intelligence as an instrument to make better use of information. *South African Journal of Information management,* 7(1), 16-28.

Vedder, R. G., & Guynes, C. S. (2002). CEO and CIO Perspectives on Competitive Intelligence. *Communications of the ACM,* 42(8), 108–116. doi:10.1145/310930.310982

Viviers, W., & Muller, M. (2004). The Evolution of Competitive Intelligence in South Africa: Early 1980s – 2003. *Journal of Competitive Intelligence and Management,* 2(2), 53–67.

Xu, K., Liao, S. S., Li, J., & Song, Y. (2011). Mining comparative opinions from customer reviews for competitive intelligence. *Decision Support Systems,* 1(50), 743–754. doi:10.1016/j.dss.2010.08.021

KEY TERMS AND DEFINITIONS

Competitive Intelligence (CI): Is the approach used for defining, gathering, analysing data, including and distributing intelligence about products, customers and competitors.

Framework: A diagrammatical design developed to guide direction of intent, in enabling goals and objectives.

Information Systems (IS): Is a computer approach for processing data by human, aimed at achieving business goals and objectives.

Innovation: Is a new idea, more effective device or process. Innovation can be viewed as the application of better solutions that meet new requirements, in articulated needs, or existing market.

Product: A product is the item offered for specific organisational purposes, to enable goals and objectives.

Services: The action of helping or doing work by different units of an organisation.

Technology: Machinery and devices developed to scientifically enable and support knowledge and data manipulation.

Compilation of References

Aalders, R. (2001). *The IT outsourcing guide*. West Sussex: John Wiley & Sons Ltd.

Adelakun, O. (2008). The Maturation of Offshore IT Outsourcing Location Readiness and Attractiveness. *Proceedings of the European and Mediterranean Conference on Information Systems*. Dubai.

Agarwal, R. (1998). Small firm survival and technological activity. *Small Business Economics*, *11*(3), 215–224. doi:10.1023/A:1007955428797

Aier, S., & Weiss, S. (2002). An institutional Framework for the Analyzing Organisational responses to the Establishment of Architectural Transformation. *In the Proceedings of the European Conference on Information Systems*.

Ajzen, I., & Fishbein, M. (1980). *Understanding attitudes and predicting social behaviour*. Englewood Cliffs, NJ: Prentice-Hall.

Akomode, O. J., Lees, B., & Irgens, C. (1998). Constructing customised models and providing information for IT outsourcing decisions. *Logistics Information Management*, *11*(2), 114–127. doi:10.1108/09576059810209973

Ali, S., & Green, P. (2005). Determinants of Effective Information Technology Governance: A Study of Intensity. In *Proceedings of International IT Governance Conference*. Auckland, New Zealand.

Ali, S., & Green, P. (2007). IT Governance Mechanisms in Public Sector Organisations: An Australian Context. *Journal of International Management*, *15*(4), 41–63.

Al-Salti, Z. (2009). *Knowledge Transfer and Acquisition in IS Outsourcing: Towards a Conceptual Framework* [Doctoral Symposium PhD]. Brunel University.

Ang, S., & Cummings, L. L. (1997). Strategic Response to Institutional Influences on Information Systems Outsourcing. *Organization Science*, *8*(3), 235–256. doi:10.1287/orsc.8.3.235

Apte, S., Mccarthy, J., Ross, C., Bartolomey, F., & Thresher, A. (2007). Shattering the Offshore Captive Center Myth. Retrieved from http://www.forrester.com/Research/Document/Excerpt/0,7211,42059,00.html

Armstrong, M. (1994). *How to be an even better manager* (4th ed.). London: Kogan Page Ltd.

Ashton, W. B., & Klavans, R. A. (1997). *Keeping abreast of science and technology: technical intelligence for business*. United States: Battelle Press.

Association for Progressive Communications. (2004). *Monitor Políticas TIC y Derechos en Internet en América Latina y el Caribe*. Retrieved October 5 2008 from http://lac.derechos.apc.org/

Avison, D., & Fitzgerald, G. (2006). *Information Systems Development Methodologies, Techniques & Tools* (4th ed.). United Kingdom: McGraw-Hill.

Avouris, N., & Page, B. (Eds.). (1995). *Environmental Informatics – Methodology and applications of environmental information processing*. Dordrecht: Kluwer Academic Publishers.

Aydin, M. N., & Bakker, M. E. (2008). Analyzing IT maintenance outsourcing decision from a knowledge management perspective. *Information Systems Frontiers*, *10*(3), 293–305. doi:10.1007/s10796-008-9084-5

Babbie, E., & Mouton, J. (2006). *The Practice of Social Research*. Cape Town: Oxford University Press.

Bakar, F. A., Suhaimi, M. A., & Huissain, H. (2009). Conceptualisation of strategic information systems planning (SISP) success model in public sector: An absorptive capacity approach. Proceeding of *European and Mediterranean Conference on Information Systems 2009 2009 (EMCIS)*. July 13 – 14, 2009. Izmir.

Balaji, S., & Ahuja, M. K. (2005). Critical team-level success factors of offshore outsourced projects: a knowledge integration perspective. *Proceedings of the 38th Hawaii International Conference on System Sciences*, Hawaii. doi:10.1109/HICSS.2005.178

Bandyopadhyay, S., & Pathak, P. (2007). Knowledge sharing and cooperation in outsourcing projects: A game theory analysis. *Decision Support Systems*, *43*(2), 349–358. doi:10.1016/j.dss.2006.10.006

Barria, D., & Araya, E. (2008). Modernización del Estado y Gobierno Electrónico en Chile 1990-2006. *Buen Gobierno*, 80-130.

Barros, A., Ruiz, C., Cerda, A., & Martínez, H. (2012). *polisDigital*. Santiago de Chile: Centro de Sistemas Públicos, Ingeniería Industrial, Universidad de Chile.

Basu, V., Hartono, E., Lederer, A. L., & Sethi, V. (2002). The impact of organizational commitment, senior management involvement, and team involvement on strategic information systems planning. *Information & Management*, *39*(6), 513–524. doi:10.1016/S0378-7206(01)00115-X

Bechor, T., Seev, N., Moshe, Z., & Glezer, C. (2010). A contingency model for estimating success of strategic information systems planning. *Information & Management*, *47*(1), 17–29. doi:10.1016/j.im.2009.09.004

Becker, J., Kugeler, M., & Rosemann, M. (2011). *Process management: A guide for the design of business processes* (2nd ed.). Berlin, London: Springer. doi:10.1007/978-3-642-15190-3

Beckinsale, M., Ram, M., & Theodorakopoulos, N. (2011). ICT adoption and ebusiness development: Understanding ICT adoption amongst ethnic businesses. *International Small Business Journal*, *29*(3), 193–219. doi:10.1177/0266242610369745

Belkin, M. (2009). *The assessment of information systems effectiveness in private and hospital pathology* [PhD Thesis]. RMIT University.

Benamati, J., & Rajkumar, T. M. (2002). A design of an empirical study of the applicability of the Technology Acceptance Model to outsourcing decisions. *Proceedings of the Special Interest Group on Computer Personnel Research*. Kristiansand, Norway. doi:10.1145/512360.512371

Benavides, P. (2011). *La Ventanilla Única de Comercio Exterior: Factores claves de éxito* [Unpublished master's dissertation]. Universidad de Chile. Santiago de Chile.

Bergeron, F., Raymond, L., & Rivard, S. (2004). Ideal Patterns of Strategic Alignment and Business Performance. *Information & Management*, *41*(5), 1003–1020. doi:10.1016/j.im.2003.10.004

Bernhardt, D. (1993). *Perfectly Legal Competitor Intelligence. How to Get It, Use It, and Profit It from It*. London: Pitman Publishing.

Compilation of References

Beyah, G., & Gallivan, M. (2001). Knowledge Management as a Framework for Understanding Public Sector Outsourcing. *Proceedings of the 34th International Conference on System Sciences*. Hawaii. doi:10.1109/HICSS.2001.927193

Beyene, A. (2002). Enhancing the Competitiveness and Productivity of Small and Medium Scale Enterprises (SMEs) in Africa: An Analysis of Differential Roles of National Governments through Improved Support Services. *Africa Development. Afrique et Developpement, 27*(3), 130–156.

Bhawan, M. D., & Marg, J. L. (2007). Telecom Regulatory Authority of India (TRAI): recommendations on infrastructure sharing. Delhi-110002.

BICEN, H. & CAVUS. (2010). The most preferred social network sites by students. *Procedia: Social and Behavioral Sciences, 2*(1), 5864–5869.

BID / Government of Chile. (2008). Chile: Evaluación del Sistema Nacional de Compras y Contrataciones Públicas. Santiago de Chile: Gobierno de Chile.

Bistričić, A. (2006). Project information system. *Tourism and Hospitality Management, 12*(2), 213–224.

Blumenberg, S., Wagner, H.-T., & Beimborn, D. (2009). Knowledge transfer processes in IT outsourcing relationships and their impact on shared knowledge and outsourcing performance. *International Journal of Information Management, 29*(5), 342–352. doi:10.1016/j.ijinfomgt.2008.11.004

Boar, H. (1998). Information Technology Strategy as Commitment. RCG Information Technology. Retrieved from http://www.rcgit.com/Default.aspx

Bolgherini, S. (2007). The Technological Trap and the Rol of Political and Cultural Variables: A Critical Analysis of E-Government Policies. *Review of Political Research, 24*(3), 259–275. doi:10.1111/j.1541-1338.2007.00280.x

Bose, R. (2008). Competitive Intelligence process and tools for Intelligence Analysis. *Industrial Management & Data Systems, 108*(4), 510–528. doi:10.1108/02635570810868362

Bowker, G., & Star, S. (1996). How things (actor-net) work: Classification, magic and the ubiquity of standards. *Philosophia, 25*(4), 195–220.

Bowler, A., Dawood, M. S., & Page, S. (2007). *Entrepreneurship and Small business Management*. Pretoria: Juta and Co. Ltd.

Bridges, L., Rempel, H. G., & Griggs, K. (2010). Making the case for a fully mobile library website from floor maps to the catalogue. *RSR. Reference Services Review, 38*(2), 309–320. doi:10.1108/00907321011045061

Brouard, F. (2006). Development of an expert system on environmental scanning practices in SME: Tools as a research program. *Journal of Competitive Intelligence and Management, 3*(4), 13–29.

Brown, I. (2008). Investigating the impact of external environment on strategic information systems planning: A qualitative inquiry. Proceedings *SAICSIT – ACM Conference*, Wilderness, 8 – 15. doi:10.1145/1456659.1456661

Brown, A. E., & Grant, G. G. (2005). Framing the Frameworks: A Review of IT Governance Research. *Communications of the Association for Information Systems, 15*, 698–712.

Brown, I., Cajee, Z., Davies, D., & Stroebel, S. (2003). Cell phone banking: Predictors of adoption in South Africa - an exploratory study. *International Journal of Information Management, 23*(1), 381–394. doi:10.1016/S0268-4012(03)00065-3

Buchda. (2007). Rulers for business intelligence and competitive intelligence: an overview and evaluations of measurement approaches. *Journal of Competitive Intelligence and Management, 4*(2) 18-30.

Buckby, S., Best, P., & Stewart, J. (2009). The Current State of Information Technology Governance Literature. In A. Cater-Steel (Ed.), *Information Technology Governance and Service Management: Frameworks and Adaptations* (pp. 1–42). UK: Information Science Reference. doi:10.4018/978-1-60566-008-0.ch001

Bunge, M. (1999). *Buscar la filosofía en las ciencias sociales*. México: Siglo XXI.

Burgess, S. (2002). Information Systems in Small Business. In S. Burgess (Ed.), *Managing Information Technology in Small Business: Challenges & Solutions* (pp. 1–17). Australia: Idea Book Publishing. doi:10.4018/978-1-930708-35-8.ch001

Burton, B., Gail, N., Newman, D., Burke, B., Allega, P & Lapkin, A. (2007). Predict 2008: Emerging trends force a clearer and deeper focus on enterprise architecture.

Butcher, D., & Clarke, M. (1999). Organizational Politics: The Missing Discipline of Management? Cranfield School of Management, Cranfield, Bedfordshire, UK. Industrial and Commercial Training, 31 (1), 9-12.

Caldeira, M. M., & Ward, J. M. (2003, June 27-29). Using Resourced-Based Theory to Interpret the Successful Adoption and use of Information Systems and Technology in the Manufacturing Small and Medium Sized Enterprises. *Proceedings of The 9th European Conference on Information Systems Bled.* Slovenia.

Calder, A. (2005). *IT Governance: Guidelines for Directors*. United Kingdom: IT Governance Publishing.

Callon, M. (1986). Some elements of the sociology of translation: Domestication of the scallops and the fisherman of St Brieuc Bay. In J. Law (Ed.), *A New Sociology of Knowledge, power, action and belief*. London: Routledge.

Callon, M. (1987). *In The Social Construction of Technological Systems New Directions in the Sociology and History of Technology*. Cambridge, Massachusetts: The MIT Press.

Callon, M., & Latour, B. (1992). *Don't throw the baby with the bath school a reply to Collins and yearly*. Chicago: The University of Chicago Press.

Callon, M., & Law, J. (1989). On the Construction of Sociotechnical Networks: Content and Context Revisited. *Knowledge and Society: Studies in the Sociology of Science Past and Present, 8*(1), 57–83.

Carmel, E., & Agarwal, R. (2001). Tactical approaches for alleviating distance in global software development. *Software, IEEE, 18*(2), 22–29. doi:10.1109/52.914734

Carmel, E., & Agarwal, R. (2002). The Maturation of Offshore Sourcing of Information Technology Work. *MIS Quarterly Executive, 1*(2), 65–77.

Carmel, E., & Tjia, P. (2005). *Offshoring Information Technology: Sourcing and Outsourcing to a Global Workforce*. New York: Cambridge University Press. doi:10.1017/CBO9780511541193

Carr, N. (2003, May). IT Doesn't Matter. *Harvard Bussiness Review*, 5-12.

Castells, M., Fernandez-Ardevo, M., Linchuan Qiu, J., & Sey, A. (2007). *Mobile Communication and Society: A Global Perspective*. Cambridge, MA: MIT Press.

Cavana, R. Y., Delahaye, B. L., & Sekaran, U. (2001). *Applied Business Research: Qualitative and Quantitative Methods*. Australia: John Wiley & Sons Ltd.

Cerpa, N., & Verner, J. M. (1998). Case Study: The Effect of Is Maturity on Information Systems Strategic Planning. *Information & Technology., 34*, 199–208.

Cha, H. S., Pingry, D. E., & Thatcher, M. E. (2008). Managing the knowledge supply chain: An organisational learning model of information technology offshore outsourcing. *Management Information Systems Quarterly, 32*(2), 281–306.

Compilation of References

Chan, Y. E., & Reich, B. H. (2007). IT Alignment: What Have We Learned? *Journal of Information Technology, 22*(4), 297–315. doi:10.1057/palgrave.jit.2000109

Chaung, C. J., & Lobberenberg, J. (2010). Challenges facing enterprise architects: a South African perspective. In the *Proceeding of the 43rd Hawaii International Conference on System Science.*

Chen, D. Q., Mocker, M., Preston, D. S., & Teubner, A. (2010). Information systems strategy: Reconceptualization, measurement, and implications. *Management Information Systems Quarterly, 34*(2), 233–259.

Chi, L., Kiku, G. J., Lederer, A. L., Pengtao, L., Newkirk, H. E., & Sethi, V. (2005). Environmental assessment in strategic information systems planning. *International Journal of Information Management, 25*(3), 253–259. doi:10.1016/j.ijinfomgt.2004.12.004

Chile Ministry of Treasury. (2005). *Informe Final Programa Proyecto Isidora.* Santiago de Chile: Ministerio de Hacienda.

Chile Presidential Comission on New Information Technologies. (1999). *Chile: hacia la sociedad de la información.* Santiago de Chile: Presidencia de la República de Chile.

Choe, J. (2003). The effect of environmental uncertainty and strategic applications of IS on a firm's performance. *Information & Management, 40*(4), 257–268. doi:10.1016/S0378-7206(02)00008-3

Christopher, D., & Tanwar, A. (2012). Knowledge Management in Outsourcing Environment: People Empowering People. *The IUP Journal of Knowledge Management, X*(2), 61–86.

Ciborra, C. U. (1996). Improvisation and information technology in organizations. *Proceedings of International Conference on Information Systems.* USA; Philadelphia.

Clarke, T. & Rollo, C. (2001). Corporate initiatives in knowledge management. *Education + Training, 43*(4/5), 206-214.

Clark, L. A., & Watson, D. (1995). Constructing validity: Basic issues in objective scale development. *Psychological Assessment, 7*(3), 309–319. doi:10.1037/1040-3590.7.3.309

Claver, E., Gonzales, R., Gasco, J., & Llopis, J. (2002). Information systems outsourcing: Reasons, reservations and success factors. *Logistics Information Management, 15*(4), 294–308. doi:10.1108/09576050210436138

Clyde, L. A. (2004). M-learning. *Teacher Librarian, 32*(1), 45–60.

Coakes, S. J. (2005). *SPSS: Analysis without anguish: Version 12.0 for Windows.* Australia: John Wiley and Sons.

Cohen, J. (2008). Contextual determinant and performance implications of information systems strategy within South African firms. *Information & Management, 45*(8), 547–555. doi:10.1016/j.im.2008.09.001

Combera, A., Fishera, P., & Wadsworth, R. (2003). Actor–network theory: A suitable framework to understand how land cover mapping projects develop? *Land Use Policy, 20*(4), 299–309. doi:10.1016/S0264-8377(03)00048-6

Cooper, D., & Schindler, P. (2006). *Business Research Methods.* New York: McGraw-Hill.

Cortés-Morales, R., & Marín-Raventós, G. (2012a). *An analytical model to measure feasibility on e-government policies. Internet Technologies & Society 2012* (pp. 69–76). Perth, Australia: IADIS Press.

Cortés-Morales, R., & Marín-Raventós, G. (2012b). *El desarrollo del gobierno digital: la perspectiva basada en actores para el caso de las compras del Estado en Costa Rica. XXXVIII Conferencia Latinoamericana en Computación e Informática 2012* (p. 91). Medellín, Colombia: CLEI.

Costa Rica General Republic Comptroller. (2012). *Informe sobre las iniciativas que impulsan el gobierno digital y una sociedad basada en la información y el conocimiento.* San José de Costa Rica: CGR.

Costa Rica Presidency of the Republic. (2006). *Gobierno Fácil.* Retrieved from http://www.gobiernofacil.go.cr/e-gob/gobiernodigital/ebooks/Decreto_Comision_de_Gobierno_Digital.pdf

Cresswell, J. W. (2009). *Research design: qualitative, quantitative and mixed methods approach* (3rd ed.). Thousand Oaks, CA: Sage Publications.

Cruz, N. M., Perez, V. M., & Cantero, C. T. (2009). The influence of employee motivation on knowledge transfer. *Journal of Knowledge Management, 13*(6), 478–490. doi:10.1108/13673270910997132

Csaszar, F., & Clemons, E. (2006). Governance of the IT Function: Valuing Agility and Quality of Training, Cooperation and Communications.*Proceedings of the 39th Hawaii International Conference on Systems Sciences.* doi:10.1109/HICSS.2006.197

Cullen, S., & Willcocks, L. (2003). *Intelligent IT outsourcing: eight building blocks to success.* Oxford: Butterworth-Heinemann.

Currie, W., & Pouloudi, A. (2000b). Evaluating the relationship between IT outsourcing and knowledge management. *Journal of Change Management, 1*(2), 149–163. doi:10.1080/714042463

Daniels, C. N. (1994). Information Technology: The Management Challenge. London; Addison-Wesley publishing Ltd

Daugherty, P. J., Myers, M. B., & Richey, R. G. (2002). Information support for reverse logistics: The influence of relationship commitment. *Journal of Business Logistics, 23*(1), 85–106. doi:10.1002/j.2158-1592.2002.tb00017.x

Davenport, T. H. (1998). Putting the Enterprise into the Enterprise System. *Harvard Business Review, 76*(4), 121–131. PMID:10181586

Davenport, T. H., & Short, J. E. (1990). The New Industrial Engineering: Information Technology and Business Process Redesign. *Sloan Management Review, 31*(4).

Davis, F. D. (1989). Perceived usefulness, perceived ease of use, and user acceptance of information technology. *Management Information Systems Quarterly, 13*(3), 319–340. doi:10.2307/249008

Davis, F. D., Bagozzi, R. P., & Warshaw, P. R. (1989). User acceptance of computer technology: A comparison of two theoretical models. *Management Science, 35*(1), 982–1003. doi:10.1287/mnsc.35.8.982

De Haes, S., & Van Grembergen, W. (2005). IT Governance Structures, Processes and Relational Mechanisms: Achieving IT/Business Alignment in a Major Belgian Financial Group.*Proceedings of the 38th Hawaii International Conference on Systems Sciences.* doi:10.1109/HICSS.2005.362

De Lone, W. L. (1988). Determinants of Success for Computer Usage in Small Business. *Management Information Systems Quarterly, 12*(1), 51–61. doi:10.2307/248803

De Moor, A., & Kleef, R. (2005). A social context model for discussion process analysis. In Hilty, L. M., Seifert, E.K., & Treibert, R. (Eds) (2005) Information systems for sustainable development. Hershey: Idea Group Publishing.

De Pelsmacker, P., Muller, M., Viviers, W., Saayman, A., Cuyvers, L., & Jegers, M. (2005). Competitive intelligence practices of South African and Belgian exporters. *Marketing Intelligence & Planning, 23*(6), 606–620. doi:10.1108/02634500510624156

Dekovic, M., Janssens, J. M., & Gerris, J. R. (1991). Factors structure and construct validity of the block child rearing practices report. *Psychological Assessment, 3*(2), 182–187. doi:10.1037/1040-3590.3.2.182

Denzin, N. K., & Lincoln, Y. S. (2005). The SAGE handbook of qualitative research (3rd ed.). London: Thousand Oaks: Sage Publications.

Compilation of References

Dervin, B. (1977). Useful theory for librarianship: Communication not information. *Drexel Library Quarterly, 13*(5), 16–32.

Devaraj, S., & Kohli, R. (2003). Performance Impact of Information Technology: Is Actual Usage the Missing Link? *Management Science, 49*(3), 273–289. doi:10.1287/mnsc.49.3.273.12736

Devellis, R. F. (2003). *Applied social research methods: scale development theory and applications* (2nd ed.). Thousand Oaks, CA: International Educational Professional Publisher.

Dibbern, J., Goles, T., Hirschheim, R., & Jayatilaka, B. (2004). Information Systems Outsourcing: A Survey and Analysis of the Literature. *The Data Base for Advances in Information Systems, 35*(4), 6–102. doi:10.1145/1035233.1035236

Dompke, M., von Geibler, J., Göhring, W., Herget, M., Hilty, L. M., Isenmann, R., et al. (2004).Memorandum Nachhaltige Informationsgesellschaft. *Stuttgart: Fraunhofer IRB Verlag.*

Donaldson, L. (2001). *The contingency theory of organisation.* Thousand Oaks, CA: Sage Publications. doi:10.4135/9781452229249

Dong, X., Liu, Q., & Yin, D. (2008). Business performance, business strategy and information systems strategy alignment: An empirical study on Chinese firms. *Tsinghua Science and Technology, 13*(3), 348–354. doi:10.1016/S1007-0214(08)70056-7

Dou, H., Leveille, V., Manullang, S., & Dou, J. M. Jr. (2005). Patent analysis for competitive technical intelligence and innovative thinking. *Data Science Journal, 4*(3), 26–38.

Drucker, P. F. (2010). *The Drucker lectures: essential lessons on management, society and economy.* McGraw-Hill.

Dugal, M. (1998). CI product line: A tool for enhancing user acceptance of CI. *Competitive Intelligence Review, 9*(2), 17–25. doi:10.1002/(SICI)1520-6386(199804/06)9:2<17::AID-CIR5>3.0.CO;2-0

Earl, M. J. (1993). Experiences in Strategic Information Systems Planning. *Management Information Systems Quarterly, 17*(1), 1–23. doi:10.2307/249507

Easty, D., & Winston, A. (2006). *Green to gold.* New Haven: Yale University Press.

ECTA (2002). Electronic and Communication Act, No. 25 of 2002.

Edersheim, E. H. (2007). *The Definitive Drucker.* New York: McGraw-Hill.

Edwards, A. R. (2005). *The sustainability revolution: portrait of a paradigm shift. Gabriola Island.* New Society Publishers.

Ee-CF. (2014). European e-Competence Framework 3.0: A common European framework for ICT professionals in all industry sectors. *European Commission.* Retrieved from http://profiletool.ecompetences.eu/

Ein-Dor, P., & Segev, E. (1982). Organisational Context and MIS Structure: Some Empirical Evidence. *Management Information Systems Quarterly, 6*(3), 1064–1077. doi:10.2307/248656

Ekeledo, I. and Bewayo, E. (2009). Challenges and Opportunities Facing African

Elliot, S. (2007). Environmentally Sustainable ICT: A critical topic for IS research? *Retrieved from*http://aisel.aisnet.org/pacis2007/114

Elloy, D. F. (2008). The relationship between self-leadership behaviors and organization variables in a self-managed work team environment. *Management Research News, 31*(11), 801–810. doi:10.1108/01409170810913015

Entrepreneurs and their Small Firms. (n. d.). *International Journal of Business Research*, 9, 3, 52-59

Epstein, M. (2008). *Making sustainability work: best practices in managing and measuring corporate social, environmental, and economic impact*. Sheffield: Greenleaf Publishing.

eSEW. (2010). *E-skills: European Week 2010 underlines e-skills' potential to help Europe's economic recovery*. Brussels. Retrieved from http://europa.eu/rapid/pressReleasesAction.do?reference=IP/10/220&format=HTML&aged=0&language=EN&guiLanguage=en

e-skills UK. (2010). Technology for growth [overview report]. *e-skills UK's 'IT and Telecoms Insights*. Retrieved from www.e-skills.com/Research-and-policy/Insights-2010/2671

eSN. (e-skills News) (2010).The e-skills Manifesto - Employers call for action on e-skills. Retrieved from www.e-skills.com/cgi-in/go.pl/newscentre/news/news.html?uid=1067

Fang, Z. (2005). Exploring the synergy between entrepreneurship and innovation. *International Journal of Entrepreneurial Behaviour & Research*, *11*(1), 25–41. doi:10.1108/13552550510580825

Farrell, D. (2005). Offshoring: Value creation through economic change. *Journal of Management Studies*, *42*(3), 675–682. doi:10.1111/j.1467-6486.2005.00513.x

Farrell, D. (2006). Smarter Offshoring. *Harvard Business Review*, *84*(6), 84–92. PMID:16770896

Fernández, O. (2002). Weber y Foucault. *Reflexiones*, *2*(81).

Fink, D., & Shoeib, A. (2003). Action: The most critical phase in outsourcing information technology. *Logistics Information Management*, *16*(5), 302–311. doi:10.1108/09576050310499309

Fitzgerald, B. (2000). Systems development methodologies: The problem of tenses. *Information Technology & People*, *13*(3), 174–185. doi:10.1108/09593840010377617

Fleisher, C. S. (2003, March/April). Competitive Intelligence Education: Competencies, Sources and Trends. *Information Management Journal*, 56-62.

Fleury, S. (2002). El desafío de la gestión de las redes de políticas. *Revista Instituciones y Desarrollo*, (12-13), 221-247.

Flick, U. (2007). *Designing qualitative research*. Sage Publications Ltd.

Foong, S. Y. (1999). Effect of end-user personal and systems attributes on computer-based information system success in Malaysian SMEs. *Journal of Small Business Management*, *37*(3), 81–87.

Fountain, J. (2001). The Virtual State: Transforming American Government? *National Civic Review*, *90*(3), 241–251. doi:10.1002/ncr.90305

Frambach, R. T., Prabhu, J., & Verhallen, T. M. M. (2003). The influence of business strategy on new product activity: The role of market orientation. *International Journal of Research in Marketing*, *20*(4), 377–397. doi:10.1016/j.ijresmar.2003.03.003

Frappaolo, C., & Capshaw, S. (1999). *Knowledge management software: capturing the essence of know-how and innovation*. Information Management Journal.

Gao, P., & Lyytinen, K. J. (2003). *China telecommunications transformation in globalization context: a structuration perspective*. Paper presented in the IFIP/TC8.2 and 9.4 Working Conference on IS Perspectives and Challenges in the Context of Globalization. Athens, Greece. doi:10.1007/978-0-387-35695-2_14

Gartner. (2007). Best practice process for creating an IT services sourcing strategy. In G00153560 (Ed.), (pp. 1-29): Gartner Inc.

Compilation of References

Gay, G., Stefanone, M., Grace-Martin, M., & Hembrooke, H. (2001). The effects of wireless computing in collaborative learning. *International Journal of Human-Computer Interaction, 13*(2), 257–276. doi:10.1207/S15327590IJHC1302_10

Gellings, C. (2007). Outsourcing Relationships: The Contract as IT Governance Tool.*Proceedings of the 40th Hawaii International Conference on System Sciences*. Hawaii. doi:10.1109/HICSS.2007.421

Ghobadian, A., & O'Regan, N. (2006). The Impact of Ownership on Small Firm Behaviour and Performance. *International Small Business Journal, 24*(6), 555–585. doi:10.1177/0266242606069267

Gibbs, B. (1994). The effects of environment and technology on managerial role. *Journal of Management, 20*(3), 581–604. doi:10.1177/014920639402000304

Giddens, A. (1984). The constitution of society: Outline of the theory of structuration. Cambridge, UK.

Giddens, A. (1979). *Central problems in social theory*. Basingstoke, UK: Macmillan.

GIIC – Global Information Infrastructure Commission. (2008). The GIIC Tokyo Declaration. *Retrieved from*www.giic.org

Gilad, B. (2000). An Ad Hoc, Entrepreneurial CI Model. *Competitive Intelligence Magazine, 3*(4), 33–39.

Glissmann, S. M., & Sanz, J. (2011). An Approach to Building Effective Enterprise Architectures. *In the Proceeding of the 44th Hawaii International Conference on System Sciences*.

Godbout, A. J. (1999, January). Filtering Knowledge: Changing Information into Knowledge Assets. *Journal of Systemic Knowledge Management (Journal of Knowledge Management Practice)*.

Godet, M. (2007). *Prospectiva Estratégica: problemas y métodos*. San Sebastián, España: Cuadernos de Liptor.

Goles, T., & Chin, W. W. (2005). Information Systems Outsourcing Relationship Factors: Detailed Conceptualisation and Initial Evidence. *The Data Base for Advances in Information Systems, 36*(4), 47–67. doi:10.1145/1104004.1104009

Goo, J., Huang, D., & Hart, P. (2008). A path to successful IT outsourcing: Interaction between service-level agreements and commitment. *Decision Sciences, 39*(3), 469–506. doi:10.1111/j.1540-5915.2008.00200.x

Gottschalk, P. (1999). Implementation Predictors of Formal Information Technology Strategy. *Information & Management, 36*(2), 77–91. doi:10.1016/S0378-7206(99)00008-7

Gottschalk, P. (2006). Research propositions for knowledge management systems supporting IT outsourcing relationships. *Journal of Computer Information Systems, 46*(3), 110–116.

Gough, I. (2013July, 8-10). The challenge of climate change for social policy.*Proceedings of Social Policy Association Annual Conference*. Sheffield, UK.

Gray, D. E. (2009). *Doing Research in the real world*. Sage Publication Ltd.

Greenhalgh, T., & Stones, R. (2010). Theorising big IT programmes in healthcare: Strong structuration theory meets actor-network theory. *Social Science & Medicine, 70*(9), 1285–1294. doi:10.1016/j.socscimed.2009.12.034 PMID:20185218

Gregor, S., Fernandez, W., Holtham, D., Martin, M., Stern, S., Vitale, M., & Pratt, G. (2004). *Achieving Value From ICT: Key Management Strategies*. Canberra: Department of Communications, Information Technology and the Arts.

Gronau, N. (2013). *Enterprise Resource Planning*. München: Oldenbourg.

Grover, S. K., & Lederer, A. L. (1999). The influence of environmental uncertainty on the strategic use of information systems. *Information & Management*, 40–68.

Guimaraes, T. (2000). The impact of competitive intelligence and IS support in changing small business organisations. *Logistics Information Management*, *13*(3), 117–125. doi:10.1108/09576050010326510

Hafner, M., & Winter, R. (2008). Process for Enterprise Application Architecture management. *In the Proceedings of the 41st Annual Hawaii International Conference on System Sciences*.

Hair, J. F., Black, W. C., Babin, B. J., Anderson, R. E., & Tatham, R. L. (2009). *Multivariate Data Analysis*. New Jersey: Pearson Education, Inc.

Hair, J., Black, W., Babin, B., Anderson, R. L., & Tatham, R. (2006). *Multivariate data analysis* (6th ed.).

Hammer, M., & Champy, J. (2006). Reengineering the corporation: A manifesto for business revolution [paperback ed., rev. and updated]. New York: Harper Collins.

Hanbury, R. (2001). Strategy Clinic: Keeping politics away from project management. Retrieved from http://www.computerweekly.com/

Hansmann, H., & Neumann, S. (2011). Process-Oriented Implementation of ERP-Systems. In J. Becker, M. Kugeler, & M. Rosemann (Eds.), *Process management: A guide for the design of business processes* (2nd ed., pp. 283–321). Berlin, London: Springer. doi:10.1007/978-3-642-15190-3_10

Hardy, C. (1994). Power and politics in organizations. In C. Hardy (Ed.), *Managing Strategic Action: Mobilizing Change*. London: Sage Publications.

Harindranath, G., Dryerson, R., & Barnes, D. (2008). ICT Adoption and use in UK SMEs: A Failure of Initiatives? *Electronic Journal Information Systems Evaluation*, *11*(2), 91–96.

Havenga, J. & Botha, D. (2004) *Developing Competitive Intelligence in the knowledge-based Organisation*, 7(1), 8-17.

Hearn, S., & White, N. (2009). Communities of practice: linking knowledge, policy and practice. Retrieved from http://www.odi.org.uk/resources/download/1129.pdf

Heeks, R. (2002). Information systems and developing countries: Failure, success, and local improvisations. *The Information Society*, *18*(2), 101–112. doi:10.1080/01972240290075039

Heiring, D., & Phillips, J. (2005). Innovation Roles: The people you need for successful innovation [White Paper].

Herring, J. P. (1999). Key intelligence topics: A process to identify and define intelligence need. *Competitive Intelligence Review*, *10*(2), 4–14. doi:10.1002/(SICI)1520-6386(199932)10:2<4::AID-CIR3>3.0.CO;2-C

Herselman, M. (2003). *ICT in rural areas in South Africa: Various case studies*. Paper presented at the InSITE Conference. Pori, Finland.

Hesford, J. W. (2008). An empirical investigation of accounting information use in competitive intelligence. *Journal of Competitive Intelligence and Management*, *4*(3), 17–49.

Hill, T. R., & Roldan, M. (2005). Toward third generation threaded discussions for mobile learning: Opportunities and challenges for ubiquitous collaborative environments. *Information Systems Frontiers*, *7*(1), 55–70. doi:10.1007/s10796-005-5338-7

Hilty, L. (2008). *Information technology and sustainability: Essays on the relationship between ICT and sustainable development*. Norderstedt: Herstellung und Verlag: Books on Demand Gmbh.

Hilty, L. M. & Ruddy, T. F. (2000). Towards a sustainable Information Society. *Informatik/Informatique 4 (2000)*, 2-9.

Compilation of References

Hilty, L. M., Binswanger, M., Bruinink, A., Erdmann, L., Froehlich, J., Köhler, A., et al. (2005).The Precautionary principle in the Information Society – Effects of pervasive computing on health and environment (2nd ed.). *Swiss Center for Technology Assessment (TA-SWISS)*. Retrieved fromwww.empa.ch/ssis

Hilty, L. M., & Aebischer, B. (2015). ICT for Sustainability: An Emerging Research Field. In L. M. Hilty & B. Aebischer (Eds.), *ICT Innovations for Sustainability. Advances in Intelligent Systems and Computing 310*. Heidelberg: Springer International Publishing. doi:10.1007/978-3-319-09228-7_1

Hilty, L. M., Schulthess, D., & Ruddy, T. F. (Eds.). (2000). *Strategische und betriebsübergreifendeAnwendungenbetrieblicherUmweltinformationssysteme*. Marburg: Metropolis.

Hirschheim, R., & Dibbern, J. (2014). *Information Technology Outsourcing: Towards Sustainable Business Value*. Springer-Verlag.

Hofstee, E. (2006). *Constructing a Good Dissertation: A Practical Guide to Finishing a Master's, MBA or PhD on Schedule*. South Africa: EPE Publishers.

Holbeche, L. (2004). *The power of constructive politics*. Horsham, United Kingdom: Roffey Park Institute Publications.

Holland, A. (2003). Sustainability. In D. Jamieson (Ed.), *A Companion to Environmental Philosophy*. Oxford: Blackwell Publishing.

Holvelja, T., Rozanec, A., & Rupnik, R. (2010). Measuring the success of the strategic information systems planning in enterprises in Slovenia. *Management, 15*(2), 25–46.

Hough, J., Thompson, A. A., Strickland, A. J. III, & Gamble, J. E. (2008). *Crafting and executing strategy* (South African ed). United Kingdom: McGraw-Hill.

Hoven, D., & Van, J. (2001). *Information Resource Management: Foundation for knowledge management*.

Huang, C. C., & Hsieh, C. C. (2011). Protect Critical Information Infrastructure Systems in Financial and Healthcare Sectors: Actor Network Theory. Proceedings of *ICONS 2011: The Sixth International Conference on Systems,83-87*.

Huang, R., Zmud, R. W., & Price, R. L. (2009). IT Governance Practices in Small and Medium-Sized Enterprises: Recommendations from an Empirical Study. *IFIP Advances in Information and Communication Technology, 301*, 158–199. doi:10.1007/978-3-642-02388-0_12

Huff, R. A., & Prybutok, V. R. (2008). Information systems project management decision making: The influence of experience and risk propensity. *Project Management Journal, 39*(2), 34–47. doi:10.1002/pmj.20050

Igben, M. J., & Akobo, D. I. (2007). State of Information and Communication Technology (ICT) in Libraries in Rivers State, Nigeria. *African Journal of Library and Information Science, 17*(2), 150–34.

Ignatov, A. A. (2004). Competitive Intelligence in Russia. *Journal of Competitive Intelligence and Management, 2*(2), 26–44.

IT Governance Institute (ITGI). (2003). *Board Briefing on IT Governance, (2nd ed.)*. Retrieved from: http://www.itgi.org

IT Governance Institute (ITGI). (2006). IT Governance in Practice: Insight From Leading CIOs. Retrieved from: http://www.pwchk.com/home/eng/it_governance_cios.html

ITWeb (2008, September). ITWeb - JCSE ICT skills survey [DVD of Powerpoint presentation].

Iyamu, T. (2009). The Factors Affecting Institutionalisation of Enterprise Architecture in the Organisation. *In the Proceeding of the 11th IEEE Conference on Commerce and Enterprise Computing*. Vienna.

Iyamu, T., & Adelakun, O. (2008). *The impact of non-technical factors on Information Technology Strategy and E-business*. Paper presented at the PACIS Conference, Suzhou, China

Iyamu, T. (2010). Theoretical analysis of Strategic implementation of Enterprise Architecture. *International Journal of Actor-Network Theory and Technological Innovation*, 2(3), 17–32. doi:10.4018/jantti.2010070102

Iyamu, T. (2011). Institutionalisation of the enterprise architecture. *International Journal of Actor-Network Theory and Technological Innovation*, 3(1), 1–27. doi:10.4018/jantti.2011010103

Iyamu, T. (2013). Underpinning Theories: Order-of-Use in Information Systems Research. *Journal of Systems and Information Technology*, 15(3), 1–13. doi:10.1108/JSIT-11-2012-0064

Iyamu, T., & Olummide, O. O. (2010). Components of the computing environment. *GESJ: Computer Science and Telecommunications*, 3(26), 144.

Iyamu, T., & Roode, D. (2010). The use of structuration theory and actor network theory for analysis: Case study of a financial institution in South Africa. *International Journal of Actor-Network Theory and Technological Innovation*, 2(1), 1–26. doi:10.4018/jantti.2010071601

Iyamu, T., & Tatnall, A. (2009). An Actor-Network analysis of a case of development and implementation of IT strategy. *International Journal of Actor-Network Theory and Technological Innovation*, 1(4), 35–52. doi:10.4018/jantti.2009062303

Iyer, B., & Gottlieb, R. (2004). The Four-Domain Architecture: An approach to support enterprise architecture design. *IBM Systems Journal*, 43(3), 587–597. doi:10.1147/sj.433.0587

Jain, P. (2009). *Strategies to Survive the Slowdown*. Retrieved from www.financialexpress.com/news/strategies-to-survive-the-slowdown/459764/0

Jain, R., & Chandrasekaran, A. (2009). Rapid system development (RSD) methodologies: Proposing a selection framework. *Engineering Management Journal*, 21(4), 30–35. doi:10.1080/10429247.2009.11431842

Jaworski, B. J., Macinnis, D. J., & Kohli, A. K. (2004). Generating Competitive Intelligence in Organizations. *Journal of Market-Focused Management*, 1(5), 279–307.

Jennex, M.E.and Adelakun, O. (2003) Success Factors For Offshore Information Systems development, in Journal of Information Technology Cases and Applications, 5(3), 12-31.

Jensen, C., & Scacchi, W. (2005). Process Modeling of the Web Information Infrastructure. *Software Process Improvement and Practice*, 10(3), 255–272. doi:10.1002/spip.228

Johns, P., & Van Doren, D. C. (2010). Competitive Intelligence in service marketing: A new approach with practical application. *Marketing & Planning*, 28(5), 551–570. doi:10.1108/02634501011066492

Jones, M. (1999). Structuration Theory. In W. L. Currie & R. D. Galliers (Eds.), *Rethinking Management Information Systems* (pp. 103–134). United Kingdom: Oxford University Press.

Jones, M. R., & Karsten, H. (2008). Giddens's Structuration Theory and information systems review. *Management Information Systems Quarterly*, 32(1), 127–157.

Jonkers, H., Lankhorst, M., Ter Doest, T., Arbab, F., Bosma, H., & Wieringa, R. (2006). Enterprise architecture: Management tool and blueprint for the organization. *Information Systems Frontiers*, 8(2), 63–66. doi:10.1007/s10796-006-7970-2

Jordan, E., & Silcock, L. (2005). *Beating the Risk*. England: John Wiley & Sons.

Kaiser, K., & Hawk, S. (2004). Evolution of Offshore Software Development: From Outsourcing to Cosourcing. *MIS Quarterly Executive*, *3*(2), 69–81.

Kaisler, S., Armour, F., & Valivullah, M. (2005). Enterprise Architecting: Critical Problems. *In the Proceedings of the 38th Annual Hawaii International Conference on System Sciences.*

Kankanhalli, A., Teo, H., Tan, B. C. Y., & Wei, K. (2003). An Integrative Study of Information Systems Security Effectiveness. *International Journal of Information Management*, *23*(2), 139–154. doi:10.1016/S0268-4012(02)00105-6

Kazooba, C. (2006). Causes of Small Business failure in Uganda: A Case Study from Bushenyi and Mbarara Towns. *African Studies Quarterly,* 8, 4, http://web.africa.ufl.edu/asq/v8/v8i4a3.htm

Kearney, A. T. (2004). Making Offshore Decisions: A.T. Kearney's 2004 offshore location Attractiveness index. Retrieved from http://kdi.mscmalaysia.my/static/reports/AT%20Kearney%202004%20Report.pdf

Kendra, S. A. (2004, May–June). Environmental scanning: Radar for success. *The Information Management Journal,* 38 – 45.

Kerlinger, F. N., & Lee, H. B. (2000). *Foundations of behavioural research.* Fort Worth: Harcourt College Publishers.

Kess, P., Torkko, M., & Phusavat, K. (2007). *Knowledge transfer for effective outsourcing relationships.* Proceedings of the 29th International Conference on Information Technology Interfaces (ITI). Cavtat, Croatia.

King, M. (2009). *King III Report on Corporate Governance.* Retrieved from: www.iodsa.co.za

King, W. R. (1988). How effective is your information systems planning? *Long Range Planning*, *21*(5), 103–112. doi:10.1016/0024-6301(88)90111-2

Klein, H., & Myers, M. (1999). A set of principles for conducting and evaluating interpretive field studies in Information Systems. *Management Information Systems Quarterly*, *23*(1), 67–93. doi:10.2307/249410

Klijn, E. (1998). Redes de Políticas Públicas: una visión general. In W. Kickert & J. F. Koppenjan (Eds.), *Managing Complex Networks* (M. Petrizzo, Trans.). London: Sage.

Kling, R., & Iacono, S. (1984). The control of Information Systems Developments After Implementation. *Communications of the ACM*, *27*(12), 1218–1226. doi:10.1145/2135.358307

Kohli, R., & Grover, V. (2008). Business value of IT: An essay on expanding research directions to keep up with the time. *Journal of the Association for Information Systems*, *9*(1), 24–38.

Korac-Kakabadse, N., & Korac-Kakabadse, A. (2001). IS/IT Governance: Need for an Integrated Model. *Corporate Governance*, *1*(4), 9–11. doi:10.1108/EUM0000000005974

Korteland, E., & Bekkers, V. (2007). Diffusion of E-government innovations in the Dutch public sector: The case of digital community policing. *Information Polity*, *12*, 139–150.

Kotlarsky, J., & Oshri, I. (2008). Country attractiveness for offshoring and offshore-outsourcing. *Journal of Information Technology*, *23*(4), 228–231. doi:10.1057/jit.2008.17

Kraus, S. E. (2005). Research paradigms and meaning making: A Primer. *Qualitative Report*, *10*(4), 758–770.

Krogh, G. v., Ichijo, K., & Nonaka, I. (2000). *Enabling Knowledge Creation: How to unlock the mystery of tacit knowledge and release the power of innovation.* New York: Oxford University Press. doi:10.1093/acprof:oso/9780195126167.001.0001

Krücken-Pereira, L., Debiasi, F., & Abreu, A. F. (2003). Technological innovation and Competitive Intelligence: an interactive process. *READ - Electronic Journal of Directors, v.7*. Retrieved from http://read.adm.ufrgs.br/read21/artigo/artigo5.pdf

Kunnathur, A. S., & Shi, Z. (2001). An investigation of the strategic information systems planning success in Chinese publicly traded firms. *International Journal of Information Management, 21*(6), 423–439. doi:10.1016/S0268-4012(01)00034-2

Kvale, S. (1996). *Interviews: An introduction to qualitative research*. London: Sage.

Kyobe, M. (2009). Factors Influencing SME Compliance with Government Regulations on Use of IT: The Case of South Africa. *Journal of Global Information Management, 17*(12), 30–59. doi:10.4018/jgim.2009040102

Kyobe, M. E. (2008). The impact of entrepreneur behaviours on the quality of e-commerce security in Urban SMEs: A comparison of Urban and Rural findings. *Journal of Global Information Technology Management, 11*(2), 58–79. doi:10.1080/1097198X.2008.10856467

Kyoto Protocol to the United Nations Framework Convention on Climate Change. (1998). *New York: United Nations*.

La Nación. (2008, July 18). Pasaportes y licencias. *La Nación*. Retrieved from http://www.nacion.com/opinion/Pasaportes-licencias_0_989301101.html

Lacerda, A. C., & et al. (2001). *Strategic technology for competitiveness: Technology in inserting the variable strategic planning*. São Paulo: Nobel.

Lacity, M. C., Khan, S., Yan, A., & Willcocks, L. P. (2010). A Review of the IT Outsourcing Empirical Literature and Future Research Directions. *Journal of Information Technology, 25*(4), 395–433. doi:10.1057/jit.2010.21

Lacity, M. C., & Willcocks, L. P. (2009). *Information Systems and Outsourcing: Studies in Theory and Practice*. Basingstoke, Hampshire: Palgrave Macmillan.

Lampel, J., & Bhalla, A. (2008). Embracing Realism and Recognizing Choice in IT Offshoring Initiatives. *Business Horizons, 51*(5), 429–440. doi:10.1016/j.bushor.2008.03.007

Lam, W., & Chua, A. (2009). Knowledge outsourcing: An alternative strategy for knowledge management. *Journal of Knowledge Management, 13*(3), 28–43. doi:10.1108/13673270910962851

Laplante, P. A., Costello, T., Singh, P., Bindiganavile, S. & Landon, M. (2004). The Who, What, Why, Where and When of IT Outsourcing. *IT Pro, IEEE, January / February*, 19-23.

Larsen, M. A., & Myers, M. D. (1999). When success turns into failure: A package driven business process re-engineering project in the financial services industry. *The Journal of Strategic Information Systems, 8*(4), 397–417. doi:10.1016/S0963-8687(00)00025-1

Latour, B. (1997). On actor-network theory: A few clarifications. Retrieved from http://www.keele.ac.uk/depts/stt/stt/ant/latour.htm

Latour, B. (1987). *Science in action: how to follow scientists and engineers through society*. Cambridge, MA: Harvard University Press.

Latour, B. (1987). *Science in Action: How to follow Scientists and Engineers through Society*. Cambridge, Massachusetts: Harward University Press.

Law, J. (1992). Notes on the theory of the actor-network: Ordering, strategy, and heterogeneity. *Systems Practice, 5*(4), 379–393. doi:10.1007/BF01059830

Layne, K., & Lee, J. (2001). Developing fully functional E-government: A four stage model. *Government Information Quarterly*, *18*(2), 122–136. doi:10.1016/S0740-624X(01)00066-1

Lederer, A. L., & Gardiner, V. (1992). The process of strategic information planning. *Journal of Strategic Information Systems (1:2)*, 76-83.

Lederer, A. L., & Sethi, V. (1996). Key Prescriptions for Strategic Information Systems Planning. *Journal of Management Information Systems*, 35–62.

Lederer, L., & Gardiner, V. (1992). The Process of Strategic Information Planning. *The Journal of Strategic Information Systems*, *1*(2), 76–83. doi:10.1016/0963-8687(92)90004-G

Lederer, L., & Sethi, V. (1988). The implementation of strategic information systems planning methodologies. *Management Information Systems Quarterly*, *12*(3), 445–461. doi:10.2307/249212

Leedy, P. D., & Ormrod, J. E. (2014). *Practical Research: Planning and Design* (10th ed.). New Jersey: Pearson Education Limited.

Lee, G. G., & Pai, J. C. (2003). Effects of organisational context and inter-group behaviour on the success of strategic information systems planning: An empirical study. *Behaviour & Information Technology*, *22*(4), 263–280. doi:10.1080/01449290310001 36548

Lee, M. K. O. (1996). IT outsourcing contracts: Practical issues for management. *Industrial Management & Data Systems*, *96*(1), 15–20. doi:10.1108/02635579610107684

Letseka, M., & Iyamu, T. (2011) The Dualism of the Information Technology Project, in the *Proceedings of the 2011 Annual Conference of the South African Institute of Computer Scientists and Information Technologists*. Cape Town. doi:10.1145/2072221.2072261

Levina, N. (2006). In or Out in an Offshore Context: The Choice Between Captive Centers and Third-Party Vendors, Cutter IT Journal Oshri, I., Kotlarsky, J. and Willcocks, L. P. The Handbook of Global Outsourcing and Offshoring, Macmillan, 2011.

Levy, M. & Powell, P. (1998). SME flexibility and the role of information systems.. *Journal of Small Business Economics*, 183 – 196.

Levy, M., & Powell, P. (2000). Information systems strategy for small and medium sized enterprises: An organisational perspective. *The Journal of Strategic Information Systems*, *9*(1), 63–84. doi:10.1016/S0963-8687(00)00028-7

Levy, M., & Powell, P. (2005). *Strategy for growth in SMEs*. Oxford: Elsevier Butterworth-Heinemann.

Lewis, D. (2002). *The place of organizational politics in strategic change*. London: John Wiley & Sons Ltd.

Leyking, K. (2010). Process Follows Strategy: Plan, Execute and Control Business Process Aligned with Corporate Strategy. Information Management and Consulting, 25, 62–68.

Lighthelm, A. A., & Cant, M. C. (2002). *Business Success Factors of SMEs in Gauteng*. Pretoria: University of South Africa.

Lindvall, M., Rus, I., Jammalamadaka, R., & Thakker, R. (2001). *Software Tools for Knowledge Management: A DACS State-of-the-art report*. Maryland: Fraunhofer Center for Experimental Software Engineering Maryland and The University of Maryland.

Liu, J., Chun-Sheng, Y., Chang, L., & Yao, J. E. (2003). Technology acceptance model for wireless internet. *Internet Research: Electronic Networking Applications and Policy*, *13*(13), 206–222. doi:10.1108/10662240310478222

Love, P. E. D., Irani, Z., Standing, C., Lin, C., & Burn, J. M. (2005). The Enigma of Evaluation: Benefits, Costs and Risks of IT in Australian Small-Medium-Sized Enterprises. *Information & Management*, *42*(7), 947–964. doi:10.1016/j.im.2004.10.004

Lucas, H. C. (1991). Methodological Issues in Information Systems Survey Research. In K. L. Kraemer (Ed.), *The Information Systems Research Challenges: Survey Research Methods* (pp. 273–285). Boston, MA: Harvard Business School Press.

Luftman, J., & Kempaiah, R. (2008). Key Issues for IT Executives 2007. *MIS Quarterly Executive*, *7*(2), 99–112.

Luftman, J., Papp, R., & Brier, T. (1999). Enablers and Inhibitors of Business-IT Alignment through a Unified Framework. *Communications of the Association for Information Systems*, *1*, 1–32.

Luoma-Aho, V., & Paloviita, A. (2010). Actor-networking stakeholder theory for today's corporate communications. *Corporate Communications: An International Journal*, *15*(1), 49–67. doi:10.1108/13563281011016831

Lynch, R. L. (2011). *Strategic management* (6th ed.). Harlow: Pearson Education Limited.

Mack, R. (2002). Creating an Information Technology (IT) Strategy: An Alternative Approach. Gartner, Inc. Retrieved from www.gartner.com

MacLean, D., Souter, D., & Creech, H. (2012). ICTs, the Internet, and Sustainability. *International Institute for Sustainable Development*. Retrieved from https://www.iisd.org/pdf/2012/changing_our_understanding_of_sustainability.pdf

Macome, E. (2008). On Implementation of an information system in the Mozambican context: The EDM case viewed through ANT lenses. *Information Technology for Development*, *14*(2), 154–170. doi:10.1002/itdj.20063

Maguire, S., & Redman, T. (2007). The role of human resource management in information systems development. *Management Decision*, *45*(2), 252–264. doi:10.1108/00251740710727278

Malhotra, Y. (2000). Knowledge Management & New Organization Forms: A framework for Business Model Innovation. *Information Resources Management Journal*, *13*(1), 5–14. doi:10.4018/irmj.2000010101

Mariano, C., & Pavesi, S. (2010). *How management can foster continuous product Innovation*. Integrated Manufacturing Systems. Retrieved from http://www.emerald-library.com

Markard, J. (2009, October 29). Characteristics of infrastructure sectors and implications for innovation processes. *Discussion paper for the workshop on environmental innovation in infrastructure sectors*. Karisruhe.

Marketplace realities in strategic outsourcing. (2002a). Gartner (pp. 1-22). Gartner Inc.

Markus, L. (1983). Power, Politics, and MIS Implementation. *Communications of the ACM*, *26*(6), 430–444. doi:10.1145/358141.358148

Markus, M. L., & Tanis, C. (2000). The Enterprise System Experience: From Adoption to Success. In R. W. Zmud (Ed.), *Framing the domains of IT management: Projecting the future through the past* (pp. 173–208). Cincinnati, Ohio: Pinnaflex Education Resources, Inc.

Martin, L. M., & Matlay, H. (2001). "Blanket" Approaches to Promoting ICT in Small Firms: Some Lessons from the DTI Ladder Adoption Model in the UK. *Internet Research: Electronic Networking Applications and Policy*, *11*(5), 399–410. doi:10.1108/EUM0000000006118

Martins, E., & Terblanche, F. (2003). Building organizational culture that stimulates creativity and innovation. *European Journal of Innovation Management*, *6*(1), 64–75. doi:10.1108/14601060310456337

Compilation of References

Martins, L., Cunha, P., Figueiredo, A., & Dias, T. (2009). IT Alignment through ANT: A Case of Sustainable Decision in the Educational Sector.*Engineering Management Conference, IEEE International*, 485-490. doi:10.1109/TIC-STH.2009.5444452

Martre, H. L., & Jean-Louis, C. P. (1994). *Intelligence and strategy business publication in the French Documentation.*

McCord, S. (2002). *Competitive Intelligence in the academic environment.* Washington State University.

Mcleod, L., & Macdonell, S. G. (2011). Factors that Affect Software Systems Development Project Outcomes: A Survey of Research. *ACM Computing Surveys*, *43*(4), 24–56. doi:10.1145/1978802.1978803

Meihami, B., & Meihami, H. (2013). Knowledge Management a way to gain a competitive advantage in firms. *International Letters of Social and Humanistic Sciences*, *3*, 80–91.

Mentzas, G. (1997). Implementing an IS strategy—a team approach. *Long Range Planning*, *10*(1), 84–95. doi:10.1016/S0024-6301(96)00099-4

Minsch, J., Feindt, P.-H., Meister, H.-P., Schneidewind, U., & Schulz, T. (1998). *InstitutionelleReformenfüreinePolitik der Nachhaltigkeit.* Marburg: Metropolis.

Mintzberg, H. (2000). *The rise and fall of strategic planning.* Englewood Cliffs, London: Prentice-Hall.

Miozza, M., & Grimshaw, D. (2005). Modularity and innovation in knowledge-intensive business services: IT outsourcing in Germany and the UK. Science Direct, 1419-1439. Retrieved from www.sciencedirect.com

Mirchandani, D. A. (2000). *Information systems planning autonomy in US-based subsidiaries of competing globally firms* [Phd Thesis]. University of Kentucky.

Mirchandani, D. A., & Lederer, A. L. (2008). The impact of autonomy on information systems planning effectiveness. *International Journal of Management Sciences*, *36*, 789–807.

Mitev, N. (2009). In and out of actor-network theory: A necessary but insufficient journey. *Information Technology & People*, *22*(1), 9–25. doi:10.1108/09593840910937463

Mitrovic, Z. (2010). Positioning e-skills within an organisation: An information systems management viewpoint. *SA Journal of Information Management*, *12*(1), 427–434. doi:10.4102/sajim.v12i1.427

Mkhomazi, S. S., & Iyamu, T. (2013). A Guide to Selecting Theory to Underpin Information Systems Studies. In Y. Dwivedi, H. Henrksen, D. Wastell, & R. De (Eds.), *Grand Successes and Failures in IT* (pp. 525–538). doi:10.1007/978-3-642-38862-0_33

Mohdzain, M. B., & Ward, J. M. (2007). A study of subsidiaries' views of information systems strategic planning in multinational organisations. *The Journal of Strategic Information Systems*, *16*(4), 324–352. doi:10.1016/j.jsis.2007.02.003

Monk, E. F., & Wagner, B. J. (2012). *Concepts in enterprise resource planning* (4th ed.). Boston, Mass, Australia: Course Technology Cengage Learning.

Monteiro, E., & Hanseth, O. (1996). Social Shaping of Information Infrastructure: On Being Specific about the Technology. In W. J. Orlikowski, G. Walsham, M. R. Jones, & J. I. DeGross (Eds.), *Information Technology and Changes in Organizational Work* (pp. 325–343). London: Chapman and Hall.

Mooney, J. G., Gurbaxani, V., & Kraemer, K. L. (2001). A Process oriented framework for assessing the business value of Information Technology. *ACM SIGMIS Database*, *27*(2), 68–81. doi:10.1145/243350.243363

Morgan, G. (1986). *Images of Organization.* London, Beverly Hills: Sage.

Morton, N. A., & Hu, Q. (2008). Implications of the fit between organisational structure and ERP: A structural contingency theory perspective. *International Journal of Information Management, 28*(5), 391–402. doi:10.1016/j.ijinfomgt.2008.01.008

Mosindi, O., & Sice, P. (2011). An Exploratory Theoretical Framework for Understanding Information Behaviour. *International Journal of Technology and Human Interaction, 7*(2), 1–8. doi:10.4018/jthi.2011040101

Muente-Kunigami, A., & Navas-Sabater, J. (2009). *Options to increase access to telecommunications services in rural and low income areas*. Washington DC, USA: World Bank working paper.

Musangu, L. M., & Kekwaletswe, R. M. (2011). Strategic information systems planning and environmental uncertainty: The case of South Africa Small, Micro and Medium Enterprises. In the Proceedings of *IADIS Information Systems Conference*, Avila, Spain 11 – 13 March, 70 – 78.

Myers, M. D. (1997). Qualitative Research in Information Systems. *Management Information Systems Quarterly, 21*(2), 241–242. doi:10.2307/249422

Myers, M. D., & Avison, D. (2002). *Qualitative Research in Information Systems*. London: Sage Publications.

National e-Skills Plan of Action. (2010). e-Skills Institute. Pretorian Department of Communications: e-Skills Institute.

National e-Skills Plan of Action. (2013). *Pretorian Department of Communications: e-Skills Institute*. Retrieved from www.doc.gov.za/documents-publications/category/14-e-skills-documents.html

NBSA (National Small Business Act). (1996). National Small Business Act, No. 106 of 1996.

NBSAA (National Small Business Amendment Act). (2003). National Small Business Amendment Act, No. 26 of 2003.

Nemutanzhela, P., & Iyamu, T. (2011). A Framework for Enhancing the Information Systems Innovation: Using Competitive Intelligence.[EJISE]. *The Electronic Journal Information Systems Evaluation, 14*(2), 242–253.

New Perspectives on ICT skills and employment. (2005). *Directorate for Science, Technology and Industry*. Retrieved from www.oecd.org/dataoecd/26/35/34769393.pdf

Newkirk, H. E. (2001). *Environmental uncertainty and strategic information systems planning comprehensiveness*. Thesis, University of Kentucky.

Newkirk, H. E., & Lederer, L. L. (2007). The effectiveness of strategic information systems planning for technical resources, personnel resources, and data security in environment of heterogeneity and hostility. *Journal of Computer Information Systems, 47*(3), 34–44.

Nickols, F. (2001). The Knowledge in Knowledge Management *Paper commissioned for Knowledge Management Yearbook 2000 - 2001*.

Niederman, F. (2005). International business and MIS approaches to multinational organisational research: The cases of knowledge transfer and IT workforce outsourcing. *Journal of International Management, 11*(2), 187–200. doi:10.1016/j.intman.2005.03.004

Nonaka, I. (1991). The Knowledge Creating Company (Harvard Business Review ed. Vol. Harvard Business Review).

Nonaka, I., Toyama, R., & Byosiere, P. (2001). A Theory of Organisational Knowledge Creation: Understanding the Dynamic Process of Creating Knowledge. In M. Dierkes, A. B. Antal, J. Child, & I. Nonaka (Eds.), *Handbook of Organizational Learning & Knowledge* (pp. 491–517). New York: Oxford University Press.

Noor, K. B. M. (2008). Case study: A strategic research methodology. *American Journal of Applied Sciences, 5*(11), 1602–1604. doi:10.3844/ajassp.2008.1602.1604

Compilation of References

North, D. C. (1990). *Institutions, Institutional Change and Economic Performance*. Cambridge, MA: Cambridge University Press. doi:10.1017/CBO9780511808678

Nyrhinen, M. (2006). *IT Infrastructure: Structure, properties and processes* [Working paper, W-403]. HSE Print Organisation for Economic Cooperation and Development.

O'Donohue, B., Pye, G., & Warren, M. J. (2009). The Impact of ICT Governance within Australian Companies. In A. Cater-Steel (Ed.), *Information Technology Governance and Service Management: Frameworks and Adaptations* (pp. 163–177). UK: Information Science Reference. doi:10.4018/978-1-60566-008-0.ch008

Oates, B. J. (2008). *Researching information systems and computing*. Los Angeles: Sage Publications.

OECD. (2004). ICT, E-Business and SMEs. Paris: Head of Publications Service, OECD.

Olivier, M. S. (1997). Information Technology Research: A practical guide for Computer Science and Informatics (Second Edition 2004 ed.). Van Schaik Publishers.

Olson, H. (1995). Quantitative 'versus' qualitative research: The wrong question. Retrieved from www.ualberta.ca/dept/slis/cais/olson.htm

Orlikowski, W. (1992). The Duality of Technology: Rethinking the Concept of Technology in Organizations. *Organization Science*, *3*(3), 398–427. doi:10.1287/orsc.3.3.398

Orlikowski, W. (1993). CASE tools as organisational change: Investigating incremental and radical changes in systems development. *Management Information Systems Quarterly*, *17*(3), 1–28. doi:10.2307/249774

Orlikowski, W. (2000). Using Technology and Constituting Structures: A Practice Lens for Studying Technology in Organizations. *Organization Science*, *11*(4), 404–428. doi:10.1287/orsc.11.4.404.14600

Orlikowski, W. J., & Baroudi, J. J. (1991). Studying Information Technology in Organisations: Research Approaches and Assumptions. *Information Systems Research*, *2*(1), 1–28. doi:10.1287/isre.2.1.1

Orlikowski, W., & Barley, S. (2001). Technology and institutions: What can research on information technology and research on organizations learn from each other? *Management Information Systems Quarterly*, *25*(2), 145–165. doi:10.2307/3250927

Orlikowski, W., & Gash, D. (1994). Technological Frames: Making Sense of Information Technology in Organisations. *ACM Transactions on Information Systems*, *12*(2), 174–207. doi:10.1145/196734.196745

Oshri, I. and van Uhm, B (2012). A historical review of the information technology and business process captive centre sector. *Journal of Information Technology*, 27(4), 270-284.

Oshri, I., Kotlarsky, J., & Liew, C. M. (2008). Four Strategies for 'Offshore' Captive Centers, Wall Street Journal.

Oshri, I. (2013). Choosing an Evolutionary Path for Offshore Captive Centers. *MIS Quarterly Executive*, *12*(3), 151–165.

Oslo Manual - Proposed guidelines for collecting and interpreting data on technological innovation [Translation of the Financier of Studies and Projects]. (2008). Retrieved from http://www.oecd.org/science/inno/2367580.pdf

Palanisamy, R. (2005). Strategic information systems planning model for building flexibility and success. *Industrial Management & Data Systems*, *105*(1), 63–81. doi:10.1108/02635570510575199

Papacharissi, Z., & Zaks, A. (2006). Is Broadband the future? An analysis of broadband technology potential and diffusion. *Telecommunications Policy*, *30*(1), 64–75. doi:10.1016/j.telpol.2005.08.001

Pappa, D., & Stergioulas, L. K. (2008). The emerging role of corporate systems: An example from the era of business process-oriented learning. *International Journal of Business Science and Applied Management, 3*(2), 38–48.

Paré, G. (2004). Investigating information systems with positivist case study research. *Communications of the Association for Information Systems, 13*(1), 233–264.

Patnayakuni, R., Rai, A., & Tiwani, A. (2007). Systems Development Process Improvement: A Knowledge Integration Perspective. *IEEE Transactions on Engineering Management, 54*(2), 286–300. doi:10.1109/TEM.2007.893997

Pawłowska, A. (2004). Failures in large systems projects in Poland: Mission impossible? *Information Polity, 9*(3), 167–180.

Pereira, C. M., & Sousa, P. (2004). A method to define an enterprise architecture using the Zachman framework. *In the Proceedings of the 2004 ACM symposium on applied computing.*

Peterson, R. (2004). Crafting Information Technology Governance. *Information Systems Management, 21*(4), 7–22. doi:10.1201/1078/44705.21.4.20040901/84183.2

Pfeffer, J. (1992). *Managing with power: Politics & influence in organizations.* Boston, USA: Harvard Business School Press.

Pita, Z. (2007). *Strategic information systems planning in Australia: Assessment and Measurement* [PhD Thesis]. RMIT University.

Polanyi, M. (1962, October). Tacit Knowing: Its Bearing on Some Problems of Philosophy. *Reviews of Modern Physics, 34*(4), 601–606. doi:10.1103/RevModPhys.34.601

Poole, C. E., & Denny, E. (2001). Technological change in the workplace: A state wide survey of community college library and learning personnel. *College & Research Libraries, 62*(6), 503–515. doi:10.5860/crl.62.6.503

Porter, M. E. (2001, March). Strategy and Internet. *Harvard Bussiness Review*.

Porter, M. E., & Kramer, M. R. (2006). Strategic and society: The link between competitive advantage and corporate social responsibility. *Harvard Business Review, 1*, 1–14. PMID:17183795

Power, M. J., Bonifazi, C., & Desouza, K. C. (2004). The ten outsourcing traps to avoid. *The Journal of Business Strategy, 25*(2), 37–42. doi:10.1108/02756660410525399

Power, M. J., Desouza, K. C., & Bonifazi, C. (2006). *The Outsourcing Handbook: How to Implement a Successful Outsourcing Process.* London: Kogan Page Limited.

Prasad, A., Heales, J., & Green, P. (2009). Towards a Deeper Understanding of Information Technology Governance Effectiveness: A Capabilities-Based Approach. *Proceedings of the International Conference on Information Systems (ICIS).* Retrieved from: http://aisel.aisnet.org/icis2009/122

Prats, J. (2001). Gobernabilidad democrática para el desarrollo humano. Marco conceptual y analítico. *Revista Instituciones y Desarrollo*, 103-148.

Premkumar, G. (2003). A Meta-Analysis of Research on Information Systems Implementation in Small Business. *Journal of Organizational Computing and Electronic Commerce, 13*(2), 91–121. doi:10.1207/S15327744JOCE1302_2

Premkumar, G., Ramamurthy, K., & Saunders, C. S. (2005). Information processing view of organisations: An exploratory examination of fit in the context of interorganisational relationships. *Journal of Management Information Systems*, 257–294.

Premkumar, G., & Roberts, M. (1999). Adoption of new information technologies in rural small businesses. *Omega International Journal of Management Sciences, 24*(5), 467–484. doi:10.1016/S0305-0483(98)00071-1

Pulkkinen, M. (2006). Systemic Management of Architectural Decisions in Enterprise Architecture Planning. Four Dimensions and Three Abstraction Levels. *In the Proceedings of the 39th Annual Hawaii International Conference on System Science.*

Pulkkinen, M. (2008). *Enterprise architecture as a collaboration tool: Discursive process for enterprise architecture management, planning and development* [PhD Thesis]. University of Jyvaskyla.

Raghunathan, B., & Raghunathan, T. S. (1994). Adaptation of a planning success model to information systems planning. *Information Systems Research, 5*(3), 326–340. doi:10.1287/isre.5.3.326

Ranganathan, C., & Balaji, S. (2007). Critical Capabilities for Offshore Outsourcing of Information Systems. *MIS Quarterly Executive, 6*(3), 147–164.

Rao, H. R., Nam, K., & Chaudhury, A. (1996). Information Systems Outsourcing. *Communications of the ACM, 39*(7), 27–28. doi:10.1145/233977.233984

Reich, B. H., & Benbasat, I. (2000). Factors that influence the social dimension of alignment between business and information technology objectives. *MIS Quartely, 24*(1), 81–111. doi:10.2307/3250980

RIA! (Research ICT Africa!). (2006). Towards an African e-Index: SMEs e-Access and Usage Across 14 African Countries. Retrieved from: www.researchictafrica.net

Robbins, S. P., Odendaal, A., & Roodt, G. (2001). *Organisational Behaviour: Global and Southern African Perspectives* (9th ed.). South Africa: Pearson Education.

Roblyer, M. D., McDaniel, M., Webb, M., Herman, J., & Witty, J. V. (2010). Findings on Facebook in higher education: A comparison of college faculty and student uses and perception of social networking sites. *The Internet and Higher Education, 13*(1), 134–140. doi:10.1016/j.iheduc.2010.03.002

Rogers, E. M. (1995). *Diffusion of Innovations* (4th ed.). New York: Free Press.

Roman, E. S. (2009). *Bringing broadband access to rural areas: A step-by-step approach for regulators, policy makers and universal access program administrators.* Paper presented at the Nineth Global Symposium for Regulators. Beirut, Lebanon.

Romani, J. C. C. (2009). 21 century literacies and OECD. *IV Congress of CyberSociety.* Retrieved from http://www.cibersociedad.net/congres2009/en/coms/21-century-literacies-and-oecd/114/

Rondeau, P. J., Ragu-Nathan, T. S., & Vonderembse, M. A. (2006). How involvement, IS management effectiveness and end-used computing impact IS performance in manufacturing firms. *Information & Management, 43*(1), 93–107. doi:10.1016/j.im.2005.02.001

Roode, J. D. (1993). Implications for teaching of a process-based research framework for information systems. *Proceedings of the 8th annual conference of the International Academy for Information Management.* Orlando, Florida

Rose, J., & Hackney, R. (2002). Towards a Structurational Theory of Information Systems: a Substantive Case Analysis. Proceeding of the 36th Hawaii International Conference on System Sciences, Track 8, vol. 8, p. 258, USA; Washington. doi:10.1109/HICSS.2003.1174746

Rosemann, M., & Schwegmann, & A.; Delfmann, P. (2011). Preparation of Process Modeling. In J. Becker, & M. Kugeler, & M. Rosemann (Ed.), *Process management: A guide for the design of business processes* (2nd ed., pp. 41-89). Berlin, London: Springer.

Rosnow, R. L., & Rosenthal, R. (1999). *Beginning behaviour research: A conceptual primer*. Englewood Cliffs: Prentice Hall.

Rosser, B., Kirwin, B., & Mack, R. (2002). Business/IT Strategy Development and Planning, Gartner Inc. Retrieved from http://www.gartner.com/DisplayDocument?doc_cd=112300

Rottman, J. W., & Lacity, M. C. (2010). Twenty Practices for Offshore Sourcing. *MIS Quarterly Executive, 3*(3), 35–46.

Rottman, J., & Lacity, M. C. (2006). Proven Practices for Effectively Offshoring IT Work. *Sloan Management Review, 47*(3), 56–63.

Sabherwall, R., & King, W. R. (1992). Decision processes for developing strategic applications of information systems: A contingency approach. *Decision Sciences, 23*(4), 917–943. doi:10.1111/j.1540-5915.1992.tb00426.x

Sachs, J. (2015). *The Age of Sustainable Development*. New York: Columbia University Press.

Sage, T. A. (2006). *A model of factors affecting business and information technology alignment enabled by enterprise architecture: a structural equation modelling analysis* [PhD Thesis]. Capella University.

SAP's plan to make money by cutting carbon. (2011). *Technology Review, Business*. Retrieved from www.technologyreview.com/business/27001/?nlid=3977

Sarapuu, K. (2015). Dangerous e-Waste is the World's Fastest Growing Municipal Waste Stream. *Let us do it World*. Retrieved from http://www.letsdoitworld.org/news/dangerous-e-waste-worlds-fastest-growing-municipal-waste-stream

Satzinger, J. W., Jackson, R. B., & Burd, S. D. (2004). *Systems Analysis and Design in a Changing World* (3rd ed.). USA: Thomson.

Scarbrough, H. (1998). *Linking strategy and IT-based innovation: The importance of the "management of expertise". Information Technology and Organisational Transformation: Innovation for the 21st Century Organisation*. West Sussex, England: John Wiley & Sons Ltd.

Schlenzig, C. (1999). Energy planning and environmental management with the information and decision support system MESAP. *International Journal of Global Energy, 12*(1–6), 81–91. doi:10.1504/IJGEI.1999.000840

Schumacker, R. E., & Lomax, R. G. (2004). *A beginner's guide to structural equation modelling*. Mahwah, NJ: Prentice Hall.

Schwegmann, A., & Laske, M. (2011). As-Is Modelling and Process Analysis. In J. Becker, M. Kugeler, & M. Rosemann (Eds.), *Process management: A guide for the design of business processes* (2nd ed., pp. 133–156). Berlin, London: Springer. doi:10.1007/978-3-642-15190-3_5

Seddon, P. B., Shanks, G., & Willcocks, L. (2003). Introduction: ERP - The Quiet Revolution? In G. Shanks, P. B. Seddon, Leslie Willcocks (Eds.): Second-wave enterprise resource planning systems. Implementing for effectiveness (pp. 1–19). Cambridge, U.K., New York: Cambridge University Press

Segars, A.H. & Grover, V. (1998, June). Strategic information system planning success: An investigation of the construct and its measurement. *MIS Quartely*, 139-163.

Segars, A. H., & Grover, V. (1999). Profiles of Strategic information system planning. *Information Systems Research, 10*(3), 199–232. doi:10.1287/isre.10.3.199

Seyal, A.H., Rahim, M. M. & Rahman, M. N. (2000). An empirical investigation of use of information technology among small and medium business organisations: a Bruneian scenario. *Electronic Journal Information Systems in Developing Countries*, 2 (2000).

Compilation of References

Shaft, T. M., Ellington, R. T., Meo, M., & Sharfman, M. P. (1997). A framework for information systems in life-cycle oriented environmental management. *Journal of Industrial Ecology*, *1*(2), 135–148. doi:10.1162/jiec.1997.1.2.135

Shepsle, K. A., & Bonchek, M. S. (2005). *Las Fórmulas de la Política*. México: Taurus.

Shiang-Yen, T., Idrus, R., & Yusof, U. K. (2011). A Framework for Classifying Misfits between Enterprise Resource Planning (ERP) Systems and Business Strategies. *Asian Academy of Management Journal*, *16*(2), 53–75.

Shtub, A., & Kami, R. (2010). *ERP: The Dynamic of Suppuly Chain and Process Management*. New York: Springer. doi:10.1007/978-0-387-74526-8

Smallbone, D. (2004). 'Institutions, governance and SME development in transition economies' Paper 5. *Working Party on Industry and Enterprise Development, Expert meeting on Good Governance for SMEs, April*. European Commission for Europe.

Sohal, A. S., & Fitzpatrick, P. (2002). IT Governance and Management in Large Australian Organisations. *International Journal of Production Economics*, *75*(1), 97–112. doi:10.1016/S0925-5273(01)00184-0

Song, Z., & Li-Hua, H. (2005). *Comparative Study of Obtaining Competitive Advantage from Information*. IEEE.

Sood, R. (2005). *IT, software and services: outsourcing & offshoring*. Austin, Texas: AiAiYo Books.

Southern, A., & Tilley, F. (2000). Small Firms and Information Systems Technologies (ICTs): Toward a Typology of ICT Usage. *New Technology, Work and Employment*, *15*(2), 138–154. doi:10.1111/1468-005X.00070

Sparrow, E. (2003). *Successful IT outsourcing: from choosing a provider to managing the project*. London: Springer-Verlag. doi:10.1007/978-1-4471-0061-4

Srinivas, H. (1999). Position Paper on Knowledge Asset Management Retrieved September, 2011, from http://www.gdrc.org/kmgmt/km-1.html

Steger, T. (2004 April, 1-2). Corporate Governance of German SMEs – A review with special regards to the situation in East Germany [Economic Commission For Europe Paper No. 6], Committee For Trade, Industry and Enterprise Development. *Proceedings of Expert meeting on Good Governance for SMEs*.

Stephen, H. (2006). *Management Information Systems for the Information Age* (3rd ed.). McGraw-Hill Ryerson.

Subirats, J., Knoepfel, P., Larrue, C., & Varonne, F. (2008). *Análisis y Gestión de Políticas Públicas*. Barcelona: Ariel.

Tallon, P., & Kraemer, K. L. (2003). Investigating the Relationship between Strategic alignment and IT Business Value: The Discovery of a Paradox. In N. Shin (Ed.), *Creating Business Value with Information Technology: Challenges and Solutions* (pp. 1–22). USA: Idea Group Publishing. doi:10.4018/978-1-59140-038-7.ch001

Teddlie, C., & Yu, F. (2007). Mixed Methods Sampling: A Typology With Examples. *Journal of Mixed Methods*, *1*(1), 77–100. doi:10.1177/2345678906292430

Teo, T. S. H., & King, W. R. (1996). Assessing the impact of integrating business planning and IS Planning. *Information & Management*, *30*(6), 309–321. doi:10.1016/S0378-7206(96)01076-2

Teo, T. S., & King, W. R. (1997). Integration between business planning and information systems planning: An evolutionary-contingency perspective. *Journal of Management Information Systems*, *14*(1), 185–214.

Terre Blanche, M., & Durrheim, K. (1999). *Research in Practice: Applied Methods for the Social Sciences*. Cape Town: UCT Press.

Tetteh, G. K., & Snaith, J. (2006). Information system strategy: Applying galliers and Sutherland's stages of growth model in a developing country. *The Consortium Journal, 11*(1), 5–16.

Teubner, R. A. (2007). Strategic information systems planning: A case study from the financial service industry. *The Journal of Strategic Information Systems, 16*(1), 105–125. doi:10.1016/j.jsis.2007.01.002

The Namibian Economist. (2012). Logistics market grows tremendously. Retrieved from http://www.economist.com.na/special-focus/1120-logistics-market-grows-tremendously

The role of communication infrastructure investment in economic recovery: Working party on communication infrastructure and services policy. (2009). OECD. Retrieved from http://www.oecd.org/dataoecd/4/43/42799709.pdf

Tolbert, C. J., & Mossberger, K. (2006, May-June). The Effects of E-Government on Trust and Confidence in Government. *Public Administration Review, 66*(3), 354–369. doi:10.1111/j.1540-6210.2006.00594.x

Tornatzky, L. G., & Fleischer, M. (1990). *The Processes of Technological Innovation*. Lexington, Massachusetts: Lexington Books.

Trade profiles 2011. (2011).Geneva: World Trade Organization.

Tsebelis, G. (2001). *Veto Players: How Political Institutions Work*. Princenton, NJ: Princeton University Press.

UGe-CF. (2008). User guidelines for the application of the European e-Competence Framework. *European Commission*. Retrieved from www.ecompetences.eu

UN. (2012, July 27). *The future we want. Resolution adopted by the General Assembly*. UN General Assembly.

UNDP-APDIP (United Nations Development Program-Asia Pacific Development Information Program). (2007). The Role of Government in Promoting ICT Access and use by SMEs: Consideration for Public Policy. Retrieved from: www.apdip.net/apdipenote/12.pdf

UNPAN. (2003). *UN Global E-Government Survey 2003*. New York: United Nations.

UNPAN. (2004). *Global E-Readiness Report 2004*. New York: United Nations.

UNPAN. (2005). *Global E-Government Readiness Report 2005: from E-Government to E-Inclusion*. New York: United Nations.

UNPAN. (2008). *UN E-Government Survey 2008: From E-Government to Connected Governance*. New York: United Nations.

UNPAN. (2010). *United Nations E-Government Survey 2010: leveragin e-goverment at a time of financial and economic crisis*. New York: United Nations.

Van Brakel, P. (2005). Innovation and Competitiveness in South Africa: the case for competitive intelligence as an instrument to make better use of information. *South African Journal of Information management, 7*(1), 16-28.

van der Raadt, B., & van Vliet, H. (2008). Van der Raadt, B. & Van Vliet, H. (2008) Designing the enterprise architecture function. *Lecture Notes in Computer Science, 5281*, 103–118. doi:10.1007/978-3-540-87879-7_7

Vedder, R. G., & Guynes, C. S. (2002). CEO and CIO Perspectives on Competitive Intelligence. *Communications of the ACM, 42*(8), 108–116. doi:10.1145/310930.310982

Verdantix. (2013, June 4). US Sustainable Business Spending 2012-2017. Retrieved from http://www.verdantix.com/index.cfm/papers/Products.Details/product_id/544/us-sustainable-business-spending-2012-2017/-

Compilation of References

Viviers, W., & Muller, M. (2004). The Evolution of Competitive Intelligence in South Africa: Early 1980s – 2003. *Journal of Competitive Intelligence and Management, 2*(2), 53–67.

Vural, I. (2010). *Success Factors in information Systems Outsourcing*. Saarbrucken, Germany: Lambert Academic Publishing.

Walsham, G., & Waema, T. (1994). Information Systems Strategy and Implementation: A Case Study of a Building Society. *ACM Transactions on Information Systems, 12*(2), 159–173. doi:10.1145/196734.196744

Wang, Q. Z., & Liu, J. (2006). Project Uncertainty, Management Practice and Project Performance: An Empirical Analysis on Customized Information Systems Development Projects. Proceedings of *Engineering Management Conference, IEEE International*, 341-345. doi:10.1109/IEMC.2006.4279882

Wang, E. T. C., & Tai, J. C. F. (2003). Factors affecting information systems planning effectiveness: Organisational contexts and planning systems dimensions. *Information & Management, 40*(4), 287–303. doi:10.1016/S0378-7206(02)00011-3

Wang, X., & Zhao, Y. (2009). An Enterprise Architecture development method in Chinese Manufacturing Industry. *IEEE Journals, 3*, 226–230.

Ward, J., & Peppard, J. (2002). *Strategic Planning for Information Systems* (3rd ed.). West Sussex, England: John Wiley & Sons.

Warr, A. (2005). A study of the relationships of strategic IS planning approaches, objectives and context with SISP success in UK organizations. Proceedings of *European Conferences on Information Systems*.

Watson, R. T., Boudreau, M., & Chen, A. J. (2010). Information Systems and Environmentally Sustainable Development: Energy Informatics and New Directions for the IS Community. *Management Information Systems Quarterly, 34*(1), 23–38.

WCED - World Commission on Environment and Development. (1987). Our common future [Brundtland Report]. Oxford University Press.

Webb, P., Pollard, C., & Ridley, G. (2006). Attempting to Define IT Governance: Wisdom or Folly?*Proceedings of the 39th Hawaii International Conference on Systems Science*. doi:10.1109/HICSS.2006.68

Weill, P., & Ross, J. W. (2004). *IT Governance: How Top Performers Manage IT Decision Rights for Superior Results*. Massachusetts: Harvard Business School Press.

Weiss, J., & Anderson, D. (2002). CIOs and IT Professionals as Change Agents, Risk and Stakeholder Managers: A Field Study, proceedings of the 36th Hawaii International Conference on System Sciences, Track 8, vol. 8, USA; Washington.

Welman, C., Kruger, F., & Mitchell, B. (1994). *Research Methodology* (3rd ed.). Cape Town: Oxford University Press Southern Africa.

Welman, J. C., & Kruger, S. J. (2001). *Research Methodology: for the Business and Administrative Sciences* (2nd ed.). South Africa: Oxford University Press.

Wernick, P., Hall, T., & Nehaniv, C. L. (2008). Software evolutionary dynamics modelled as the activity of an actor-network. *The Institution of Engineering and Technology, 2*(4), 321–336.

Whittaker, B. (1999). Unsuccessful information technology projects. *Information Management & Computer Security, 7*(1), 23–29. doi:10.1108/09685229910255160

William, J., & Baumol. (2010). *The Free-Market Innovation Machine: Analyzing the Growth Miracle of Capitalism*.

Wixom, B. H., & Watson, H. J. (2001). An Empirical Investigation on the factors affecting Data Warehouse success. *MIS Quaterly*, *2*(1), 17–41. doi:10.2307/3250957

Wolff, S., & Sydor, K. (1999). Information Systems Strategy Development and Implementation: A Nursing Home Perspective. *Journal of Healthcare Information Management*, *13*(1), 2–12. PMID:17283848

World Bank. (2012a). *Exportaciones de productos de TIC (% de las exportaciones de productos)*. Retrieved from http://datos.bancomundial.org/indicador/TX.VAL.ICTG.ZS.UN

Xu, K., Liao, S. S., Li, J., & Song, Y. (2011). Mining comparative opinions from customer reviews for competitive intelligence. *Decision Support Systems*, *1*(50), 743–754. doi:10.1016/j.dss.2010.08.021

Yi, L., & Thomas, H. R. (2007). A review of research on the environmental impact of e-Business and ICT. *Environment International*, *33*(6), 841–849. doi:10.1016/j.envint.2007.03.015 PMID:17490745

Yin, R. K. (2009). Case Chapter Research: Design and Methods (4th ed.). SAGE Publications Inc.

Yu, E., Strohmaier, M., & Deng, X. (2006). Exploring intentional modelling and analysis for Enterprise Architecture. *In the Proceedings of the Enterprise Distributed Object Computing conference workshop*.

Zelt, S., Wulf, J., Uebernickel, F., & Brenner, W. (2013). *The Varying Role of IS Capabilities for Different Approaches to Application Services Outsourcing*. Paper presented at the 19th Americas Conference on Information Systems (AMCIS).

About the Contributors

Tiko Iyamu holds a PhD in Information Systems. Currently, he is at Cape Peninsula University of Technology, Cape Town, South Africa. He was a Professor of Informatics, Chair of Health Informatics at the Namibia University of Science and Technology, Windhoek, Namibia. He also serves as a Professor Extraordinaire at the Department of Computer Science, University of the Western Cape, South Africa. In 2013 and 2014, he was a visiting professor at the Flensburg University of Applied Sciences, Germany. Prior to his fulltime appointment in academic in 2009, Tiko held several positions in both Public and Private Institutions in South Africa. He was System Analyst and Technologist at both Nedcor Investment Bank and Metropolitan Life, respectively. He became the Chief Architect at the City of Cape Town in 1999. Thereafter, he joined Old Mutual as IT Architect, from 2001 to 2008. Iyamu's last corporate experience was at a Telecommunication company (MWeb), as Head of IT Architecture & Governance. Iyamu's interests and focus areas include Mobile Computing, Enterprise Architecture, Information Technology Strategy, Actor Network Theory and Structuration Theory. He has published widely in books, book chapters, journals and conference proceedings. Tiko is an Associate Editor of the International Journal of Actor-Network Theory and Technological Innovation (IJANTTI).

* * *

Olayele Adelakun is an Associate professor of MIS at DePaul University Chicago, Illinois, College of Computing and Digital Media (CDM). His research focuses on IT Outsourcing, Telemedicine, ERP systems implementation, Information Systems Quality, and IT Leadership. He has conducted studies in both medium size companies and large multinational companies in Europe, Africa and the United States. He has chair several academic and industry focus conferences. He started the study abroad program in the school CDM in 1994. He has organized several executives' presentations. He has published over eighty articles in conferences, books and journals. He holds an M.S. in Information Processing Science from University of Oulu, Oulu, Finland and Ph.D. in Information Systems from the Turku School of Economics and Business Administration, Turku, Finland and MBA from DePaul University, Chicago, IL.

Charles Boamah-Abu holds a BSc Hon degree in Computer Science from Rhodes University and MCom in Information Systems from University of Cape Town. His interests in computing spans software engineering, human computer interaction and IT management. He has experience in software development and evaluation of user interfaces, and has consulted for many organizations. He is currently a lecturer of Information Technology at Durban University of Technology. His duties include teaching software development and user interface design. His research interests include strategic use of IT in organisations.

Roberto Cortés-Morales is an associated professor at Costa Rica Institute of Technology (ITCR). PhD in Government and Public Policies from Costa Rica University (UCR). Master in Computer and Informatic Sciences from UCR. Researcher on digital government at the ITCR. Current Coordinator of the Graduate Unit of the Computer Engineering School at ITCR. Professor of Strategic Use of Information Technology at the Computer Master Program at ITCR. Professor of Software Engineering at the BS Program of Computer Engineering at ITCR.

Stephan Hofmann completed a BA Business Administration and MA focussing on Procurement, Logistics and Supply Chain Management from 2007 to 2013 at Flensburg University of Applied Sciences. He is currently working as a research assistant on projects concerning process management and IT business solutions at Flensburg University of Applied Sciences.

Ray Kekwaletswe is a rated IS researcher. He is currently with the School of Economic and Business Sciences at the University of the Witwatersrand, South Africa. As an Information Systems researcher, his core areas include Systems Planning, digital disruption, strategic IT leadership, information systems management, IT strategy alignment, information security awareness, IT governance, mobile technologies, IT value and cost. He has contributed to the local and international IT research and innovation landscapes through ICT workshops and training, publications in journals, conference proceedings and chapters in books. He has, in the last 4 years, successfully supervised and graduated over 60 doctoral and masters' candidates. Prof Kekwaletswe has MSc in Computer Information Systems, BSc in Audio Technology and BA in Communication and multimedia, all three from the American University, Washington DC, USA. He earned his PhD in Information Systems from the University of Cape Town, South Africa.

Paula Kotzé is a Chief Researcher and the Research Group Leader of the Enterprise Knowledge Engineering and Management Group at the Meraka Institute of the Council for Scientific and Industrial Research (CSIR) in South Africa; Adjunct Professor at the Nelson Mandela Metropolitan University and Extraordinary Professor at North-West University. Before joining the CSIR in 2008, she was Professor, Director of the School of Computing and Director of the Centre for Software Engineering at the University of South Africa. Her background is multidisciplinary combining computer science, information systems, industrial psychology, and education. She holds a PhD in Computer Science with specialization in Human-Computer Interaction from the University Of York (UK), which she obtained in 1997. She specialises in human factors engineering, enterprise engineering, design thinking, design research, and health informatics, as reflected in an extensive publication record, and is a regular speaker at international and national conferences.

Michael Kyobe is Professor of Information System. He holds a PhD in Computer Information Systems and an MBA. Michael worked as a project manager and IT manager for several years and has consulted extensively with the public, and SMEs.

Marianne Loock received her PhD in Computer Science from the University of Pretoria, South Africa in 2013. She is a Senior Lecturer in the School of Computing at the University of South Africa, Johannesburg and has been a full-time member of this School since 1987. She writes and presents on issues of information security, access control and security, cyber security awareness, secure knowledge management, secure data mining and databases.

About the Contributors

Phathutshedzo Nemutanzhela is a senior manager in the information technology (IT) division at Avis group of companies. She has over ten years of experience in the field of IT. She has heard various positions, such as Business Analyst and Technology Manager over the years, in different organisations. Ms Nemutanzhela holds a Master's degree and she currently enrolled for a Doctoral program in Informatics. Nemutanzhela is an author of numerous peer-reviewed journal and conference proceeding articles. Her research interests include Competitive Intelligence, Mobile Health, Information Systems, and focuses on Diffusion of Innovation theory (DoI).

Zoran Mitrovic is the Head of Research at the Mitrovic Development and Research Institute and senior academic at the University of the Western Cape, South Africa. His research and consulting praxis encompasses e-skills and e-competences in the developmental context, realising organisational benefits for ICT investment, application of ICT for local socio-economic development, e-government, open government and open data policies and praxis, and the use of ICT for sustainability development. He is the author of a number of academic papers as well as funded research reports. Among others, Dr Mitrovic is the leading author of the South African National e-Skills Plans of Action (NeSPA 2010 and NeSPA 2013).

Sharol Sibongile Mkhomazi received her Master's degree in Business Information Systems from Tshwane University of Technology, Pretoria, South Africa in 2009 and her Doctoral Degree in Computer Science and Data Processing in 2013 from the same institution. She is currently an HOD in the Department of Office Management and Technology, Faculty of Management Sciences at Tshwane University of Technology. Her main research activities involve Telecommunication Infrastructure management, Knowledge Management and Research methodology. She has published articles in book chapters and international conferences.

Relebohile Moloi is an Information and communication Technology (ICT) practitioner. In the last ten years of her practice, Ms Moloi has held several positions such as Business Analyst and Decision Support Analyst at Telecommunication and Technology Service Provide companies, respectively. Currently, she is an IT Operations Manager for IT Consulting Company in South Africa. Ms Moloi also lectures on part-time at Tshwane University of Technology, Pretoria, South Africa. Relebohile holds a Master's degree in Business Information System.

Leshoto Mphahlele is currently an IT senior manager for one of the government departments in South Africa. He has over 8 years working experience in the field of IT. During this period, Leshoto has held various senior positions, including in the areas of consulting, in both private and public institutions. Also, he once lectured on part-time at Tshwane University of Technology, South Africa. Leshoto areas of interests and focus include enterprise architecture, IT strategy and software development. Mr Mphahlele holds a Master's degree in Informatics. He has interest in research, and has thus published articles in conference proceedings and journals.

Eunice Mtshali is a Librarian at Tshwane University of Technology, Pretoria, South Africa. She has 15 years working experience in academic libraries as an Information librarian and research librarian. She holds Master's degree in Business Information Systems. In her academic and research works, she focuses on the use of mobile technologies for the management of library process and activities, and the application of technology acceptance model (TAM) in information systems studies. She has published research papers in both local and international journal and conference proceedings, including book chapters.

Thomas Schmidt holds a Master in Industrial Engineering from the Technical University Karlsruhe (now Karlsruhe Institute of Technology) and a PhD in Information Systems from the University of Bamberg. He started his career as a scientific assistant at the Fraunhofer Institute for Production Technology and Automation with specialization in shop floor control and maintenance organisation. As a senior management consultant with CSC Ploenzke he developed and implemented logistics and IT-strategies for clients in small and large-scale projects for various industry sectors. Since 1995 Thomas Schmidt is a Professor for Business Informatics at Flensburg University of Applied Sciences. The main focus of his work is lecturing and applied research on IT-strategies, supply chain management, information logistics and management information systems. In these fields he has supported companies in technology-transfer projects and has vast experience as a consultant. He has lectured and completed research as a visiting professor in the United States, Sweden, France, China and Namibia.

Tefo Sekgweleo is an Information Technology (IT) practitioner. He has been in the IT industry for the past 17 years. He started his career as a software developer and moved to software testing. Currently, he is a test manager at one of the biggest power utility in South Africa. He renders multiple IT services and conduct researches within the software testing space to ensure that the organisation standards are aligned with the latest IEEE standards. He has also published articles in several journals as well as chapters in books. He is pursuing his doctoral studies with Polytechnic of Namibia in Windhoek. Tefo has a passion in research and would like to become a supervisor in one of the higher learning institutions in South Africa. I would like help my fellow South Africans and other nationalities to achieve their post graduate qualifications. Apart from IT, Tefo Sekgweleo also enjoys drawing, taking pictures, fixing and driving his classic vintage cars.

Hanlie Smuts is the General Manager for Product and Digital at Mobile Telephone Networks (Pty) Ltd in South Africa. Her main focus is business transformation and the outcomes of her role aim to empower customers through convenient and effective self-service, to drive growth through personalised digital offerings and to strengthen brand association between MTN and digital services. She holds a PhD in Information Systems from the University of South Africa with specialisation in knowledge management and specifically the impact on Information Systems outsourcing. She is associated with multiple business schools and universities in Johannesburg where she is appointed as external examiner and where she oversees Masters students as study leader.

About the Contributors

Alta van der Merwe is currently the Head of the Department of Informatics at the University of Pretoria. She serves on several international research working groups, steering committees, advisory boards and editorial boards. She is the founder and past chair of the South African IEEE SMCS Chapter, specialist editor of the SAIEE journal (Software Engineering track) and co-founder and past chair of the Enterprise Architecture Research Forum. On International level she was involved in the proposal and acceptance of the Open Group Academic Forum and also the IEEE Enterprise Engineering and Enterprise Architecture Technical Committee, where she still acts as co-chair. Prof van der Merwe focuses on research related to Enterprise Architecture; Data Analyitics (Social media); Use of Mobile Technologies in the South African Domain and Design and Innovation. She is the current president of the South African Institute of Computer Scientists and Information Technologists (SAICSIT).

Index

A

Actor-Network 51, 63, 66, 75, 152
Architecture 41, 63, 67, 81, 88, 115, 171-172, 177, 187, 261, 269, 286, 288
assessing strategic information 1-2, 14, 24-25

B

Best Practices 106, 108, 110, 112, 117, 119-120, 124, 164, 180, 201
Business Strategy 1-3, 8, 11, 14, 20, 23, 25, 30, 42, 59, 63-64, 66, 82-83, 92, 155, 190-191, 206-207, 213, 217, 260

C

Capital University 226-230, 232-234, 236-237
captive center 106, 109-110, 117
Captive Offshore 106-111, 117, 120
CI products 265, 273, 280-290
Competitive Intelligence (CI) 260-262, 264, 269-273, 275-277, 279-286, 288, 292
Competitive Intelligence Information 273
computing environment 33, 35-38, 40-47, 51, 53, 55, 57-69, 72, 76
contingency 1-3, 5, 7-8, 10, 12-16, 18, 20, 24-25, 30, 190-191
Contingency Theory 1, 10, 25, 30
Costa Rica 153-154, 159, 161-162, 165-168
critical tasks 37, 47

D

data collection 34, 48, 54, 88, 110, 136, 202, 209, 262
Descriptive statistics 15-16, 18, 196
developing countries 106, 189, 209, 223, 243-244
Diffusion of Innovation (DoI) 262, 279

E

E-Competences 242, 244-246, 250-253, 255, 258-259
empirical data 7, 35, 40, 110
Engineering 214, 217, 226, 241
Enhancement 82, 87, 236, 280, 285
enterprise architecture 171-172, 177
Enterprise Conceptual Model 121-123, 125-126, 128, 130, 132-134
Environmental Information System 246, 258
Environmental Management Information System 246, 258
Environmental Uncertainty 1-3, 8, 14, 20, 23, 30
ERP System 122-130, 132-134
European e-Competence 242, 244, 250, 253
Explicit Knowledge 84, 86, 97, 105
Externalisation 85, 105

F

Feasibility 156-160, 164-167, 170, 269
Fortune 1000 106, 109
Fortune 1000 companies 106

G

German Informatics 246, 255
Governance 81, 96, 99, 112, 154, 174, 178, 181-182, 184-185, 187-195, 197, 199-202, 206, 235-236, 238, 288-290

H

Human action 31, 33, 35, 75, 212, 224

I

Implicit Knowledge 105
Individual choices 32-33

Information and Communication Technologies (ICT) 241-243, 258
Information Systems Lifecycle 105
Information Systems Outsource Model 105
Information Systems Outsourcing 79, 87, 105
Information Technology Strategy 51, 134
Innovation 8, 68, 79, 82, 87, 143-146, 148, 188, 210, 229, 232, 234, 260-277, 279, 282, 292
Innovation-decision process 262-263
Intelligence Information 273
Internalisation 85, 105
IS Strategy 30, 83, 120, 187
IT Governance 188-195, 197, 199-202, 206
IT Governance Practices 188-189, 191, 193, 195, 197, 199-202, 206
IT Outsourcing 106, 108, 117, 120, 190
IT Performance Management 190, 194, 206
IT Resource Management 188, 190, 194, 199-200, 206
IT Risk Management 190, 194, 201, 206
IT Strategic Alignment 35, 199, 206
IT Strategy 31-48, 50-54, 57-70, 72-76, 78, 190, 196, 199, 201, 210

K

Knowledge-Based Assets 80, 105
Knowledge creation 84, 86
Knowledge management 79-84, 86-87, 90-91, 96, 99, 115, 252, 275, 281
Knowledge requirements 79-80, 83-84, 87-88, 90, 97, 100
Knowledge Transfer 80, 82, 86-87, 91-93, 96, 105

L

legal compliance 247, 252
Legitimacy 37, 156-160, 164-167, 170
life cycle 125, 248, 277

M

management team 7, 36, 106, 108, 110, 112-114, 116, 217
material flow 247, 252
maturation process 107-108
Medium Enterprise 2, 23, 30
Mobile Technology 226, 228-231, 234, 236-239, 241
Moderating Role 1, 12-14, 16, 25

N

Namibian freight 121-123, 126-128, 132-133
National e-Skills 244
Network Theory 55, 78, 135-136, 138, 152
Non-Technical Factors 31-32, 34-35, 37, 46-48, 50, 53, 57, 59, 78, 145, 147, 149, 212, 238

O

official languages 37, 46-47
Offshore 81, 96, 106-110, 112, 116-117, 119-120
Organisational politics 51-54, 69-71, 73-76
outsource vendor 79-83, 86-88, 90-91, 96-97, 99-100, 105

P

parent company 106-110, 120
performance contracts 47, 58-60, 62, 64, 70, 72-74
personal interests 32, 36, 39, 52, 61, 65, 68, 70, 74, 180
policy makers 201, 208
program management 108, 114, 119
Public policy 153, 155, 159-161, 170

R

respondent demographics 34, 53-54
rural areas 193, 208-209, 212, 215-217, 219-220, 222-224

S

SISP 2-9, 12-16, 18-19, 22-25, 53
Small and Medium Enterprises (SMEs) 188-189, 192-193, 195, 199-202, 207
social dynamics 172, 174
Software Deployment 135, 137, 139, 145-147, 149, 152
South Africa 14, 23, 34, 53, 80, 88, 100, 128, 136, 173, 188-189, 192, 194, 208-209, 212, 216-217, 223, 244
strategic information 1-5, 7-9, 14, 24-25, 30, 53, 282
Strategic Information Systems Planning 1-5, 7, 14, 24-25, 30, 53
structural equation 12, 15, 25
Structuration Theory (ST) 32-35, 40, 48, 50-51, 55, 57, 75, 78, 135-136, 138, 152, 171-174, 187, 208-209, 211
Sustainability 148, 157, 160, 164-165, 167, 170-171, 215, 217, 222, 242-253, 255, 259, 267

Sustainability e-Competences 244-245, 253, 255, 259
systems planning 1-5, 7, 14, 24-25, 30, 53

T

Tacit Knowledge 82, 84, 97, 105, 268
Technology Acceptance Model 228, 232, 241
telecommunication company 80, 100

telecommunication infrastructure 208-224, 226-228, 237
third party 80, 106-109, 111, 113, 117
thought processes 32-33

V

value creation 80, 82, 122
Veto Power 154-159, 163, 167, 170